MACQUARIE BOOK OF
SLANG

MACQUARIE BOOK OF SLANG

Australian Slang in the 90s

GENERAL EDITOR
James Lambert

Published by the Macquarie Library Pty Ltd
The Macquarie Dictionary, Macquarie University, NSW 2109 Australia

First published 1996

© Copyright The Macquarie Library Pty Ltd
© Copyright Macquarie University

Typeset in Australia by Docupro

Printed in Australia by McPherson Printing Group

National Library of Australia Cataloguing-in-Publication Data

> Lambert, James, 1965-.
> The Macquarie book of slang.
>
> ISBN 0 949757 87 X
>
> 1. English language–Australia–Slang–Dictionaries.
> 2. Australianisms–Dictionaries. I Title. II. Title: Book of slang.

427.994

All rights reserved. No part of this publication may be reproduced, stored in a retrieval system, or transmitted in any form, or by any means, electronic, mechanical, photocopying, recording or otherwise, without the prior written permission of the publisher.

■ INTRODUCTION ■

English-speaking Australians have always had a love affair with slang. The early convicts, settlers and military all spoke the slang current in their home country, Britain of the 18th century, and this was transported with them to the Great South Land, starting a tradition of Australian slang that is still very much with us today. The *Macquarie Book of Slang* is the most up-to-date account of Australian slang and colloquial language.

The *Macquarie Book of Slang* has as its base all those definitions in *The Macquarie Dictionary* which are labelled *Colloquial*. These were short-listed, and then added to from the most up-to-date resources currently available. Happily, today computer technology makes lexicographical life much easier than it used to be. Much more information can be gathered for analysis with much less effort than the laborious reading through of material and writing out of citation slips. At the Macquarie Dictionary a corpus of Australian language has been created. Called *Ozcorp,* it comprises over twenty million words of Australian writing, from colonial times to the present, including novels, short stories, poetry, newspapers, magazines, oral transcripts, student essays, history texts, sociological texts, and private correspondence. This is an immensely useful research tool. It can be used to ascertain the meaning of a word, the age or currency of a term, settle questions as to the commonest spelling, or even simply to confirm that a term does actually exist. The Internet is also a useful exploratory tool for the modern-day lexicographer, especially one dealing with counter-cultures and the latest and coolest developments in popular culture.

Slang is an unruly beast and to generalise about it is difficult. The differences between slang, colloquialism and jargon are not clear-cut. In the expressions *turf slang, student slang, political slang, kids' slang, skater slang,* etc., the term *slang* may be replaced with *jargon*. The term *Australian slang* is often used loosely to refer to what is simply an Australianism. In fact, what one person may think of as a slang word may seem to be perfectly standard English to another. In this introduction and in this dictionary's title the term *slang* is used in the widest possible sense. Thus in this dictionary you will find numerous colloquial phrases, jargon terms from various fields (including the Internet), sporting terms, horseracing lingo, vulgarisms old and new, and a good smattering of historical slang terms that are of cultural significance, even if they are somewhat out-moded or downright obsolete these days. However, the slant is definitely towards slang of the 1990s. There is a judicial selection of prison and underworld terms, the inclusion and defining of which owe much to the information available in Gary Simes' excellent *Dictionary of Australian Underworld Slang* (1993). Many words are included solely because they are terms of an urban counter-culture or subculture, and are thus not part of standard English. These are particularly useful since most of them are, to my knowledge, not recorded elsewhere. Absent are many rural words and those of the jargon of shearing, which are well covered in numerous other dictionaries such as Sidney J. Baker's *The Australian Language,* G.A. Wilkes' *A Dictionary of Australian Colloquialisms* and W.S. Ramson's *The Australian National Dictionary.*

Despite the inexactitude of the term *slang,* there are still some strongly-held myths about slang which need debunking. It used to be quite popularly believed that slang is just poor English, and to be avoided at all costs. *Blackie's Standard Shilling Dictionary* of the early 20th century defines slang as "a class of expressions not generally approved of, as being inelegant and undignified". However, in recent years slang has become much more accepted and much less reviled. This is well and good, because slang is not "poor" English. That is to say, people using slang are on the whole quite capable of speaking normal, "good" English and their use of a slang phrase or word is a quite deliberate action to step outside the normal register. The use of slang certainly does not mean that the user does not know other ways of saying what they mean or is deficient in language attainment. Slang words have quite distinct meanings and connotations that other words do not, and very often using slang is the only way of expressing these meanings. On the whole, the words generally conceived of as slang have an impact that other words do not. For this reason it is apposite to use other slang words when defining slang terms, for often it is only another slang term that captures the essence of the word being defined. Slang is fresh and alive, racy and very often ironic and humorous.

It is often said that slang is ephemeral and changes extremely quickly. It is indeed true that a slang dictionary written in the 1980s will by 1996 seem quite dated and quaint, quite, well, 80s. However, having said this, one can point to numerous current slang terms with a long slang history. For instance, the word *bloke* was first recorded in 1829 and is still with us, some 167 years later. The word *grog* is to be found used in the logbook of the *Hillsborough,* a convict transport ship that left for Sydney in 1798. And there is an example of an Australian *grog shop* as early as 1799. Other terms such as *beak,* for judge, and *prat,* meaning buttocks, date back to the 1500s. They were slang (or rather, cant) then and are still slang today. In fact the word *slang* was itself originally a slang word.

Canting was the practice of speaking the secret language used by the criminal class or underworld of England in the 16th century. It was created in order to give those people acting outside the law the ability to discuss their underhand business without the risk of divulging any damning information. Cant has been well recorded in many glossaries from the 16th century on, by honest, upright souls who thought it would foil the criminals in their plan if the police, magistrates and good citizens were conversant with this secret language. The desire to assist the authorities by publishing glossaries of cant or the "flash" language found expression in the early days of the Australian colony with the publication of a *New and Comprehensive Vocabulary of the Flash Language* compiled in 1812 by the transportee James Hardy Vaux. This records thieves' slang that would have been current in both England and Australia at the time. A later glossary, dating from 1882, is the anonymous *Slang Phrases [or] The Detective's Handbook, comprising the Quaint Slang Words and Flash Dialogues in use in Australian Shadows of Life,* which was followed still later by *The Australian Slang Dictionary,* compiled by a Melbourne policeman by the name of Cornelius Crowe in 1895. Some of the words recorded in these glossaries are now widespread colloquialisms.

This history of cant lexicography has contributed in part to a widely held misconception about slang, namely, that slang is used as a secret language known only to the members of a select group: that slang is a crypto-language. This belief is commonly cited by journalists and amateur lexicographers, and is especially directed at the slang of school-age children. It is claimed that adults cannot understand the language of their children, that the children have intentionally set out to create a crypto-language, and that if an adult does cotton on to a term and attempt to make use of it then it is quickly dropped by the original users. This is a nice, neat little theory, but unfortunately quite untrue. Maybe many people don't remember being a child or teenager, but I do, and I am certain that when I or my peers spoke slang it was never so that our elders wouldn't understand. If I didn't want them to hear something, I took the expedient of absenting myself from their presence. Sure, there are cryptolanguages available, such as pig Latin and alibi, but these are, on the whole, little used in comparison with ordinary slang. Most slang terms used by children, whilst not actually used by adults, are still understood by adults, a fact of which children are completely aware. Which adult in constant contact with school children doesn't understand the meaning of *cool, daggy, a total babe, unreal, dork,* or *fatso?* Who will put their hand up and admit to this? None, but these are the very words teenagers use.

The last common *bête noire* relating to slang is that it is, along with the rest of our culture, becoming Americanised. This is partly true and there is little to be done about it. The phenomenon is nothing new. As far back as the gold rushes Australians were exposed to Americanisms from the great influx of American prospectors. During World War II another influx of Americans brought many new terms, and from this time till now the flow of American English to our shores has been constant, what with the advent of rock'n'roll, the beat generation, hippie culture and finally television.

Perhaps too much is made of the distinction between US, British and Australian English. There are differences, but once a word is disseminated throughout the English-speaking world what does its origin really matter? Who could do without such common words as *floozy, gobbledegook, jinx, phoney,* and *stooge?* Words which have been with us, and also with the British, so long that most people could not spot them as Americanisms. Should these words be considered Americanisms still, or is it more appropriate to think of them as general English slang words? Such recent arrivals as *wimp, geek, dork,* and *wuss* are commonly used by teenagers and young adults, and amongst those users they are not considered Americanisms. In another ten years, who will know, or much less care, about their US origin?

Much of the latest American idiom is used by teenagers, and in a very conscious manner. Skateboarders and surfers use much American slang, because it is in the States that the major group of their subculture exists. In this subculture such words as *gnarly* and *rad* are par for the course. They have a specific application in that subculture which other words don't have. A *gnarly* set (of waves) cannot be called a *bonzer* set. Fine word that bonzer is, it doesn't have the same connotations. In such a subculture the American idiom is cool, even if actual Americans are considered only *bloody yanks* or *seppos*. In time, these Americanisms lose their American flavour. Even blatant Americanisms, like *chill out* and *awesome,* when used in Australia, with Australian intonation, Australian accent, Australian stress patterns, and in a distinctly Australian sentence, do not grate on the nerves as they do when heard on Ricki Lake. The process of borrowing is an integral part of language, and so is objection to such borrowings. Over time the hubbub dies down about certain words, or, more correctly, is moved onto different, newer borrowings. It's all part of that verbal workbench, melting pot and mosaic known as slang.

However, for those still worried about the American cultural invasion of our language, there is hope and happiness to be found in looking at the latest trends of Australian English. Australian humour and inventiveness is alive and well, as is much traditional Australian slang. The term *cobber,* while pretty much anachronistic on the mainland is widely used throughout Tasmania (often shortened to *cob*), and is, as many have noted, also widely used by Australians abroad. It is still a part of our linguistic culture, and mateship is still a part of our cultural mythos. But the story does not end here, for apparently cobber is still in use amongst some Australian children. The *Macquarie Dictionary* has recently set up a free Internet site called K*I*D (the Kids' Internet Dictionary **http://www.dict.mq.edu.au/kid**) which allows children from Australia and the rest of the world to make their own dictionary by recording their words in their own words. Basically, it is a blank form in which a term may be recorded, with definitions and comments on usage, pronunciation, etc. Surprising to many may be the fact that one schoolkid from Victoria chose to enter *Cobber* into K*I*D as the nickname of a female schoolmate, adding that it "is a word used to describe good friends", and that "it can be used by anyone in Australia". Other classic Australianisms entered by Australian children are *berko, dag, dodgy, dunny, hurl (vomit), mullet, sconed, slack, spaz, up the creek* and that perennial description of stupidity, *silly as a two bob watch.*

But, not only is such venerable Australian slang surviving well, new Australian slang inventions are in plentiful supply. A *billy* was once used by bushies to boil water, nowadays it can also refer to an apparatus for smoking marijuana. And a *billy lid* is a kid, proving that rhyming slang is still very much with us. The Australian *hoon* has moved from being a pimp, to being a lout, to being, in current speech, a speeding petrolhead. We have shortened *gossip* to *goss* and a *government flat* to a *govie,* and our medical practitioners have had their cumbersome titles cut in a typically Australian way, thus the *chiropractor* is a *chiro*, the *physiotherapist* is a *physio* and the *gynaecologist* is a *gyno*. The great Australian -o ending, as in *garbo* and *milko,* has recently been used to create *ambo* (an ambulance or ambulance officer), *femmo* (a feminist), *lammo* (a lamington) and *servo* (a service station). It has also been added to give emphasis to expression of taste, with *yucko* and *yummo*. How Aussie is that?

All in all, Australian slang is brilliant. Not only does it pay homage to its roots, it is also keeping well abreast of the times.

J. L.

■ ACKNOWLEDGMENTS ■

I would like to thank all those people who gave their time and effort in helping me in many ways. I would especially like to mention Scott Fitzgerald, Julia Wokes, Sarah Ogilvie, Kris Burnet, Michael Free, and the editors of *Tracks* magazine. Thanks must also go to all my workmates whom I annoyed from time to time with various queries regarding lexicographical style, grammar, etc. Finally I would like to thank Diana Jarosiewicz for all her support, love and intelligence, and for setting me straight on many things outside my limited ken.

■ EXPLANATORY NOTES ■

LABELLING

The dictionary section of the *Macquarie Book of Slang* employs a number of restrictive labels which give the user extra information about the word that is not covered in the definition. These labels can restrict the definition(s) to a particular sphere of interest or endeavour, as *Cricket, Surfing*, etc., or to a certain region, as *WA* or *Tas,* and are fairly self-explanatory. However, there are some restrictive labels that will need explaining.

Firstly, there are labels which place definitions in time.
Hist.
The *Hist.* label is used for the various Australianisms that are important enough historically to be retained in this dictionary. Thus various terms to do with convict or colonial life, bushranging and humping swags are labelled *Hist.* – the sort of stuff that is the heart of the Australian bush/outback mythology.

Obsolete

This refers to words or meanings that are no longer alive, but are not old enough to be labelled as historical. They are generally words to do with Australian urban culture rather than the bush.

Obsolescent

This refers to those words which are dying out but are deemed to be not quite dead yet. In fact, one of the hardest decisions a lexicographer faces is that of deciding if a relatively recent word truly merits being labelled as obsolete. The mere fact of not having any evidence that a word is in use at the present time is in no way an assurance that the word is dead. It may be alive and kicking on the lips of people next door, across the street, a few suburbs away or in another state.

Older slang

This refers to those terms which, while no longer in use by in current colloquial speech, were used within living memory of many people of the older generation and are more than likely not yet totally obsolete. Generally, terms labelled *Older slang* date from the 1940s, 50s, to a lesser extent, the 1960s and 70s.

Secondly, there are the labels *Offensive, Crass, Derogatory* and *Racist,* all of which relate to the attitude or the feelings of the speaker or the person spoken to.

Offensive

This label is reserved for words that in general usage are thought of as "swear words" or as being "rude". Thus words such as *fuck, cunt, turd,* etc. are labelled *Offensive*. These words are stigmatised as being able to cause offence — when one wants to swear, these are the words one will inevitably use. This is not to say that one should avoid using these terms, it is merely pointing out that this is a function that these terms can perform. The choice to use or not use these words is up to the individual.

Crass

This label is applied to those words which embody some off-colour concept. A good example is the term *axemark* for vagina. The term itself is a compound of two perfectly ordinary words "axe" and "mark", neither of which are derogatory or offensive by themselves, nor as a compound. However, the equating of the female genitalia with a wound caused by an axe is a very off-colour metaphor. To say that this term is blatantly crude and crass is a statement that would brook very little argument. Sure, some people may find this term to be somewhat humorous, but the very essence of this term's success is its deliberate crassness. Many people enjoy being crass and purposefully use terms such as this in order to shock, offend or upset those of greater sensitivities about such things. The labelling of terms as such is not necessarily condemning them as inherently bad, rather it is merely noting one of the linguistic functions of the terms.

Derogatory

This refers to words that are strongly deprecating or disparaging. The word *fuck* is an offensive word, but it is not derogatory, whereas *dole-bludger* is derogatory but not offensive since neither "dole" nor "bludger" are swear words. On the other hand, the term *fuckhead* is both offensive and derogatory since not only is it highly disparaging, but it also uses the word "fuck" which is already labelled offensive.

Racist

This label is more easily assigned than *Offensive*, *Derogatory* or *Crass*. It records that the term is a derogatory term that specifically singles out one racial group. The *Racist* label includes the concept of the *Derogatory* label.

ABBREVIATIONS

abbrev.	abbreviation	*pl.*	plural
ACT	Australian Capital Territory	*prep.*	preposition
adj.	adjective	*pron.*	pronoun
adv.	adverb	Qld	Queensland
Brit.	British	SA	South Australia
Comp.	computing	*Tas.*	Tasmania
Cf.	compare	US	United States
Hist.	history	*v.*	verb
interj.	interjection	*Vic.*	Victoria
n.	noun	WA	Western Australia
NSW	New South Wales	WWI	World War I
NT	Northern Territory	WWII	World War II
phr.	phrase		

ACRONYM

Thankfully the mania for inventing *acronyms* that occurred in the 80s has passed. Creations like *yuppies* (Young Urban Professionals) and *dinks* (Double Income, No Kids) spawned a veritable host of relatively useless terms such as: *arpies* (Asset Rich Parents), *bobos* (Burnt Out But Opulent), *lombards* (Lots Of Money But A Real Dork), *zuppies* (Zestful Upscale People in their Prime), etc. We also got a number of acronyms for things other than social groups, such as *nimby* (Not In My Back Yard) and the computer term *wysiwyg* (What You See Is What You Get). The 90s has seen a slowing down in the proliferation of acronyms, but there are still some new ones around. There is the *snag*, the Sensitive New Age Guy, quite a positive term for the same sort of bloke who was ridiculed as a *quiche-eater* in the 80s!

The increasing popularity of the Internet portends that a good many new acronyms are headed our way in the not too distant future, though perhaps none as long as *veronica,* the Very Easy Rodent-Oriented Net-Wide Index of Computerised Archives – whatever that may be!

A BIG ASK

This phrase has only recently become common, especially in the media where it began appearing with regularity at the beginning of the 1990s. Of course, for all those people who vehemently object to verbs being turned into nouns, the phrase is anathema. They think it is *a big ask* to have to accept this bastardisation of language! But, perhaps this innovation is not so new after all. The changing from verb to noun is quite a common occurrence not only in modern English, but throughout the whole history of the language. And thus it is not surprising that the word *ask* was used as a noun as far back as 1000 AD, even before William the Conqueror started his tricks. And, hang on a sec, isn't *bastardisation* a bastardisation of language anyhow?

ANKLE-BITER

billy, billy lid, brat, bub, cub, joey, kid, kiddie, kiddo, laddie, lassie, little Johnny, little vegemite, littley, munchkin, nipper, nointer (Tas), piccaninny, rug-rat, runt, snork, sonny, sprag, sprog, squirt, tacker, tiddler, tin lid, tiny, tiny tot, tot, tyke, youngie

STUCK FOR WORDS

ABC *n.* a Chinese person born and raised in Australia. [standing for *Australian-Born Chinese*; in the US it is similarly used to stand for an *American-Born Chinese*]

Abo *n. Racist.* **1.** an Aborigine. *–adj.* **2.** Aboriginal. [shortened form of *Aborigine*]

abs *n. Weights.* the abdominal muscles.

acca *n.* an academic. Also, **acker**.

accident *n.* a person born from an unplanned pregnancy: *I was definitely an accident.*

AC/DC *adj.* attracted to both males and females as sexual partners; bisexual.

ace *adj.* **1.** excellent; first in quality; outstanding: *The kids think he's ace.* *–v.* **2.** to successfully achieve, complete, etc.: *You aced that exam.*

acid[1] *phr.* **put the acid on, a.** to ask (something) of (someone) in such a manner that refusal is difficult; pressure (someone). **b.** to pressure (someone) for sexual favours.

acid[2] *n.* **1.** LSD. *–phr.* **2. drop acid**, to take LSD.

acid head *n.* one who takes LSD.

acid house *n.* a type of dance music.

acidic *adj.* (of dance music) having an acid house influence.

acker *n.* **1.** a pimple. [abbreviated from *acne*] **2.** Also, **acca**. an academic.

action *n.* potentially sexually available people: *checking out the action.*

adios *interj.* the Spanish word for 'goodbye'.

ADO *n.* an accumulated day off.

aerial *n. Surfing.* See **air**.

aesthetically challenged *adj. Jocular.* ugly.

Afghani dark *n.* a type of marijuana.

afternoon delight *n.* sexual intercourse in the afternoon.

aggers *adj.* aggressive: *aggers to the max.*

aggro *adj.* **1.** aggressive; dominating. *–n.* **2.** aggression; violence. **3.** aggravation.

agricultural shot *n. Cricket.* a wild slog of the ball, usually over square leg or mid wicket. [so called as it is the sort of shot a farmer might make]

ai caramba *interj.* an exclamation of dismay. [from Spanish; first recorded in English in the 19th century, but recently popularised by the television show *The Simpsons*]

ai chihuahua *interj.* an exclamation of surprise.

air *n.* **1.** *Surfing.* Also, **aerial.** a manoeuvre in which the rider and board become airborne, and then land and continue surfing. *–phr.* **2. off the air, a.** crazy. **b.** very angry.

air guitar *n.* the pretence of playing an imaginary guitar: *alone in his room playing air guitar.*

airhead *n.* an empty-headed, scatterbrained or frivolous person.

alibi *n.* a secret language used by schoolchildren in which normal words are modified by adding into each syllable the sounds 'ullab'; thus *hug* becomes *hullabug*; *You are a pig* becomes *Yullaboo ullabar ullaba pillabig*. Also **nullabat**.

alkie *n.* a heavy drinker; an alcoholic. Also, **alco, alko**.

3

alley oop *interj.* an exclamation of encouragement, exhortation, etc., some vigorous action or forceful effort. Also, **alleyoop, allez oop**. [from French *allez hop*]

alot *adv.* 1. a great deal. *–adj.* 2. many; a great number or amount of. [a common spelling error, but also used deliberately as a marker of informal or cool (i.e. anti-authoritarian) writing and ethos]

alrighty *adv.* yes; okay.

also-ran *n.* 1. *Horseracing.* an unplaced horse in a race. 2. a nonentity.

alterna- *prefix.* alternative; unconventional; not an ordinary or run-of-the-mill example of: *alternababe; alternateens; alternadom; alternarock.*

alternative *adj.* 1. (of music) different to any of the mainstream genres, such as that available on indie labels. 2. (of any aspect of popular culture) not having a mainstream following.

altogether *phr.* **in the altogether,** naked; in the nude.

amber fluid *n.* beer. Also, **amber liquid.**

ambient *adj.* 1. of or pertaining to a genre of music designed to induce a calm mood in the listener. *–n.* 2. Also, **ambience**. a type of electronic dance music.

ambo *n.* 1. an ambulance officer. 2. an ambulance.

amigo *n.* a friend. [from US, from Spanish]

ammo *n.* 1. *Military.* ammunition. *–phr.* 2. **wouldn't use (someone) for ammo at a shit fight,** an expression stating that (someone) is hopeless, worthless, etc.

amp *v.* to get excited; become thrilled: *keep amping; totally amped.*

amyl *n.* the drug amyl nitrate, used as a sexual stimulant.

anal *adj.* obsessive; finicky; fussy; having to have everything in strict order, set up perfectly neatly, etc.: *Don't be so anal.* [from psychoanalytical terminology, relating to an *anal character* or the *anal stage*]

anal floss *n.* G-strings or other items of skimpy underwear that ride up the anal cleft.

anally retentive *adj.* excessively meticulous and rigid about minor things.

anal retent *n.* an excessively anal person. Also, **retent.**

anchor *n.* (*pl.*) brakes: *hit the anchors; throw the anchors out.*

angel gear *n. Motoring.* neutral gear, especially when used to coast downhill to save fuel.

Anglo *n. Often derogatory.* an Australian of Anglo-Saxon or Anglo-Celtic descent.

animal *n.* 1. a disgusting person. 2. a highly-sexed person. 3. *Car sales.* a very dirty car.

ankle biter *n.* a young child.

anthem *n.* a song or piece of music seen indicative of, or encapsulating the feelings and ideas of, a particular subculture.

anthemic *adj.* (of music) regarded as an anthem.

any *phr.* **get any,** to obtain sexual intercourse: *Are you getting any?*

A-OK *adj.* very good; functioning correctly. Also, **A-okay.**

APC *n.* a quick wash. [initialism from the phrase *Arm Pits and Crotch,* punning on the brandname of a former headache powder]

ape *n.* **1.** a large, uncouth, boorish man. **2.** *phr.* **go ape (over),** to react with excessive and unrestrained pleasure, excitement, etc.

ape hangers *pl. n.* motorcycle or bicycle handlebars so curved that the handles are above the level of the rider's shoulders.

apeshit *phr.* **go apeshit,** to go crazy.

app *n. Computing.* an application.

apple *phr.* **she's apples** or **she'll be apples,** all is well. [from rhyming slang *apples and spice* nice]

-a-rama *suffix.* See **-o-rama**.

argue *phr.* **argue the toss,** to dispute a decision or command.

aristotle *n.* **1.** a bottle. **2.** the arse. Also, **aris, aras.** [def 1 straight rhyming slang; def 2 secondary rhyming slang *bottle and glass* arse]

-aroonie *suffix.* used to make colloquial or slang forms of nouns and adjectives: *It was a buzzaroonie; a complete stifferoonie; smitheroonies.* Also, **-eroonie.** See **-eroo**.

arse *n. Sometimes offensive.* **1.** rump; bottom; buttocks; posterior. **2.** a despised person. **3.** impudence: *What arse!* **4.** a person considered as a sex object: *What a nice bit of arse!* **5.** good luck. *–phr.*
6. arse about, in reverse or illogical order: *He did the exercise completely arse about.*
7. arse about (or **around**), to act like a fool; waste time.
8. arse over tit, a. upside down. **b.** fallen heavily and awkwardly usually in a forward direction.
9. arse up, to spoil; cause to fail.
10. cover one's arse, to protect oneself.
11. get one's arse into gear, to become organised and ready for action.
12. give (someone) the arse, a. to reject or rebuff (someone). **b.** to dismiss from employment.
13. kick arse, to be totally amazing; to really go off.
14. kick (someone's) arse, a. to beat convincingly. **b.** to reprimand severely; tell off.
15. kiss my arse! an expression of derision.
16. not to care a rat's arse, not to care at all
17. pain in the arse, an annoying person or thing.
18. think the sun shines out of one's arse, See **sun**.
19. up your arse! See **up**.
[from Middle English *ers*, from Old English *aers*]

arse bandit *n. Derogatory.* a male homosexual.

arse end *n.* **1.** the tail end; the base. **2.** the worst part: *This place is the arse end of the world.*

arsehole *n.* **1.** the anus. **2.** a despised person, especially a male; a person who is selfish, rude, unkind, etc. *–v.*
3. to remove a person from a place quickly and without ceremony; throw someone out. **4.** to dismiss; sack. *–phr.*
5. arsehole about, to fool around.
6. as ugly as a bagful (or **hatful**) **of arseholes,** unattractive; very ugly, especially of a person.

7. from arsehole to breakfast time, completely.

8. while one's arsehole points to the ground, while one is alive: *I'll never come at it, not while my arsehole points to the ground.*

arse-licking *adj. Offensive.* **1.** sycophantic. **2.** extremely good: *the most arse-licking bass you'll ever hear.*

arse-up *adj.* **1.** wrong side up; topsy-turvy; incorrect. *–adv.* **2.** in a clumsy fashion.

arsewipe *n.* a despicable person. [from US English *asswipe* toilet paper]

arsy *adj.* lucky. Also, **arsey, arsie.** [from *tin arse* a lucky person, from *tin* money]

artist *n.* a person noted or notorious for a reprehensible aspect of their behaviour: *a booze artist; a bullshit artist.*

arvo *n.* the afternoon. Also (less commonly), **arvie, aftie.**

as *conj.* **1.** used after an adjective to denote that what is being described is a superb or extreme example of its kind: *he was as fickle as; this place is hot as; I'm tired as. –phr.* **2. as if,** used to express complete disbelief or disagreement; in your dreams: *Would I come on a date with you? As if!*

ask *phr.* **a big ask,** a request or expectation of large magnitude which is difficult to fulfil.

ass[1] *n.* a stupid person. [from *ass* donkey]

ass[2] *n. US (rare in Australia)* arse. [originally an English dialect variant. In the US *arse* is often used as a euphemism]

attitude *n.* excessively aggressive and dominating behaviour: *a band with attitude; no attitude, just heaps of fun; hardcore attitude.*

aunty *n.* **1.** the Australian Broadcasting Corporation. **2.** an effeminate or homosexual older male. Also, **auntie.**

Aussie *adj.* **1.** Australian. *–n.* **2.** an Australian. **3.** Australia. **4.** the Australian dollar. Also **Ozzie, Ossie.**

Aussie battler *n.* See **battler**.

Australian *phr.* **the great Australian adjective,** the word *bloody*, used as an intensifier signifying approval, as in *bloody beauty*, or disapproval, as in *bloody bastard*; once ubiquitous in Australian colloquial speech.

Australian salute *n.* the movement of the hand and arm to brush away flies from one's face.

avoid list *n.* a putative list of people one wishes not to socialise with; a list of geeks.

awake *phr.* **awake (up) to,** fully aware: *He's awake up to what's going on; they're awake to our plan.*

awesome *adj.* extremely impressive; of high quality; totally excellent.

axe *n.* **1. a.** an electric guitar. **b.** *Jocular.* an acoustic guitar. **c.** *Jazz.* any instrument for playing jazz. *–v.* **2.** to cut out; abolish (a project, etc.). **3.** to reduce (expenditure, etc.) sharply. **4.** to dismiss from a position.

axe man *n.* a man who plays guitar.

axe mark *n. Offensive.* (a crass term for) the vagina.

axe woman *n.* a woman who plays guitar.

BOOFHEAD

This word first appeared in the 1940s when *Boofhead* was the name of a comic strip character in the Sydney newspaper *The Mirror*. Australians have always enjoyed a light-hearted dig at their mates and friends, and *boofhead* is a fine example of this type of friendly insult. You can generally call someone a *boofhead* without getting a biff on your own *boofhead*, though I wouldn't suggest testing this with just anyone. Perhaps this is due to the apparent meaninglessness of the word. *Fathead*, *meathead*, and *bullethead* are all similar insults, and we are all familiar with the words *fat*, *meat* and *bullet* – but just what is a *boof*? Well, nothing really. If there ever was a meaning of *boof* it is now lost in time. One theory is that *boofhead* is a shortening of an earlier insult *bufflehead*. That this was once used in Australia, is attested to in the writing of Norman Lindsay.

It comes from English dialect, meaning, literally, *bullock head* since *buffle* was an old term, borrowed from French, for a *bullock*.

BLUEY

There are those amongst us who always like to call a spade "a spade", but there are others who follow a perverse and twisted path, who call black "white" and white "black", often in jest or playfulness. In this game of contraries, irony plays a major part, so that the nickname "Shorty" could be given to someone who is very short, but equally to someone who is very tall. Black may be the opposite of white, but for the other colours it is a bit difficult to decide what's what. Certainly Australians seem to feel that blue is the opposite of red, and so the nickname for a redhead is "Bluey" or "Blue". Maybe it works as a kind of verbal underlining, a way of highlighting the most obvious and noticeable thing about someone. This way of arriving at a nickname is common to English speakers around the world, but it does seem that this particular nickname for redheads is linked to Australians and has been most popular here since the late 1800s.

BACK OF BOURKE

back of nowhere, Bandywallop, beyond the black stump, Bullamakanka, land where the crows fly backwards, Outer Mongolia, six-finger country, Snake Gully, tthe boondocks, the Never-Never, tiger country, Woop Woop

STUCK FOR WORDS

babbling brook *n.* a cook. Also, **bab, babbler.** [rhyming slang]

babe *n.* **1.** a familiar term of address to a woman: *Hey, babe. How've you been?* **2.** a sexually attractive female. **3.** a sexually attractive male.

babefest *n.* a place or event at which there are many sexually attractive females or males.

babelicious *adj.* absolutely gorgeous; incredibly attractive. [blend of *babe* and *delicious*]

babe-slayer *n.* a ladies' man.

Babewatch *n. Jocular.* the television show *Baywatch.*

baby *n.* **1.** an affectionate term of address to a woman, especially a partner, lover, etc. **2.** an invention, project, creation, job, etc. which one proudly considers as their own: *This book is my baby.* –*phr.*
3. leave (someone) holding the baby, a. to leave (the mother) with the sole responsibility of bring up a child. **b.** to abandon (someone) with a problem or responsibility not rightly theirs.
4. make babies, *Jocular.* to have sexual intercourse (not for the purpose of having children).

-baby *suffix.* a diminutive element added to the end of a name, or a familiar shortening of a name, in order to make it more informal and colloquial: *Chuck-baby; Gorby-baby.*

baby blues *pl. n.* blue eyes.

baby-poo brown *n.* a yucky brown colour, reminiscent of baby's faeces. Also, **baby-cack brown.**

bach *v.* **1.** to keep house alone or with a companion when neither is accustomed to housekeeping: *She was baching with a friend at North Sydney.* **2.** to live alone: *an old hand at baching.* Also, **batch.** [shortened from *bachelor*, i.e. to live as a bachelor who has moved out of home]

back *phr.*
1. backs to the wall, a homophobic catchphrase used supposedly to warn men that a particular male is homosexual.
2. back up for, to seek a second share of (a commodity being distributed).
3. see the back of, a. to be rid of (a person). **b.** to be finished with (a situation, task, etc.).

backblocks *pl. n.* **1.** remote, sparsely inhabited inland country. **2.** the outer suburbs of a city.

backburner *phr.* **put on the backburner,** to delay immediate action on.

backchat *n.* **1.** impertinent talk; answering back. –*v.* **2.** to answer someone back, especially in a cheeky manner.

backhander *n.* **1.** a bribe: *He slipped the witness a backhander.* **2.** a blow to the face with the back of the hand.

back of beyond *n.* **1.** a remote, inaccessible place. **2.** the far outback. –*adv.* **3.** in the outback. Also, **back o' beyond, back of sunset, back of Bourke.**

bad *adj.* **1.** *Originally US Black English.* wonderful; excellent; good: *You look bad, man; You're the baddest.* –*phr.*
2. bad call, an exclamation proclaiming that someone has made a really poor decision.

bad | **ball**

3. not bad, a. pretty good; fair; acceptable: *He's a good fighter, not bad for a monk.* **b.** very good, even excellent: *You just won $500? Not bad, eh?* [the seemingly paradoxical def 1 is actually a development of an earlier sense in which *bad* meant 'tough', 'mean', 'rugged']

bad hair day *n.* **1.** a day in which one cannot get one's hair to look good. **2.** a day in which one is in a bad mood and nothing goes right: *Having a bad hair day, are we?* See **good hair day**.

bad karma *n.* **1.** bad luck **2.** uneasy feelings associated with something; bad vibes.

badmouth *v.* to speak unfavourably of; criticise with malice.

bad trot *n.* a period of ill fortune.

bag *n.* **1.** (*pl.*) a lot; an abundance: *bags of money.* **2.** Also, **old bag.** *Derogatory.* a disagreeable and unattractive woman. **3.** *Cricket.* a good haul of wickets obtained by a bowler. **4.** a measure of marijuana, heroin, etc. *–v.* **5.** Also, **bag out.** to criticise sarcastically or harshly; knock. *–phr.*
6. bag of tricks, a. a miscellaneous collection of items. **b.** a tool box.
7. get a bag, *Cricket.* a sarcastic remark made to a cricketer who has dropped a catch.
8. in the bag, a. secured; certain to be accomplished: *The contract is in the bag.* **b.** (of a jockey) to be set up to receive money for not letting his or her mount run on its merits. **c.** (of a horse) going to be run to lose.
9. rough as bags, (of a person) extremely rough in either manners or looks.

baggy green *n.* **1.** the Australian Test Cricket cap. **2. don/wear the baggy green,** to represent Australia at Test cricket.

bagman *n.* **1.** *Hist.* **a.** a swagman; tramp. **b.** a travelling pedlar. **2.** a bookmaker's change clerk.

bag of fruit *n.* a suit. [rhyming slang]

bags *interj.* **1.** an exclamation by which one establishes right by virtue of making the first claim: *Bags I have first ride; Bags the window seat.* **2.** *v.* to claim priority rights by making the first claim: *It's not fair, I bagsed it first!* [originally also *bag*; extended from the sense of *bag* to kill game and hence claim it as one's own, literally, to add it to one's bag]

bagswinger *n.* a bookmaker's change clerk.

bail *v.* **1.** to depart, leave: *Come on, let's bail.* **2.** to withdraw in a cowardly manner from (a contest, a dare, the riding of a large wave, etc.); pike out. *–phr.* **3. bail on (someone),** to abandon (someone).

baldy *n.* **1.** *Derogatory.* (a term of address for) a bald person. **2.** a worn tyre having little or no tread. **3.** a coin with Edward VII on the obverse, traditionally used in the game two-up.

Bali belly *n.* diarrhoea, as suffered by travellers to South-East Asia.

ball *n.* **1.** a testicle: *kicked smack-bang in the left ball.* *–v.* **2.** (of a man) to have intercourse with (someone). *–phr.*
3. a ball of muscle, a person who is very healthy and in good spirits.
4. balls and all, aggressively and enthusiastically.

5. do (one's) balls on, (of a man) to become infatuated with (someone).

6. have (someone) by the balls, to have (someone) in one's power.

7. stick out like dog's balls, to be blatantly obvious.

ball and chain *phr.* **the old ball and chain,** *Derogatory.* the wife.

ballistic *phr.* **go ballistic,** to become crazy; get furious.

balls *pl. n.* **1.** courage, moral strength. **2.** the testicles. *–interj.* **3.** an exclamation of repudiation, ridicule, etc.

balls-out *adj.* aggressive in a masculine way.

balls-up *n.* **1.** confusion arising from a mistake; a mess. **2.** the mistake itself. *–v.* **3.** to bring to a state of hopeless confusion or difficulty.

ballsy *n.* **1.** showing great courage. **2.** aggressively masculine.

ball-tearer *n.* something extremely good or dynamic: *a ball-tearer of a book.*

Balmain kiss *n.* See **Liverpool kiss**.

baloney *n.* nonsense; insincere or idle talk; waffle. Also, **boloney**.

banana *phr.* **1. go bananas, a.** to become uncontrollably angry. **b.** to become mentally unbalanced. **2. nice try, but no banana,** a phrase indicating that someone has made a good, but nevertheless incorrect, guess.

bananabender *n.* a Queenslander.

bandicoot *v.* **1.** *Obsolete.* to dig up (root vegetables, potatoes, etc.) leaving the top of the plant undisturbed. *–phr.* **2. bald as a bandicoot,** remarkably bald.

B and S *n.* a ball held for young people who are unmarried. Also **B and S ball**, **B&S**. [standing for *Bachelor and Spinster*]

Bandywallop *n.* an imaginary remote town.

bang *n.* **1.** an act of sexual intercourse. **2.** a person rated according to their sexual ability: *a good bang.* *–v.* **3.** to have sexual intercourse. *–phr.* **4. bang out,** to play (music) loudly.

banger *n.* **1.** a sausage: *bangers and mash. –phr.* **2. three bangers short of a barbie,** See **barbie**.

banging *adj.* (of dance music) having a strong beat. Also, **bangin'**, **bang** *n.*

bank *n.* an amount of money used for betting when out gambling.

banker *phr.* **run a banker,** (of a river) to be flowing up to the top of the banks.

barbed wire *n.* brand Fourex beer. [referring to the four Xs displayed on the label (XXXX), resembling barbed wire]

barbie *n.* **1.** a barbecue. *–phr.* **2. a couple** (or **three**) **bangers short of a barbie,** dull-witted; weak of intellect; stupid. Also, **barby**.

Barbie *n. Derogatory.* a young, empty-headed, woman who is tall, slim, well-endowed and attractive in a stereotypical way, with peroxide-blonde hair. Also, **Barbie doll**. Cf. **Ken doll**. [Trademark: name of a children's doll]

barf *v.* to vomit; spew. [imitative]

bargain *interj.* an exclamation of great approval, pleasure, etc.

barge *n.* **1.** any old or unwieldy boat. **2.** a cumbersome surfboard.

barmy *adj.* mad; stupid; silly.

barn *phr.* **were you born in a barn** (or **field**) (or **tent**), a phrase used to reprimand a person who has forgotten to close a door.

barney *n.* **1.** an argument; fight. *–v.* **2.** to argue or fight. [from British dialect]

barrack *v.* **1.** to shout encouragement for (a player, team, etc.). *–phr.* **2. barrack for,** to support or go for: *I barrack for St. George; I barracked for Whitlam back in '72.* [? Nth Ireland dialect *barrack* to brag, to boast of fighting powers]

barrel *n.* **1.** *Surfing.* the hollow tube of a wave. *–v.* **2.** to knock over by running into or striking hard: *I'll barrel the bloke.* **3.** *Surfing.* to ride inside the tube of a wave.

barrier rogue *n.* a horse that is difficult to manage in the starting barriers.

barro *adj.* embarrassing: *It was heaps barro.*

base *n.* **1.** the rump; the buttocks. *–phr.* **2. base over apex,** fallen heavily and awkwardly, usually in a forward direction.

bash *n.* **1. a.** a party. **b.** a drinking spree. **2.** an attempt; a try: *had a bash at is last night; give it a bash.* **3.** an act of sexual intercourse.

bash hat *n.* a felt hat. [so called because they are normally moulded into a personalised shape by bashing with the hand]

basin cut *n.* See **bowl cut.**

basket case *n.* a person in an advanced state of nervous tension or mental instability.

basketweaver *n. Derogatory.* a person who advocates simple living, natural foods, avoidance of high-technology, etc.

bastard *n.* **1.** an unpleasant or despicable person. **2.** (*used without negative connotations*) any person. *–adj.* **3.** bad; pathetic: *a bastard thing to do. –phr.*
4. don't let the bastards grind you down, an exhortation to keep one's resolve and remain firm and cheerful in the face of difficulties. Often jocularly rendered in mock Latin, as *nil carborundum bastardis.*
5. happy (or **lucky**) **as a bastard on Father's Day,** (*ironic*) unhappy; unlucky.

bat¹ *n.* **1.** *Two-up.* the piece of wood used in tossing the coins; the kip. **2.** rate of motion: *to go at a fair bat.*

bat² *n.* **1.** *Derogatory.* an ugly woman: *She's an old bat. –phr.* **2. like a bat out of hell,** at speed; quickly.

bat-pad *n. Cricket.* a close-in fielder.

bats *adj.* mad; crazy.

battery *n.* an illegal device which delivers an electric shock to a racehorse when racing in order to make it run faster.

battery-trained *adj.* (of a racehorse) having been trained with a battery device used continually on a certain part of the body, so that it will respond similarly from a smart smack in that area while racing.

battle *v.* **1.** to courageously struggle to make ends meet in the face of adversity. *–phr.* **2. battle on,** to continue a struggle; endure.

battleaxe *n. Derogatory.* a domineering woman.

battler *n.* **1.** a decent and fair person who struggles continually and persistently against heavy odds; a doer. **2.** Also, **(little) Aussie battler.** a typical member of the working class in Australia. **3.** a conscientious worker, especially one living at subsistence level. **4.** *Hist.* an itinerant worker reduced to living as a swagman. **5. a.** a small time punter who tries to live on their winnings. **b.** a small time horse owner who is always struggling to make a living. **6.** a prostitute.

bazoomas *pl. n. Originally Brit.* a woman's breasts. Also, **bazooms.** [alteration of *bosom*]

BD *abbrev.* (in personal ads) bondage and discipline.

beach bum *n.* one who spends most of his or her life lazing about on a beach.

beak *n.* a judge. [from British slang, earlier (16th century) as *beck*; origin unknown]

beamer *n. Cricket.* a full toss which goes towards the head of the person batting. Also, **beam ball.**

bean *n.* **1.** anything of the least value: *I haven't a bean.* –*phr.*
2. full of beans, energetic; vivacious.
3. spill the beans, to divulge information, often unintentionally.

bean ball *n. Cricket.* a full toss which goes towards the head of the person at bat. Also, **beam ball, beamer.**

bean counter *n.* an accountant.

beanpole *n.* a tall, lanky person.

bear *n.* **1.** *Homosexual slang.* a large and hairy homosexual man. –*phr.*
2. like a bear with a sore head, intensely irritable; grumpy.

bear pit *n.* an arena for fierce political debate, as parliament house or a council chamber. Also, **bearhouse.**

bear-up *n. Obsolete.* an approach to a female for the purpose of engaging in amorous banter. [i.e. fronting up boldly and uncouthly as a *bear*; cf. the rare variant *bull-up*]

beast *n.* **1.** a large, usually old, car. **2.** *Derogatory.* an ugly person. **3.** *Surfing.* **a.** a thick surfboard. **b.** a very large wave. –*phr.* **4. beast with two backs,** two people having sexual intercourse.

beastly *adj.* absolutely wonderful; terrific; excellent.

beat *n.* **1.** a public area where a street prostitute solicits. **2.** a public place which homosexual men frequent to pick up casual sexual partners. –*v.*
3. *Criminal.* to be acquitted from a charge. –*adj.* **4.** exhausted; worn out. –*phr.*
5. beat it, (*frequently in the imperative*) to go away; depart.
6. beat off, to masturbate.

beat queen *n.* a male homosexual who frequents beats.

beaut *adj.* **1.** fine; good: *a beaut car.* –*interj.* **2.** an exclamation of approval, delight, enthusiasm, etc. –*n.* **3. a.** something successful or highly valued. **b.** a pleasant, agreeable, trustworthy person. –*phr.*
4. you beaut! an exclamation of elation.

beautiful people *pl. n. Derogatory.* a social set of young, affluent, people having a self-centred view of the world.

beauty *interj.* **1.** an exclamation of

beauty approval, delight, enthusiasm, etc. –*n.* **2. a.** something successful or highly valued. **b.** a pleasant, agreeable, trustworthy person. –*phr.* **3. you (little) beauty!** an exclamation of elation. Also, **bewdy.**

beaver *n. Chiefly US. Offensive.* **1.** the female pubic region; the vulva or vagina. –*phr.* **2. beaver shot,** a pornographic picture of the vulva or vagina.

bed flute *n.* the penis.

be-diddle *v. Frisbee.* to spin (a frisbee, etc.) on the point of a finger.

beef *n.* **1.** weight, as of human flesh: *He's got plenty of beef on him.* **2.** *Originally US.* a complaint. –*v.* **3.** *Originally US.* to complain; grumble.

beef bayonet *n. Crass.* an erect penis. Also, **beef bugle.**

beefcake *n.* photographs of men in newspapers, magazines, etc., posed to display their bodies and emphasising their sex appeal. See **cheesecake.**

Beemer *n.* a BMW car. [pronunciation of the letters *BM* + *-er*]

beer gut *n.* a paunch associated with excessive beer drinking. Also, **beer belly.**

beetle *n.* **1.** a Volkswagen car of the first type produced. [so called due to its shape] –*v.* **2.** Also, **beetle off** (or **along**), to move swiftly; leave quickly.

Beezer *n.* a vehicle manufactured by the British Small Arms company. [pronunciation of the letters *BSA*]

beg *phr.*
 1. beg, beg, grovel, grovel, *Jocular.* an exclamation used to plead, as for a favour.
 2. beg pardon, a colloquial shortening of the phrase *I beg your pardon.*
 3. no beg pardons, no time for pleasantries or niceties; no pussyfooting around.

bell *n.* a telephone call: *to give someone a bell.*

belly-ache *n.* **1.** a complaint. –*v.* **2.** to complain or grumble.

bellybuster *n.* a painful dive in which one's stomach hits the water first. Also, **bellywhacker.**

bellyflop *n.* **1.** Also, **bellyflopper.** a bellybuster. –*v.* **2.** to dive so that one's stomach hits the water first.

belt *v.* **1.** to move quickly: *to belt along.* –*phr.*
 2. add (something) to one's belt, to acquire a favourable point.
 3. below the belt, against the rules; unfairly: *hitting below the belt.*
 4. belt up, to stop making noise; be quiet.

bench warmer *n. Sport.* a reserve in a team who does not get many games.

bender *n.* a drinking spree.

benny *n.* a benzedrine pill.

bent *adj.* **1.** having little or no regard for the law; dishonest; corrupt. **2.** diverging from what is considered to be normal or conservative behaviour, as having some strange sexual predilection, etc. –*phr.* **3. get bent,** to get stoned on marijuana, etc.

bent cop *n.* a dishonest police officer, especially one who takes bribes.

berk *n. Originally Brit. Derogatory.* a despicable person. Also, **birk, burk, burke**. [from 19th century rhyming slang, *Berkeley* (or *Berkshire*) *Hunt* cunt]

berko *adj.* berserk.

bestest *n. Jocular.* a mock superlative of *best*; the best of the best: *He's my bestest, bestest friend.*

bet *phr.*
  1. **bet your boots,** See **boot.**
  2. **bet your bottom dollar,** to be so sure of something as to be willing to bet one's last piece of money.
  3. **you bet (your life),** you may be sure; certainly; indeed.

betcha *interj.* bet you: *Betcha she'll win.*

better half *n.* 1. one's wife. 2. one's spouse or partner.

bev *n.* a drink; a beverage. Also, **bevvie**.

bevan *n.* a stupid or unfashionable male; a geek or dork. [from *Bevan* a male name]

bewdy *n., interj.* See **beauty.**

Bex *phr.* **a cup of tea, a Bex, and a good lie down,** a stock formula used to describe a once popular method of relaxation. Also, **a Bex, a cuppa and a lie down.** [from *Bex*, a brand of pain killer]

bhang *n.* marijuana. [from Hindi, from Sanskrit]

bi *adj.* 1. bisexual. –*n.* 2. a bisexual.

bible-basher *n.* a person of excessive religious, especially evangelical, zeal.

bickie *phr.*
  1. **big bickies,** a lot of money.
  2. **bite short of a bickie,** not very intelligent. Also, **bikkie**.

biddy *n.* a woman, especially an old or fussy one.

biff *n.* 1. a blow; punch. 2. fighting: *a bit of biff.* –*v.* 3. to punch. –*phr.* 4. **go the biff,** to fight. [originally imitative of the sound of a punch]

biffo *n.* 1. fighting: *He got into a bit of biffo.* –*adj.* 2. aggressive: *a biffo style of football commentating.*

big C *n.* cancer.

big girl *n. Derogatory.* an effeminate male. *I reckon blokes who don't take on dares are big girls.* Also, **big girl's blouse.**

big gun *n.* 1. a powerful or influential person. 2. *Surfing.* a long surfboard for big waves. –*adj.* 3. influential or important: *big gun designers.*

big hair *n.* hair styled to add volume.

big head *n.* 1. a conceited person. –*phr.* 2. **get/have a big head,** to be a conceited person: *Don't get a big head about it.*

big O *n.* sexual orgasm.

big one *n.* 1. *Originally US.* a thousand dollars. 2. (*usually ironic*) a dollar coin or that amount of money. [a US slang term for a thousand-dollar note]

big shot *n.* a very important person.

big smoke *n.* the city, or any built-up or closely settled area. [originally Aboriginal pidgin]

big spit *n.* vomit: *to go for the big spit.*

big sticks *pl. n. Australian Rules.* the goal posts: *He's dobbed it through the big sticks.*

big swinging dick *n.* an aggressively powerful businessman.

big time *adv.* (used post-positively) to a great degree or extent: *You owe* *me big time; plunged into it big time.*

big-time *adj.* **1.** at the top level in any business or pursuit: *big-time executive.* **2.** (of criminals, prostitutes, etc.) involved in organised vice.

big whoop *interj.* a sarcastic expression of surprise, etc. Also, **big whoops, big whoopsie.**

bike *n. Derogatory and offensive.* **1.** a woman who has sexual relations with many men of her acquaintance; a woman who sleeps around. [i.e. everyone 'rides' her; see *ride* def 1] –*phr.*
2. get off one's bike, to get angry; lose control of oneself.
3. on your bike, a direction or order to someone to leave immediately.

bikie *n.* a member of a gang of motorcycle riders. Also, **biker.**

bikkie *n.* See **bickie.**

bilk *v.* **1.** to cheat or swindle; defraud; rip off. **2.** to evade payment of a debt, etc.

billy *n.* **1.** a tin with a lid and a wire handle used for boiling water, making tea, etc. over an open fire. **2.** a bong for smoking marijuana or hash. **3.** a child. [from rhyming slang *billy lid* kid] –*phr.*
4. boil the billy, a. to make tea, not necessarily with a billy can. **b.** to stop for refreshments.
5. swing the billy, a. *Originally.* to put the billy on the fire and make some tea. **b.** to take a billy full of tea and swing it around in a great circle at arm's length, done in order to help settle the leaves.

billy lid *n.* a child; kid. [rhyming slang]

billyo *phr.*
1. go to billyo, get lost!
2. like billyo, a. with gusto: *We laughed like billyo.* **b.** with great speed: *He rode like billyo.*
3. off to billyo, a. off course; astray; in error. **b.** a long way ahead.
4. to billyo, to a great degree: *scared me to billyo.* Also, **billyoh, billy-oh.**

bimbo *n. Derogatory.* **1.** an attractive but empty-headed woman. See **himbo. 2.** (during the Depression) a younger male homosexual companion of a tramp. **3.** *Obsolete.* a baby. [from Italian *bimbo* baby, from *bambino* a baby boy]

bin *v.* to throw into a bin.

bint *n. Derogatory.* a young woman. [originally services slang during both World Wars, from Arabic]

bird *n.* **1.** *Horseracing.* a certainty to win; a cert. **2.** *Derogatory.* a woman. –*phr.*
3. give (someone) the bird, to ridicule (someone).
4. the birds and the bees, human sexual reproduction, as explained metaphorically to children.

birdwatcher *n. Jocular.* a male who perves at women.

birthday suit *n.* the naked skin; the state of nakedness.

bishop *phr. Crass.*
1. beat the bishop, (of a male) to masturbate.
2. bury the bishop, (of a male) to have sexual intercourse.

bit *n.* **1.** sexual intercourse: *Fancy a bit?* –*phr.*
2. a bit, a modest sum of money: *Reg had a bit on the winner of the*

last race; Ann was left a bit when her grandmother died.
3. a bit of all right, a sexually attractive person.
4. a bit of how's your father, See **father.**
5. a bit on the side, sexual relations outside of a marriage or monogamous relationship.

bitch *n.* **1.** *Derogatory and offensive.* a disagreeable or malicious woman; often, any self-assertive woman. **2.** *Derogatory and offensive.* any female: *You bitches stay in the car.* **3.** (in soap operas, etc.) a stock character of a calculating and manipulating woman: *She plays the new bitch in next season's offering.* **4.** something that causes great displeasure: *the bitch of a thing won't work.* **5.** a complaint; a gripe. *–v.* **6.** to complain. **7.** to spoil; bungle. *–interj.* **8.** an exclamation, used as an accusation when someone, either male or female, has said some cruelly cutting remark, or has acted in a very mean way. *–phr.* **9. life's a bitch, (and then you die),** a catchphrase expressing a dismal outlook on life, used when one feels that things are peculiarly bad.

bitchin' *adj.* excellent. Also, **bitchin.**

bitchy *adj.* **1.** (of a person) acting in a nasty manner; inclined to make snide comments. **2.** (of a comment, action or the like) cruelly cutting; malicious; extremely snide.

bite *v.* **1.** to trouble; worry; disturb: *What's biting him?* **2.** to react to a provocative statement: *I knew if I hassled you enough, you'd bite eventually.* **3.** to borrow money from (someone). *–n.* **4.** a person from whom one anticipates borrowing money: *He'd be a good bite.* **5.** a reaction: *Did you get a bite from Robin? –phr.* **6. put the bite on,** to cadge.

bitser *n.* a mongrel dog. Also, **bitzer.** [from the phrase *bits of this, and bits of that*]

bizzo *n.* worthless or irrelevant ideas, talk, writing, etc.: *politics, and all that bizzo.*

blab *v.* **1.** to talk, especially vacuously: *Quit blabbing!* **2.** to reveal some information that one is supposed to keep quiet; gossip.

black and tan *n.* a drink made by mixing beer and stout.

black stump *phr.*
1. back of (or **beyond**) **the black stump,** in the far outback; in any remote region.
2. this side of the black stump, a loose measure of comprehensiveness or distance: *I make the best pumpkin soup this side of the black stump; He is the biggest bore this side of the black stump.*

blading *n.* (the sport of) using rollerblades; rollerblading.

blank *phr.* **fire** (or **shoot**) **blanks,** (of a male) **a.** to experience orgasm but not ejaculate. **b.** to ejaculate infertile sperm.

blast *interj.* **1.** an exclamation of anger or irritation. *–v.* **2.** to criticise someone abusively. **3.** to shoot with a firearm. *–n.* **4.** a curt piece of abuse or criticism: *gave him a blast over the phone.* **5.** a quickly taken alcoholic drink. *–phr.* **6. blast off,** to begin: *The party blasts off at 9pm.*

blimey *interj.* an exclamation expressing surprise or amazement.

Also, **blimy, bli'me, blimey Charlie**. [shortened form of *gorblimey*, from *God blind me*]

blind *adj.* **1.** drunk. **2.** (of a pimple) not having formed a well-developed core near the surface, and hence not able to be burst or popped.

blinder *n.* something incredibly amazing: *a blinder of a game; one of the rumours was a blinder.*

blind Freddy *n.* **1.** an imaginary person representing the lowest level in perception or competence. *–phr.* **2. even blind Freddy could see that,** an expression used to indicate that something needs no explanation or defence. Also, **blind Freddie.**

blink *phr.* **on the blink,** not working properly.

blitz *n.* **1.** *Sport.* a bombardment of scoring, great play, etc. **2.** a concerted effort to curb some specific crime or misdemeanour waged by some authority: *a ticket blitz; a blitz of drink driving.* *–v.* **3.** to beat convincingly: *blitzing the field in the final heat.*

blob *n.* **1.** *Cricket.* nought; no runs: *out for a blob.* **2.** a fat person.

block *phr.*
1. lose (or **do**) **one's block,** to become very angry; lose one's temper.
2. off one's block, insane.

blockhead *n.* a stupid or slow person.

bloke *n.* **1.** man; fellow; guy. **2.** an affectionate term used to refer to a male animal. **3.** *Obsolete.* a person in charge; boss. **4.** *Obsolete.* a prostitute's pimp. [formerly also spelt *bloak*; from British working class slang, ? from Shelta (a tinkers' jargon of Ireland and parts of Britain); cf. British underworld slang *gloak* a man; Celtic *ploc* large stubborn person]

blokette *n. Jocular.* a blokey woman: *all the blokes and blokettes.*

blokey *adj.* crassly masculine.

blood oath *interj.* an exclamation usually expressing agreement, affirmation, etc. Also, **(my) bloody oath!**

bloody *adj.* **1.** a word used to add emphasis in signifying approval, as in *bloody beauty,* or disapproval, as in *bloody bastard.* **2.** (of events) cruel; unjust; unbearable. **3.** inserted between syllables to add emphasis: *abso-bloody-lutely; vege-bloody-mite.* *–adv.* **4.** very; extremely: *a bloody wonderful game; a bloody awful thing to happen.*

blotto *adj.* very drunk.

blouse *n. Derogatory.* an effeminate or ineffectual man. Also, **big girl's blouse; girl's blouse.**

blow *v.* **1.** to fail in something; ruin; wreck: *to blow an exam.* **2.** to ejaculate; experience orgasm. **3.** Also, **blow out.** *Horseracing, etc.* (of odds on a horse offered by bookmakers) to lengthen. **4.** (past participle: **blowed**), (*euphemism*) to damn: *Well I'll be blowed; Blow that!* *–n.* *–phr.*
5. blow in, to make an unexpected visit; drop in.
6. blow it out your arse! an exclamation of contempt.
7. blow up, a. to scold or abuse. **b.** to lose one's temper.
8. blow (someone) out, to amaze someone.
9. blow (someone's) mind, a. (of

a drug) to produce an altered state of consciousness. **b.** to totally amaze.

blowie *n.* **1.** a blowfly. **2.** a blowfish.

blow-in *n.* an unexpected visitor or newcomer to an area.

blow job *n.* an act of fellatio. Also, **blow-job**.

blown-out *adj.* amazed, usually from delight. Also, **blown-away**.

BLT *n.* a bacon, lettuce and tomato sandwich.

blubber *n.* jellyfish.

bludge *v.* **1.** *Originally.* to pimp; live on the earnings of a prostitute. **2.** to waste time, as lesson time or work time. **3.** to cadge: *Can I bludge a piece of your pie?* –*n.* **4.** a job, task, etc. which entails next to no work: *This class is an absolute bludge.* –*phr.*
5. bludge on, to impose on others.
6. on the bludge, actively engaged in bludging; cadging for something; imposing on someone. [backformation from *bludger*]

bludger *n. Derogatory.* **1.** *Originally.* a man living on the earnings of a prostitute. **2.** someone who imposes on others, evades responsibilities, does not do a fair share of the work etc. [a variant of earlier thieve's slang *bludgeoner* a thug who uses a bludgeon]

blue *adj.* **1.** dismal: *I'm feeling blue.* **2.** obscene; pertaining to obscenity: *a blue joke; blue movie.* –*n.* **3.** a fight; a dispute; a row. **4.** an error. –*v.* **5.** to fight, dispute or argue. **6.** *Obsolete.* to spend wastefully; squander: *blued his cheque.*

blue balls *pl. n.* a painful, temporary condition of the testicles which may follow a long period of unrelieved sexual arousal. Also, **lover's balls**.

blue blazes *pl. n.* an intensifier: *What the blue blazes are you doing?; drove like blue blazes.*

blue-flame *v.* to ignite a burst of flatulence.

blue mouldy *adj. Obsolete.* out of sorts; stale: *a bloke goes blue mouldy in a place like this.*

blue movie *n.* a pornographic film.

blues *pl. n.* despondency; melancholy.

blue-singlet *adj.* working-class.

blue swimmer *n.* a $10 note.

bluey *n.* **1.** *Hist.* a rolled blanket (originally blue) containing the possessions carried by a traveller through the bush; swag; shiralee. **2.** (an ironic nickname for) a redheaded person. –*phr.* **3.** *Hist.* **hump the bluey** or **humping bluey, a.** to carry a swag in the outback. **b.** to be unemployed and on the road, as an itinerant worker.

Blunnies *pl. n.* a pair of leather boots of the *Blundstone* brand, very popular in Tasmania, where the company originated in 1870.

BO *n.* body odour, especially due to excessive perspiration. [standing for *Body Odour*]

boarder *n.* a person who snowboards.

boardies *pl. n.* board shorts.

boatie *n.* a person who owns and runs a small craft.

boatrace *n.* **1.** the face. [rhyming slang] **2.** a competition between teams of beer drinkers to see which team can drink its beer the fastest.

bob *n.* (*pl.* **bob**). **1.** *Obsolete.* one shilling; a coin of this value. **2.** ten cents; a ten cent coin. **3.** (*pl.*) money: *saving a few bob.* –*phr.* **4. bob in,** (formerly) a subscription of one shilling to a common fund. [18th century British slang for a shilling; origin unknown]

bobby *n.* **1.** a police officer. **2.** *Prison.* a prison officer; screw. [special use of *Bobby* for Sir *Robert* Peel, who as British Home Secretary, organised the Metropolitan Police Force (1828)]

bobby-dazzler *n.* an excellent thing or person: *you little bobby-dazzler.* Also, **ruby-dazzler.**

Bob Hope *n.* **1.** soap. **2.** dope. [rhyming slang from Bob Hope, well-known American comedian]

Bob's your uncle *interj.* a response in conversation expressing compliance; it's all right; there you are.

bod *n.* **1.** a person: *an odd bod.* **2.** a body: *He's got a cute bod!*

bodacious *adj.* remarkable; outstanding. [from US, from British dialect *boldacious*, a blend of *bold* and *audacious*]

bodge *v.* **1.** to do something incorrectly but so as to make it appear right; to do something or make something in a sloppy manner: *I bodged together a few examples.* **2.** to ruin; wreck: *Now you've really bodged it.* Also, **bodge up.** [back-formation from *bodgie*]

bodger *n. Obsolete.* **1.** a worthless person. –*adj.* **2.** inferior; false; second-rate (as a name, receipt, etc.) [obsolete British *bodge* to patch or mend clumsily]

bodgie *adj.* **1.** inferior; worthless; bad: *a bodgie repair job.* **2.** (of names, etc.) false; assumed. –*n.* **3.** Also, **bodge.** (in the 1950s and 60s) a young man belonging to an anti-social subculture (known as **bodgies and widgies**) that rejected the morality and general worldview of the time. Bodgies were especially noted for violent behaviour, free sexuality and being influenced by American fashions. They characteristically had long hair, wore drape style, waistless jackets, and rode motorcycles. See **widgie.** –*v.* **4.** Also, **bodgie up.** to repair superficially; to quickly remove any obvious defects. [from *bodg(er)* + *-ie*]

bodice ripper *n.* a paperback romance novel with a pictorial cover featuring a man and woman in a steamy pose.

boff *v.* to have sexual intercourse.

boffin *n.* a person who is enthusiastic for and knowledgeable in any pursuit, activity, study, etc., especially a research scientist.

bog[1] *n.* **1.** an act of defecation. **2.** *Chiefly Brit.* a lavatory; toilet. –*v.* **3.** to defecate. –*phr.* **4. hang a bog,** to defecate. [British slang of the 18th century, recorded earliest in the compound *boghouse*; origin uncertain]

bog[2] *n.* **1.** a putty-like material applied to the body of a motor vehicle to patch up a hole after the rust has been cut out. –*v.* **2.** *WA Mining.* to work shovelling ore underground. –*phr.*
3. bog down, to sink in or as in a bog: *I'm bogged down with work today.*

4. bog in, a. to eat voraciously. **b.** to begin a task with enthusiasm.
5. bog it in, to win easily or perform a task easily. [from *bog* wet, spongy ground, from Gaelic]

bogan *n.* **1.** a fool; idiot. **2.** *WA.* a lout or hooligan, especially of a particular social group noted for wearing black shirt and jeans. **3.** *Tas.* a rough lout or hooligan. In Hobart equivalent to a **Chigga**. [probably from *Bogan* a river in NSW]

bogey[1] *n.* **1.** a swim or bath in a creek, waterhole, dam, etc. **2.** Also, **bogeyhole.** a swimming hole. *–v.* **3.** to take a bath or swim in a bogeyhole. Also, **bogie**. [from the Aboriginal language Dharuk]

bogey[2] *n.* **1.** a piece of nasal mucus: *You got a bogey on your chin. –v.* **2.** to expel snot from the nose: *Don't bogey on it.* Also, **bogie, booger, boogie.** [in British dialect *bug, boggart, boggle* mucus]

boghouse *n.* a toilet, especially an outside toilet.

bog standard *adj.* not containing any special features. Also, **bog stock**.

bogus *adj. Originally US.* very bad; unfair; no good; worthless: *That was a bogus stunt you pulled; Your dad is totally bogus.* [from *bogus* counterfeit; origin uncertain, cf. Hausa (an African language) *boko* deceit; Louisiana French *bogue* fake]

boil *v.* **1.** to feel very hot. *–phr.* **2. on the boil,** *Football.* running at full speed.

boilover *n.* **1.** a win by long-priced entrant in horse or greyhound race. **2.** a sudden conflict between persons.

boil-up *n.* **1.** *Prison.* an illegal brewing of tea or some other hot beverage in one's cell. **2.** a sudden excitement or conflict.

bollocks *pl. n.* **1.** the testicles. **2.** rubbish; nonsense. *–interj.* **3.** an exclamation decrying the verity of another's statement. Also, **ballocks, bollicks**. [from Middle English *ballokes*, Old English *beallucas* the testicles]

bollocky *adj.* **1.** completely naked: *stark bollocky. –phr.* **2. in the bollocky,** naked. Also, **bollicky, bols.**

boloney *n.* See **baloney**.

bolt *phr.*
1. bolt (it) in, *Originally horseracing.* to win easily.
2. bolt home, *Originally horseracing.* to win by a large margin.
3. do the bolt, to run away, especially when caught committing a misdemeanour.
4. shoot one's bolt, See **shoot**.
5. have shot one's bolt, to have reached the limit of one's endurance or effort.

bomb *n.* **1.** an old car. **2.** a jump into water with the knees tucked into the chest and the arms clasped about the knees, with the intent of making a large splash, especially to annoy nearby swimmers. *–v.* **3.** to fail a test, exam, etc. **4.** to jump into a pool, waterhole, etc., in a tucked up position so as to create a large splash. **5.** to spray (a train, etc.) with graffiti.

bombie *n.* a bombora. Also, **bommie, bommy**.

bombshell *n.* **1.** a sudden or devastating action or effect: *His resignation was a bombshell.* **2.** a woman who is physically well-endowed. *–phr.* **3. drop a bombshell,** to make a startling or unexpected announcement.

Bondi *phr. Older slang.* **shoot through like a Bondi tram, a.** to depart in haste. **b.** *WWII Military.* to go A.W.L. (absent without leave). [from *Bondi,* a beach and suburb of Sydney]

Bondi cigar *n.* a floating piece of human excrement in the ocean. [referring to an effluent outlet near *Bondi* beach, Sydney]

Bondi whistler *n.* a tweaking of the nipple.

bone *n.* **1.** Also, **boner.** an erect penis. *–phr.* **2. jump on someone's bones,** to have sexual intercourse with someone. **3. make old bones,** to reach a great age. **4. point the bone at, a.** to bring or wish bad luck upon (someone). **b.** to indicate (a guilty person).

bonecrusher *n. Rugby Football.* a heavy tackle.

bonehead *n.* a stupid, obstinate person; a blockhead.

boner *n.* **1.** a mistake: *You made a boner that time.* **2.** a difficult question. **3.** Also, **bone.** an erect penis.

bong *n.* **1.** an apparatus for smoking marijuana or hashish consisting of a container, partially-filled with water, with a pipe passing into it. The harsh smoke is made smoother as it passes through the water. **2.** an instance of smoking through a bong. *–v.* **3.** to smoke marijuana or hashish through a bong. *–phr.* **4. bong on, a.** to take part in a dope smoking session. **b.** (as a credo, often seen in graffiti) smoke marijuana. [from Thai *baung,* literally, a cylindrical wooden tube]

bonk *v.* **1.** to administer a blow to someone; hit: *She bonked her little brother on the head.* **2.** to have sexual intercourse (with someone). *–n.* **3.** an act of sexual intercourse.

bonkable *adj.* sexually attractive.

bonker *n.* a large marble.

bonkers *adj.* **1.** crazy; insane; out of control: *He's gone bonkers. –n.* **2.** a type of marble game using a bonker.

bonk song *n.* a song played while having sex in order to enhance the experience: *One of the greatest bonk songs of all time.* Also, **bonking song**.

bonus *interj.* an exclamation of strong approval, pleasure, etc.

bonzer *adj.* **1.** excellent; attractive; pleasing. *–interj.* **2.** an exclamation of joy, elation, etc.; excellent! Also, **bonza**. [origin unknown; cf. the equivalent obsolete terms *bontosher, bonster, boshter, bosker*]

boob[1] *n.* **1.** prison. *–adj.* **2.** jail issue, and hence poor quality: *boob tea, boob tobacco.* [shortening of *booby-hatch* a prison]

boob[2] *n.* a woman's breast. Also, **boobie**. [from earlier *bub*]

boob happy *adj. Prison.* suffering from a form of neurosis brought about by the strain of jail routine; stir crazy.

boobhead *n. Prison.* a recidivist. Also, **boob head**.

boobjob *n.* any cosmetic surgery done to the breasts.

boob tube *n.* **1.** a television set. **2.** a woman's strapless, tubular, elasticised upper garment primarily covering the breasts; bandeau top. [def 1 from *boob*[1]; def 2 from *boob*[2]]

boofhead *n.* a large, stupid fellow, esp. having an out-sized head. [a variant of earlier *bufflehead*, literally, buffalo head, and popularised by the cartoon character *Boofhead* as appearing in the Sydney *Daily Mirror* from 1941]

boofy *adj.* **1.** brawny but stupid: *the boofy boys in the gym.* **2.** (of the hair) having lots of volume. **3.** puffed out: *big boofy sleeves.*

booger *n.* **1.** *Surfing.* a bodyboard rider. **2.** See **bogey**[2].

boogie[1] *n., v.* See **bogey**[2].

boogie[2] *v.* to dance: *boogieing all night long; Get down and boogie.*

book *n.* **1.** a bookmaker. *–phr.* **2. make a book,** *Horseracing.* to lay and receive bets at such odds that whichever horse wins, a profit is made. **3. wrote the book on,** to be an expert at, especially a self-proclaimed expert: *Do I know anything about picture-hanging? I wrote the book on it!*

bookie *n.* a bookmaker.

bookie's runner *n. Horseracing.* a bookmaker's assistant engaged in collecting prices and laying off bets with other bookmakers, etc.

boomer *n.* **1.** something large, as a surfing wave. **2.** something successful or popular: *a boomer of a welcome.* **3.** a mature male kangaroo. [from Warwickshire dialect]

boomerang *n.* **1.** a scheme, plan, argument, etc., which rebounds upon the user. **2.** a small fish that is thrown back into the water. **3.** that which is expected to be returned by a borrower. *–v.* **4.** to return or recoil upon the originator: *The argument boomeranged.* [from the Aboriginal language Dharuk]

boomerang bender *n.* a teller of tall stories.

boong *n. Racist.* **1.** an Aboriginal. **2.** a black person of any race or nationality; a Negro. [from the Aboriginal language Wemba Wemba]

booshit *adj.* very good; excellent: *booshit surf.*

boot *n.* **1.** a kick: *a swift boot up the khyber.* *–v.* **2.** to kick. **3.** to dismiss; expel; discharge: *booted out of the club.* *–phr.* **4. bet your boots,** to be certain. **5. boot home, a.** *Horseracing.* to ride to win, kicking the horse to greater speed. **b.** to emphasise strongly. **c.** to push into position forcibly. **6. boots and all,** completely; with all one's strength or resources: *Go in boots and all.* **7. get the boot,** to be discharged. **8. order of the boot,** a dismissal; an order to leave.

booty *n.* the buttocks or rump; the arse: *get your booty on down this Saturday night; get your booty shakin'.*

booze *n.* **1.** alcoholic drink. *–v.* **2.** Also, **booze up.** to drink immoderately. *–phr.* **3. on the booze,**

drinking immoderately. [Middle English, from Middle Dutch *busen*]

booze artist *n.* a heavy drinker.

booze bus *n. NSW.* a mobile police unit used for random breath tests.

booze cruise *n.* an outing on a boat which stops at various wharves while the participants patronise a local pub; a pub-crawl via water.

boozer *n.* 1. one who drinks immoderately. 2. a hotel.

booze-up *n.* a drinking session.

boozing mate *n.* a drinking partner. Also, **boozing buddy, boozing friend**.

bop *v.* 1. to dance to pop or rock music: *bopping all night long. –phr.* 2. **bop till ya drop,** to dance all night long. [from *bebop,* a type of jazz music]

bo-peep *n.* a peep, view: *Have a bo-peep at that!*

bosie *n. Cricket.* a delivery bowled by a wrist-spinner which looks as if it will break one way but in fact goes the other; a googly. Also, **bosey**. [from BJT *Bos(anquet)*, an English cricket player renowned as the inventor of this bowl + *-ie*]

bosker *adj. Obsolete.* excellent; delightful. Also, **boshter**. [origin unknown; cf. *bonzer*]

bosom buddy *n.* a sworn friend; a best friend and companion.

boss *n.* 1. *Rural.* the male owner of a country station; traditionally having jurisdiction over the running of the property except for the homestead, run by the **missus**. 2. the principal of a school. *–v.* 3. to lord it over (someone), especially when one has no real jurisdiction; to meanly and overtly order (someone) about. [Dutch *baas* master]

bot[1] *n. Older slang.* 1. a person who cadges persistently. *–v.* 2. to cadge. *–phr.* 3. **on the bot,** cadging. [perhaps because a cadger is parasitic like the *bot* a parasitic insect larva]

bot[2] *n.* the bottom; the buttocks.

bot[3] *n.* a computer program which performs a simple task somewhat resembling human activity, as greeting a user by name, etc. [from *(ro)bot*]

bottle *v.* 1. to knock over people as though they were bottles: *Bottle 'im! –phr.*
2. **hit the bottle,** to drink heavily; become an alcoholic.
3. **on the bottle,** on a drinking binge; intoxicated.

bottle blonde *n.* a person with dyed blonde hair.

bottler *n.* something exciting admiration or approval: *You little bottler.* [origin unknown]

bottle-washer *phr.* **chief cook and bottle-washer,** a person who, as well as being responsible for some enterprise, also does much of the work, especially manual work for it.

bottom *n.* 1. the passive partner in homosexual anal sex. *–interj.* 2. an exclamation of mild disappointment, annoyance, etc.

botty *n.* the bottom; the buttocks.

bounce *v.* 1. (of cheques) to be dishonoured and be returned unpaid. 2. (of e-mail) to come back to the sender because it could not be received by the addressee's e-mail program. *–phr.* 3. **the bounce,** *Australian Rules Football.* the start of the game, when the umpire bounces the ball to begin play.

bouncy-bouncy *n.* sexual intercourse.

Bourke *phr.* **back of Bourke,** any remote, unsettled outback area. [from *Bourke* a town in north-west NSW]

bovver boot *n.* any large, tough, lace-up boots, as army boots.

bovver boy *n.* **1.** *Brit.* an aggressive skinhead type. **2.** any male who is aggressive, antagonistic, etc. [Cockney pronunciation of *bother*]

bower bird *n.* a person who collects trivia and useless objects.

bowl cut *n.* a poor haircut, which appears as though the barber merely placed an inverted bowl on the head and trimmed the hair that hung below the rim. Also, **basin cut.**

box *n.* **1.** *Offensive.* the vagina or vulva. –*v.* **2.** to place a bet so that one receives a return whether the horse or dog wins or runs a place. –*phr.*
3. nothing out of the box, not remarkable; mediocre.
4. one out of the box, an outstanding person or thing.
5. the box, a television set.

boxer *n.* one who runs a two-up school and receives a set proportion, usually twenty percent, of the spinner's earnings; ringie.

boxhead *n.* one who has a large, squarish head; a bullethead.

boy *n.* **1.** a man; a lad: *the boy from Brunswick; the boys down the pub.* –*interj.* **2.** Also, **(boy) oh boy!** an exclamation of mild surprise, amazement, wonder, etc. –*phr.*
3. boy in the boat, Also, **man in the boat.** *Crass.* the clitoris.
4. boys in blue, the police force.
5. jobs for the boys, a. a system of male nepotism in which one looks after the interests of one's mates in preference to other people's interests. **b.** any similar system in which preferential treatment is given to friends, associates, supporters, etc.
6. old boy, a. one's father. **b.** one's boss. **c.** one's husband. **d.** the penis.
7. old boy network, a system of male nepotism in which ties formed at school or college are maintained in business, politics, etc.
8. send the boys around, a mock threat, role-playing a criminal who is threatening to send around thugs to administer a beating.
9. the boys, a group of male friends: *out with the boys.*

boyf *n.* one's boyfriend.

boy's germs *n.* (*amongst children*) a supposed contagion of boyness avoided by girls. See **girl's germs.**

bozo *n.* a fool; idiot. [? originally the name of a circus clown]

bpm *abbrev.* beats per minute.

brace and bits *pl. n.* a woman's breasts. [rhyming slang]

Brahms *adj.* drunk. [rhyming slang *Brahms and Liszt* pissed]

brain *n.* **1.** a highly intelligent or well-informed person. **2.** (*pl.*) intelligence. –*v.* **3.** to hit someone hard, especially about the head; cuff: *If you do that again I'll brain you!* –*phr.*
4. pick (someone's) brains, to question (someone) in order to gain information in an area or subject that they are very knowledgeable in.

brain dead *adj.* 1. stupid; moronic. 2. mentally exhausted.

brains trust *n.* a group of people engaged in nutting out a problem, or employed to think of strategies, plans, etc.

brasco *n.* a toilet.

brass *n.* 1. money. 2. Also, **top brass. a.** high ranking military officers. **b.** the people in the most senior positions in an organisation.

brass monkey *phr.*
1. **cold enough to freeze the balls off a brass monkey,** extremely cold.
2. **brass monkey weather,** extremely cold weather. [originally referring to a brass figure of a monkey; not, as widely believed, referring to a device for holding cannonballs]

bread *n.* money; earnings.

break *n.* 1. an opportunity; chance. –*v.* 2. *Aeronautics.* to dismantle for use as spare parts: *a contract to break nine Boeing 727s.* –*phr.*
3. **break it down,** (used imperatively) **a.** stop it. **b.** calm down; be reasonable.
4. **break up, a.** to collapse with laughter. **b.** to cause (someone) to laugh uncontrollably.
5. **them's the breaks,** that is how life is.

breakbeat *n.* a type of dance music evolving out of hip-hop, but with more complex beat patterns.

breakfast *phr.*
1. **all over the place like a madwoman's breakfast,** See **madwoman.**
2. **bushman's** (or **dingo's**) **breakfast,** no breakfast at all; jocularly defined as 'a piss and a good look round'. 3. See **dog's breakfast.**

bred *n. Derogatory.* a person from a small town, remote place, etc. [shortened form of *inbred*, a common slur directed at people of a remote area]

brekkie *n.* (*originally children's speech*) breakfast. Also, **brekky.**

brew *n.* a pot or cup of tea or coffee.

brewer's droop *n.* alcohol-induced sexual impotence in men.

brick *n.* 1. a good person. 2. *Obsolete.* **a.** the sum of 10 pound. [so called from the colour of the Australian 10 pound note] **b.** the sum of $10. 3. *Prison.* a prison sentence of ten year's duration. –*v.* 4. to falsify evidence. –*phr.* 5. **a brick short (of a load),** simple-minded.

brickie *n.* a brick layer.

bricking *n.* the falsification of evidence against someone in order to substantiate a criminal charge.

brief *n.* a barrister.

brill *adj., interj.* brilliant. Also, **brillo.**

Brisso *n.* a person who lives in Brisbane.

Brissy *n.* Brisbane. Also, **Brizzie.**

Brit *n.* a person from Britain. [short for *British*]

bro *n.* 1. a brother. 2. a close male friend, especially a member of one's gang. 3. (as a form of familiar greeting) brother.

broad *n. Derogatory.* a woman. [from US slang; earlier meaning 'prostitute', used by pimps in the sense of 'meal-ticket', from *broad* a ticket, from *broads* playing cards]

broke *adj.* 1. out of money. –*phr.*

2. broke to the wide, out of money; bankrupt.
3. go for broke, a. (gambling, investment, etc.) to risk all one's capital in the hope of a very large gain. **b.** to take a major risk in pursuing an activity, objective, etc., to its extreme; to go all out.

brolly *n.* an umbrella. [19th century British slang]

bronzed *adj.* sun-tanned.

brothel *n.* **1.** any room in a disorderly state. *–phr.* **2. couldn't organise sex in a brothel,** (someone is) totally pathetic.

brother *n.* **1.** a close male friend, especially a member of a gang. **2.** used as a form of familiar greeting. *–interj.* **3.** a mild exclamation of surprise, amazement, etc.

brown dog *phr.* **kill** (or **choke**) **a brown dog,** (of food) to be disgusting.

browned off *adj.* bored; discontented; fed up; annoyed. Also, **browned-off.**

browneye *n.* an obscene gesture of contempt in which one bends over and presents the bared anus.

brownie point *n.* an imaginary point scored to one's credit or in one's favour.

brownnose *v.* **1.** to flatter servilely. *–n.* **2.** a self-seeking servile flatterer; one who curries favour.

brown noser *n.* a sycophantic crawler.

Bruce *n.* **1.** *Obsolescent.* (a name for) a typical Australian male. [from a Monty Python sketch] **2.** Also, **Brucie.** a name given to a male as an accusation that they are homosexual. [because 'Bruce' was a common camp name]

bruiser *n.* a tough fellow; bully.

brumby *n.* a wild horse, especially one descended from runaway stock. [? from Irish *bromaigh* gen. of *bromach* a horse]

bub *n.* **1.** Also, **bubba,** a baby. **2.** a child in their first years of school, as in kindergarten or infants. **3.** an affectionate name for a woman, girlfriend, wife, etc. *–phr.* **4. the bubs,** kindergarten.

bubbler *n.* a drinking fountain.

buck[1] *v.* **1.** to resist obstinately; object strongly: *to buck at improvements.* **2.** to have sexual intercourse. *–phr.* **3. buck up, a.** to become more cheerful, vigorous, etc. **b.** to make more cheerful, vigorous, etc.

buck[2] *phr.*
1. pass the buck, to shift the responsibility or blame to another person.
2. the buck stops here, the acceptance of final responsibility. [originally US, from *buck* an object used in poker to remind the winner of some privilege or duty at the next deal, from *buckhorn knife,* once often used for this purpose]

buck[3] *n. Originally. US.* **1.** a dollar. *–phr.*
2. a fast buck, money earned with little effort, often by dishonest means.
3. big bucks, lots of money. [shortened form of *buckskin,* the skin of a buck or deer, formerly an accepted form of exchange on the US frontier]

bucket *v.* **1.** to criticise or make

scandalous accusations about (someone). *–phr.*
2. empty (or **tip**) (or **drop**) **the bucket on,** to make scandalous accusations or revelations about (someone); criticise strongly.
3. kick the bucket, See **kick**.

bucket bong *n.* a type of bong for smoking marijuana in which a bottomless plastic softdrink bottle is sunk partially into a bucket of water, the chamber is filled with smoke and then consumed all at once with the release of air pressure.

Buckley's *phr.*
1. to have Buckley's, (or **Buckley's chance**), to have no chance at all.
2. to have two chances - Buckley's and none, *Jocular.* to have no chance at all. [def 1 possibly referring to a famous escaped convict William *Buckley*; def 2 a pun on *Buckley and Nunn,* a Melbourne store]

bucko *n. Chiefly US.* (as a term of address) a person, usually a male.

buck's night *n.* a party held on the eve of a wedding for the bridegroom by his male friends. Also, **buck's ding, buck's party, buck's turn**. See **hen's night**.

bud *n.* the budding heads of the marijuana plant prepared for smoking.

buddha *n.* marijuana.

buddy *n.* comrade; mate. [from *bud*, alteration of *brother*]

budgie *n.* a budgerigar.

buff *phr.* **in the buff,** in the nude; naked.

bug *n.* **1.** a malady, especially a virus infection. **2.** an idea or belief with which one is obsessed. **3.** a microphone hidden in a room to tap conversation. **4.** (*cap.*) a Volkswagon car of the first type produced. *–v.* **5.** to install a bug in (a room, etc.). **6.** to cause annoyance or distress to (a person).

bugger *n.* **1.** a person: *Come on, you old bugger.* **2.** a foul, contemptible or annoying person: *little buggers; stupid bugger.* **3.** a nuisance; a difficulty; something unpleasant or nasty: *That recipe is a real bugger; It's a bugger of a day.* *–v.* **4.** to damn or curse, as an indication of contempt or dismissal: *Bugger him, I'm going home.* **5.** to cause inconvenience to someone; to ruin; wreck. *–interj.* **6.** a strong exclamation of annoyance, disgust, etc.: *Oh, bugger!* *–phr.*
7. bugger about (or **around**), to mess about; fiddle around.
8. bugger me dead, an exclamation of surprise.
9. bugger off, to remove oneself; depart.
10. bugger up, to cause damage, frustration or inconvenience to.
11. play silly buggers, to engage in time-wasting activities and frivolous behaviour. [from *bugger* one who practises bestiality or sodomy, from Middle Latin *Bulgarus* a Bulgarian, a heretic; certain Bulgarian heretics of the Middle Ages being charged with this activity]

bugger-all *n.* very little; nothing: *He's done bugger-all all day.* Also, **bugger all**.

buggered *adj.* **1.** tired out; exhausted. **2.** broken; wrecked. **3.** damned: *I'm buggered if I'll do that.*

buggerise *phr.* **buggerise about** (or **around**), to behave aimlessly or ineffectually.

buggerlugs *n.* a mock abusive term, used affectionately.

buggery *phr.*
1. **as buggery,** an intensifier: *gentle as buggery; hot a buggery.*
2. **go to buggery!** go away; leave me alone.
3. **like buggery,** an intensifier: *It hurts like buggery.*

bug house *n.* a picture theatre; cinema.

bugle *n.* 1. the nose. *–phr.* 2. **on the bugle,** smelly.

built *adj.* 1. (of a woman) large-breasted. *–phr.* 2. **built like a tank** or **a brick shit-house,** having a thick, strong, muscular physique.

bulbing *n.* the inhalation of nitrous oxide gas from bulbs in soda siphon.

bulk *adj.* 1. a great many; a great amount: *We've got bulk people staying at our place;* 2. immense: *It was bulk fun.*

bull *n.* 1. nonsense. 2. trivial or boastful talk. *–v.* 3. to boast; exaggerate. *–interj.* 4. Also, **bulls.** an exclamation implying that what has been said is nonsensical or wrong. [shortened form of *bullshit*]

Bullamakanka *n.* an imaginary remote town; any remote place.

bull artist *n.* one notorious for excessive talk which is usually boastful, exaggerated and unreliable. Also, **bullshit artist.**

bulldust *n.* a euphemism for *bullshit.*

bull dyke *n.* a butch lesbian.

bullet-head *n.* 1. a person with a large, squarish head. 2. an obstinate or stupid person.

bullshit *n.* 1. nonsense. 2. something totally amazing or excellent; something so excellent as to be almost unbelievable: *This movie is complete bullshit - well worth seeing.* *–v.* 3. to deceive; to lie to. *–interj.* 4. an expression of disgust, disbelief, etc.

bullshit artist *n.* See **bull artist.**

bullswool *n.* (*euphemistic*) 1. nonsense. *–interj.* 2. an exclamation of disbelief, disgust, etc.

bully[1] *interj.* an exclamation indicating approval, often used sarcastically: *Bully for you.*

bully[2] *n.* a bulldog.

bum *n.* 1. the rump; buttocks. 2. a shiftless or dissolute person. 3. a habitual loafer and tramp. *–v.* 4. to get for nothing; borrow or take without expectation of returning: *to bum a cigarette; bum a ride.* 5. to annoy or upset: *We were totally bummed that the club has stopped putting on bands.* 6. to sponge on others for a living; lead an idle or dissolute life. *–adj.* 7. of poor, wretched, or miserable quality; bad: *a bum deal. –interj.* 8. an exclamation of mild disappointment, annoyance, etc.

bum chum *n. Derogatory.* one of a pair of males in a homosexual relationship.

bum crawl *v.* to be servile and fawning.

bum crawler *n. Derogatory.* a sycophant; arselicker.

bumfluff *n.* light hair growing on the face of an adolescent male.

bum-fuck *v. Offensive.* to sodomise; to perform sodomy.

bummer *n.* 1. a bad outcome, situation, or the like. 2. a big disappointment: *Couldn't get tickets for Friday. Major bummer.*

bump *phr.*
1. **bump off,** to kill.
2. **bump uglies,** See **ugly**.

bump and grind *n.* sexual intercourse.

bum rap *n.* 1. an unjust or false conviction. 2. an unfair assessment or review.

bum-root *v. Offensive.* to perform anal intercourse.

bum's rush *n.* 1. the peremptory dismissal or bodily removal of an unwanted person. 2. the peremptory rejection of an idea or proposal.

bum steer *n.* incorrect information or advice.

bun *phr.* **have a bun in the oven,** to be pregnant.

bunch of fives *n.* the fist.

bundy *phr.*
1. **bundy on,** to begin work.
2. **bundy off, a.** to finish work. **b.** *Prison Talk.* to die, especially from a drug overdose.
3. **punch the bundy, a.** to begin work. **b.** to be in regular employment. [from *Bundy* a time clock used to record the arrival and departure times of employees. Trademark]

Bundy *n.* Bundaberg rum.

bunfight *n.* 1. noisy or disorganised gathering of people, as at a crowded party. 2. a scrap or row between a group of people, especially a petty fight. Also, **bun fight.**

bung[1] *v.* 1. to put: *Bung it in the cupboard.* 2. to toss to another person; throw. *–phr.*
3. **bung it on,** to behave temperamentally.
4. **bung on, a.** stage; put on: *bung on airs and graces.* **b.** to prepare or arrange, especially at short notice: *We'll bung on a party.*
5. **bung on side,** to behave in a pompous and overbearing manner. [from *bung* a stopper]

bung[2] *adj.* 1. not in good working order; impaired; injured. *–phr.* 2. **go bung, a.** *Obsolete.* to die. **b.** to break down; cease to function. **c.** to fail. **d.** become bankrupt. [from the Aboriginal language Jagara]

bunk[1] *n.* 1. any bed. *–phr.* 2. **bunk down,** to go to bed.

bunk[2] *phr.* **do a bunk,** to run away; take flight. [19th century British slang; perhaps referring to an escape made by taking a *bunk* on a ship]

bunny *n.* 1. *Cricket.* a person who is not very good at batting. 2. one who accepts the responsibility for a situation, sometimes willingly: *to be the bunny.*

bunny-hop *n.* See **kangaroo**.

buns *pl. n.* the buttocks.

burbs *phr.* **the burbs,** the suburbs of a city. Also, **'burbs**.

burl *n.* 1. an attempt. *–v.* 2. to move quickly: *to burl along.* [northern British dialect *birl* to spin]

burn *v.* 1. to drive at a high speed. 2. to play brilliantly. 3. to successfully outplay an opponent; torch. 4. *US.* to be electrocuted in an electric chair. *–n.* 5. a drive at high speed: *took it for a burn around the block. –phr.*
6. **burn off,** to beat another vehicle

in a race, such as from the traffic lights.

7. burn out, to become exhausted; to become deficient in energy or drive: *Many Olympic swimmers are burnt out before they are 20.*

burnt offering *n. Jocular.* overcooked food.

burst *phr.*
  1. burst a blood-vessel, to become excited; to be very keen; to become agitated.
  2. on the burst, *Rugby football.* running at full speed.

bus *n.* **1.** a motor car, especially when giving a lift to someone. **2.** *Prison.* a large police or prison van used to transport prisoners, as from court to jail, etc.

bush *n.* **1.** the pubic hair. –*v.* **2.** to rough it; camp out: *bushing it under the stars.* –*phr.*
  3. beat about the bush, to fail to come to the point; prevaricate.
  4. go bush, a. to turn one's back on civilisation; adopt a way of life close to nature. **b.** Also, **take to the bush.** to disappear suddenly from one's normal surroundings or circle of friends.

bush-bash *v.* **1.** to flatten the bush so as to clear the way for a path, farming land, etc. **2.** to drive a vehicle through virgin bush. Also, **scrub-bash**.

bush bashing *n.* **1.** clearing virgin bush. **2.** (in bush walking) making a path through virgin bush. **3.** driving a vehicle through virgin bush. Also, **scrub bashing**.

bush bellows *n.* a hat (as used to fan camp fires).

bushed *adj.* **1.** lost. **2.** exhausted. **3.** confused.

bushie *n.* **1.** a person, usually unsophisticated, who lives in the bush. **2.** a member of a volunteer bush fire brigade. Also, **bushy.**

bush-lawyer *n.* **1.** a person with a good knowledge of the law, but without legal qualifications. **2.** a person who uses casuistry when arguing, especially by inventive interpretation of rules, terms, etc.

bushman's breakfast *n.* See **breakfast.**

bushman's hanky *n.* the act of blowing nasal mucus through one nostril while closing the other off with a finger. Also, **bush hanky, bushman's handkerchief.**

bush pig *n. Derogatory.* an ugly girl or woman.

bush telegraph *n.* an unofficial chain of communication by which information is conveyed and rumour spread, by word of mouth. Also, **bush telegram, bush wire, bush wireless.**

bush tucker *n.* **1.** simple fare, as eaten by one living in or off the bush. **2.** food gathered from nature in the bush.

bush week *n.* **1.** a fictitious week when country people come to town. **2.** circumstances in which unsuspecting people are imposed upon: *What do you think this is - bush week?*

bushwhacked *adj.* **1.** extremely fatigued; beaten; exhausted. **2.** astonished; annoyed. Also, **bushwacked.**

bushwhacker *n.* one who lives in the bush; a bushie.

bush wire *n.* See **bush telegraph.** Also, **bush wireless.**

business *n.* 1. defecation. *–phr.* 2. **business end,** the dangerous part of something: *the business end of a snake.* 3. **mean business,** to be in earnest.

bust *v.* 1. to catch (someone) doing something illegal; to cop: *We were busted smoking behind the dunnies.* 2. to reduce in rank or grade; demote. 3. to raid (an illegal establishment). *–n.* 4. a police raid. 5. an arrest. *–adj.* 6. bankrupt. *–phr.* 7. **bust a gut,** to overexert oneself.

buster *n.* 1. a term of address to a man or boy, either casually friendly or covertly aggressive. *–phr.* 2. **come a buster,** to fail, usually because of a misfortune.

busting *adj.* 1. badly needing to urinate or defecate. 2. completely eager: *He's busting to have a go.*

but *adv.* 1. however; though (used at the end of a sentence): *We never win but; I cannot confirm or deny any of your points but; I never did it but.* *–phr.* 2. **no buts,** (as a pre-emptory remonstrance) do not object. 3. **no buts about it,** without restriction or objection.

butch *adj.* 1. (of a woman or homosexual man) having strong masculine attributes. *–n.* 2. a woman or homosexual male who has strong masculine characteristics. [a shortening of *butcher*, originally used as a nickname for a tough young man]

butchers *n.* 1. a look. *–adj.* 2. ill. *–phr.* 3. **go butchers (hook) at,** to become angry with. [rhyming slang *butcher's hook* look; crook]

butt *n.* 1. the rump; the buttocks. *–phr.* 2. **kick butt,** to be totally amazing; to go off. 3. **kick (someone's) butt, a.** to beat convincingly. **b.** to reprimand severely. 4. **work one's butt off,** to work very hard or diligently. [from Middle English *bott* buttock]

butt-fuck *v. Offensive.* to sodomise; to perform sodomy.

butthole *n. Offensive.* the anus.

butthole surfer *n. Derogatory and offensive.* a male homosexual.

buttinski *n.* a stickybeak; an interfering person. [in the form of a mock Russian name, from *butt in* to interrupt + *-ski* a Russian name element]

buttplug *n. Offensive.* an anal plug.

buy *n.* 1. a bargain: *a good buy; the buy of the century.* 2. a purchasing of goods: *I was out on a buy this morning.* *–v.* 3. to accept (something untrue, dishonest, dubious, etc.): *Do you think he'll buy the idea? –phr.* 4. **buy it,** to die: *He bought it at Bathurst.* 5. **buy into,** to choose to become involved in: *buy into an argument.*

buzz *n.* 1. a telephone call. 2. a feeling of exhilaration or pleasure: *It was such a buzz.* 3. a bodily sensation induced by drugs, anything from a nice tingling in the nerves, to the strong euphoric feelings brought on by hard drugs. *–v.* 4. to call (someone) on the telephone.

buzzy *adj.* (of a drug) giving a strong buzz.

CHUNDER

This peculiarly Australian term has been with us for roughly fifty years. There once was a popular notion that it was derived from the phrase *watch under*, used by seasick sailors on the upper decks as a warning to those on the lower decks. But a nautical origin would mean that the word would have travelled throughout the seven seas rather than staying put in Australia. No, actually, it is more likely that *chunder* is a piece of good old Australian rhyming slang. The illustrator and cartoonist Norman Lindsay created a character known as Chunder Loo of Akim Foo who appeared in the *Bulletin* in the 1910s and 20s. *Chunder Loo*, of course, rhymes with "spew"! And naturally, as with most rhyming slang, the rhyme word is dropped thus making the word intelligible to only those in the know.

CORNSTALK

Rivalries between the States seem to be as strong as ever, but the term *Cornstalk* for someone from New South Wales seems to have dropped completely out of fashion. *Sandgropers* (Western Australians) still abound, as do *Croweaters* (South Australians). There are still some references to *Bananabenders* (Queenslanders). *Apple islander* (for a Tasmanian) has understandably faltered, as the Tasmanians pulled up their apple trees and took to growing other more lucrative crops. But why the disappearance of *Cornstalk*? It is such a splendid image after all, the youngster growing straight and tall like the corn in the fields. It applied to women as well as men, although it depended what side of the fence you were on whether you regarded it as a friendly or a mocking greeting. "The Australian ladies may compete for personal beauty and elegance with any Europeans, although satirised as 'corn-stalks' from the slenderness of their forms", *Currency Lad*, 1832. As an epithet it is positively romantic, compared with the black humour of *Sandgroper* and *Croweater*. Perhaps that is its downfall in this unromantic age.

CHUNDER

barf, bring up, call God on the big white telephone, chuck, chuck up, cry ruth, drive the porcelain bus, dry retch, feed the fishes, fetch up, go for the big spit, have a liquid laugh, have a technicolour yawn, herk, hurl, perk, puke

STUCK FOR WORDS

Cabbage Gardener *n.* a Victorian. Also, **Cabbage Patcher, Cabbage Stater.**

cab sav *n.* cabernet sauvignon wine.

cack *n.* **1.** faeces. **2.** a very funny person: *That guy's such a cack.* –*v.* **3.** to laugh uncontrollably. **4.** to defecate; to soil with excrement: *The baby cacked its nappy.* –*phr.*
5. cack oneself (laughing), to laugh uncontrollably.
6. cack one's pants (or **corduroys**), to be extremely scared. Also, **kack.** [from Middle English *kakken*]

cackle berry *n.* an egg.

cactus *adj.* **1.** ruined; useless. –*phr.* **2. in the cactus,** in difficulties, in trouble.

Cadbury *n. Derogatory.* a person who needs little alcohol to get drunk. [from the phrase 'a glass and a half' used in advertising *Cadbury* chocolate]

cakehole *n.* the mouth.

call *n.* **1.** a decision to say or do something or act in a certain way: *He swore at the footballers drinking at the bar - a dodgy call in anyone's books.* –*v.* **2.** to make a decision about; work out in one's mind: *I couldn't tell if he was joking or not. It was hard to call.* –*phr.*
3. bad call, See **bad.**
4. call a spade a spade, to state things as they are; to be bluntly matter-of-fact.
5. call a spade a fucking shovel, *Offensive.* to exaggerate.
6. call of nature, the need to urinate or defecate.
7. call the shots, See **shot.**
8. good call, See **good.**
9. the call, *Two-up,* the right to call, i.e. to nominate either heads or tails to win the toss.

calories *pl. n.* food: *time for some calories.*

camel *phr.* **a man's not a camel,** a saying denoting that one is in need of a drink.

camel driver *n. Horseracing.* an unsuccessful jockey.

camel jockey *n. Racist. Car sales.* an Arab customer.

camo *adj.* in a military camouflage pattern: *camo clothing.*

camp *adj. Originally gay slang.*
1. (of a male) exaggeratedly effeminate; ostentatiously homosexual. **2.** (of a male) homosexual. **3.** (of behaviour, music, films, etc.) exaggerated and outrageous in a fun way: *A camp bit of music.* –*n.* **4.** exaggeratedly effeminate behaviour and mannerism. **5.** a man displaying this quality; a male homosexual. –*v.* **6.** (of a male) to act in a camp manner. –*phr.*
7. camp as a row of (pink) tents, (of a male) homosexual.
8. camp it up, a. (of a male) to make an ostentatious or affected display of one's homosexuality. **b.** (of a performer) to play a role in an outrageous manner; to ham it up. [probably from French *se camper* to posture, behave in an exaggerated manner]

campy *adj.* having camp elements; in a camp style.

can *n.* **1.** jail. **2.** *Originally US.* the toilet or bathroom. **3.** *US.* dismissal. **4.** *US.* the buttocks. –*v.* **5.** to criticise harshly: *absolutely canned the film.* **6.** *US.* to dismiss; fire. –*phr.*

7. can it, to be or become silent.
8. can of worms, a situation, problem, etc., bristling with difficulties.
9. carry the can, See **carry**.
10. in the can, (of a film) completed; finished.

canary *n. Hist.* a convict. Also, **canary bird.** [named from yellow colour of the prisoner's clothing in the early days of the colony]

cancer stick *n.* a cigarette.

cane *v.* to beat severely in a competition, game, etc.

cane toad *n.* a player for the Queensland state team in the Rugby League State of Origin football competition.

canned *adj.* **1.** recorded: *canned laughter.* **2.** prepared in advance. **3.** drunk.

caper *n.* **1.** occupation; job; career. **2.** behaviour: *all that kind of caper.*

capital *phr.* **with a capital,** used to add emphasis to a statement: *It's up-market, with a capital 'u'.*

captain *n.* a person buying the drinks.

Captain Cook *n.* a look. Also, **Captain, captain.** [rhyming slang]

caramba *interj.* See **ai caramba**.

carcass *n.* **1.** a living body. *–phr.* **2. move** (or **shift**) **one's carcass,** to move away; get out of the way.

cardboard cut-out *n.* a dull, boring, lifeless, one-dimensional person.

cark *v.* **1.** to die. *–phr.* **2. cark it, a.** to collapse; die. **b.** (of a machine) to fail; break down. Also, **kark**. [? shortened form of *carcass* body of a slaughtered animal]

carn *interj.* a sporting barracker's cry; come on!: *Carn the Blues!* [altered form of *come on*]

carnie *n.* **1.** a person who works in a carnival. *–adj.* **2.** in the style of or suitable for a carnival. [*carn(ival)* + *-ie*]

carrot-top *n.* a red-headed person.

carry *v.* **1.** to be pregnant: *Is she carrying again? –phr.*
2. carry a torch for, See **torch**.
3. carry on, a. to behave in an excited, foolish, or improper manner. **b.** to flirt.
4. carry the can, to do the dirty work; bear the responsibility; take the blame.

carve *v.* **1.** *Surfing, snowboarding, etc.* **a.** to make a wake with the board along the wall of a wave, etc. **b.** to surf, snowboard, etc., exceptionally well. *–phr.* **2. carve up, a.** to slash (a person) with a knife or razor. **b.** to distribute profits, a legacy, illegal gain, an estate, etc. **c.** to defeat, as in a match.

cas *n.* a casualty ward.

case[1] *n.* a peculiar or unusual person; a weirdo: *He's a case.* [short for *nut case*]

case[2] *v.* to examine or survey (a house, bank, etc.) as in planning a crime.

caser *n. Obsolete.* **1.** a five shilling coin; a crown. **2.** *Prison.* a five year sentence. [British slang, from West Yiddish, literally, crown, from Hebrew; in Australia possibly influenced by *Casey's cartwheel*]

Casey's cartwheel *n. Obsolete.* a 1937 five shilling coin commemorating the coronation of King George VI. [from the then Federal Treasurer, Richard *Casey* (later

Lord Casey) + *cartwheel* any coin of extraordinary size]

cash *phr.*
1. **cash in,** to obtain a financial advantage.
2. **cash in on, a.** to gain a return from. **b.** to turn to one's advantage.
3. **cash in one's chips,** to die.

cashed-up *adj.* having ready money.

casting couch *n.* a supposed couch in a film or stage director's office for the seduction of those auditioning.

castle *n. Cricket.* the stumps.

castor *n.* **1.** *Obsolete.* a hat. –*adj.* **2.** pleasing; excellent: *She'll be castor!* [def 1 originally a hat made of beaver-skin, from Latin *castor* beaver; def 2 possibly in reference to a code in tick-tack in which the hat was touched to signify that all was okay]

cat[1] *n.* **1.** *Prison.* an inmate who, while heterosexual outside of prison, submits to the passive role in homosexual sex. **2.** *Derogatory.* a homosexual. **3.** *Derogatory.* an effeminate male. –*phr.*
4. **cat on a hot tin roof,** See **hot**.
5. **go like a cut cat,** See **cut**.
6. **kick** (or **flog**) (or **whip**) **the cat,** to give way to suppressed feelings of frustration by venting one's irritation on someone.
7. **look like something the cat dragged in,** something horrid or abhorrent.
8. **raining cats and dogs,** to be raining very heavily.
9. **the cat's pyjamas** (or **whiskers**) (or **miaow**), an excellent person, proposal, etc.
10. **too much of what the cat licks itself with,** very talkative (too much tongue).

cat[2] *n. Older slang.* a person, especially a young jazz musician or devotee of jazz. [originally US black English; cf. Wolof (an African language) -*kat* a person]

catch *n.* **1.** a person of either sex regarded as a highly-desirable person for a relationship or marriage: *The young doctor was the best catch in town.* **2.** a difficulty, usually unseen: *What's the catch?* –*phr.*
3. **catch it,** to get a scolding or a beating.
4. **catch out, a.** to trap somebody, as into revealing a secret or displaying ignorance. **b.** to surprise.
5. **catch you later,** a common phrase of farewell.

catch-22 *n.* a situation or rule which prevents the completion of an operation and may establish a futile self-perpetuating cycle. [from the title of the novel (1961) by J Heller, American novelist]

catfight *n.* a fight between two women.

Catho *n.* a member of the Catholic church.

cattle dog *n. Jocular.* a catalogue.

Cazaly *phr.* **up there Cazaly,** a cry of encouragement. Also, **up there Cazzer.** [from Roy *Cazaly*, 1893-1963, an Australian Rules Football player]

ceiling *phr.* **hit the ceiling,** See **hit**.

celeb *n.* a celebrity.

cellar dwellers *n. Sport.* the team at the bottom of the competition table.

centre *n.* **1.** *Two-up.* **a.** the one who

holds all bets in a game of two-up made by the spinner. **b.** the amount of money bet by the spinner which must be covered before any side bets can be made. –*phr.* **2. the (red) centre,** the remote interior of Australia.

cert *n.* something regarded as certain to happen, to achieve a desired result as winning a race, etc.; a certainty: *a cert to win; an absolute cert for the last race.*

chalkie *n.* a schoolteacher.

champ *n.* a champion.

champers *n.* champagne.

champion *adj.* first-rate.

champy *adj.* feeling like a champion; in good spirits.

chancy *adj.* uncertain; risky. Also, **chancey.**

Changa *n. Racist.* a Chinese person. Also, **Chonga.**

channel surf *v.* to change television channels repetitively in order to find something interesting to watch.

chap *n.* a male person; a bloke. Also, **chappie.** [16th century abbreviation of *chapman* a customer, a pedlar]

charge *n.* **1.** a thrill; a kick. –*v.* **2.** *Surfing.* to surf extremely well. –*phr.* **3. charge like a wounded bull,** to ask prices that are excessively high.

charlie[1] *n.* **1.** a fool; a silly person: *a right charlie.* [? from Cockney rhyming slang *Charley Ronce* ponce]

charlie[2] *n.* a girl or woman. [rhyming slang *Charlie Wheeler* sheila]

Charlie *n. Military.* an enemy Asian solider, especially a Vietnamese soldier. Also, **Charley**. [from military signals code *Victor Charlie* representing VC, for Viet Cong]

chat *phr.* **chat up,** to talk to in order to obtain a sexual relationship with; to schmooze.

chateau cardboard *n. Jocular.* cask wine.

chatty *adj.* rough; dirty; in poor condition. [from *chat* a louse, hence, the same as *lousy*]

cheap *phr.*
   1. cheap and nasty, (of merchandise) of very poor quality.
   2. cheap as chips, **cheap as dirt**, extremely cheap.
   3. cheap at half the price, (*ironic*) not very cheap.
   4. cheap at twice the price, very cheap.
   5. cheap drunk, one who easily becomes intoxicated.
   6. on the cheap, done in a substandard manner.

cheapie *n.* a cheap product.

cheapies *n.* cheap thrills: *He get's his cheapies looking at lingerie ads.*

cheat *n.* **1.** Also, **cheat code.** a special code which allows a player to access levels of a computer game without playing through the lower levels, or to play in a mode without the normal rigmarole of attaining the mode. –*phr.* **2. cheat on,** to be sexually unfaithful to (one's spouse or lover).

check *v.* **1.** take a look at: *Check the nose on that guy!* –*phr.* **2. check you later,** a common phrase of farewell.

checkout chick *n.* a woman, especially a young woman, serving at a

cheese *phr.*
  1. cheese off, to upset or annoy.
  2. hard cheese (or **cheddar**), **a.** bad luck. **b.** an off-hand expression of sympathy. **c.** a rebuff to an appeal for sympathy.
  3. old cheese, one's wife.

cheese and kisses *n.* one's wife. [rhyming slang for 'missus']

cheesecake *n. Originally US.* photographs of attractive women in newspapers, magazines, etc., posed to display their bodies, and emphasising their sex appeal.

cheesed-off *adj.* irritated; annoyed. Also, **cheesed off, cheesed.**

cheesy *adj.* smelly: *cheesy socks; cheesy undies.*

cheesy grin *n.* an exaggerated smile. [from the request by a photographer to say 'cheese', to produce an apparent smile in the subject]

cherry *n.* **1.** virginity. **2.** the hymen. **3.** a virgin. **4.** *Cricket.* a cricket ball, especially a new one. **5.** *Cricket.* the red mark made on the bat by hitting a new ball or by a vigorous stroke. *–phr.* **6. two bites of** (or **at**) **the cherry,** two attempts.

Chevvie *n.* a Chevrolet motor car. Also, **Chev, Chevvy.**

chew *phr.*
  1. chew (someone's) ear, to talk to (someone) insistently and at length.
  2. chew (someone) out, to verbally criticise or rouse on (someone).
  3. chew the fat (or **rag**), to gossip.

chewie *n.* **1.** chewing gum. *–phr.* **2. chewie on your boot!** *Football.* a cat-call intended to disconcert a player taking a kick.

chew-'n'-spew *n. Derogatory.* any fast-food establishment viewed as selling poor-quality food. Also, **chew and spew.**

chiack *v.* **1.** to jeer; taunt; deride; tease. *–n.* **2.** jeering cheek. Also, **chyack.** [British dialect *chi-hike* a salute, exclamation]

chick *n.* **1.** *Derogatory.* a young woman. **2.** (amongst teenage girls) an extremely attractive male; a hunk. *–phr.* **3. pull a chick,** (of a man) to attract a woman for sexual intercourse.

chicken *n.* **1.** a coward. **2.** See **spring chicken.** *–adj.* **3.** cowardly. *–phr.*
  4. chicken out, to withdraw because of cowardice, tiredness, etc.
  5. play chicken, a. to perform a dangerous dare. **b.** (of a person) to stand in the path of an approaching vehicle daring the driver to run them down. **c.** (of the drivers of two vehicles) to proceed along a collision course, as a test of courage.

chickenfeed *n.* a meagre or insignificant sum of money.

chickenshit *n. Offensive.* **1.** something worthless or pathetic. *–adj.* **2.** worthless; pathetic. **3.** cowardly.

chickey babe *n. Offensive.* **1.** a term of familiar address from a male to a girl or young woman. **2.** an attractive female. Also, **chicky babe.**

chick-magnet *n.* a male whom many women find sexually attractive.

Chigga *n. Tas. Derogatory.* a person from the Hobart suburb of

Chigwell, viewed as uncultured. See **bogan**.

chill *v.* **1.** to relax; to chill out. *–n.* **2.** a chill-out room at a dance party, rave, etc.: *He spent most of the night in the chill.* **3.** a relaxing time: *a great chill after a hard night.*

chill out *v. Originally US.* to let go of emotional tension and stressful engagement; relax.

chill-out *adj.* **1.** designed or used for relaxing: *This is my favourite chill-out record.* *–phr.* **2. chill-out room,** an area at a dance party where people can rest and cool down from the exertions of dancing.

chill pill *phr.* **take a chill pill,** calm down!

china *n.* a mate; friend. [rhyming slang *china plate* mate]

Chinaman *n.* **1.** *Cricket.* a left-hand bowler's googly. *–phr.* **2. must have killed a Chinaman,** *Older slang.* a fanciful explanation for a run of bad luck: *He must've killed a Chinaman.*

Chinese cut *n. Cricket.* an inside edge wide of leg stump. Also, **French cut.**

Ching *n. Racist.* (*especially with school children*) a Chinese person. Also, **Ching-chong, Ching-chong-changa.**

Chink *n. Racist.* (*sometimes l.c.*) a Chinese person. Also, **Chinkie.**

chinless wonder *n.* a feeble, pathetic male.

chip *v.* **1.** to reprimand: *He chipped me for being late.* *–phr.*
2. cash in one's chips, See **cash.**
3. chip in, a. to contribute money, help, etc. **b.** to interrupt; enter uninvited into a debate or argument being conducted by others.
4. chip off the old block, a person inheriting marked family characteristics.
5. chip on the shoulder, a grudge.
6. spit chips, See **spit.**
7. the chips are down, the moment of decision has been reached.

chipper *adj.* lively; cheerful.

chippie *n.* a carpenter.

chiro *n.* a chiropractor.

chisel *n.* **1.** an old, paper $5 note. [see *Chisholm*] *–v.* **2.** to cheat; swindle. **3.** to get by cheating or trickery.

chiseller *n.* a swindler.

Chisholm *n.* an old, paper $5 note. [because it had a picture of Caroline *Chisholm* on it]

chiv *n.* a knife. [Romany *chiv* a blade]

Chloe *phr.* **drunk as Chloe,** very drunk. [origin unknown; clearly not derived from the famous painting of *Chloe* in Young and Jackson's Hotel, Melbourne, as the expression appeared many years before the painting was actually painted]

choc-attack *n.* an acute desire to eat a great deal of chocolate.

chock-a-block *adj.* **1.** full; overcrowded. *–adv.* **2.** in a jammed or crowded condition. *–phr.*
3. chock-a-block up, Also, **chockers up.** (of a male) fully engaged in sexual intercourse.

chocker *adj.* **1.** completely full. **2.** replete; stuffed. Also, **chocka, chockers, chock-full.**

chockie *n.* chocolate. Also, **choc, chokkie**.

choco *n. Offensive.* a member of a dark-skinned race. Also, **chocko**.

chocoholic *n.* someone whose constant craving for and delight in chocolate suggest addiction. Also, **chocaholic**.

chocolate frog *n. Racist.* a person of Mediterranean descent. [rhyming slang for 'wog']

choice *adj.* **1.** (with teenagers) fantastic; wonderful; excellent: *What a choice dress.* –*interj.* **2.** (with teenagers) an expression of extreme pleasure: *Would you like to go to the movies? Choice!* –*phr.* **3. choice language,** colourfully vulgar language.

choke *v. Sport.* **1.** to fail from nervousness when one had previously been succeeding: *Norman choked on the last day of play.* –*n.* **2.** the act of choking: *What a choke!* –*phr.*
3. a bit more choke and you would've started, a put-down directed at someone who has farted loudly.
4. choke a brown dog, See **brown dog**.

choker *n.* a sports player who is in a position to win or achieve a high score, as in golf or cricket, but who is overwhelmed by the pressure of the game and does not clinch the promised victory; one who snatches defeat from the jaws of victory.

chompers *pl. n.* the teeth.

Chonga *n. Racist.* a Chinese person. Also, **Changa**.

choof *phr.* **choof off,** to go away.

chook *n.* **1.** a woman: *a nice old chook.* **2.** an affectionate name for a young female. **3.** a silly person. –*phr.*
4. how are your mother's chooks? *Older slang.* a general expression of greeting.
5. I hope your chooks turn into emus and kick your dunny down, a phrase wishing ill luck upon someone. [from earlier *chuckey,* from British dialect, ultimately imitative of the cackling of a chicken]

chook chaser *n. Derogatory.* **1.** a trail bike or other small road motorcycle. **2.** a person who rides such a bike.

chop[1] *n.* **1.** a share, cut: *in for one's chop.* **2.** the sack; dismissal. –*v.* **3.** to dismiss; give the sack to; fire. –*phr.* **4. chop off,** to finish suddenly; put an abrupt end to.

chop[2] *phr.* **not much chop,** no good. [Hindi *chhap* impression, stamp]

chop chop *interj.* hurry up. [Pidgin English *chop* quickly]

chopper *n.* **1.** a helicopter. **2.** a large, powerful, customised motorcycle with wide handlebars. **3.** a push-bike popular in the 70s with wide handlebars and having the front wheel smaller than the back. **4.** (*pl.*) teeth or false teeth. **5.** Also, **chopper tailor.** a small tailor (fish). [def 2: because they were *chopped* customised]

chop shop *n.* a panel beater's.

chow *n.* **1.** food. –*phr.* **2. chow down,** to begin eating. [from *chow-chow,* originally nautical slang of SE Asia]

Chow *n. Racist.* a Chinese person. [Pidgin English *chow-chow;* origin uncertain]

Chrissie *n.* Christmas. Also, **Chrissy**.

christen *v.* to use something for the first time: *to christen the new bathroom.*

Christmas *phr.*
 1. **as regular as Christmas,** regularly.
 2. **done up like a Christmas tree,** overdressed; garish.
 3. **have all one's Christmases come at once,** to have extreme good fortune.
 4. **think one is Christmas,** to be pleased with oneself; be elated.

Christmas hold *n. Wrestling, etc.* a hold in which one grabs the opponent's testicles. [a Christmas hold is 'a handful of nuts', i.e. *nuts* testicles]

chrome dome *n.* a bald person.

chromo *n. Older slang.* a prostitute; a criminal's woman. Also, **chrome, cromo**. [short for *chromo(lithograph)* a coloured lithograph, referring to the painted faces of prostitutes]

chuck *v.* 1. to do or perform right away: *chuck a U-ie, chuck a mental, chuck a wobbly.* 2. Also, **chuck up**. to vomit. *–phr.*
 3. **chuck in,** to resign from: *He's chucked in his job.*
 4. **chuck it in,** to desist; give up (something begun) without finishing: *There were so many problems with the job that finally she just chucked it in.*
 5. **chuck one's weight about,** to be overbearing; interfere forcefully and unwelcomely.

chucker *n. Cricket.* a bowler who throws the ball instead of bowling it, or (technically) who bends the arm during bowling.

chucker-out *n.* one employed at a place of public entertainment to eject undesirable persons; a bouncer. Also, **chucker-outer**.

chuffed *adj.* pleased; delighted: *She was really chuffed about her exam results.* [originally British, from *chuff* proud, elated, swollen with pride, fat, chubby]

chug-a-lug *n.* a bout of drinking; a booze-up.

chum *n.* 1. a mate or friend. *–phr.* 2. **chum up (with),** to become friendly with. [17th century British slang; origin unknown]

chump *n.* 1. a blockhead or dolt. 2. the head.

chunder *v.* 1. to vomit. *–n.* 2. the act of vomiting. 3. the substance vomited. [? rhyming slang *Chunder Loo* spew, from the advertising character drawn by Norman Lindsay, Australian artist]

chunderous *adj.* revolting, unpleasant.

chyack *v., n.* See **chiack**.

ciao *interj.* goodbye. [Italian, alteration of *schiavo* at your service]

cigarette swag *n. Hist.* a swag rolled into a long, thin shape like a cigarette.

cinch *n.* something certain or easy.

cinchy *adj.* easy to do; no problem; a snack.

city slicker *n.* a person living the slick, fast-moving lifestyle of a large city.

clackers *pl. n.* false teeth.

clap *n.* gonorrhoea, or any other

venereal disease. [Middle English *clapier* brothel]

clapped-out *adj.* **1.** exhausted; weary. **2.** broken; in a state of disrepair.

clapper *phr.* **go like the clappers,** to move very rapidly.

classic *adj.* **1.** excellent; brilliant; unreal: *That joke was classic.* *–interj.* **2.** used to express great appreciation of something: *I just won $40. Classic!*

Claytons *adj., adv.* an imitation or substitute: *a Claytons government; Claytons sex.* [from *Claytons* tradename of a non-alcoholic drink which was advertised as 'the drink you have when you're not having a drink']

clean *adj.* **1.** free from addiction to drugs. **2.** free from sexually transmitted diseases. **3.** not carrying concealed weapons. *–phr.*
4. clean out, a. to use up; exhaust. **b.** to take all money from, especially illegally: *to clean out the bank.*
5. clean up, a. to make (money, or the like) as profit, gain, etc.: *to clean up at the races.* **b.** *Sport, etc.* to defeat crushingly: *Carlton cleaned up Richmond last Saturday.* **c.** to be totally wrecked from a collision: *I was almost cleaned up by a semi.*

cleaner *phr.* **take (someone) to the cleaners,** to strip (someone) of all assets, money, etc., usually in gambling.

cleaner upper *n. Jocular.* the person responsible for cleaning or tidying up. Also, **cleaner upperer**.

cleanskin *n.* **1.** *Originally.* an unbranded animal. **2.** one who is free from blame, or has no record of police conviction.

clerk *phr.* **dressed up like a pox doctor's clerk,** See **pox doctor**.

clever dick *n.* a conceited, smug person, who displays their prowess at the expense of others.

click *n.* **1.** (*pl.*) Also, **klicks.** kilometres. *–v.* **2.** to make a success; make a hit. **3.** to fall into place or be understood: *His story suddenly clicked.* **4.** to establish an immediate affinity with, especially with amorous intentions: *They clicked right away.*

clinah *n. Obsolete.* one's girlfriend. Also, **cliner**. [German *kleine* little]

clink *n.* a prison; jail. [apparently from *Clink* Prison in Clink Street, Southwark, London]

clinker *n.* something first-rate or worthy of admiration.

clit *n.* the clitoris.

clobber[1] *v.* to batter severely; maul: *Say that again and I'll clobber you.* [20th century US slang; ? frequentative of *clob*, variant of *club*]

clobber[2] *n.* clothes or gear: *Sunday clobber.* [19th century British slang; origin unknown]

clock *v.* **1.** to record the speed of a racehorse, racing car, runner, etc. **2.** (on pinball machines, computer games, etc.) to make the digital read-out of the scoreboard return to the initial position of zeros in a single game of continuous play. **3.** to drive a car until its odometer has returned to the initial position reading all zeros. *–n.* **4.** a speedometer or odometer: *100km/h on the clock.*

clocker *n. Horseracing.* a person who frequents the racetrack in the early morning when horses are being trained and times the runs in order to get useful information for betting.

clock-watcher *n.* an employee who spends a lot of time thinking about the end of the working day.

clod *n.* a stupid person; a blockhead; dolt.

clodhopper *n.* 1. a country bumpkin or rustic boor. 2. (*pl.*) large, ungainly boots. [17th century British slang]

clone *n. Derogatory.* a person who imitates another: *a Jana Wendt clone.*

close out *v. Surfing.* (of a wave) to break simultaneously along the entire length, thus offering no practical surface for surfing.

closet *adj.* 1. secret: *a closet drinker; a closet queen.* –*phr.*
2. **come out of the closet,** to make public one's erstwhile hidden sexual preferences, usually used in reference to admitting one's homosexuality.
3. **in the closet,** keeping one's sexuality from the public eye.

closeted *adj.* not letting one's sexual preferences be known publicly.

cloud-suck *n. Hang-gliding.* the increase of lift often found at the base of a cloud, sometimes strong enough to cause a glider to unavoidably enter the cloud.

clubber *n.* one who regularly attends nightclubs; one who goes clubbing.

clubbie *n.* a member of an organised surf life saving club.

clubbing *n.* going out to nightclubs.

clucky *adj.* 1. wanting to have children. 2. fussy and over-protective of children. [from *clucky* (of a hen) broody]

clued-up *adj.* well-informed.

clueless *adj.* patently stupid; ignorant.

cluey *adj.* 1. well-informed. 2. showing good sense and keen awareness.

clunky *adj.* 1. not running smoothly: *a clunky engine.* 2. unsophisticated or unpolished; not smooth: *delivering some really clunky lines.*

coast *v.* to travel in neutral gear in order to save fuel.

coat *phr.*
1. **on the coat,** *Prison.* ostracised.
2. **pull the coat,** a signal to avoid (someone).

Coathanger, the *n.* the Sydney Harbour Bridge.

cobber *n.* 1. a mate; friend. Also, **cob.** [origin uncertain, probably related to British dialect *cob* to form a friendship with]

cobber-dobber *n.* one who informs on a mate.

cobblers *pl. n.* 1. balls, testicles. –*phr.* 2. **a load of old cobblers,** a lot of nonsense. [rhyming slang *cobbler's awls* balls]

cock *n.* 1. *Offensive.* the penis. 2. *Derogatory and offensive.* a despicable male. 3. *Tasmania.* a term of address for a mate or friend. –*phr.* 4. **cock up,** to make a mess of; ruin: *You really cocked that up.* [def 1 dates back to Middle English (at least 15th century) where this meaning was a metaphorical exten-

cock / **Collins Street cocky**

sion of cock meaning 'rooster'; in the 14th century *pilkoc*, later *pillicock* (from northern dialect *pill* the penis); see also German *hahn* rooster, penis]

cockamamie *adj.* crazy; ridiculous; muddled. [from US, originally meaning 'decal', from *decalcomania*]

cockatoo *n.* one who keeps watch during a two-up game, or other illegal activity. [so called because the *cockatoo* is known for its habit of posting 'sentries' to noisily warn the feeding flock of any approaching danger]

cockatoo farmer *n.* a farmer, especially one who farms in a small way. Also, **cocky.**

cock breath *n. Offensive and derogatory.* a despicable person. [imputing that one has performed fellatio]

cocked *adj. Car sales.* (of a car) cleaned and ready for display.

cock-head *n. Offensive and derogatory.* a despicable person.

cock-headed *adj. Offensive.* despicable.

cockie *n.* a cockroach.

cockroach *n.* a player for the New South Wales state team in the Rugby League State of Origin football competition.

cock rock *n.* aggressive, masculine rock and roll.

cocksucker *n. Offensive and derogatory.* 1. a fellator. 2. a despicable person. 3. a male homosexual.

cocksucking *adj. Offensive.* awful; disgusting (an intensifier indicating extreme disapproval).

cockteaser *n. Offensive.* See **prickteaser.**

cocky *n.* 1. a cockatoo, or other parrot. 2. See **cockatoo farmer.** –*v.* 3. to follow the occupation of a farmer. [abbreviation of *cockatoo*]

coconut *n. Racist.* an Aboriginal person brought up by white people. [so called because coconuts are brown on the outside and white on the inside]

codger *n.* 1. a mean, miserly person. 2. an odd or peculiar (old) person: *a lovable old codger.* 3. a fellow; a chap. [18th century British slang]

cods *pl. n.* the testes.

codswallop *phr.* **a load of old codswallop,** rubbish or nonsense. [first recorded in the 1960s in British English; origin unknown]

coffin nail *n.* a cigarette.

coit *n.* 1. the anus. 2. the buttocks. Also, **quoit.**

coke *n.* cocaine.

Coke bottle glasses *n.* spectacles with thick lenses. Also, **Coke bottom glasses.**

coldie *n.* a glass, bottle or can of cold beer.

cold-turkey *n.* 1. a method of withdrawal from a drug addiction in which the drug is given up completely, and no other drugs are used as substitutes. –*adv.* 2. without the aid of other drugs: *come off cold turkey*; *go cold turkey.*

collect *n.* 1. a winning bet. –*v.* 2. to win a bet: *collected on a 100-1 winner.* 3. to run into or collide with, especially in a motor vehicle.

Collins Street cocky *n. Vic.* one who owns a country property, often

45

for purposes of tax avoidance, but who lives and works in Melbourne. See also **Pitt Street farmer, Queen Street bushie**. [from *Collins Street* a major street in Melbourne]

collywobble *n.* an aquatic insect larva; wriggler.

collywobbles *n.* **1.** stomach-ache. **2.** diarrhoea. **3.** a mythical ailment once affecting the Collingwood team in the AFL which caused them to not be able to win a premiership despite getting to the grand final. [*colic* + *wobbles*]

colour gang *n.* a gang of street youths.

combo *n.* **1.** a combination. **2.** *Northern Australia.* a white man who lives with an Aboriginal woman. –*phr.* **3. go combo,** to begin such a relationship.

come *v.* **1.** to orgasm. **2.** to play the part of: *Don't come the great lady with me.* –*n.* **3.** Also, **cum.** semen; sperm. –*phr.*
4. come across, a. to pay or give. **b.** (of a woman) to give sexual favours.
5. come again? a request to repeat, expand or explain (a statement, etc.).
6. come clean, to confess.
7. come down, to come off a drug.
8. come in, (of odds on a horse, dog, etc.) to become lower.
9. come nothing, *Prison Talk.* to make no admissions.
10. come off it, a request that someone be reasonable: *Come off it, mate!*
11. come on, an exclamation of encouragement.
12. come on to, to attempt to seduce.
13. come one's guts, to confess.
14. come out, to admit openly one's homosexuality.
15. come that on, to attempt to hoodwink (someone) with an argument, device, etc., which is blatantly a deception: *Don't come that on me.*
16. come the raw prawn, See **prawn.**

comeback *n.* **1.** a retort; repartee. **2.** a ground for complaint.

comedown *n.* a letdown; disappointment.

come-fuck-me *adj. Offensive.* sexually alluring: *my best come-fuck-me look; come-fuck-me pose.*

come-fuck-me boots *pl. n. Offensive.* a snide term for trendy boots or shoes worn by a woman when dressed up for going out, especially when seeking sexual partners. Also, **come-fuck-me's**.

come-on *n.* **1.** an inducement; lure: *The free drinks were just a come-on.* **2.** an attempt at seduction.

comp *n.* competition: *a regular at the Monday night comp.*

compo *n.* **1.** *Cricket.* a composite ball made from cork and rubber. **2.** compensation for injury at or in connection with a person's work; workers' compensation. –*phr.* **3. on compo,** in receipt of such payment.

con[1] *adj.* **1.** confidence: *con game, con man.* –*n.* **2.** a confidence trick; swindle. –*v.* **3.** to swindle; defraud. **4.** to deceive with intent to gain some advantage. [from *con(fidence)*]

con[2] *n.* a prisoner. [from *con(vict)*]

conchie *n.* **1.** a conscientious objector. **2.** one who is overly conscientious. *–adj.* **3.** incredibly conscientious. Also, **conch, conchy, conshie, conshy**. [short for *conscientious*]

cone *n.* **1.** the conical piece of a bong in which the drug is placed. **2.** an amount of marijuana smoked from a cone: *having a few cones. –phr.* **3. cone on,** to have a marijuana smoking session.

cone-head *n.* a heavy user of marijuana; a dope addict.

congrats *interj.* a congratulatory remark.

coning *n.* the smoking of marijuana.

con job *n.* a practised confidence trick; a swindle.

conk *n.* **1.** the nose. *–phr.* **2. conk out, a.** (of an engine) to break down. **b.** to faint; collapse. **c.** to die. Also, **konk**. [origin unknown]

con man *n.* one who swindles by gaining the victim's confidence and then inducing the victim to part with property or money; confidence man.

cooee *phr.*
1. not within cooee, far from achieving a given goal: *He is not within cooee of finishing the job by Friday.*
2. within cooee, a. within calling distance. **b.** close to achieving a given goal. [originally from the Aboriginal language Dharuk *guwi* come here]

cook *v.* **1.** to be going along well: *now you're cooking; this really cooks. –phr.*
2. cook up, to prepare heroin for injection.
3. cook up a storm, to cook an amazing meal.
4. cooking with gas, to be doing things correctly and well: *now you're cooking with gas.*
5. what's cooking? a request to be told what is happening.

cookie *phr.*
1. a smart cookie, a particularly intelligent person.
2. that's the way the cookie crumbles, that's how things are. Also, **cooky**.

cool *adj.* **1.** suave and sophisticated; as opposed to *daggy*. **2.** up-to-date and in fashion; stylish. **3.** excellent; radical; unreal: *You'll meet me there? Cool!* **4.** all right; okay: *Don't worry, it's cool.* **5.** composed; under control: *be cool about it; stay cool.* **6.** (of a number or sum) without exaggeration or qualification: *a cool thousand. –n.* **7.** composure: *lost his cool.* **8.** sophistication and stylishness: *the very essence of cool. –phr.*
9. cool as a cucumber, calm; not excited; level-headed.
10. cool it, stop doing (something); take it easy; relax.
11. cool off (or **down**), to become calmer; to become more reasonable.
12. play it cool, be cautious and shrewd; keep composure under difficult circumstances. Also (for defs 1-3), **kewl, kool**.

cool bananas *interj.* an exclamation of understanding and agreement.

cooler *n.* a prison.

cool hand *n.* a person who is aloof and calmly calculating.

coon *n. Racist.* a dark-skinned person, as a Negro or Aborigine.

[originally US; shortening of *raccoon*]

coot *n.* **1.** a fool; simpleton: *rich coots with tons of money.* **2.** a man: *poor old coot.* [an allusion to the bird]

cootie *n. US.* a head-louse.

cop *n.* **1.** a police officer. **2.** a profit or gain: *He could sell it now and make a cop out of it; taking a cop.* –*v.* **3.** to catch out doing something illegal; to bust: *copped us nicking apples.* **4.** to receive or obtain: *cop a feel; copped a gong.* **5.** to accept resignedly; put up with: *Would you cop a deal like that?* **6.** to be allotted; receive: *She copped more than her fair share; cop a fine of $200; he dished it out and he copped it.* **7.** to steal. –*phr.*
8. a sure cop, something certain.
9. a sweet cop, an easy job.
10. cop a load, to contract venereal disease.
11. cop it, to be punished.
12. cop it sweet, a. to endure or put up with an unpleasant situation. **b.** to have a lucky break.
13. cop out, a. to opt out of (something). **b.** to fail completely.
14. cop the lot, to bear the brunt of some misfortune.
15. cop this! Also, **cop this** (or **that**) **lot!** look at this! (implying **a.** admiration. **b.** astonishment. **c.** contempt.)
16. cop you later, a common phrase of farewell. [with a pun on the word *copulator*]
[Old English *coppian*, lop, steal]

cop-out *n.* a way out of a situation of embarrassment or responsibility: *Her going overseas was a bit of a cop-out.*

copper *n.* a police officer. [from *cop*]

copper's nark *n.* a police informer.

cop shop *n.* a police station.

copspeak *n.* police jargon.

copter *n.* a helicopter.

cor *interj.* an exclamation of surprise, grief, etc. [shortened from *cor blimey*, variant of *gorblimey*]

cork *phr.* **put a cork in it,** to be quiet; cease to talk.

corker *n.* **1.** something striking or astonishing. **2.** something very good of its kind. **3.** *Cricket.* a cork ball.

corn *n.* a trite or sentimental writing or style.

cornball *n.* one who is corny; a sentimentalist.

Cornstalk *n.* **1.** a person native to or resident in New South Wales. **2.** a tall, thin person. **3.** *Obsolete.* a native-born Australian, being generally taller and thinner than the immigrant.

cosmic *adj.* **1.** of or pertaining to universal forces which have an effect on human behaviour: *the cosmic payback; cosmic powers.* **2.** of the nature of one that believes in such powers: *He was a bit cosmic for my liking.*

cossie *n.* a swimming costume. Also, **cozzie.**

cot *phr.* **hit the cot,** to go to bed.

cot case *n. Jocular.* someone who is exhausted, drunk, or in some way incapacitated, and fit only for bed.

cotton-picking *adj. Originally US.* unworthy; simple: *out of one's cotton-picking mind.*

couch potato *n.* a dull and inactive person, especially one who spends a lot of time watching television.

cougan *n.* a person who drinks much alcohol and acts in a rowdy manner; a party animal; a yobbo.

counterjumper *n.* a salesperson at a counter.

country *n. Sport.* any part of the ground on which a sporting event takes place which is far from the main area of activity, as the outfield in cricket, or the part of the course away from the stands in horseracing.

country cousin *n.* a person, sometimes a relative, from the country.

country mile *phr.* **by a country mile,** by a great extent: *She won by a country mile.*

couth *adj. Jocular.* civilised, well-mannered. [backformation from *uncouth* uncivilised]

cove *n.* **1.** a man: *a rum sort of cove; some old cove.* **2.** *Obsolete.* a boss, especially the manager of a sheep station. [British criminal cant; said to be from Romany *kova* creature]

cow *n.* **1.** *Derogatory.* an ugly or bad-tempered woman: *mean old cow.* **2.** *Derogatory.* a despicable person: *You miserable cow. –phr.*
3. a cow of a (something or **someone),** a difficult, unpleasant, disagreeable (thing or person): *That's a cow of a thing to say.*
4. a fair cow, anything regarded as disagreeable or difficult.
5. chase (or **hunt**) **up a cow,** to find a dry spot outdoors, usually with sexual intentions.
6. don't have cow, don't get unduly upset. [originally US (1960s); currently popularised by the television show *The Simpsons*]

cowabunga *n. Originally US (esp. Surfing).* an exclamation of enjoyment, excitement, exhilaration, encouragement, etc.: *Cowabunga dudes! What a rad set!* [a fanciful coinage by writer Eddie Kean and used in the US television show *Howdy Doody*; in the 1960s used by surfers in the US and Australia; revived in the 1980s by the *Teenage Mutant Ninja Turtles* phenomenon and used mainly by young schoolchildren]

coward's castle *n.* parliament when used as an arena in which to vilify and abuse others while under parliamentary privilege.

cow corner *n. Cricket.* the area of the field over mid wicket. [so called because this is where an *agricultural shot* is aimed at]

cow juice *n.* milk.

cow shot *n. Cricket.* a stroke made without style or discrimination.

cozzie *n.* See **cossie**.

CP *n.* (in personal ads) corporal punishment.

crack *v.* **1.** to break into (a safe, vault, etc.). **2.** to gain unauthorised access to a computer; to break the security code on a piece of software; to break an encryption code. **3.** to solve (a mystery, etc.). **4.** to obtain: *crack an invite.* **5.** to tell (a joke); say (something humorous): *cracked a funny.* **6.** to open and drink (a bottle of wine, etc.): *Let's crack a bottle of champers.* **7.** to give way to pressure. **8.** to win a free game on a pinball machine. *–n.* **9.** a try; an opportunity or chance: *I'd like a*

crack at that job. **10.** the anal cleft; the anus. **11.** a joke; gibe. **12.** a highly-addictive form of cocaine prepared for smoking. **13.** *Offensive.* the vagina or vulva. **14.** *Comp.* a file with information about cracking computer games, giving cheat codes, instructions, patches, etc. *–adj.* **15.** of superior excellence; first-rate: *a crack rider. –phr.*
8. crack a fat, to get an erection.
9. crack it, a. to obtain sexual intercourse. **b.** to be successful.
10. crack on to, to seduce (someone).
11. crack up, a. to suffer a physical, mental or moral breakdown. **b.** to break into controllable laughter. **c.** to cause to laugh uncontrollably; to amuse.
12. cracked up to be, (something) as described; as it is supposed to be: *It isn't all it's cracked up to be.*
13. fair crack of the whip, a. a fair chance. **b.** an appeal for fairness.

cracker *n.* **1.** someone who breaks a computer security system. *–phr.*
2. not to have a cracker, to be without money.
3. not worth a cracker, (something) of little worth.

crackerjack *n.* **1.** a person of marked ability; something exceptionally fine. *–adj.* **2.** of marked ability; exceptionally fine.

crackers *adj.* insane; crazy.

crackhead *n.* a user of the drug crack cocaine.

cracking *adj.* **1.** first-rate; fine; excellent. **2.** fast; vigorous: *a cracking pace. –phr.* **3. get cracking,** to start an activity, especially energetically.

crackpot *n.* **1.** an eccentric or insane person. *–adj.* **2.** eccentric; insane; impractical.

cradle snatcher *n.* one who shows romantic or sexual interest in a much younger person.

Craft's disease *n. Jocular.* forgetfulness brought on by old age. [acronym from the phrase *Can't Remember A Fucking Thing*]

crank *n.* **1.** an eccentric person, or one who holds stubbornly to eccentric views. *–adj.* **2.** false; phoney: *crank calls; a crank letter. –v.* **3.** to be excellent: *the surf's really cranking. –phr.*
4. crank out, to sing, perform, or play music loudly.
5. crank up, to put into motion; to start.

cranky *adj.* **1.** in a bad mood. **2.** angry.

crap *n. Often offensive.* **1. a.** excrement. **b.** a piece of excrement; a turd. **c.** an act of defecation. **2.** nonsense; rubbish. **3.** junk; odds and ends. *–adj.* **4.** worthless; of poor quality; crappy: *a crap magazine. –v.* **5.** to defecate. **6.** to be mightily scared: *I was crapping myself at the thought of it. –phr.*
7. crap artist, one who tells tall tales; a bullshit artist.
8. crap off, to annoy; disgust.
9. crap on, a. to talk nonsense. **b.** to go on at length.
10. crap out, to fail.
11. the crap, used as an intensifier: *scared the crap out of me.* [from British slang, from dialect *crap* a scrap, remnant, from Middle English *crappe* chaff]

crapola *n. Originally US.* rubbish; nonsense.

crappy *adj.* **1.** of poor quality: *a crappy magazine.* **2.** soiled: *a crappy nappy.* **3.** badly done or executed: *a crappy performance.*

crash *v.* **1.** to come uninvited to (a party, etc.). **2.** to sleep over: *You can crash at my place.* **3.** Also, **crash out.** to collapse or fall asleep with exhaustion. *–adj.* **4.** characterised by all-out, intensive effort, especially to meet an emergency: *a crash program; a crash diet. –phr.*
5. crash out, to get knocked out of a contest.
6. crash through or crash, make a do-or-die attempt.

crash-hot *adj.* excellent. Also, **crash hot.**

crate *n.* a run-down, dilapidated vehicle.

crater-face *n.* **1.** a person suffering from acne. **2.** a person with a pock-marked face.

crawler *n.* an person who behaves ingratiatingly to another; a sycophant. **1.** *Obsolete.* a person who is slow, or lazy, or unfit to work.

cream *v.* **1.** to beat up in a fight. **2.** to beat convincingly. *–phr.* **3. cream one's jeans, a.** to have an orgasm while dressed. **b.** to become extremely (sexually) excited.

creamed *adj.* **1.** beaten up in a fight. **2.** beaten convincingly. **3.** *Surfing.* wiped off one's surfboard by a wave.

cred *n.* credibility.

creek *phr.* **up the** (or **shit**) **creek** (**in a barbed wire canoe** or **without a paddle**), in a dire predicament; in trouble.

creepy *adj.* **1.** (of a person) unpleasant, obnoxious, repulsive. **2.** scary in an eerie way.

crew *n.* **1.** a gang of youths, homeboys, or the like; a posse. **2.** a group of surfies, skaters, snowboarders, etc. **3.** a band, pop group, etc.: *Melbourne's finest rap crew.*

crim *n.* a criminal.

critter *n.* **1.** *Derogatory.* an ugly or despised person. **2.** *Chiefly US.* an insect. [variant of the word *creature*]

croak *v.* to die.

croc *n.* a crocodile.

crock[1] *n.* **1.** a worn-out, decrepit old person; a person laid-up by ill health. **2.** an old motor car or boat. [from *crock* an old ewe, an old horse]

crock[2] *n.* **1.** nonsense; a load of rubbish: *That's the biggest crock I've ever heard. –phr.* **2. a crock of shit,** nonsense; lies; a load of rubbish. [def 1 is an abbreviation of def 2]

crocodile skin *n.* badly sun-damaged skin.

cronk *adj. Older slang.* dishonest; illegal; crooked. [see British dialect *crank* infirm, weak, ailing]

crook *n.* **1.** a dishonest person; a swindler. *–adj.* **2.** fraudulent. **3.** sick; disabled. **4.** bad; inferior: *That food was crook.* **5.** unpleasant; difficult: *a crook job. –phr.*
6. crook as a (mangy) dog (or **a dog's hind leg**), feeling extremely unwell.
7. crook as Rookwood, extremely

unwell; very sick. [from *Rookwood*, a cemetery in Sydney]

8. go crook at (or **on**), to upbraid noisily.

crooked[1] *phr.* **crooked on,** angry with.

crooked[2] *phr.* **crooked as a dog's hind leg,** very crooked; not straight.

crool *v.* See **cruel.**

cropper *phr.* **come a cropper, a.** to fall heavily, especially from a horse. **b.** to fail; collapse, or be struck by misfortune.

crow *n.* **1.** *Derogatory.* an unattractive woman: *an old crow.* –*phr.*
2. as the crow flies, in a straight line.
3. land where the crow flies backwards, the remote outback.
4. starve (or **stiffen**) (or **stone**) **the crows,** an exclamation of astonishment.

crowd surf *v.* to be carried across the top of a crowd of moshing audience members.

crowd surfer *n.* a person crowd surfing.

Croweater *n.* a South Australian. Also, **croweater**.

crown jewels *n.* the testicles. Also, **family jewels.**

crucify *v. Sport.* to beat convincingly.

crud *n.* **1.** rubbish; junk; nonsense: *Who scripted this crud?* **2.** Also, **crud-face.** a reprehensible person. [from British dialect *crud* curd]

cruddy *adj.* inferior; unworthy.

cruel *v.* **1.** Also, **crool.** to impair, spoil: *to cruel one's chances.* –*phr.*
2. cruel someone's pitch, to spoil someone's opportunity.

cruet *n.* **1.** the head. **2.** (*pl.*) the testicles. –*phr.* **3. do one's cruet,** lose one's head; become angry.

cruise *v.* **1.** to go out with a view to picking up a sexual partner. **2.** to wander about in a relaxed, cool way. –*phr.* **3. cruise on** (or **along**), to maintain a moderate level of activity; lead an uneventful life.

cruising *n.* the frequenting of bars and parties in search of casual sex.

cruisy *adj.* **1.** of or befitting the nature of someone on the lookout for a casual sexual partner. **2.** relaxed and cool, as of a person just cruising around: *just cruisy fun in the sun down at the beach.*

crumb *n.* a horrible person: *He's a real crumb.*

crummy *adj.* very inferior, mean, or shabby.

crumpet *n.* **1.** a woman considered as a sexual object: *a nice bit of crumpet.* **2.** (of a male) sexual intercourse with a woman: *Had any crumpet lately?* **3.** the head: *soft in the crumpet.* –*phr.*
4. off one's crumpet, crazy.
5. not worth a crumpet, worthless; of little or no value.

crunch *n.* a moment of crisis.

crusty *adj.* **1.** *Derogatory.* (of a person) shabbily dressed and unwashed. –*n.* **2.** *Derogatory.* a dirty person dressed in old clothes. **3.** dried semen on men's underwear.

crystal cylinder *n. Surfing.* the tube of a breaking wave.

crystally *adj. Derogatory.* having a world view which incorporates such notions as alternative healing, crystal power, etc.

cub *n.* a child.

cuckoo *adj.* crazy; silly; foolish.

cum *n.* semen. Also, **come**.

cunt *n. Offensive.* **1.** the vagina or vulva; a woman's genitals. **2.** women in general, regarded as sexual objects. **3.** *Derogatory.* a despicable person. **4.** any person. **5.** sexual intercourse. *–phr.* **6. cunt off,** (used imperatively) go away; fuck off. [Middle English *cunte, counte*, in Old Norse *kunta*, Old Frisian *kunte*]

cunt-hair *n. Chiefly Military. Offensive.* (used in communicating measurements) a very small fraction of the smallest graduation on a scale: *59.2mm and a cunt-hair.*

cunt-head *n. Offensive and derogatory.* a despicable person.

cunt-lapper *n. Offensive and derogatory.* a despicable person.

cunt-lapping *adj. Offensive.* (of a person) despicable: *those cunt-lapping bastards.*

cunt-starver *adj. Prison. Offensive.* a person convicted for neglecting maintenance payments. Cf. **wife-starver**.

cunt-struck *adj. Offensive.* infatuated with women.

cup of cheeno *n. Jocular.* a cappuccino. Also, **cup of chino**.

cuppa *n.* a cup of tea or coffee: *It's time for a cuppa!*

curl *phr.* **curl the mo,** *Older slang.* **a.** to succeed brilliantly. **b.** an exclamation indicating surprised admiration.

curly *adj.* (of a problem) difficult.

currency *n. Hist.* **1.** one born in Australia. *–adj.* **2.** born in Australia, as opposed to *sterling*, one born in Britain or Ireland. *–phr.* **3. currency lad** (or **lass**), a man (woman) born in Australia.

curry muncher *n. Racist. Car sales.* an Indian or Pakistani customer.

curse *phr.* **the curse,** menstruation.

curtains *pl. n.* the end, especially of life.

cushy *adj.* easy; pleasant. [Anglo-Indian, from Hindustani *khush* excellent]

cuss *n. Originally US.* **1.** a curse. **2.** a person or animal: *a decent old cuss.* *–v.* **3.** to curse.

custard brains *n.* a stupid person.

cut *v.* **1.** to dilute a drug with another substance. **2.** to renounce; give up: *to cut the grog.* **3.** to be hurt or offended by another's actions: *He was really cut because she didn't phone.* *–adj.* **4.** upset; angered; annoyed: *Don't get cut about it, I was only kidding.* **5.** circumcised. **6.** diluted; adulterated; impure: *cut heroin.* *–n.* **7.** a share: *His cut was 20 per cent.* **8.** a recording of a song, etc. *–phr.*

8. cut a dash, *Older slang.* to make an impression by one's ostentatious or flamboyant behaviour or dress.

9. cut and run, to leave unceremoniously and in great haste.

10. cut in, a. to allow oneself (or someone else) a share: *He cut his brother in on the deal.* **b.** to begin to shear sheep. **c.** to join a card game by taking the place of someone who is leaving.

11. cut it, make the grade; be competent: *She couldn't cut it in her new job.*

12. cut no ice with, See **ice**.

13. cut loose, to free oneself from restraint.

14. cut one's losses, to abandon a project in which one has already invested some part of one's capital, either material or emotional, for no return, so as not to incur more losses.

15. cut one's stick, *Older slang.* to be off.

16. cut out, a. *Prison.* to serve time instead of paying a fine. **b.** *Prison.* to serve a short sentence. **c.** to spend (an amount of money).

17. cut the mustard, *Originally US.* to achieve success in line with the expectations of others.

18. cut up, a. to criticise severely. **b.** to upset or cause distress to.

19. cut up rough (or **nasty**), to behave badly; become unpleasant.

20. go like a cut cat, to go very fast.

21. in for one's cut, participating in the expectation of a share in the spoils or profit.

22. the cuts, a caning.

cute *adj.* **1.** sexually pleasing or attractive; gorgeous; used of either males or females, or specific bodily features: *such a cute face; cute buns; He's so cute I could die.* –*phr.* **2. cute as a button,** extremely cute. [originally an aphetic variant of *acute*, meaning 'shrewd', 'clever'; def 1 is not recorded in other dictionaries, presumably because it is not regarded as a distinct sense; however, there is quite a distinct semantic difference between a *cute puppy* and a *cute butt*; the often quoted 'true' or 'dictionary' definition of *cute* as 'ugly but interesting' does not exist in any actual dictionary and most probably originally arose as a joke]

cutie *n.* a pleasing person; one with a winning personality. Also, **cutey.**

cutie-pie *n.* **1.** a woman or girl who is cute. **2.** an endearment for such a woman or girl.

cut-lunch commando *n. Military.* a member of the Army Reserve.

cutsie-pie *adj.* appealing in a coy or affected way.

cyber- *prefix.* **1.** a word element denoting computers, computing or the Internet. **2.** a word element denoting futuristic robotics, technology, or science: *cyber-clothing*.

cyberbabe *n.* a cool female user of the Internet. Also, **cyberchick; cybergirl**.

cyberdude *n.* a cool male user of the Internet. Also, **cyberboy**.

cyberpunk *n.* **1.** a science-fiction genre, generally accepted as beginning with William Gibson's 1984 novel, *Neuromancer.* **2.** a popular culture movement influenced by the cyberpunk science-fiction genre.

cybersex *n.* sexual interaction via the Internet; sex in cyberspace or virtual reality.

cyberspace *n.* **1.** the perceived space of a virtual reality system. **2.** the metaphorical space in which the information available on the Internet exists; hence, the Internet itself. [coined by William Gibson in the science-fiction novel *Neuromancer* (1984) in which it referred to a world-wide computer matrix to which human brains could directly link]

DUNNY

Of all the terms for the toilet, the word *dunny* is the one that has the most Australian flavour (or should that be odour?). The extremely lonely are described by the phrase *as lonely as a country dunny*. To wish ill upon another you can employ the dreaded conjuration *I hope your chooks turn into emus and kick your dunny down*. Also, amongst the school-aged, the *dunnies* was always the place behind which amorous assignations were concluded (unless it was behind the weathershed). This Australianism is a shortening of the earlier *dunniken* which occurs in many British dialects. In this word, the final element *ken* means house, and the first element *dunne–* is presumably a variant of the word *dung* – thus the word *dunniken* is equivalent to that other oft-heard Australian term, *shithouse*.

DUDE

Dude is, as we all know, an American word. It originally referred to a refined or pretentious man who was more concerned with grooming and effete manners than with being macho. Later on it came to be used to mean any male person – equivalent to the Australian *bloke*. Then, as with the word *guys*, teenagers started using *dudes* to refer to both sexes. People may think that this a recent borrowing which sadly reflects the Americanisation of our culture, but the word has been in Australia for many a year. You can find early examples of *dude*, in its original sense, in such noted writers as Henry Lawson, Henry Handel Richardson, and Ion L. Idriess. Still, despite this history, it has to be admitted that the current teenage use probably is due largely to American TV shows. However, there may be a distinct Aussie twist to this word, for now the word, as used by kids, doesn't simply mean "a person", but rather a *cool* person. A *dude* is the opposite, the very antithesis, of a dag, nerd, gumby, wuss, etc. This meaning may exist in America, but certainly none of their slang dictionaries record it.

DROP-DEAD HONEY

alternababe, alternahunk, babe, babe-magnet, bombshell, chickey babe, chick-magnet, DDH, dish, doll, glamour, guy-magnet, handbag, head-turner, himbo, honey, hot property, hunk, megababe, megahunk, sex on legs, spunk, spunkrat, stunner

STUCK FOR WORDS

D *n.* **1.** *Basketball.* defence: *come on, play D!* **2.** *Ultimate frisbee.* a defensive play: *Great D!* –*phr.*
3. D out, *Ultimate frisbee.* to successfully mark an opposition player so that they do not get the disc.
4. D up, *Basketball.* **a.** to set up a defence. **b.** to mark up on the opposition.

dack *v.* to pull (someone's) trousers or pants down: *I was dacked in front of everyone.*

dacks *n.* See **daks**.

dadah *n.* illegal drugs. [Malay: medicinal herb]

Dad'n'Dave *n.* a shave. [rhyming slang; from the two comical characters featured in the short stories by Australian writer Steele Rudd (1868-1935)]

dag[1] *n.* **1.** a lump of excrement-matted wool on a sheep's rear. –*phr.* **2. rattle your dags,** a command to hurry up. [from British dialect; ultimate origin unknown]

dag[2] *n.* **1.** a person who is neat in appearance, conservative in manners, and lacks style and sophistication. **2.** an untidy, slovenly person. [originally applied to an eccentric person, a character, from British dialect *dag* a feat of skill amongst children used in dares]

daggy *adj.* **1.** dirty; slovenly; unpleasant. **2.** conservative and lacking style and sophistication in manners, interests, etc.; uncool. **3. a.** conservative or unfashionable in dress. **b.** slovenly in appearance; taking no effort to dress smartly or well.

dago *n. Racist.* **1.** an Italian. **2.** any person of Latin ethnic origin. [originally nautical slang, from Spanish *Diego* James]

daisy chain *n.* **1.** a continuous chain of homosexual males engaged in having sex, each performing anal intercourse with the next. **2.** any group people engaged in lovemaking forming some chain-like formation.

daisy-cutter *n.* (in cricket, football, tennis, etc.) a ball which, after being struck or kicked, skims near the ground.

dak-dak *n.* a Volkswagon car of the first type produced. [imitative of the engine noise]

dakka *n.* marijuana. [from South African English, from Afrikaans, from Hottentot *dachab*]

daks *pl. n.* trousers. Also, **dacks**. [Trademark]

dame *n.* a woman of mature age: *a wily Toorak dame.*

dance party *n.* **1.** an entertainment event similar to a rave, but more commercial and not so underground. See **rave**. **2.** (used also to refer to) a disco: *Friday night dance party at Hornsby RSL.*

dancer *phr.* **Spanish dancer,** cancer. Also, **disco dancer, Jack the dancer, Jimmy dancer, tap dancer.** [rhyming slang]

D&C *n.* a dilatation and curettage.

D&M *n.* **1.** a deep and meaningful conversation, usually about problems in interpersonal relationships. –*v.* **2.** to have such a conversation: *They were D and M-ing all night.* Also, **D and M.**

Dapto dog *n. Racist.* a person of Mediterranean background. [rhym-

Dapto dog   **dead marine**

ing slang for 'wog'; from the dog races held at Dapto, NSW]

darbies *pl. n. Hist.* handcuffs. [from British slang; in the 16th century known as *Father Darbie's bands*]

darkie *n.* **1.** *Offensive and derogatory.* a dark-skinned person. **2.** a stool; a turd. *–phr.* **3. drop** (or **choke**) (or **strangle**) **a darkie,** to defecate. Also, **darky, darkey**.

darl *n.* darling. Also, **darls**.

Darwin rig *n. NT.* See **Territory rig**.

Darwin stubby *n.* **1.** (formerly) an 80oz bottle of beer. **2.** a 2.25 litre bottle of beer.

date *n.* **1.** the anus. *–v.* **2.** to poke or prod in the buttocks. [from *date* the fruit of the date palm]

date roll *n.* toilet paper.

DDH *n.* (amongst teenagers) an incredibly attractive male. [initialism from *Drop-Dead Honey*]

dead *adj.* **1.** very tired; exhausted. **2.** quiet: *Business is dead today.* **3.** used to add emphasis to a statement; completely: *dead right; a dead shot; dead stupid.* **4.** sexually dull: *a dead root.* **5.** *Horseracing, etc.* (of a racetrack) not conducive to fast racing. **6.** *Horseracing.* (of a horse) not being run on its merits. *–phr.*

7. dead and won't lie down, refusing to give in.

8. dead from the neck up, lacking intelligence; stupid.

9. dead on, exactly right.

10. dead set, quite true.

11. dead to the world, asleep.

12. left for dead, left behind; surpassed; outstripped.

13. run dead, *Horseracing.* (of a horse) to be deliberately pulled up so that it does not run at its best.

14. wouldn't be seen dead with, to refuse to have any association with.

15. you're dead! a threat of violence towards someone: *You touch my pencil case and you're dead!*

deadbeat *n.* **1.** a person down on their luck; a jobless and homeless person. *–adj.* **2.** shabby and grungy as a deadbeat; down and out. **3.** not offering good future prospects; going nowhere: *a deadbeat job.*

dead cert *n.* a certainty: *He's a dead cert to win; it's a dead cert that they'll get married.*

dead duck *n.* **1.** a person lacking good prospects; a failure. **2.** something useless, or worthless, or utterly without promise. *–phr.* **3. to look like a dead duck in a thunderstorm,** to be unattractive, untidy, etc.

dead eye *phr.* **dead eye and horse,** a pie and sauce. [rhyming slang]

deadhead *n.* **1.** a dull and ineffectual person. **2.** *Aviation.* a pilot, flight attendant, etc., travelling on a plane as a passenger.

dead heart *n.* the arid central regions of Australia. Also, **Dead Heart.**

dead horse *n.* tomato sauce. [rhyming slang]

dead-leg *n.* **1.** a cork of the thigh muscle. *–v.* **2.** to cork (someone's) thigh.

deadly *adj.* excellent; fantastic; cool: *a deadly spunk; a deadly skirt.*

deadman's float *n.* the faking of a drowned person effected by floating face down in the water.

dead marine *n.* a bottle which had

dead marine / **deliver**

contained beer, whisky, etc., but is now empty.

dead ringer *n.* a person or thing that closely resembles another: *He was a dead ringer for the local policeman.*

deadshit *n.* **1.** *Derogatory* a despicable person. **2.** a no-hoper; a dullard. *–adj.* **3.** despicable: *It was a deadshit thing to do.*

dead spit *n.* the image, likeness, or counterpart of a person, etc.

dead'un *n.* **1.** a dead person or animal. **2.** *Horseracing.* a racehorse which is deliberately made to lose; a horse not run on its merits.

deal *n.* **1.** a measured quantity, as of marijuana. **2.** a purchase of drugs. *–phr.*
3. a big deal, an important event; a serious matter.
4. big deal! an ironic exclamation indicating contempt, disbelief, etc.

deaner *n.* See **deener**.

death adder *phr.* **have a death adder in one's pocket,** to be mean or parsimonious.

death-knock *n.* the end; the last minute: *right at the death-knock.*

death seat *n.* **1.** the front passenger seat in a motor car. **2.** (in a trotting race) a position on the outside of the leader, from which it is very hard to win.

debag *v.* to remove the trousers of, as a joke or punishment.

deck *v.* **1.** to knock (someone) to the ground. *–n.* **2.** *Cricket.* the wicket; pitch. **3.** the top surface of a surfboard. **4.** the top surface of a skateboard, or the skateboard itself.
5. (*pl.*) the turntables used by a DJ. *–phr.*
6. below decks, in the genital region.
7. hit the deck, a. to fall to the ground or floor. **b.** to rise from bed.
8. not playing with a full deck, mentally inadequate or unsound; insane.

dee *n.* a detective or police officer.

deejay *n.* **1.** a radio station disc jockey. **2.** a disc jockey at a nightclub, dance party, etc. *–v.* **3.** to perform as a disc jockey at a night club or dance party. Also, **DJ**.

deener *n.* **1.** *Hist.* a shilling; twelve pence. **2.** *Obsolescent.* a ten cent piece; ten cents. Also, **deaner**. [originally British slang]

deep house *n.* a type of dance music.

deep north *n.* (*sometimes caps*) Queensland. [so called on analogy with the deep south (of the United States), because of supposed conservative and racially intolerant attitudes]

deep throat *n.* fellatio. [derived from the title of a pornographic movie about fellatio]

def *adj.* cool; excellent; unreal.

dekko *n.* a look or view. Also, **dek**. [Hindi *dekko* look!]

Delhi belly *n.* diarrhoea, as suffered by travellers.

delish *adj.* delicious.

deliver *v.* **1.** to perform a task competently and professionally; come up to expectations: *He seems to have the qualifications, but can he deliver? –phr.*
2. deliver a serve, to make an

59

deliver

opening statement as part of a planned debate.
3. deliver the goods, come up with the goods.

delo *n.* a delegate.

delts *pl. n. Weights.* the deltoid muscles.

demo *n.* a demonstration.

demolish *v.* to eat or drink greedily.

demon *n.* a detective; a police officer, especially a motorcycle police officer.

department *n.* an aspect of a person: *a bit light in the brains department; got what it takes in the legs department.*

deppie *n. Car sales.* a deposit.

der *interj.* **1.** a mocking exclamation indicating faked and exaggerated stupidity or bewilderment. *–adj.* **2.** blatantly stupid. *–n.* **3.** a stupid person. Also, **derr, dur.**

derro *n.* a vagrant. Also, **dero.** [shortened form of *derelict*]

Derwent duck *n. Hist.* a convict at Hobart on the river Derwent, Tasmania.

Derwenter *n. Hist.* an ex-convict from Tasmania. [from the convict settlement on the Derwent River, Tasmania]

desk wallah *n. Derogatory.* one who works at a desk, especially a government official or bureaucrat.

desperado *n.* a person, usually a male, who is desperate for sex.

desperation *adj.* exhibiting extreme keenness or urgency, especially in sport: *a desperation tackle.*

destructo *n.* a person who causes great havoc or destruction, as by being oafish, or through unrestrained behaviour.

devo *n.* **1.** a deviant. **2.** an objectionable person.

DFE *adj.* extremely easy; offering no challenge. [standing for *Dead Fucking Easy*]

dial *n.* **1.** the face. *–phr.* **2. off one's dial,** incredibly drunk or stoned, or affected by some other drug.

diamond duck *n. Cricket.* See **duck.**

dice *v.* **1.** to throw away, reject. *–phr.* **2. dice with death,** to act dangerously or take a risk.
3. no dice, of no use; unsuccessful; out of luck.

dicey *adj.* dangerous; risky; tricky.

dick[1] *n.* a detective. [shortened form of *detective*]

dick[2] *n.* **1.** the penis. **2.** (*with small children*) Also, **girl's dick.** the female genitals. **3.** a cretinous, annoying person; a dickhead. *–phr.* **4.** See **big swinging dick.**
5. have had the dick, to be finished or ruined.
6. have shit on one's dick, *Crass.* an expression used by homophobes to accuse someone of being a male homosexual. [from 19th century US slang, from *Dick* a variant of the name *Richard*]

dick[3] *n.* a dictionary.

dick-brain *n.* a fool; idiot.

dick-brained *adj.* foolish.

dick-eye *n.* an annoying, foolish person; a jerk. [referring to the meatus, or *eye*, of the penis]

dick-flop *n.* an annoying, foolish person; a jerk. [referring to a flaccid penis]

dickhead *n.* **1.** a stupid, annoying, horrible person; a jerk: *I couldn't care less what all the dickheads up the pub reckon.* *–adj.* **2.** Also, **dickheaded.** stupid; foolish; befitting a dick-head: *It was a dickhead thing to do; You dick-headed nob.*

dickie *n.* (*in children's speech*) a penis.

Dickless Tracy *n.* a female police officer. [a humorous reference to the comic strip character *Dick Tracy,* + *dick* penis]

dick-nose *n.* an annoying, foolish person; a dickhead. Also, **dick-shit, dick-wad.**

dick-rash *n.* an annoying, foolish person; a jerk. [referring to a supposed sexually transmitted disease]

dick-shitty *adj.* despicable.

dickstickers *pl. n.* a pair of tight-fitting men's swimming costume.

dick-wit *n.* an annoying, foolish person; a jerk. [a blend of *dick*² + *fuckwit*]

dicky¹ *adj.* **1.** unsteady, shaky; in bad health; in poor condition: *a dicky ticker; a dicky knee.* **2.** difficult; untenable: *a dicky position.* [origin unknown; not originally rude]

dicky² *adj.* stupid and annoying; characteristic of a dickhead: *That was a dicky thing to do.* [from *dick*²]

did *n.* a toilet. Also, **diddy, didee.**

diddle *v.* **1.** to cheat; swindle; victimise. **2.** to have sexual intercourse with (someone). **3.** to sexually stimulate (a woman) manually.

diddly-squat *n.* absolutely nothing; none.

diddums *interj.* an exclamation indicating that the speaker thinks that the person addressed is being childish and petulant. [in speech to children *did 'ems* did they?]

die *v.* **1.** to desire or want keenly or greatly: *I'm dying for a drink.* *–phr.* **2. die in the bum** (or **arse**), to fail completely.
3. die on (**someone**), **a.** to fall asleep while in the company of (someone). **b.** to let (someone) down; fail to keep a promise.
4. to die for, extremely desirous: *It is chocolate cake to die for.*

diesel dyke *n.* See **bull dyke.**

dig¹ *n.* a cutting, sarcastic remark.

dig² *n.* a form of casual address among men. [abbreviation of *digger*]

dig³ *v.* **1.** to understand or find to one's taste. **2.** to take notice of; pay attention to. [originally US black English; possibly from Wolof *deg, dega* understand]

digger *n.* **1.** an Australian soldier, especially one who served in World War I. **2.** a form of casual address among men; cobber; mate. [a term originating on the goldfields]

dill *n.* a fool; an incompetent. Also, **dill-brain, dill-pot.** [backformation of *dilly*]

dill-brained *adj.* completely stupid; idiotic.

dilly *adj.* queer; mad; crazy. [blend of *d(aft)* + *(s)illy*]

din-din *n.* (*originally in children's speech*) dinner. Also, **din-dins.**

dine *phr.* **dine at the Y,** to engage in cunnilingus.

ding *v.* **1.** to dent; damage. *–n.* **2.** a damaged section on a car, bike, surfboard, etc. **3.** a minor accident involving a car, bike, surfboard, etc. **4.** an argument. **5.** the penis. **6.** Also, **dinger**, the backside or anus.

ding-a-ling *n.* a fool; idiot; eccentric person.

dingbat *n.* an eccentric, peculiar, or stupid person. [from US slang; popularised in this sense by a cartoon strip *The Dingbat Family* begun by George Herriman in 1909; earlier meaning 'a stiff drink' or 'a projectile for throwing']

ding-dong *adj.* **1.** vigorously fought with alternating success: *a ding-dong contest.* –*n.* **2.** a loud and vigorous argument.

dinger *n.* **1.** Also, **ding.** the buttocks; arse; the anus. **2.** a shanghai; catapult.

dingo *n.* **1. a.** a contemptible person; coward. **b.** one who shirks responsibility or evades difficult situations. –*v.* **2.** to act in a cowardly manner. **3.** to shirk, evade, or avoid; to spoil or ruin. –*phr.*
4. dingo's breakfast, See **breakfast.**
5. put on a dingo act, act in a cowardly way.
6. turn dingo on (someone), to betray (someone). [from *dingo* the Australian wild dog which is said to be treacherous and cowardly]

dink[1] *v.* **1.** to carry or convey a second person on a horse, bicycle or motorcycle. –*n.* **2.** such a ride. Also, **double-dink.**

dink[2] *n.* one of a couple, married or unmarried, who have separate incomes and no children. [acronym from *double* (or *dual*) *income no kids*]

dink[3] *n. Racist.* **1.** *Esp. Military.* a person from South-East Asia. **2.** *Vietnam War.* a member of the Viet-Cong. [origin unknown]

dinks *n.* abbreviation of *dinkum*. See **fair dinkum, true dinks.**

dinkum *adj.* **1.** Also, **dinky-di, dinky.** true; honest; genuine: *dinkum Aussie; the dinkum article.* **2.** seriously interested in a proposed deal, scheme, etc. –*adv.* **3.** truly. See **fair dinkum.** –*n.* **4.** an excellent or remarkable example of its kind: *You little dinkum.* –*phr.* **5. dinkum oil,** See **oil.** [earliest used (1890s) in the phrase *fair dinkum*, from British dialect (Derbyshire and Lincolnshire) *dinkum* work, a due share of work; there is no evidence to support that the Cantonese *din kum*, meaning 'real gold', was ever in use on the goldfields]

dinky[1] *adj.* **1.** of small size. **2.** neat; dainty; smart: *a dinky beard.* –*n.* **3.** a small tricycle. **4.** a small rowing or sailing boat, sometimes inflatable; dinghy.

dinky[2] *adj., adv., n.* dinkum.

dinky-di *adj.* true; honest; genuine: *he's a dinky-di Aussie.* [alteration of *dinkum*]

dinnyhayser *n.* anything superior or excellent. [from *Dinny Hayes,* pugilist]

dip *n.* **1.** *Prison.* a pickpocket. –*phr.*
2. dip into one's pocket, to spend money.
3. dip one's lid to (someone), a. to raise one's hat. **b.** to pay honour to or congratulate (someone).
4. dip out, a. to miss out, **b.** to fail: *He dipped out in his exams.*

dip   **divvy**

5. dip out on, to remain uninvolved; avoid.
6. dip the wick, *Crass.* (of a male) to have sexual intercourse.

dipshit *n. Offensive.* a stupid person.

dipso *n.* one who suffers from an insatiable craving for alcoholic drink; a dipsomaniac.

dipstick *n.* **1.** an idiot; jerk. **2.** the penis.

dirt-ball *Derogatory. n.* a despicable person.

dirty *adj.* **1.** morally unclean; indecent. **2.** angry. *–adv.* **3.** very; extremely: *dirty big. –phr.*
4. be dirty on, to be angry with.
5. do the dirty on. to behave unfairly or wrongly towards (someone).

dirty old man *n.* a man, usually of mature years, who is considered to have an unhealthy interest in sexual matters.

dirty weekend *n.* **1.** a clandestine weekend spent away by a couple to engage in illicit sex. **2.** *Jocular.* any weekend spent away by a couple.

dirty word *n.* **1.** a vulgar or rude word. **2.** something one doesn't mention because it is as objectionable as if it were a vulgar word: *Work is a dirty word around here.*

dis *v.* to criticise; to disparage; put down. Also, **diss.** [originally US black English; probably extracted from *disrespect*]

disc *n. Ultimate frisbee.* **1.** a frisbee. **2.** the amount of time spent catching and throwing the frisbee during play: *Didn't get much disc last point.*

disco dancer *n.* cancer.

discombobulate *v.* to upset, confuse (a person). [mock Latin formation, from *discompose* or *discomfort*]

dish *n.* **1.** an attractive woman or man. *–v.* **2.** to abandon; discard; sack.

dishlicker *n.* a greyhound dog.

dishwater *n.* **1.** any weak drink. *–phr.* **2. dull as dishwater,** very boring.

dishy *adj.* physically attractive.

dit *n. Naval slang.* a yarn or story, especially used in the phrase **spin a dit**, to tell a yarn. [? from morse code slang for a dot]

ditch *v.* to discontinue a relationship with (someone); drop.

dits *n.* a flighty, stupid person, especially a woman. [backformation from *ditsy*]

dit-spinner *n. Naval slang.* a person who tells tall stories.

ditsy *adj.* (of a woman) flighty; empty-headed. [originally US; ? blend of *dotty* and *dizzy*]

diva *n.* an outstandingly glamorous woman or drag queen, especially a performer: *a dance diva; disco divas.*

dive *n.* a disreputable place, as for drinking, gambling, etc., especially a cellar or basement.

dive-bomb *v.* **1.** to jump into water, as a swimming pool, creek, etc., with the knees tucked under the chin, in order to make a large splash. *–n.* **2.** the action of dive-bombing. Also, **bomb.**

divvy *n.* **1.** a dividend. **2.** (*pl.*) rewards; profits; gains. **3.** Also, **divvy van.** a police van. *–phr.*
4. divvy up, to share: *divvy up the proceeds.*
5. divvy with, to share with.

DJ *n., v.* See **deejay**.

do *n.* **1.** a festivity or party: *We're having a big do next week.* **2.** a hairdo: *traded her long locks for a short do.* **3.** a swindle. *–v.* **4.** to have a meal with someone as a social or business occasion: *do lunch; do dinner.* **5.** to injure: *did his ankle jumping from a train.* **6.** to take (an illegal drug). **7.** to cheat or swindle. **8.** to commit burglary; steal. **9.** to use up; expend: *He did his money at the races.* **10.** to beat up. **11.** to have sexual intercourse with. *–phr.*
8. do a (**someone**), to imitate (someone): *He did a Kennett.*
9. do away with, to kill.
10. do for, a. to accomplish the defeat, ruin, death, etc., of. **b.** *Obsolescent.* to cook and keep house for. **c.** to charge with a certain offence: *I've been done for speeding again.*
11. do in, a. to kill; murder. **b.** to exhaust; tire out. **c.** to ruin.
12. do it, to have sexual intercourse: *Everyone knows they're doing it.*
13. do one's thing, to act according to one's own self-image.
14. do or die, of supreme effort: *a do or die attempt at the record.*
15. do out of, to deprive, cheat, or swindle of.
16. do over, a. to redecorate; renovate: *to do a room over.* **b.** to assault.
17. do the bolt, See **bolt**.

dob *v.* **1.** *Football.* to kick, usually accurately, especially in shooting for goal: *He's dobbed another goal.* *–phr.*
2. dob in, a. to betray, report (someone) as for a misdemeanour. **b.** to contribute money to a common fund: *We'll all dob in and buy him a present.* **c.** to nominate (someone absent) for an unpleasant task.
3. dob on, to inform against; betray. [dialect variant of *dab* to set down abruptly, from Middle English *dabben*]

dobber *n.* an informer; telltale.

doc *n.* a doctor.

docking *n.* the sexual act of stretching the foreskin of the penis over the glans of another.

doco *n.* a documentary.

Docs *pl. n.* a brand of heavy lace-up walking boots or shoes with an air cushioned sole. Also, **Doc Martens**. [Trademark; from the name of their German Inventor, Dr Klaus *Maertens*]

doctor *n.* **1.** an expert; one who makes the final decision: *You're the doctor.* *–v.* **2.** to repair or mend. **3.** to tamper with; falsify; adulterate. **4.** to castrate or de-sex an animal. *–phr.* **5. go for the doctor, a.** to bet all one's money on a race. **b.** to go all out.

dodgy *adj.* **1.** difficult; awkward; tricky. **2.** unsound: *Those foundations look a bit dodgy.* **3.** dishonest: *a dodgy salesperson.*

doer *n.* **1.** a hard and keen worker; one who succeeds through hard, honest work. *–phr.* **2. hard doer,** *Older slang.* a doer that works particularly hard, or has had a particularly hard life.

dog *n.* **1.** *Derogatory.* a despicable fellow. **2.** *Derogatory.* an ugly woman. **3.** *Prison.* an informer. *–adj.* **4.** used as a measurement of coldness when camping out in the open: *It was a three-dog night, four-dog night,* etc. [referring to how

dog

many dogs one needs to snuggle around one's person to keep warm] –*phr.*
5. a dog tied up, an outstanding account.
6. get a dog up you, an abusive expression; go to hell; fuck off.
7. to have a dog's chance, to have no chance.
8. put on (the) dog, to behave pretentiously; put on airs.
9. see a man about a dog, to leave a room for the purpose of urination.
10. the dogs are barking, one's feet are tired and sore.
11. try it out on the dog, to make a sample or trial of a dubious project, procedure, etc., in order to test its feasibility.
12. turn dog, to turn traitor or begin acting cowardly.

dog and bone *n.* the telephone. [rhyming slang]

dogbox *n.* **1.** the last carriage on a train. **2.** cramped quarters; a kennel-like room.

dog collar *n.* a stiff collar, fastened behind, as worn by a priest.

doggie bag *n.* a bag provided by a restaurant or the like, for carrying home leftovers. Also, **doggy bag.**

doggie do *n.* the faeces of a dog.

doggie style *n.* sexual intercourse in which the recipient is on all fours and entered (either vaginally or anally) from behind. Also, **doggy style; doggy fashion.**

doggo *phr.* **lie doggo,** to hide; remain in concealment.

doghouse *phr.* **in the doghouse,** in disgrace; in trouble; unpopular.

do-gooder *n.* a well-intentioned, but often clumsy social reformer.

dolly

dogs, the *pl. n.* greyhound racing; greyhound races.

dog's breakfast *n.* a mess; a confused state of affairs. Also, **dog's dinner.**

dog squad *n. Prison.* undercover police.

dog's vomit *n.* horrible food.

dog tag *n.* an identity disc. Also, **meat tag, dead meat ticket.**

d'oh *interj.* a self-reprimanding grunt used when one has done something stupid. [as used by Homer Simpson of *The Simpsons* television cartoon; cf. *der* and *duh*]

do-hickey *n.* any device or gadget, the name of which is unknown or temporarily forgotten; doodad. Also, **dohickey.**

doing –*phr.*
1. doing over, a beating.
2. drop of the doings, alcohol; grog.
3. nothing doing, an exclamation indicating refusal.

dole bludger *n. Derogatory.* one who is unemployed and lives on social security payments without making proper attempts to find employment.

doll *n.* **1.** an attractive woman. –*phr.*
2. doll up, to dress (oneself or another) smartly.
3. knock over a doll, to incur the consequences of one's actions.

dollar *n.* **1.** *Obsolete.* the sum of five shillings. **2.** (*pl.*) money: *advertising dollars.* –*phr.* **3. bottom dollar,** the last of a person's money: *I'm down to my bottom dollar.*

dolly *v.* **1.** to falsify evidence against: *The police dollied Joe.* –*phr.*

2. dolly up, to dress up smartly: *all dollied up for the night.*

dolly catch *n. Cricket.* a simple catch.

dolly's wax *phr.* **full up to dolly's wax,** replete; full of food: *I couldn't eat another crumb, I'm full up to dolly's wax.* [a reference to dolls of the 18th and 19th centuries with heads made of wax]

dolt *n.* a stupid person.

dome *n.* a person's head.

domestic *n.* an argument with one's spouse.

donah *n. Hist.* a young woman; a sweetheart or girlfriend; (specifically) a female counterpart of a larrikin (def 1). Also, **dona.** [from British slang, from Italian *donna* woman]

done *interj.* **1.** agreed; settled. *–phr.* **2. done for, a.** dead. **b.** close to death. **c.** utterly exhausted. **d.** deprived of one's means of livelihood, etc.; ruined.
3. done in, very tired; exhausted.
4. done out of, cheated; tricked.
5. done up, a. dressed smartly. **b.** finished; ruined.
6. get done, to be completely defeated.

dong *v.* **1.** to hit, punch. *–n.* **2.** a heavy blow. **3.** Also, **donger.** the penis.

donk *n.* **1.** an engine of a motor vehicle. **2.** a donkey. **3.** the penis.

donkey *v. SA.* **1.** to carry a second person on a bicycle, horse, etc.; double. *–n.* **2.** a ride where one is carried as a second person on a bicycle, horse, etc.; a double.

donkey drop *n. Cricket.* a slow, high ball which looks easy to hit. Also, **donkey shot.**

donkey-lick *v. Horseracing, etc.* to defeat (another contestant in a race) with ease.

donnybrook *n.* a fight or argument; a brawl. Also, **donneybrook, donny.** [originally with reference to a fair held annually until 1855 at *Donnybrook*, Dublin, famous for rioting and dissipation]

dood *n.* See **dude.**

doodad *n.* **1.** See **do-hickey. 2.** (*pl.*) any trifling ornaments or bits of decorative finery.

doodette *n.* See **dudette.**

doodle *n.* **1.** the penis. **2.** a silly fellow.

doofus *n. Originally US.* a stupid, dull-headed person; a fool; a gumby. [see earlier US *doof*, from Scottish]

dook *n.* **1.** *Older slang.* a hand. *–v.* **2.** *Older slang.* to hand over; to give. **3.** *Older slang.* to give as a bribe. *–phr.*
4. dook it out, to fight.
5. put up your dooks, an invitation to fight. Also, **duke.** [from British slang; spelling variant of *dukes*, according to Hotten (who wrote a slang dictionary in the 19th century), from rhyming slang *Dukes of Yorks* forks = fingers, hands, which he says is 'a long way round, but quite true']

doormat *n.* an uncomplaining person who meekly accepts ill-treatment or bullying.

doover *n.* any object (often used jocularly in place of the usual name). Also, **doovah, doofer,**

dooverlackie, doovahlackie. [alteration of *do for* in such phrases as *that will do for now*]

doozey *n.* anything especially pleasing: *It's a doozey of a camera; Watch that first step, it's a doozey.* [from *doozey* fancy, splendid, ? influenced by Italian actress Eleonora *Duse*]

dope *n.* **1.** marijuana. **2.** any drug, especially a narcotic. **3.** a stimulating drug, as one illegally given to a racehorse to induce greater speed. **4.** information or data. **5.** a stupid person. *–v.* **6.** to affect with dope or drugs. *–adj.* **7.** very cool and sophisticated: *the dopest nightclub around.* [originally meaning 'sauce', 'gravy', from Dutch *doop* dipping sauce]

dope fiend *n.* a person addicted to marijuana.

dopey *adj.* slow-witted; stupid.

dorba *n.* a stupid person, especially someone who is physically or socially clumsy or inept. Also, **dorb**.

dork *n. Originally US.* a fool, especially someone who is physically or socially clumsy or inept. [from *dork* the penis; ? alteration of *dick*]

dorky *adj.* befitting a dork; dweeby.

Dorothy *phr.* See **friend of Dorothy**.

dorothy dixer *n.* a question asked in parliament specifically to allow a propagandist reply by a minister. [from *Dorothy Dix* a well-known column of advice to people with emotional problems, the questions are said to have been devised by the columnist, and not sent in by readers]

dose *n.* venereal disease.

dosh *n.* money. [origin unknown]

doss *n.* **1.** a place to sleep, especially in a cheap lodging house. *–v.* **2.** to sleep in a dosshouse. **3.** to make a temporary sleeping place for oneself. [from French *dos* back, from Latin *dorsum*]

dosser *n.* one who sleeps in a dosshouse.

dosshouse *n.* a cheap lodging house, usually for men only; flophouse.

dot ball *n. Cricket.* a maiden ball. [so called from being marked with a dot on the scoring sheet]

dotty *adj.* crazy; eccentric.

double-dink *v.* to carry or convey a second person on a horse, bicycle, or motorcycle. Also, **double, double bank, dink**.

double-header *n.* **1.** a double-headed coin. **2.** two attractions, events, etc., featured on the one program, day, etc.

doubletalk *n.* evasive or ambiguous language.

double whammy *n.* See **whammy**.

douche-bag *n. Chiefly US.* a contemptible or despicable person.

dough *n.* **1.** money. *–phr.* **2. do one's dough, a.** to lose one's money, especially in some speculation or gamble. **b.** to throw away a last chance.

doughnut *phr.* **do a doughnut,** to perform a manoeuvre in which a car or motorcycle is driven in a very tight circle so that the front remains almost stationary while the rear wheels, spinning wildly, pivot around the front, leaving a circle marked on the ground.

dover *n. Obsolete.* **1.** a bush knife. *–phr.*
2. flash one's dover, to prepare to eat.
3. the run of one's dover, as much to eat as one wants. [originally from brand name on blade of both knife and shears]

down *adj.* **1.** in prison: *He is down for a few months.* *–v.* **2.** to drink, especially quickly: *down a few.* *–phr.*
3. down below, the private parts.
4. down on, over-severe; unnecessarily ready to detect faults and punish harshly.
5. down the plughole (or **drain**) (or **gurgler**), wasted (as effort, money, etc.).
6. down time, a. time lost. **b.** *Comp.* the amount of time a computer is shut down or not supporting users.
7. down with, accepting of; cool about: *That would be cool if he was down with it.*
8. go down, a. to practise fellatio or cunnilingus. **b.** to be ruined or disgraced: *If I'm going down, I'm taking you with me.*
9. go down on (**someone**), to practise fellatio or cunnilingus on (someone).
10. have a down on, to hold a grudge against.
11. put (**someone**) **down, a.** to humiliate or rebuke (someone). **b.** to record someone's name: *Put me down for six please; I'll put you down for next Wednesday.*
12. take (**someone**) **down,** to disgrace or ruin (someone).

downbeat *adj.* dull and slow.

downer *n.* **1.** a depressant or tranquilliser, as Valium, etc. **2.** a depressing experience; a bummer.

down-under *n.* Australia, New Zealand, and adjacent Pacific Islands (viewed from or as from the Northern Hemisphere). Also, **Down Under.**

DQ *abbrev.* **a.** a drama queen. **b.** a drag queen.

drack *adj.* **1.** unattractive; dressed in a slovenly manner: *a drack sort. –n.* **2.** *Obsolete.* a police officer. **3.** an unattractive person, especially a woman. [perhaps from *Drac*, short for *Dracula*; but cf. *dreck*]

drag *n.* **1.** somebody or something that is extremely boring. **2.** a puff or a pull on a cigarette. **3.** women's clothes, worn by men; transvestite costume. **4.** a drag queen. **5.** a prison sentence of three month's or less duration. **6.** a drag race. **7.** a road or street: *the main drag. –phr.*
8. drag off, to beat in a drag-race, especially starting from traffic-lights.
9. drag up, a. (of a child) to bring up or raise in a socially unacceptable way. **b.** to raise an unpopular or disturbing topic.

dragon *phr.* **1. drain the dragon,** to urinate. **2. chase the dragon,** to inhale the smoke of heated heroin.

dragon slayer *n.* a person employed to put out burning oil wellheads.

drag queen *n.* a male who dresses in drag.

drama queen *n.* a person who overreacts regularly to minor problems.

dreads *pl. n.* dreadlocks.

dream *n.* **1.** *Prison.* a period of

imprisonment of six months. *–phr.* **2. dream on,** Also, **in your dreams!** an expression denoting that someone has unrealistic expectations.

dreamboat *n.* an overwhelmingly attractive person.

dreck *n. Originally US.* trash; rubbish; junk. [from Yiddish *drek* human excrement, shit, rubbish]

dribble *n.* **1.** a very small amount of some liquid. **2.** *Surfing.* poor surfing waves.

drinkies *n.* a social gathering, as at a pub after work, for the purpose of sharing a few drinks.

drinky-poo *n.* an alcoholic drink.

drip *n.* an insipid or colourless person; a fool.

drippy *adj.* (of a person) colourless; insipid; stupid.

drongo *n.* **1.** *Originally.* a raw recruit in the Royal Australian Air Force. **2.** a slow-witted or stupid person. [origin uncertain; probably from *drongo* a type of bird, though widely believed to be from *Drongo* the name of a racehorse in the early 1920s which was famed for its poor form and used as a character in political cartoons by Sammy Wells appearing in the *Melbourne Herald*]

drool *phr.* **drool over,** to show excessive pleasure at an object or at the prospect of enjoying something.

drool value *n.* physical attractiveness.

drool-worthy *adj.* extremely physically attractive. Also, **droolsome**.

droopy drawers *n.* a sluggish, apathetic person.

drop *n.* **1.** the gallows. **2.** *Cricket.* the fall of a wicket. **3.** stolen goods. **4.** a place of temporary storage for stolen goods, drugs, etc. *–v.* **5.** to take (drugs) orally. **6.** to stop, terminate (a topic of conversation, etc.): *Drop it!* **7.** to receive stolen goods. **8.** to fell (a tree, etc.). **9.** *Prison.* to inform on (someone). *–phr.*
10. drop dead, a. to die. **b.** an imprecation used to insult the person addressed.
11. drop in, *Surfing.* to cut across the path of another surfer who has priority.
12. drop (or **shoot**) **one's load,** (of a male) to ejaculate.
13. get (or **have**) **the drop on,** to get or have at a disadvantage.
14. till one drops, until one is exhausted: *shop till ya drop.*

drop-dead *adj.* exceedingly attractive: *a drop-dead hunk.* Also, **drop-dead gorgeous**.

drop-in *n.* **1.** a drop-in centre. **2.** a place visited casually: *a favourite drop-in of mine.*

dropkick *n.* an obnoxious person. [rhyming slang *dropkick and punt* cunt]

dropsy *n. Jocular.* a bout of accidentally dropping things.

drop test *n. Jocular.* an attempt to fix a faulty piece of equipment, usually electronic, by dropping it.

drover's dog *n.* **1.** a person of no importance, anybody at all. *–phr.* **2. work like a drover's dog,** to work hard and in a determined way.

druggie *n.* one who takes drugs habitually. Also, **druggo**.

drum *n.* **1.** *Hist.* a swagman's rolled blanket and the belongings it con-

tains. **2.** *Obsolescent.* a brothel. **3.** information. *–phr.*
4. give (someone) the drum, to give (someone) information or advice, usually confidential or profitable.
5. hump one's drum, *Hist.* to carry a swag.
6. tight as a drum, (of the stomach) completely full of food.

drum and bass *n.* See **jungle**.

drunk *phr.* **drunk as a lord, drunk as a skunk, drunk as Chloe,** very drunk.

druthers *pl. n.* choice; preference: *If I'd had my druthers I'd be in bed.* [from the phrase *(I)'d rather*]

dry *phr.*
1. dry out, a. to subject (an alcoholic or other drug addict) to a systematic process of detoxification. **b.** (of alcoholics, and other drug addicts) to rid the body of the drug of dependence.
2. dry up, (used in the imperative) stop talking!

dry-hump *v.* **1.** to engage in sexual activities while fully clothed, esp. imitating sexual intercourse but only indulging in frottage. **2.** to insert and rub the penis between the thighs or breasts, but not ejaculate. Also, **dry-root**.

DTs *pl. n.* delirium tremens.

dub *n.* **1.** an instrumental version of a Jamaican reggae song emphasising drums and bass as well as a variety of production effects, often used as a backing for toasting. **2.** a musical genre based on such songs.

Dub *n.* a Volkswagon of the type first produced.

dubbo *adj.* **1.** stupid; imbecilic. *–n.* **2.** an idiot or imbecile. [from *Dubbo* a town in NSW]

dubby *adj.* (of dance music) dub influenced: *some fine dubby tracks.*

duck *n.* **1.** *Cricket.* Also **duck's egg.** a score of zero runs. *–phr.*
2. diamond duck, *Cricket.* a dismissal without having faced a ball, e.g. run out, knocking the bails off before facing a ball, etc.
3. golden duck, *Cricket.* a dismissal with the first ball.
4. fuck a duck, *Offensive.* an exclamation of vexation, surprise, etc.

duckhouse *phr. Obsolete.*
1. that's one up against your duckhouse, an exclamation identifying a score against someone in one-upmanship.
2. upset (someone's) duckhouse, to upset (someone's) plans or calculations.

ducks and drakes *pl. n.* **1.** the shakes (as induced by excessive consumption of alcohol). [rhyming slang]

duck's disease *n.* shortness of stature.

duckshove *v.* **1.** to use unfair methods; to be unscrupulous in dealings. **2.** (of a taxi driver) to solicit passengers along the roadside, rather than waiting in turn at a rank.

dud *n.* **1.** any thing or person that proves a failure. **2.** an empty bottle. *–v.* **3.** to swindle; deceive. *–adj.*
4. useless; defective: *a dud cheque.*
5. that fails: *a dud joke.* *–phr.*
6. dud up, a. to cause someone to fail. **b.** to misinform someone deliberately.

dudder *n. Car sales.* a customer with no credit standing.

dud-dropper *n.* one who sells inferior goods as superior goods, in a manner suggesting that they are high-priced goods being sold cheaply because they are stolen.

dude *n.* **1.** an adult male; fellow: *Some dudes at the pub were selling raffle tickets.* **2.** a person who is fashionable, up-to-date and socially acceptable: *Jason's such a dude, man.* **3.** a term of familiar address: *Hey dude, what's happening?* **4.** *Originally.* a person who is stylishly and ostentatiously dressed; a dandy. **5.** *US West.* a city person unfamiliar with the West. Also, **dood**. [origin uncertain; originally referring to dress, thus perhaps related to *duds*]

dudette *n. Jocular.* a female dude. Also, **doodette**.

dudical *adj.* excellent; fantastic; incredibly cool.

duds *pl. n.* **1.** trousers. **2.** clothes, especially old or ragged clothes. **3.** belongings in general.

due *phr. Surfing.* **pay one's dues,** to earn a place in the line-up.

duff *v.* **1.** to steal: *duffing cattle.* **2.** to mess up; fluff. *–phr.* **3. up the duff, a.** pregnant. **b.** ruined; broken.

duffer *n.* a plodding, stupid, or incompetent person.

duh *interj.* **1.** an exclamation used to express a grunt, such as one gives when receiving a blow, being winded, etc. **2.** an exclamation representing a filler used when thinking, usually implying stupidity.

duke *n., v.* See **dook**.

dumbcluck *n.* a fool; idiot.

dumb fuck *n. Offensive and derogatory.* a foolish, ignorant person. Also, **dumbfuck**.

dumdum *n.* (*especially in children's speech*) a stupid person. Also, **dumb-dumb**.

dummy *n.* **1.** a stupid person; dolt. **2.** (especially in buying land) one put forward to act for others while ostensibly acting on their own behalf.
3. sell a dummy, *Football.* to successfully make a feigned or pretended manoeuvre; make a dummy pass.
4. spit the dummy, a. to give up or opt out of a contest or the like before there is reasonable cause to do so. **b.** to throw a tantrum.

dump[1] *n.* **1.** a place, house, or town that is poorly kept up, and generally of wretched appearance. **2.** an act of defecation: *taking a dump.* *–v.* **3.** to end a relationship with (someone); drop. **4.** to defecate. *–phr.* **5. dump on (someone),** to criticise, put down or scold (someone).

dump[2] *n.* **1.** *Hist.* a round piece cut from the centre of a silver dollar, and used as a coin. *–phr.* **2. not give a twopenny dump,** not to care. [origin uncertain]

dumper *n.* **1.** a tip-truck. **2.** a wave which, in shallow water, instead of breaking evenly from the top, crashes violently down, throwing swimmers or surfers to the bottom.

dung-puncher *n. Derogatory and crass.* a male homosexual. Also, **dung-pusher**.

dunlop overcoat *n.* a condom.

dunno *v.* contraction of *don't know.*

dunny *n.* **1.** *Originally.* an outside toilet, found in unsewered areas,

usually at some distance from the house it serves and consisting of a small shed furnished with a lavatory seat placed over a sanitary can, or pit. **2.** a sanitary can or toilet bowl. **3.** the toilet or bathroom. –*phr.*
4. all alone like a country dunny, completely alone; isolated.
5. the dunnies, a toilet block, as in a school yard, camping ground, etc. [from earlier *dunniken*, from British dialect and cant, from *danna* excrement + *ken* house]

dunny can *n.* **1.** a sanitary can. **2.** a toilet bowl.

dur *n.* See **der**.

durry *n.* a cigarette. [possibly from Bull *Dur*(*ham*) a brand of roll-your-own tobacco + -*y*]

Dutch oven *n.* a prank in which one holds another's head under the covers of a bed they have just farted in.

Dutch treat *n.* a meal or entertainment in which each person pays their own way. Also, **Dutch shout**.

dweeb *n. Originally US.* a person who is stupid, lacks style, or is otherwise annoying; a dag. [origin unknown]

dweeby *adj.* befitting a dweeb; daggy.

dyke[1] *n.* a lesbian. [originally US, from earlier *dike, dike out* (of a woman) to dress up (like a man); cf. *decked out* all dressed up; formerly used derogatorily by homophobes, but now reclaimed as a positive term, especially in self-reference]

dyke[2] *n.* a lavatory. [Old English *dic* a ditch for water]

dykefest *n.* **1.** an organised lesbian event, dinner, etc. **2.** *Derogatory.* any social or formal gathering of women.

dykey *adj.* having a lesbian quality.

ESKY

This word is a classic example of a trademark that has gained popular currency in the language. There are many other similar words, some of which many people no longer recognise as being originally trademark terms, *alfoil, araldite, bandaid, biro, bowser, cellophane* and *doona,* just to name a few. The *Esky* was originally released onto the market by Malleys Ltd in the 1950s. This was the sturdy metal type, with a drainage hole near the base. It was a huge success. They obviously coined the name by shortening the word *eskimo,* with the ending assimilated to the common colloquial noun suffix *–y* or *–ie*. Later on they were made of various materials, even styrofoam – which whilst being lighter and much easier to carry are not very useful when sat upon by someone who has drunk the contents of the beer cans that had been contained within.

E G G

The simple, everyday *egg*, whilst enriching cakes and other culinary items, has served to enrich our language at the same time. It's so versatile! For instance, a *fried egg*, apart from being served for breakfast, is also a colloquial name for the once-common small, yellow domes seen at intersections, otherwise known as silent cops. A person who is good is a *good egg*, and a bad person is a *rotten egg* or a *bad egg* – and if you've ever had the displeasure of smelling a bad egg you'll know how obnoxious an appellation this is! The phrase *go teach your grandmother to suck eggs* is used to admonish someone who is intent on showing you something you already know. Of course, all grandmothers know the way to suck out the contents of an egg without cracking the shell and getting it all over the place. And amongst the teenagers *egg roll* is an epithet for a moron, idiot, gumby, etc. This may be an allusion to that particular sort of half-squashed, half-squished, plastic-wrapped, from-the-bottom-of-the-schoolbag, sort of egg roll that schoolchildren are familiar with, rather than the gourmet one sold at the local sandwich shop.

ELEPHANTS

blind, blotto, Brahms, drunk as Chloe, hammered, legless, Molly the Monk, off one's dial, off one's tits, paralytic, pissed as a parrot, plastered, rotten, shickered, shit-faced, sozzled, under the table, written-off

STUCK FOR WORDS

e *n.* **1.** the drug ecstasy. **2.** used in respelling of words to indicate that the drug ecstasy was being taken: *a groove-E nite; happee birthday.* Also, **E**.

earbash *v.* **1.** to harangue (someone). **2.** to talk insistently and for a long time.

earful *n.* **1.** a quantity of oral advice, especially unsolicited advice. **2.** a stern rebuke, especially lengthy or abusive.

earhole *n.* the ear.

early mark *n.* a leaving work before normal knock-off time.

early opener *n.* a hotel which opens for bar trading before normal hours.

earn *n.* an earning: *made a nice little earn from it.*

earwig *n. Prison.* an eavesdropper; stickybeak.

Eastern Stater *n. WA. Often derogatory.* a person who comes from any of the eastern states of Australia.

easy *adj.* **1.** having no firm preferences in a particular matter: *I'm easy.* **2.** promiscuous; free with sexual favours. **3.** susceptible, as to a loan or a swindle: *easy take.*

easybeat *n. Sport.* **1.** a person who is easily beaten. **2.** (*pl.*) a team which is easily beaten.

easy wicket *n.* **1.** *Cricket.* a pitch of slow pace which favours the batsmen. **2.** an easy task; a comfortable position in life: *The manager is on an easy wicket here.*

eat *v.* **1.** to cause to worry; trouble: *What's eating you?* **2.** to perform fellatio or cunnilingus on. *–n.* **3.** (*pl.*) food. *–phr.*
  4. eat dirt, an expression of triumph, said to a vehicle overtaken in a race.
  5. eat my shorts, a contemptuous riposte. [popularised by the character Bart Simpson of the television program *The Simpsons*]
  6. eat (someone) out, to perform fellatio or cunnilingus on (someone).
  7. eat shit, *Offensive.* to be subservient or submissive.

eating irons *pl. n.* eating utensils.

eccy *n.* ecstasy, a recreational drug based on MDMA. Also, **eccie, e**.

echo *n.* **1.** one who reflects or imitates another: *What are you? An echo?* **2.** *SA.* a small returnable beer bottle.

Edgar Britt *n.* **1.** the act of defecating. **2.** (*pl.*) an attack of diarrhoea. Also, **Jimmy Britt**. [rhyming slang *Edgar Britt* shit]

eelerspee *n. Obsolete.* a confidence trickster; a con artist. [the word *spieler* as rendered in pig-Latin]

eelie *n. Obsolete.* a confidence trick. See **healy**. [probably extracted from *eelerspee* + *-ie*]

eff *v., n., interj.* **1.** a euphemism for the word *fuck*: *Eff off. –phr.* **2.** to use the word *fuck* in swearing: *been effing all evening.*

effem *n.* an effeminate person.

egg *v.* **1.** to pass wind; to fart. *–phr.*
  2. bad egg, a person of reprehensible character.
  3. break eggs with a big stick, to act in an ostentatious or flamboyant manner, usually well beyond the requirements of the given situation.
  4. have egg on one's face, to be exposed in an embarrassing situation.

5. suck eggs, a derisive exclamation; sucked in!

egghead *n.* an intellectual; highbrow.

egg roll *n.* a stupid person; idiot.

eggshell blonde *n.* a bald person.

eh *interj.* **1.** an exclamation of surprise; hey! **2.** a tag used at the end of a statement in order to assure that the listener is in agreement, not necessarily requiring a reply or answer, but offering the option of agreeing or disagreeing: *Wasn't it lucky, eh? Great fun, eh? Blessing in disguise, eh?* Also, **ay**. [the usage in def 2 is very common, and dates back to colonial times. It is neither restricted, nor excessively more common, to New Zealand, Queensland, or any other particular region, as often claimed]

eight ball *phr.* **behind the eight ball,** in an awkward or disadvantageous position.

eighteen *n.* an eighteen-gallon keg.

elastics *n.* a girls' schoolyard game in which a long loop of elastic is held, usually between two children, and a set of various trick manoeuvres with the legs is performed by a third. After the completion of a set without mistakes the elastic is moved up higher thus increasing the difficulty.

elastic sides *pl. n.* boots similar to riding boots, with a piece of elastic inset into the sides. Also, **laughing-side boots**.

elbow *phr.* **bend one's elbow,** to drink (especially beer).

el cheapo *adj.* **1.** of or relating to that which is cheap and/or inferior, as a restaurant, amplifier, record, etc. *–n.* **2.** any such article. **3.** a cheap restaurant. [mock Spanish]

electro *n.* a type of dance music.

elephant gun *n.* a surfboard used for riding big waves.

elephant juice *n.* a narcotic analgesic used to immobilise large animals such as the elephant or the rhinoceros, but now used illegally in small doses to stimulate racehorses.

elephants *adj.* drunk. [rhyming slang *elephant's trunk* drunk]

elevator *phr.* **(someone's) elevator** (or **lift**) **doesn't go to the top floor,** (someone) is intellectually weak or stupid.

el primo *adj.* first rate; very good; the top quality, especially used of marijuana.

Elvis Presley *n.* **1.** *Car sales.* a car with many dents in the body and scratches in the duco. [i.e. it has had many hits] **2.** *Fishing.* a leatherjacket.

emcee *n.* **1.** a performer at a nightclub, dance party, etc., who raps over the top of the deejay's music. *–v.* **2.** to perform as an emcee. Also, **MC**. [from *Master of Ceremonies*]

emma chisit *phr. Strine.* the question 'how much is it?'

emoticon *n.* a representation of a facial expression made with the characters of a qwerty keyboard, for example (viewed sideways) :-) happy, :-(sad, ;-) a wink. [from *emot(ion)* + *icon*]

emu-bobber *n.* a person employed to pick up sticks lying around on land which has been cleared or burnt off.

emu parade *n.* **1.** *Military.* a parade to clean up an area by emu-bobbing. **2.** the picking up of litter in a camping area, school playground, etc., by a group of people organised for this purpose. **3.** *Police.* Also, **emu walk.** a combing of an area for clues, suspects, etc.

end *phr.*
 1. at a loose end, Also, **at loose ends.** unoccupied; with nothing to do: *She asked him to dinner because he seemed to be at a loose end.*
 2. get one's end in, (of a male) to have sexual intercourse.
 3. go off the deep end, to become violently agitated; to lose control of the emotions.
 4. no end, very much; greatly: *The news of the lottery win thrilled them no end.*

envelope *phr.* **push the envelope,** to extend beyond the normally accepted bounds; to take ideas, art, music, life, etc. to an extreme.

Enzedder *n.* a New Zealander.

E-pal *n.* a penpal corresponding via e-mail. Also, **e-pal**.

equaliser *n.* a gun.

-erer *suffix. Jocular.* added pleonastically to make agent nouns from compound verbs: *fixer-upperer, hanger-onerer, sorter-outerer, washer-upperer.*

-eroo *suffix.* added to the end of words to make colloquial or slang forms: *switcheroo; smackeroo.* Also, **-aroonie, -eroonie**. [originally US, from the 1930s; popularised by US newspaper columnist Walter Winchell; origin uncertain, possibly mimicking such words as *buckeroo, kangaroo,* etc., however, earlier appearing in the form *-erine* and *-erino*]

esky *n.* a portable icebox. [Trademark; from *esk(imo)* + *-y*]

esky lid *n. Surfing. Derogatory.* a bodyboard.

esky-lidder *n. Surfing. Derogatory.* a bodyboard rider.

euchre *v.* **1.** to outwit; get the better of, as by scheming. **2.** to ruin or spoil: *That euchred it.* [from the card game *euchre*]

euchred *adj.* beaten; exhausted.

Euro *adj.* European.

Euro-dance *n.* a type of fast, pop-oriented techno dance music; hi-NRG.

evac *n.* **1.** *Military.* evacuation time. **2.** time to leave: *How long till evac?*

ever *phr.* **do I ever!** an exclamation used to express a positive answer to a question; certainly: *'Do you remember?' 'Do I ever!'*

evil weed *n.* marijuana.

evo *n.* evening: *What're you doing tomorrow evo?*

ex *n.* **1.** one's former husband or wife. **2.** one's former boyfriend or girlfriend.

excellent *adj.* **1.** terrific; wonderful; unreal. *–interj.* **2.** used to express great appreciation of something. *Mum said it was okay to go. Excellent!*

exec *n.* an executive.

ex-govie *n. ACT.* a house built by the Commonwealth Government but now privately owned.

exo *adj.* **1.** excellent. *–interj.* **2.** excellent!

ex-pug *n.* a retired boxer. [from *pug* short for pugilist, a boxer]

extra-curricular *adj.* of or pertaining to sexual activities outside of a relationship.

eye *phr.*
  1. **easy on the eye,** attractive to look at.
  2. **eye off,** to watch or look at with interest, attention, etc.
  3. **get one's eye in,** to adapt oneself to a situation.
  4. **go eyes out,** to work very hard.
  5. **lay** (or **clap**) (or **set**) **eyes on,** to catch sight of; see.
  6. **make eyes at,** to gaze flirtatiously at.
  7. **pick the eyes out of,** to select the best parts, pieces, etc., of (a collection).
  8. **sight for sore eyes,** a welcome sight; an agreeable surprise.
  9. **turn a blind eye to,** to pretend not to see; to avoid noticing that which one should oppose or condemn.
  10. **up to the eyes in,** very busy with; deeply involved in.

eyeball *v.* 1. to look at: *to eyeball a room.* –*phr.*
  2. **eyeball to eyeball,** aggressively face to face; in confrontation.
  3. **greasy eyeball,** Also, **hairy eyeball**. a disdainful look: *He gave her the greasy eyeball.*

eyeful *n.* 1. a person of striking appearance. –*phr.* 2. **get an eyeful of,** to look at.

eye-opener *n.* 1. an enlightening or startling disclosure or experience. 2. a highly attractive person. 3. **a.** an alcoholic drink, especially one taken early in the day. **b.** any drink, as coffee, taken before one begins the day's activities. **c.** a drug addict's first injection or smoke of the day.

eyewash *n. Older slang.* nonsense.

e-zine *n.* a magazine in electronic form available on the Internet. Also, **ezine**.

F

FANG

Fangs have been with us since the days of Adam and Eve and they've retained a relatively nasty connotation ever since. *Fangs* are sharp, dangerous and tenacious, and once they are sunk in it is hard to get them out again. Thus the phrase *to put the fangs into someone* meant to try and borrow money from them. It is also known as *fanging* someone, which is the same as to *biting* them, for cash! The human teeth are sometimes jocularly called *fangs,* and thus *to sink the fangs into* a meat pie, is to eat it, and to *go the fang* means to begin eating, to hoe into your food.

Another quite different meaning of *fang* is to drive a car, often at high speed. Young louts, lairs, and larrikins, who have nothing better to do will just *fang around* in their cars, doing wheelies, screechies, and hopefully charming members of the opposite sex. However, when they *fang* it up the street, they *put the pedal to the metal* and really *burn rubber*. They may even *fishtail* the car (make the rear-end swerve from side to side) or do *doughnuts* (leave circular layers of wheel rubber). This meaning of *fang* supposedly derives from the name of the famous racing car driver Juan *Fangio*, whom all these young heroes attempt to emulate.

FOSSICK

Fossick is a word that sounds very much like what it is. You can almost hear in *fossick* someone rummaging through lots of little bits of things, searching here and there. It is a word from a British dialect that had its start in Australian English in the goldmining days when miners fossicked through mullock heaps, turning over the dirt that other miners had tossed aside, in the hope that, if they searched diligently enough, they'd find that little bit of gold that the previous miner had missed. In British dialect, *fossick* meant "to find something out by asking around". Lots of patient fossicking might turn up the information you wanted. To *fussick* or *fursick* was "to potter over one's work", while to *fussock* was "to make a fuss or bustle about".

FAIR DINKUM

dead set, dinkum, dinky, dinky-di, fair dink, fair dinks, grouse, ribuck (obs.), ridge, ridgy-didge, ridgy-didgy, straight wire, straight, the real McCoy, true blue, true dinks

STUCK FOR WORDS

f *v., n., interj.* a euphemism for the word *fuck*. Also, **eff**.

fab *adj.* fabulous; excellent. Also, **fabbo**.

face *n.* **1.** facial make-up: *Wait while I put on my face; when I have my face on.* –*phr.*
2. in someone's face, annoyingly close when face to face with someone; invading someone's personal space in an aggressive way.
3. off one's face, incapacitated as a result of taking drugs, alcohol, etc.; really drunk, stoned or tripping out.

face-ache *n.* an extremely ugly or irritating person.

face fungus *n.* facial hair, as a moustache, beard, etc.

face plant *n.* a heavy fall off a skateboard, snowboard, skis, etc., in which the face hits the ground front on.

fade *v. Surfing.* to change the direction of a surfboard towards the breaking part of a wave.

fag *n.* **1.** a cigarette. [probably from *fag-end* the last part] **2.** *Derogatory.* a male homosexual. [shortening of *faggot*] –*v.* **3.** to smoke a cigarette.

fagged out *adj.* completely exhausted.

faggot *n. Derogatory.* a male homosexual. [originally a term of abuse applied to a woman]

fag hag *n. Derogatory.* a woman who socialises with male homosexuals.

fair *phr.*
1. a fair cop, a. a just sentence. **b.** the discovery of a wrongdoer in the act or with their guilt apparent.
2. fair and square, honest; just; straightforward.
3. fair suck, an appeal for fairness or reason. Also, with various extensions, **fair suck of the sav,** (or **saveloy**), (or **sauce bottle**), (or **Siberian sandshoe**).

fair dinkum *adj.* **1.** true; genuine; dinkum: *Are you fair dinkum?* –*interj.* **2.** Also, **fair dink, fair dinks.** (an assertion of truth or genuineness): *It's true, mate, fair dinkum.* [from British dialect (North Lincolnshire), from *dinkum* hard work]

fair enough *adj.* **1.** acceptable; passable. –*interj.* **2.** a statement of acquiescence or agreement.

fair go *n.* **1.** a fair or reasonable course of action: *Do you think that's a fair go?* **2.** an adequate opportunity: *He never had a fair go.* –*interj.* **3.** an appeal for fairness or reason: *Fair go, mate!*

fairy *n.* **1.** *Derogatory.* an effeminate male. **2.** *Derogatory.* a male homosexual. –*phr.*
3. away (or **off**) **with the fairies** (or **pixies**), **a.** daydreaming. **b.** mentally unsound or eccentric. **c.** not in touch with reality.
4. shoot a fairy, to fart.

fakie *adv. Skateboarding and snowboarding.* **1.** backwards. –*n.* **2.** a backwards ride; a trick done moving backwards. –*adj.* **3.** (of a trick) performed whilst travelling backwards.

fall *phr.*
1. fall for, a. to be deceived by: *Don't fall for that old story.* **b.** to fall in love with.
2. fall off the back of a truck, to be obtained by questionable or illegal means.

3. fall out, a. to disagree; quarrel. **b.** to occur; happen; turn out.
4. fall over oneself, a. to become confused in attempting to take some action. **b.** to be excessively enthusiastic.
5. go over the falls, *Surfing.* to wipe-out from the top of a wave going over with the lip.

fall guy *n.* an easy victim; scapegoat.

falsies *pl. n.* **1.** padding worn to enlarge the apparent size of the breasts. **2.** false eyelashes. **3.** false teeth.

fam *n.* family: *fun for the whole fam.*

family *n.* **1.** *Obsolete.* the criminal fraternity. *–phr.* **2. in the family way,** pregnant.

family jewels *n.* the testicles. Also, **crown jewels.**

fan *phr.* **fan the breeze,** to engage in idle talk.

fang[1] *n.* **1.** a tooth. **2.** the act of eating: *go the fang.* **3.** the penis. *–v.* **4.** to borrow. *–phr.*
5. be good on the fang, to be a hearty eater.
6. put the fangs (or **nips**) **into,** to attempt to borrow from; to make demands on.

fang[2] *v.* **1.** to drive one's car or motorbike at great speed; to hoon. *–n.* **2.** such a drive: *taking it for a fang around the block.* [from Juan *Fangio* Argentinian racing-car driver]

fang carpenter *n.* a dentist. Also, **fang farrier.**

fanny *n.* **1.** the vagina or vulva; the female genitals. **2.** *Chiefly US.* the buttocks; the arse.

fantabulous *adj.* marvellous; wonderful. [blend *fantastic* + *fabulous*]

fanzine *n.* a magazine for fans or enthusiasts of a particular star, band, etc.

FAQ *n. Internet.* a file containing answers to frequently asked questions about a particular topic.

far *phr.* **far out! a.** an exclamation of surprise or wonder. **b.** an exclamation of annoyance, frustration, etc. **c.** used as a euphemism for *fuck!*

farnarkel *v.* Also, **farnarkel around.** to indulge in farnarkeling: *While politicians farnarkel around, the economy gets steadily worse.*

farnarkeling *n.* activity which creates an appearance of productivity but which has no substance to it. [coined by comedian John Clarke for a fictitious team sport for which he acted as sports commentator in the 1980s television series *The Gillies Report*]

fart *n.* **1.** an emission of wind from the anus, either audible or inaudible. *–v.* **2.** to emit wind from the anus. *–phr.*
3. fart about (or **around**), to behave stupidly or waste time.
4. old fart, an old person. [Middle English *ferten*, Old English *feortan* to fart]

fart-arse *n.* **1.** an ineffectual person. *–phr.* **2. fart-arse about** (or **around**), to waste time; to idle.

fart-face *n.* a despicable or annoying person. Also, **fart-head.**

fart-mobile *n.* a car which makes a muffler noise resembling that of farting.

fart sack *n.* a sleeping bag.

fast *adj.* **1.** sexually promiscuous. **2.** *Horseracing.* (of a track) conducing to fast racing. *–phr.* **3. pull a fast one,** to act unfairly or deceitfully.

fastie *n.* **1.** a deceitful practice; a cunning act. *–phr.* **2. pull** (or **put**) **over a fastie,** to deceive; to take an unfair advantage.

fat *n.* **1.** an erect penis. *–adj.* **2.** *Originally US.* Also, **phat.** excellent; cool; unreal: *the fattest, funkiest soul. –phr.* **3. fat chance,** little or no chance. **4. fat lot,** little or nothing. **5. it isn't over till the fat lady sings,** the outcome is unknown until the end; it's not over until it has finished. [originally US; reputedly coined by San Antonio sports editor Dan Cook in 1978]

fat cat *n.* a person who expects special comforts and privileges because of their position or wealth: *the fat cats of the Public Service.*

fat farm *n.* a resort where one goes to lose weight.

fat green *n.* a type of marijuana.

father *phr.*
1. a bit of how's your father, sexual intercourse.
2. the father of a (something), the biggest or greatest example of: *gave him the father of a hiding.*

fave *adj.* **1.** favourite. *–n.* **2.** a favourite.

faze *v.* to disturb; discomfit; daunt. Also, **phase.** [variation of obsolete *feeze* disturb, worry]

fazzo *adj.* fabulous; wonderful.

feather duster *phr.* **a rooster one day and a feather duster the next,** See **rooster.**

-features *suffix.* a word element used to make insulting compounds: *dweeb-features; snot-features.*

fed *n.* **1.** a federal police officer. **2.** any police officer.

feeding *phr.* **feeding time at the zoo,** a disorderly rabble.

feeding frenzy *n.* a disorderly group of people all getting and eating food, as at a function.

feet *n.* See **foot.**

feisty *adj.* high-spirited and volatile. [from *feist* a silent fart; in this sense originally applied to a breed of small, aggressive dog known as a *fisting dog*, from Middle English *fyst* to fart]

felch *v.* **1.** to perform anilingus; to lick or suck a partner's anus, especially after anal intercourse. *–phr.* **2. felch you later,** *Crass.* a deliberately crude version of the phrase *catch you later*. Also, **velch.** [from homosexual slang of the late 60s, originally a jocular term; origin unknown]

fem *n.* **1.** a homosexual person, especially a lesbian, who is feminine. *–adj.* **2.** Also, **femmy.** feminine.

femmo *n.* **1.** a feminist, especially a woman. *–adj.* **2.** feminist.

fence *n.* **1. a.** a person who receives and disposes of stolen goods. **b.** the place of business of such a person. *–v.* **2.** to receive stolen goods.

fencing *n.* the receiving of stolen goods.

feral *n.* **1.** a person with strong environmentalist views, who lives a very rugged, commodity-free, low-technology lifestyle, and who usually shows little adherence to the

feral

normal societal notions of sartorial or personal hygiene. –*adj.* **2.** living as, looking like a feral. **3.** disgusting; gross. **4.** cool; excellent; unreal.

ferret *n.* **1.** the penis. **2.** *Cricket.* a player placed at the tail-end of the batting order. [so called since they follow the *bunnies* or *rabbits* in] –*phr.*
3. give the ferret a run, (of a male) to urinate.
4. run the ferret up the drainpipe, *Crass.* (of a male) to have sexual intercourse.

fess up *v.* to confess to something. Also, **'fess up**.

fester *v.* to waste time while you are meant to be studying or working; to bludge.

festy *adj.* **1.** dirty; grubby; unclean and smelly. **2.** extremely bad; awful; dreadful. [from *festering*]

FF *n.* (in personal ads) fist fucking.

fiddle-fart *v.* to waste time in frivolous activity. Also, **fiddle-arse**.

fiddley *n. Obsolete.* a pound note. [rhyming slang *fiddley-did* quid]

field *n. Horseracing.* **1.** all of the horses running in a race: *running at the tail end of the field; not hampered by a big field.* –*v.* **2.** to lay odds; to work as a bookmaker. –*phr.*
3. field a book, or, **field 'em,** to be a bookmaker.
4. (a certain odd) the field, a call used by bookmakers in order to drum up business, meaning that the favourite is offered at the odds called out and all other horses are at better odds: *Six to four the field!*

fielder *n. Horseracing.* a bookmaker.

finagle

fifth wheel *n.* any extra or superfluous person or thing.

fifty-fifty *n.* **1.** Also, **fifty.** a glass of beer, half old and half new. **2.** a dance, usually held in a country or suburban hall, in which the dancing and music is half old-time and half modern.

fight *phr.*
1. couldn't fight one's way out of a (wet) paper bag, said of someone who is extremely weak, cowardly or incompetent.
2. fight shy of, to keep carefully aloof from (a person, affair, etc.).

File-o-phile *n.* a fan of the television show *The X-files*.

filly *n.* a girl or young woman. [from *filly* a female foal]

filth *n.* **1.** *Originally Brit.* the police. **2.** people one does not approve of; annoying or disgusting people: *Filth like you shouldn't be allowed on the streets.* **3.** something excellent: *the waves were absolute filth.*

filthy *adj.* **1.** excellent; very good: *a totally filthy concert; the filthiest spunk on the planet.* **2.** highly offensive or objectionable: *filthy pollies; filthy mongrel bastards.* **3.** lurid; sexually depraved: *You've got a filthy mind.* –*phr.* **4. filthy rich,** very rich.

fin *n. Obsolete.* **a.** a five pound note. **b.** ten dollars. [originally British thieve's slang; from *finnup, finnuf,* from West Yiddish *finef,* from German *f:unf* five]

finagle *v.* **1.** to practise deception or fraud. **2.** to trick or cheat (a person). **3.** to wangle: *to finagle free tickets.* [from British dialect *fainaigue* to renege at cards, to cheat]

finger *v.* **1.** to point out; accuse. **2.** to sexually feel a woman's genitals, especially to place a finger, or fingers, into the vagina. *–phr.*
3. burn one's fingers, to get hurt or suffer loss from meddling with or engaging in anything.
4. finger up, to stimulate erotically with the fingers.
5. have a finger in the pie, to have a share in the doing of something.
6. pull one's finger out, to become active; hurry.
7. put the finger on, a. to inform against or identify a criminal to the police. **b.** to designate a victim, as of murder or other crime.
8. the finger, an offensive gesture made by holding up the index finger, wishing upon someone that they get something unpleasantly inserted into their anus.
9. twist round one's little finger, to dominate; influence easily.

finito *interj.* an exclamation proclaiming the completion of something. [from Italian]

fink *n.* a contemptible or undesirable person, especially one who reneges on an understanding. [originally US; probably from German *Fink* a student not belonging to the students' association, hence a 'bad guy', literally, 'finch']

fire *v.* to go extremely well; to really go off: *she was really firing in the second half.*

fire-ie *n.* a fire fighter. Also, **firee**.

First Fleeter *n.* a person whose family can be traced back to someone who came to Australia with the First Fleet in 1788.

fish *n.* **1.** *Surfing.* a type of wide surfboard with a swallow tail. **2.** (with an adjective) a person: *a queer fish, a poor fish. –phr.*
3. feed the fishes. a. to be seasick. **b.** to drown.
4. what's that got to do with the price of fish, a phrase used to question the relevance of a piece of information.

fisho *n.* **1.** a person who fishes. **2.** (formerly) a street vendor selling fish.

fishy *adj.* **1.** improbable, as a story. **2.** of questionable character.

fist fucking *n. Offensive.* **1.** the insertion of a hand into the vagina, as a form of sexual intercourse. **2.** Also, **fisting**. the insertion of a hand into the anus, as a form of sexual intercourse.

fit *v.* **1.** to bring a person before the law on a trivial or trumped-up charge while really intending to victimise them: *He had been trying to fit Chilla for years. –n.* **2.** the equipment used to prepare and inject drugs.

five *phr.* **take five,** to take a break, originally of five minutes, for rest or refreshment, especially as of a performing group in rehearsal.

five-finger discount *n.* stealing; shoplifting.

fiver *n.* **1.** *Obsolete.* a five-pound note. **2.** a five dollar note; five dollars. **3.** anything that counts as five.

fix *v.* **1.** to arrange matters, especially privately or dishonestly, so as to secure favourable action: *to fix a jury or a game.* **2.** to put in a condition or position to make no further trouble. **3.** to get even with; get revenge upon. *–n.* **4.** a shot of heroin or some other drug.

fixed *adj.* arranged privately or dishonestly.

fizgig *n.* **1.** a police informer. *–v.* **2.** to inform on criminals to the police. Also, **fizz-gig**.

fizzer *n.* **1.** a firecracker which fails to explode. **2.** a failure; fiasco.

fizzle *n.* **1.** a fiasco; a failure. *–phr.* **2. fizzle out,** to fail ignominiously after a good start.

flabbie *n.* a fat person.

flack *n. Originally US.* a publicity agent; press secretary; public relations officer. Also, **flak**.

flag *n.* **1.** Also, **Australian flag.** part of a shirt, which has come untucked and hangs out over the trousers. *–phr.*
2. hoist the flag, *Prison Talk.* to appeal against a conviction or the severity of a sentence.
3. keep the flag flying, to appear courageous and cheerful in the face of difficulty.
4. raise the flag, *Prison Talk.* to lodge an appeal against a conviction.
5. raise the flags, a. *Rugby, Australian Rules.* to score a conversion. **b.** to accomplish something.
6. take the flag, *Australian Rules.* to win the premiership pennant.

flak *n.* reactions, repercussions or publicity, usually poor, to some action, decision, etc.: *to cop a lot of flak.* Also, **flack**. [from *flak* anti-aircraft fire, from German]

flake *v.* **1.** Also, **flake out.** to collapse, faint, or fall asleep, especially as a result of complete exhaustion, or influence of alcohol, drugs, etc.

–n. **2.** one who is strange or eccentric.

flame *v. Internet.* to send a person an abusive message through e-mail, newsgroup postings, etc.; to be abusive over the Internet.

flame war *n. Internet.* a dispute full of caustic and negative abuse conducted over the Internet.

flaming *adj.* used to add emphasis to a statement, often as a euphemism for swear words: *Stone the flaming crows; a flaming bore.*

flaming fury *n. Rural.* a toilet constructed over a pit, the contents of which are periodically doused with oil and burnt.

flannie *n.* a flannelette shirt. Also, **flanno**.

flap *n.* **1.** a state of panic or nervous excitement: *in a flap.* **2.** (*pl.*) *Crass.* a woman's vaginal lips.

flash *adj.* **1.** pretentious. *–phr.*
2. flash as a rat with a gold tooth, (of a person) showy or ostentatious.
3. flash in the pan, something which begins promisingly but has no lasting significance.

flasher *n.* a man who exposes his genitals in public.

flash language *n. Obsolete.* the cant or jargon of thieves.

flat *adj.* **1.** *Prison.* tobacco other than jail issue. **2.** *Obsolete.* honest (opposed to *sharp*). *–n.* **3.** *Obsolete.* an honest person. **4.** a police officer. [? from *flatfoot*] *–phr.*
5. flat out, a. as fast as possible. **b.** very busy. **c.** lying prone. **d.** exhausted; unable to proceed.

flat chat *adv.* at full speed: *He drove*

flat chat down the road. Also, **flat strap.**

flatfoot *n.* a police officer.

flatline *v.* (of a person) to cease heart function as registered on an eletrocardiograph.

flattie *n.* **1.** a flathead fish. **2.** a flat-bottomed dinghy. **3.** a flatmate.

flea *phr.*
  1. could crack a flea on it, (of one's stomach) distended from having eaten a great deal.
  2. flea in one's ear, a. a discomforting rebuke or rebuff; a sharp hint. **b.** a blow to the ear; a cuff.

fleabag *n.* **1.** a sleeping bag. **2.** a dog; any worthless creature ridden with fleas. **3.** a despicable person; a swine.

fleapit *n.* a shabby, dirty room or building, especially a cinema. Also, **flea house.**

fleas-and-itches *n.* pictures; the cinema. [rhyming slang]

flick[1] *n.* **1.** a movie or film. **2.** *Ultimate frisbee.* a forehand throw. **3.** (*pl.*) a picture theatre. **4.** (*pl.*) a schoolyard game using bubblegum cards, basketball cards, or the like, in which the cards are flicked towards a wall, with certain conditions being applied to where or in what position they land. *–adj.* **5.** *Car sales.* to turn back the reading on the odometer.

flick[2] *phr.*
  1. give (someone) the flick, a. to dismiss or sack (someone). **b.** to end a romantic relationship with (someone); to drop (someone).
  2. give (something) the flick, to give up an activity, job, etc. [rhyming slang *flick pass* arse]

flied lice *n.* a mocking representation of a Chinese pronunciation of 'fried rice'.

fling *n.* a brief sexual affair.

flip *n.* **1.** a giddy, irresponsible, silly person. *–v.* **2.** Also, **flip out.** to amaze: *The results will flip you.* **3.** to become angered or enraged. *–phr.*
  4. flip one's lid, to become angry.
  5. flip oneself off, to masturbate.

flipper *n.* **1.** *Jocular.* the hand. **2.** *Cricket.* a delivery similar to a wrong'un, which pitches short like a long hop, but actually kicks forward upon striking the pitch, stays low and comes through quicker than, hopefully, the person batting expects.

flipping *adj., adv.* a euphemism for the word *fucking*, used as an intensifier: *a flipping headache.*

flipwreck *n. Derogatory.* a male who masturbates very often.

floater *n.* **1.** a meat pie served in pea soup. **2.** a cheque which is not honoured. **3.** one who often changes their job; a temporary employee; one of the floating population. **4.** *Two-Up.* Also, **butterfly.** a coin which when tossed fails to spin. **5.** *Prison.* an item, such as a book or magazine, that is kept illegally by prisoners and smuggled from cell to cell. **6.** *Wharfie slang.* a worker not attached to a gang. **7.** *Police.* a dead person found floating in the ocean, a creek, etc. **8.** *Surfing.* a manoeuvre in which one surfs on top of the curl of a wave as it breaks. **9.** a piece of excrement that floats.

flog *v.* **1.** to sell or attempt to sell. **2.** to steal. **3.** (of a male) to masturbate. –*n.* **4.** an act of male masturbation.

flogger *n. Australian Rules.* a short stick with a bunch of crepe paper streamers (in team colours) attached, waved to approve a score, or to distract a member of the opposing team.

flogging *adj., adv.* a euphemism for the word *fucking*, used as an intensifier: *Starve the flogging crows!*

flooze *v. Derogatory.* **1.** to have sex casually; sleep around. **2.** to flirt openly. [backformation from *floozy*]

floozy *n. Derogatory.* **1.** a woman or man who has sex casually. **2.** a woman or man who flirts openly. Also, **floosy, floosie, floozie.** [originally US, a prostitute, ? from *flossie* a young woman]

flop *v.* **1.** to fail. –*n.* **2.** a failure. **3.** a place to bed down.

flophouse *n.* a dosshouse.

fluff *n.* **1.** a blunder or error in execution, performance, etc. **2.** something intellectually lightweight. **3.** a fart. –*v.* **4.** to fail to perform properly: *to fluff a golf stroke.* **5.** to blunder; fail in performance or execution. **6.** to break wind. –*phr.* **7. bit** (or **piece**) **of fluff,** *Derogatory.* a woman, especially one who is superficially attractive.

flunk *v.* to fail, as a student in an examination. [originally 19th century US]

flute *n.* the penis.

flutter-by *n.* a butterfly. [jocular spoonerism, punning on the phrase *flutter by*]

fly[1] *n.* **1.** an attempt: *Give it a fly.* –*phr.* **2. fly a kite, a.** to attempt to obtain reactions to a proposal for a course of action by allowing it to be circulated as a rumour or unconfirmed report.
3. go fly a kite, a phrase used to rebuff someone; get lost!

fly[2] *phr.*
1. drink with the flies, to drink alone in a pub.
2. fly in the ointment, a slight flaw that greatly diminishes the value or pleasure of something.
3. no flies on (someone), a. (someone) is not easily tricked. **b.** *Obsolete.* honest.

fly[3] *adj.* **1.** knowing; sharp; cunning and crafty. **2.** stylish; sophisticated; cool: *she's fly.* [? special use of *fly*[1]]

flyblown *adj.* **1.** *Older slang.* broke; penniless. **2.** in a hopeless state; cactus.

Flynn *phr.* **in like Flynn,** successful in a particular enterprise, especially sexual. [from the popular belief in the sexual prowess of Errol *Flynn*, Australian-born US movie actor]

foamie *n.* a surfboard made from plastic foam.

foggiest *phr.* **not have the foggiest,** not to have the least idea.

foil *n.* a saleable measure of marijuana wrapped in aluminium foil.

folding stuff *n.* banknotes; paper (now plastic) money. Also, **folding**.

folkie *n.* one who likes or performs folk music.

folks *pl. n.* **1.** one's parents. **2.** the persons of one's own family; one's relatives: *My folks are having a big bash tonight.*

follicularly enhanced *adj. Jocular.*

follicularly enhanced   **frame**

having had hair replacement therapy.

f-one-j-one *n.* Fiji. [a fanciful spelling-out of *Fiji* with *one* (1) substituted for *i*]

foodie *n.* a connoisseur of food.

foot *phr.*
1. **feet first, a.** dead. **b.** thoughtlessly; impetuously.
2. **have one foot in the grave (and the other on a banana peel),** to be near death.
3. **keep one's feet on the ground,** to retain a sensible and practical outlook.
4. **put one's best foot forward, a.** to make as good an impression as possible. **b.** to do one's very best.
5. **put one's foot down,** to take a firm stand.
6. **put one's foot in one's mouth** (or **in it**), to make an embarrassing blunder.
7. **stand on one's own (two) feet,** to be self-sufficient.

footie *n.* football. Also, **footy, footer**.

footslogger *n.* an infantry soldier.

footsy *n.* **1.** (*especially in children's speech*) a foot. *–phr.* **2. play footsies,** to touch in secret a person's feet, knees, etc. with one's feet, especially as part of amorous play.

footy *n.* football.

for *phr.* **for it,** about to suffer some punishment, injury, setback, or the like: *You'll be for it if you don't behave!*

foreman *phr.* **get the foreman's job,** to take a white collar job as in management, politics, etc., such usually regarded as a betrayal of a working class background. [from the rhyme 'the working class can kiss my arse, I've got the *foreman's job* at last', often sung to the tune of 'The Red Flag']

fork *n.* **1.** the crotch. *–phr.*
2. **fork over** (or **out**), to hand over; to pay.
3. **get some pork on your fork,** (of a male) to obtain some sexual intercourse.
4. **the forks,** an offensive gesture made by holding up the pointer and index finger, wishing upon someone that they get something unpleasantly inserted into their anus.

fossil *n.* **1.** an outdated or old-fashioned person or thing. **2.** a very old person.

foul *adj.* (of a person) gross; disgusting.

four-by-two *n.* **1.** a Jew. **2.** a prison warder; screw. Also, **four-by, fourbie, forbie**. [rhyming slang]

four-eyes *n.* a person who wears glasses.

four-legged lottery *n.* a horse race.

four-letter word *n.* **1.** a swear word. **2.** anything which is distasteful or unpleasant: *Housework is a four-letter word.* [so called since a number of important taboo words happen to be spelt with four letters in modern English]

four-on-the-floor *n.* a gear shift with four forward gears located on the floor of a car (as opposed to **three-on-the-tree**).

foxy *adj.* sexy and stylish; having animal attraction and sophistication.

frame *n.* **1.** an emaciated stock animal. **2.** a frame-up. *–v.* **3.** to incriminate (someone) unjustly by manufacturing evidence.

frame-up *n.* that which is framed, as a plot, or a contest whose result is fraudulently prearranged; fix-up. Also, **frame.**

franger *n.* a condom. [origin unknown]

freak *n.* **1.** a person who is enthused about a particular thing: *a Jesus freak; a drug freak.* **2.** an unusually amazing person. **3.** a weirdo. *–v.* **4.** Also, **freak out. a.** to have an extreme reaction, either favourable or adverse, to something. **b.** to panic. **c.** to frighten: *Spiders really freak her out.* **5.** to experience the effects of a psychoactive drug: *She's really freaking, man.*

freaking *adj., adv.* a euphemism for the word *fucking*, when used as an intensifier.

freak-out *n.* **1.** an extreme experience, usually terrifying, produced by hallucinogenic drugs. **2.** any unusual or unexpected experience.

Fred Astaire *n.* **1.** a chair. **2.** hair. [rhyming slang]

Fred Nerk *n.* an imaginary person regarded as the archetypal fool or simpleton.

freebie *n.* a service or item provided without charge.

freestyle *n.* **1.** a type of dance music; Latin hip-hop. **2.** the art of performing trick manoeuvres on skateboards, snowboards, BMX bikes, etc. *–v.* **3.** to practise freestyle manoeuvres.

French *n.* **1.** a humorous term for mild swear words: *Pardon my French.* **2.** oral sex. *–adj.* **3.** relating to oral sex.

French cut *n. Cricket.* See **Chinese cut.**

French kiss *n.* a kiss in which the tongue enters the partner's mouth.

French letter *n.* a condom. Also, **Frenchy, Frenchie.**

French tickler *n.* a condom with an attachment on the end to give extra stimulation.

fried egg *n.* a traffic dome. Also, **silent cop.**

friend of Dorothy *n.* a homosexual man. [from *Dorothy* the protagonist in the movie *The Wizard of Oz*, played by Judy Garland, a US actor very popular amongst gay men]

friends *pl. n.* menstrual periods.

frig *v.* **1.** to masturbate. **2.** to have sexual intercourse. *–interj.* **3.** an exclamation of vexation, surprise, etc.; often used as a euphemistic substitution for *fuck.* *–phr.*
4. frig around, to behave in a stupid or aimless manner.
5. frig up, to confuse; muddle. [from Middle English *frigg* to rub, to agitate the limbs, ? from *frike*, Old English *frican* to dance]

frigging *adj., adv.* **1.** a euphemism for *fucking.* *–n.* **2.** masturbating. **3.** having sex. *–phr.* **4. frigging in the rigging,** wasting time.

frig-up *n.* a confusion; muddle; mess.

frisbee *v.* to throw something flat so that it spins about its centre: *just frisbee it over here.*

frog *n.* **1.** (*cap.*) a French person. **2.** *Obsolete.* Also, **frogskin.** a pound note. [def 1 possibly because the French are famed for eating *frog*'s legs; def 2 because the Australian pound note was green]

frog and toad *n.* a road. [rhyming slang]

frog's eggs *pl. n.* boiled sago or tapioca, especially as served in institutions.

front *v.* **1.** to head a band or group (of musicians). **2.** Also, **front up.** to arrive; turn up. **3.** to confront (someone) about some problem you have with them.

front man *n.* a man who is the lead singer or key person of a band.

front woman *n.* a woman who is the lead singer or key person of a band.

froth and bubble *n.* **1.** trouble. **2.** *Horseracing, Gambling.* the double. [rhyming slang]

fruit *n.* **1.** *Derogatory.* a male homosexual. **2.** someone eccentric; a strange person; a weirdo. *–phr.* **3. fruit for** (or **on**) **the sideboard, a.** something extra; a luxury item. **b.** an additional source of income.

fruitcake *n.* **1.** a nut-case; a ratbag. **2.** *Derogatory.* a homosexual man. *–adj.* **3.** mad; insane. *–phr.* **4. nutty as a fruitcake,** foolish; very eccentric.

fruit loop *n.* a loony; someone of unsound mind.

fruit salad *n. Military.* a large collection of medal ribbons.

fry *v.* **1.** *US.* to execute in an electric chair. *–phr.* **2. fry one's brain,** to be strongly affected by a psychoactive drug.

fuck *v. Often offensive.* **1.** to have sexual intercourse; to insert or rub the genitals on; to engage in sexual activity. A word having wide application, referring to not only to straight heterosexual vaginal sex, but equally to hetero- or homosexual anal sex, and a variety of other sexual acts, as oral sex, bestiality, the use of dildos, the fingers, etc. Also used, often with little semantic force, as a swear word or word of abuse. *–n.* **2.** an act of sexual intercourse. **3.** a person rated according to their sexual performance: *a good fuck; a lousy fuck.* **4.** a person with whom one has sexual intercourse. **5.** *Derogatory.* a stupid or annoying person; a despicable person: *Leave me alone you stupid fuck; a sick fuck.* *–interj.* **6.** an exclamation of disgust or annoyance, often used as a mere intensifier. **7.** an exclamation of amazement, wonder, delight, etc. *–phr.*

8. fuck about (or **around**), **a.** to treat (someone) unfairly; deceive, or cause inconvenience, distress, etc., to. **b.** to behave stupidly or insanely.

9. fuck a duck, an exclamation of surprise, etc.

10. fuck me (dead), an exclamation of surprise, etc.

11. fuck up, to make a mess of; ruin.

12. fuck up and die, a strong request to be left alone by someone, or for someone to stop annoying you.

13. fuck off, a. to go away; depart: *we fucked off down to the beach.* **b.** (used imperatively) a harsh expression of abuse; piss off; rack off; go to hell.

14. fuck (someone) over, to take advantage of (someone); to swindle, or cheat (someone).

15. fuck the legs off (someone),

to have sex with someone energetically; to have sex with someone to the point of exhaustion.
16. fuck with, to meddle with; tamper with.
17. go fuck yourself, a strong request to be left alone by someone, or for someone to stop annoying you.
18. not give a (flying) fuck, not to care at all.
19. the fuck, used to as an intensifier: *Who the fuck are you?*
20. what the fuck! an exclamation of surprise.
21. would fuck a hole in the ground if it smiled at him, an phrase used to deride a sexually desperate male.
[early modern English *fuc*, *fuk*, from a presumed Middle English *fuken* (of a male) to have sex. Cognate with Middle Dutch *fokken*, Norwegian dialect *fukka*, Swedish dialect *focka*, and possibly German *ficken*. From earliest recorded times considered a taboo word. Absolutely nothing to do with a supposed acronym: For Unlawful Carnal Knowledge]

fuckable *adj. Offensive and crass.* sexually desirable.

fuckalicious *n. Offensive.* extremely sexually desirable. [blend of *fuck* and *delicious*]

fuck-all *n. Offensive.* very little; nothing: *They've done fuck-all all day.*

fucked *adj. Often offensive.* **1.** exhausted. **2.** done for; in an impossible situation. **3.** broken; out of order; wrecked. **4.** suffering heavily from the effects of too much alcohol, marijuana, etc. *–phr.*
5. fucked in the head, mad; insane; crazy; stupid.
6. get fucked, (*offensive*) go away; leave me alone.

fucked-up *adj. Often offensive.* **1.** (of a person) emotionally or mentally wrecked. **2.** completely bad; in a state of total abnormality: *this is a fucked-up town.*

fucken *adj., adv. Often offensive.* a variant spelling of *fucking*.

fucker *n. Offensive.* **1.** one who fucks; one much given to fucking. **2.** *Derogatory.* a contemptible person or thing. **3.** any person.

fuckface *n. Derogatory and offensive.* a despicable person.

fuckfest *n. Offensive.* an event, party, etc., where there is much sexual coupling.

fuckhead *n. Derogatory and offensive.* a despicable person; fuckwit.

fuck hole *n. Offensive and crass.* the vagina.

fucking *adj. Often offensive.* **1.** an intensifier signifying approval, as in *It's a fucking marvel* or disapproval, as in *fucking bastard*. **2.** inserted between syllables to add emphasis: *abso-fucking-lutely; Kings-fucking-Cross; Aca-fucking-pulco. –adv.* **3.** very; extremely: *fucking ridiculous. –n.* **4.** an act or instance of sexual intercourse: *a good and proper fucking. –adv.* **5.** Also, **fucking-well**. used as an intensifier: *too fucking right!; You fucking-well did run into me! –phr.* **6. fucking A!** an exclamation of pleasure or total agreement.

fuck-knuckle *n. Derogatory and offensive.* a stupid person; dickhead. Also, **fucknuckle**.

fuckstick *n. Offensive.* 1. a penis. 2. *Derogatory.* a stupid or annoying person.

fuck truck *n. Offensive and crass.* a panel van decked out in the back for sexual liaisons; a shaggin' wagon.

fuck-up *n. Offensive.* 1. a miscalculation; a bad mistake. 2. a person who is mentally or emotionally unstable.

fuckwit *n. Derogatory and offensive.* 1. an incredibly stupid person. 2. a mean, despicable person.

fuckwitted *adj. Derogatory and offensive.* foolish; stupid: *a fuckwitted suggestion.*

fudge *interj.* 1. a euphemism for the exclamation *fuck! –n.* 2. faeces.

fugging *adj., adv.* a euphemism for *fucking.*

fugly *adj. Derogatory.* extremely unattractive. [blend of *fucking* + *ugly*]

full *adj.* 1. intoxicated. *–phr.* 2. **full of oneself,** conceited; egoistic. 3. **full up to dolly's wax,** or **full up to pussy's bow,** extremely full; replete with food.

full bore *adv.* to the maximum; all out.

full-on *adj.* 1. enthusiastic; full of energy; unrestrained. 2. requiring complete involvement or total commitment. *–adv.* 3. as fast, strong, committed, as possible.

full points *pl. n. Australian Rules.* a goal.

full tilt *adv.* 1. at top speed: *The bus was going full tilt for the station. –adj.* 2. aggressive; strong; forceful: *smacking out full tilt lyrics.*

fully *adv.* 1. completely; without reservation: *Do you like this shirt? Oh yeah, fully.* 2. very strongly; totally: *It fully reminds you just where you are in the scheme of things.*

fun *v.* 1. to make fun; joke: *I was just funning. –adj.* 2. relating to fun; amusing; lively: *a fun thing to do; Perth is a fun city. –phr.* 3. **like fun,** not at all.

fun bags *pl. n. Crass.* the female breasts.

fundie *n. Derogatory.* a fundamentalist Christian, especially one who is very vocal about their conservative, right-wing views on society.

funeral *n.* business; worry; concern: *That's his funeral.*

fungus face *n.* a person with a beard or other facial hair.

funk[1] *n.* 1. cowering fear; state of fright or terror. 2. one who funks; a coward. *–v.* 3. to be afraid of. 4. to frighten. 5. to shrink from; try to shirk. [originally 18th century British university slang, ? from Flemish *fonck*]

funk[2] *n. Music.* a type of up-tempo soul music with much syncopation. Also, **phunk.** [backformation from *funky*]

funk-hole *n.* a place of refuge from something feared.

funkster *n.* a person who performs funk or is a fan of funk; a cool person.

funky *adj.* 1. *Originally.* (of jazz) earthy; bluesy; down to earth. 2. having a funk rhythm. 3. fashionable; hip; cool: *a funky jacket.* Also, **phunky.** [Originally US Black English meaning 'excellent', and (earlier) 'bad', 'worthless', from British dialect *funky* filthy, musty, bad-smelling, from Northern French *funquier* to give off smoke]

funky-drummer *n.* a funky piece of drumming, first heard in the James Brown song *Funky Drummer*, and extensively sampled into much dance music.

funny business *n.* 1. foolish behaviour. 2. underhand, dubious, or dishonest dealings. 3. sexual intercourse or any amorous behaviour.

funny farm *n.* a lunatic asylum; psychiatric hospital.

funny money *n.* 1. money made by dubious or dishonest means. 2. counterfeit money.

furburger *n. Crass.* 1. cunnilingus. 2. the female genitals.

furgle *v.* to have sexual intercourse. [from German slang *vogeln*]

furniture *n. Cricket.* the stumps.

furphy *n.* a rumour; a false story. [from John *Furphy* manufacturer in Victoria of water carts, which during WWI were centres of gossip]

fuzz *n.* the police force or a police officer.

f-word *phr.* **the f-word,** a euphemism for the word *fuck*.

GOBSMACKED

This term, meaning astonished or flabbergasted, started appearing in English newspapers in the mid–1980s. It actually originated in the north of England where it was probably used for quite a while in the spoken language before moving south, and into print. There are two theories about the origin of the phrase. One suggests that the image being invoked is that of a person clapping their hand over their mouth as a sign of surprise, usually accompanied by a sharp intake of breath. This is a stock gesture in both the theatre and in comic strips. The other theory is that the astonished look is that of one who has just been smacked in the mouth. Either way, it is clear that *gobsmacked* is a piece of body language translated into the English language.

GONE TO GOWINGS

The retail store *Gowing Bros. Ltd*, still to be found in Sydney, came up with a very witty, and hence quite influential, advertising campaign in the 1940s. It ran a series of cartoons which featured comic scenes in which someone had just hastily departed, with the only explanation being that they had *gone to Gowings*. One such ad shows a stunned wedding party looking at the bargain-hunter wife-to-be's note that she had *gone to Gowings*.

One classic use was by the criminal Darcy Dugan. Apparently when he made his famous escape from jail he left a short note scrawled on the cell wall. It read: *gone to Gowings!*

COME A GUTSER

bomb, bomb out, bum out, clap out, come a buster, come a cropper, crap out, crash, die, die in the hole, die standing up, draw a blank, fall flat, fall flat on one's face, fizzle, flop, go over like a lead balloon, go to the pack, go under, have had it, lay an egg, lose the plot, not be able to take a trick

STUCK FOR WORDS

gabber *n.* a type of extremely fast dance music. Also, **gabba**.

gaff *phr.* **blow the gaff,** *Older slang.* to disclose a secret; reveal the truth, often unintentionally.

gaffer *n.* **1.** an old man; an old bloke: *some silly old gaffer.* **2.** a foreman or boss. **3.** a cigarette. [variant of late Middle English *godfar* (contracted form of *godfather*)]

gaga *adj.* **1.** senile; stupid. **2.** mad; fatuously eccentric. **3.** besotted: *He is gaga about his new car.* Also, **gah gah**. [French: senile, a senile person; probably imitative of meaninglybabble]

gal *n.* used to represent the American pronunciation of *girl*. See **gel**.

galah *n.* **1.** a fool; simpleton. **2.** a show-off. *–phr.* **3. mad as a gumtree full of galahs,** quite stupid. [from the name of the pink and grey cockatoo, from the Aboriginal language Yuwaalaraay]

galah session *n.* a time set aside for the people of isolated outback areas to converse with one another by radio. [from the noisy sounds made by large groups of galahs]

galoot *n.* an awkward, silly fellow: *silly galoot; big galoot; great galumphing galoot.* [origin unknown]

gamarouche *n.* the act of fellatio. Also, **gamo**. [from French *gamahucher*]

game *n.* **1.** business or profession: *Andrew is in the building game now. –phr.*
2. game as Ned Kelly, game as Phar Lap, with fighting spirit; plucky; resolute.
3. game plan, the overall strategy.
4. game, set and match, a convincing victory; complete triumph.
5. on the game, working as a prostitute.
6. the game is up, said to inform someone that they have been caught doing something illegal, wrong, naughty, etc.

gander *n.* a look: *take a gander at it.*

gang bang *n. Crass.* an occasion on which a number of males have sexual intercourse with one female. Also, **gangie, gang slash, gang splash.**

gangsta rap *n.* a type of rap music with harsh anti-authoritarian lyrics.

ganja *n.* marijuana. Also, **ganga**. [from Hindi]

gank *n.* to steal.

gaol-bait *n.* See **jail-bait**.

garage *n.* **1.** a type of dance music. *–adj.* **2.** (of pop or rock music) quite raw and unpolished, as that produced by bands which characteristically practise in a band member's garage.

garage door *phr.* **the garage door is open,** a phrase used to politely inform someone that their fly is undone.

garbage guts *n.* a person who eats to excess or will eat any food.

garbo *n.* **1.** one employed to collect garbage; a garbage collector. **2.** a garbage bin.

garbologist *n. Jocular.* a garbage collector.

gargle *n.* a drink, usually alcoholic.

gasbag *n.* **1.** an empty, voluble talker; a windbag. *–v.* **2.** to talk volubly; chatter.

gas guzzler *n.* a car which consumes an inordinate amount of fuel.

gash *n.* **1.** *Offensive.* the vagina or vulva. **2.** *Derogatory and offensive.* women in general, viewed as sex objects. [from 19th century British slang]

gawk *v.* **1.** to stare stupidly. *–phr.* **2. gawk at,** to stare: *What are you gawking at?* [cf. Middle English *gaw* to stare, from Old Norse]

gay *adj.* **1.** *Originally US homosexual slang.* homosexual, especially of a man. **2.** (especially with teenagers) uncool, unattractive, not socially acceptable: *What a gay haircut.; That band is so gay.* *–n.* **3.** a homosexual male. [for a long time used by homophobic people as a derogatory term, reclaimed as a positive word by the gay community and now pretty much an item of standard English]

gay bar *n.* a bar which caters to a gay clientele.

gay boy *n.* a young male homosexual.

gazunder *n.* **1.** a chamber-pot that goes under the bed. **2.** *Cricket.* a mullygrubber. Also, **gozunder**. [alteration of *goes under*]

gear *n.* **1.** various items, paraphernalia, especially as associated with a particular activity, task, job, etc.: *Grab your gear, we're off; we left all the gear back at the house; where's me fishin' gear?* **2.** any illegal drug of addiction, often marijuana or heroin. **3.** the apparatus used to prepare and inject drugs, especially heroin. **4.** clothes: *get your gear off.* **5.** used loosely to refer to whatever is being discussed; stuff; type of thing: *and all that gear; I don't like any of that mucking about gear.* *–phr.* **6. gear up,** to get prepared: *all geared up for the big race.*
7. on the gear, taking heroin.

gee[1] *interj.* an exclamation of surprise, wonderment, etc. [from *Jesus!*]

gee[2] *phr.* **gee up,** to incite; urge: *he was geeing up the crowd; all geed up and raring to go.*

gee[3] *n.* a thousand dollars. [from *g* standing for *grand*]

gee-gee *n.* **1.** (*in children's speech*) a horse. *–phr.* **2. the gee-gees,** the horseraces.

geek[1] *n.* a look: *Have a geek at this.* [from British dialect *geek* to peer, stare, peek]

geek[2] *n.* **1. a.** (*generally*) a nerd; an uncool person. **b.** (*in school contexts*) a reviled diligent, studious student; a book-worm. **2.** (*in computing contexts, on the Internet, etc.*) **a.** a complete fanatic; one whose whole life revolves around their computer. **b.** (*often used jocularly in a positive sense*): *I'm a big computer geek, the geekiest of them all.* [originally US, from British dialect, variant of *geck* a fool, simpleton, from Low German *geck*, Dutch *gek*]

geekboy *n.* a male computer geek, especially on the Internet.

geekgirl *n.* a female computer geek, especially on the Internet.

geek-speak *n.* computer jargon.

geekster *n.* a computer geek, especially on the Internet.

geeky *adj.* of the nature of a geek; befitting a geek; socially awkward; dorky.

gee up *n.* **1.** a lift (as of spirits, enthusiasm, etc.): *The big crowd gave the players a gee up.* –*v.* **2.** to excite or stir up.

gee whiz *interj.* **1.** Also, **gee whizz.** an exclamation expressing surprise, admiration, etc. –*adj.* **2.** (of a device, etc.) technologically sophisticated: *a gee whiz computer game.* [a euphemistic variation of *Jesus*]

geez[1] *interj.* gee; gee whiz. [alteration of *Jesus*]

geez[2] *n.* a look: *give us a geez, will ya?*

geezer[1] *n.* an odd or funny old man. [? from dialect pronunciation of *guiser*, from *guise* to go in disguise]

geezer[2] *n.* a look: *Give us a geezer at your new bike.* Also, **geez.**

gel[1] *v.* to come together in a comprehensible way.

gel[2] *n.* used to represent British or high-faluting pronunciation of *girl.* See **gal.**

gen *n.* **1.** general information. **2.** all the necessary information about a subject: *give me the gen.* –*phr.* **3. gen up,** to become informed (about); to learn or read up (about).

geri *n.* an old person. Also, **gerry; jerry.** [short for *geriatric*]

germ *n.* an annoying, obnoxious person, especially a small person or one in a low position of authority: *a smug little germ behind the counter.*

Geronimo *interj.* a cry used when making a parachute jump.

get *v.* **1.** to have someone in a corner, especially when arguing a point; to catch out: *I've got you there, haven't I?* **2.** to amuse: *that really gets me.* **3.** to exact revenge: *I'll get you for that.* **4.** to understand, comprehend: *What I don't get is, why?* **5.** to trick or deceive: *Gets 'em every time.* –*phr.* **6. get a (fucking) life!** an exhortation to someone to become worthwhile; start living an interesting and fulfilling life.
7. get a dog up you, See **dog.**
8. get a move on, to hurry up and start; to begin right away.
9. get any, See **any.**
10. get at, a. to imply: *What are you getting at?* **b.** to tamper with: *Don't let the kids get at that cord.* **c.** to annoy: *What's got at you?*
11. get into (someone's) pants, to have sex with (someone).
12. get it, a. to be killed. **b.** to get into trouble.
13. get it off with (someone), to have sex with (someone).
14. get it up, to achieve an erection.
15. get it up (someone), a. (of a male) to have sex with (someone). **b.** to successfully stir or annoy (someone).
16. get lost, to go away; desist: *Get lost, will you!*
17. get off on, a. to be sexually stimulated by someone or something. **b.** to be excited by something.
18. get (on) one's goat, to annoy or irritate one.
19. get one's end in, (of a male) to have sex.
20. get out, to not lose money on: *If she wins this race we'll get out okay; the stable got out and didn't lose so much at all.*
21. get set, to place a bet (in two-up, horseracing, etc.).
22. get the axe (or **boot**) (or **chop**) (or **spear**) etc., to be dismissed from a job.

23. get this! an expression asking someone to listen and comprehend; to pay attention to and accept: *Get this – ninety-five of kids in the ACT wear surf clothes.*
24. get up, (of a competitor) to win a race, game, etc.
25. get up (someone), a. (of a male) to have sex with (someone). **b.** to successfully stir or annoy (someone).
26. get with, to engage in kissing and petting.
27. where does (someone) get off? what gives (someone) the right? Where does (someone) get the effrontery?

GI *adj.* (of a person or place) inconveniently located; inaccessible. [standing for *Geographically Impossible*]

gig[1] *n.* a stupid person; a fool. [British dialect *gig* to laugh at, taunt]

gig[2] *n.* **1.** a booking for an entertainer to perform at a venue. **2.** the performance itself. **3.** any job or occupation. *–v.* **4.** (of a musician or group) to play gigs. [originally jazz slang]

gig[3] *v.* **1.** to watch; stare. *–n.* **2.** a look; geek. [shortened from *fizgig*]

gig[4] *n. Computers.* a gigabyte.

gillion *n.* a very large number or sum of money. Also, **jillion, squillion, zillion**.

ginger *n.* **1.** the backside; the bum: *a swift kick up the ginger. –phr.* **2. be on (someone's) ginger,** to be chasing (someone). [from rhyming slang *ginger ale* tail]

gink[1] *n. Older slang.* a silly person. [origin unknown]

gink[2] *n.* a look: *Have a gink at this.* [nasalised variant of *geek* a look]

ginormous *adj.* incredibly huge. [blend of *gigantic* and *enormous*]

gippo *n. Racist.* **1.** an Egyptian. *–adj.* **2.** Egyptian. Also, **gyppo**.

girl *n.* **1.** a woman: *seeing a girl from work.* **2.** one's girlfriend. **3.** Also, **big girl.** a derogatory term for a male, especially used by males in sporting contexts: *Make a decent effort, ya girl! –phr.* **4. old girl, a.** an affectionate form of familiar address to a woman. **b.** one's wife.

girlie *adj.* **1.** illustrating or featuring nude or nearly nude women: *a girlie magazine.* **2.** of or befitting a girl; effeminate: *girlie designer beers.* *–phr.* **3. girlie sick,** suffering period pain.

girl's blouse *n. Derogatory.* a timid, ineffectual male; a wuss. Also, **big girl's blouse**.

girl's germs *n.* (*amongst children*) a supposed contagion of girlness avoided by boys. See **boy's germs**.

girls' night out *n.* an evening on which a group of women have a night out together.

girl's week *n.* the menstrual period.

girly-girly *adj.* effusively effeminate in the manner of a small girl.

gism *n.* semen. Also, **jism**. [origin unknown]

git *n.* a fool; a stupid person.

gizmo *n.* a gadget. Also, **gismo**. [origin unknown]

glad[1] *phr.*
1. the glad eye, an inviting or flirtatious look: *She gave him the glad eye.*
2. the glad hand, (*usually ironic*) an effusive welcome, often public: *to give someone the glad hand.*

glad² *n.* gladiolus, a type of flower. Also, **gladdie**.

glam *adj.* **1.** glamorous. *–n.* **2.** glamour: *all the glitz and glam.*

glam rock *n.* a type of rock'n'roll of the 70s characterised by performers dressed in a showy, glittering, outrageous style.

glass can *n.* a small squat beer bottle; a stubby.

glass jaw *phr.* **have a glass jaw,** to be defeated easily; to be a push-over. [from boxing slang *glass jaw* a boxer's jaw that is broken easily]

glitch *n.* a minor problem; a hiccup; a snag or hitch.

glitz *n.* conspicuous luxury and opulence of a phoney nature. [back-formation from *glitzy*]

glitzy *adj.* outwardly glamorous and glittery. [*glit(ter)* + *(rit)zy*]

glory hole *n.* a hole in a wall, as of a male toilet cubicle, used for sexual purposes, as the insertion of penis, or to peep through.

glum bum *n.* a pessimistic person.

gnarly *adj.* **1.** difficult; awkward: *a gnarly problem.* **2.** excellent; terrific: *a gnarly surf.* **3.** annoyed and difficult to deal with: *getting a bit gnarly*. Also, **narly**.

go *v.* **1.** to say, especially used when reporting speech: *So I go to him, 'Shut your face!'* **2.** to have some specified food or drink: *I could really go a beer right now. –n.* **3.** a fight: *Then there would be some goes; Do you want a go, mate?* **4.** something that goes well; a success: *to make a go of something. –phr.*
5. fair go, a. adequate opportunity.
b. a request for fairness: *fair go, mate!*
6. from go to whoa, from beginning to end.
7. go all the way, to have sexual intercourse.
8. go it, *Surfing.* to take off on a wave.
9. go down, a. to occur; happen: *What's going down?* **b.** to perform fellatio or cunnilingus. **c.** be received: *that went down well.* **d.** to be so notable as to be well remembered: *That'll go down as the best goal of the season.*
10. go down on, to perform fellatio or cunnilingus on.
11. go for it! an exhortation to action.
12. go jump (in the lake/creek), an expression of dismissal; piss off!
13. go off, a. (of a party, dance party, etc.) to be excellent; to be successful; to fire: *It was a great night, it really went off; the place was going off.* **b.** *Surfing.* (of the surf) to produce many good riding waves; to really pump. **c.** (of an illegal establishment) to be raided by the police.
14. go off at, to criticise or scold.
15. go off the deep end, to go insane.
16. go out, to be in an amorous or sexual relationship: *they've been going out for donkey's years.*
17. go places, to be successful, especially in one's career.
18. go through, to leave, abscond, escape speedily.
19. go through the roof, to become incredibly angry.
20. go through (someone),

go

Crass. (of a man) to have sex with (a woman).

21. go to bed with, to have sex with.

22. go to pieces, to break down with emotion.

23. go to water, to lose courage.

24. go walking, (of an inanimate object) to disappear: *My pen's gone walking.*

25. go with (someone), to be in an amorous or sexual relationship with (someone).

26. open go, a. a situation in which fair play prevails and no unfair restraints or limiting conditions apply: *The election was an open go.* **b.** a situation in which normal restraints do not apply: *It was open go at the bar that night.*

27. touch and go, dangerous; difficult; likely to fail as succeed.

28. what's the go? how does one proceed from here?

goal sneak *n. Australian Rules.* **1.** a player who catches the opposition unawares and scores a goal. **2.** a full-forward.

goanna *n.* a piano. [rhyming slang *goanna* 'pianner']

goat *n.* **1.** a fool. *–phr.*
2. get (on) one's goat, to annoy; enrage; infuriate.
3. run like a hairy goat, a. to run very slowly. **b.** to run very fast.

goat boat *n.* a surf ski.

gob *n.* **1.** the mouth. **2.** a sticky mass of slimy substance. *–v.* **3.** to spit or expectorate. [Gaelic or Irish]

gobble *phr.* **gobble off,** *Crass.* to perform fellatio on. Also, **gob off.**

gobbledegook *n.* written or spoken nonsense. [originally US military slang for 'red tape', from the earlier slang phrase *gobble the goop* to perform fellatio]

gobsmacked *adj. Originally Brit.* astonished; flabbergasted.

God *interj.* **1.** an oath or exclamation used to express weariness, annoyance, disappointment, etc. *–phr.*
2. God damn (someone or **something),** an oath wishing ill to befall the person or thing it is directed at.
3. God's gift to, (*often ironic*) a truly wonderful person in a particular sphere of interest: *god's gift to the business world*; *He thinks he's God's gift to women.*
4. God's own, a. an intensifier: *It'll be God's own misery next winter.* **b.** (of a country) the best; a paradise. Cf. **Godzone.**

goddamn *adj.* used as an intensifier: *the whole goddamn night long.* Also **Goddamn, God-damn, goddam.**

Godzone *n.* one's own country, viewed as the best on earth: *I can't wait to get back to Godzone.*

goer *n.* **1.** a person who displays great energy and drive. **2.** a horse, vehicle, etc., which goes very fast. **3.** one who engages in sex vigorously and with gusto. **4.** any activity, project, etc., having evident prospects of success.

goey *n.* the drug speed.

goggles *n.* glasses, especially strong ones.

go-in *n.* a fight: *They had a bit of a go-in behind the pub.*

going-over *n.* **1.** a thorough examination. **2.** a severe beating or thrashing.

gold-digger *n.* a man or woman who

gold-digger / **goofy**

has a sexual relationship with or marries someone in order to obtain some financial gain.

golden arches *n.* a McDonald's Family Restaurant.

golden duck *n. Cricket.* See **duck**.

golden handshake *n.* a gratuity or benefit, given to employees as a recognition of their services on the occasion of their retirement or resignation, or as a sop when they are dismissed.

golden shower *n.* urination on someone for sexual pleasure.

goldfish *phr.* **throw the goldfish another cat,** a humorous invitation to be extravagant.

gold head *n. Car sales.* a home owner, having good credit standing.

golly *v.* **1.** to spit. *–n.* **2.** spittle. [? related to British dialect *golls* mucus dripping from children's noses]

gonads *pl. n.* the testicles.

gone *adj.* **1.** incapacitated through laughter, drugs, alcohol, overexcitement, etc. *–phr.*
 2. far gone, a. deeply infatuated. **b.** extremely mad. **c.** extremely drunk. **d.** almost exhausted. **e.** almost dead; dying.
 3. gone on, infatuated with.

goner *n.* a person or thing that is dead, lost, or past recovery or rescue.

gong *n.* a medal or other award.

goober *n.* a stupid or annoying person. [from US slang, from *goober* peanut]

gooby *n.* snot. Also, **goobie, gorby**.

good *phr.*
 1. deliver the goods, to produce what one has promised or what is expected of one.
 2. good call, an encouragement denoting that one has made the right decision.
 3. good guys, the characters of a play, novel, movie, etc. that are on the ostensible side of right.
 4. good one, a. an exclamation of delight, approval, etc. **b.** often used ironically: *Oh, good one! You great berk.*
 5. good shit, a. excellent quality marijuana. **b.** an exclamation of praise.
 6. good thing, a racehorse tipped to win.
 7. have the goods on, to have knowledge about someone that places you in a position of power.

good hair day *n. Jocular.* a day in which one's hair is manageable. See **bad hair day**.

good oil *n.* correct (and usually profitable) information, often to be used in confidence; the drum. Also, **dinkum oil**. See **oil**.

goody-goody *n.* a person who is excruciatingly good. Also, **goody-two-shoes**.

goof *n.* **1.** a foolish or stupid person. *–v.* **2.** to blunder; slip up. *–phr.*
 3. goof around, to play the fool to entertain others.
 4. goof off, to daydream; fritter away time.
 5. goof up, to bungle; botch.
[apparently variant of obsolete *goff* a dolt]

goofy *adj.* **1.** dull, stupid, clumsy, etc., in an inoffensive way. **2.** uncool: *a goofy 80s T-shirt.* **3.** pathetically amorous: *he's gone all goofy.*

4. *Surfing, snowboarding, etc.* left-footed. *–n.* **5.** a goofy-foot surfer, snowboarder, etc.

goofy-foot *n.* **1.** Also, **goofy-footer**. a surfboard rider who surfs with their right foot as the lead foot. *–adj.* **2.** pertaining to this style of surfing. Also now applied to snowboarding.

googly *n. Cricket.* a delivery bowled by a wrist-spinner which looks as if it will break one way but in fact goes the other; wrong'un. [origin unknown]

gook *n. Racist.* **1.** *Originally US Military.* an South-East Asian, especially a national of a country in which Western soldiers fought, as a Japanese, a Korean or a Vietnamese. **2.** a South-East Asian. *–adj.* **3.** South-East Asian: *gook food; gook speak.* [possibly from US *goo-goo* a derogatory term for a Filipino person]

goolie *n.* **1.** a stone. **2.** a testicle. **3.** a glob of phlegm.

goom *n.* methylated spirits (used as an alcoholic drink as by derelicts). [? from the Jagara word for fresh water]

goomie *n.* a person addicted to drinking methylated spirits.

goon[1] *n.* **1.** a stupid person. **2.** a hired thug or bouncer. **3.** a hooligan or tough. [originally US; probably a backformation from *gooney* a stupid person, from dialect *goney*]

goon[2] *n.* a flagon of wine. Also, **goonie**.

goose[1] *n.* **1.** a silly or foolish person; a simpleton. *–phr.*
 2. (**someone's**) **goose is cooked,** (someone) is definitely going to get into trouble.
 3. a wigwam (or **whim-wham**) **for a goose's bridle,** a fanciful, non-existent object, used as an answer to an unwanted question.

goose[2] *v.* **1.** to poke someone between the buttocks, usually in fun and unexpectedly. *–n.* **2.** an unexpected poke between the buttocks. [originally meaning 'to have sex with', from rhyming slang *goose and duck* fuck]

gorby *n.* See **gooby**.

gorilla *n.* **1.** an ugly, brutal fellow. **2.** the sum of $1000.

gormless *adj.* (of a person) dull; stupid; senseless. [variant of dialect *gaumless,* from *gaum* attention]

Gosford dog *n.* See **Dapto dog**. [from *Gosford* a town north of Sydney]

Gosford skirt *n.* a very short tight-fitting skirt. [so called because *Gosford* is close to 'The Entrance' (two NSW towns); punning on *entrance* = vagina]

goss *n.* the latest news or gossip: *So, give us all the goss.*

got *phr.*
 1. have got 'em bad, a. to be in a nervous condition. **b.** to be suffering from withdrawal symptoms, especially from alcohol.
 2. have got into (**someone**), to be causing (someone) to display anger, irritation, etc.: *What has got into that man?*
 3. have got it bad for, to be infatuated with.

gotcher *interj.* **1.** an exclamation accompanying the capture of a person. **2.** an exclamation indicating comprehension and agreement.

Also, **gotcha**. [contraction of *(I have) got you*]

goth *n.* a person of the goth sub-culture, affecting the style and look found in Gothic novels.

Gowings *phr.* **gone to Gowings**, used as an intensifier for any slangy sense of the word *gone*, as specifically: **a.** deteriorating financially. **b.** ill, especially with a hangover. **c.** failing dismally. **d.** departed hastily or without a specific destination in mind. **e.** drunk. **f.** insane; idiotic. [from an advertising slogan of *Gowing Bros Ltd* a Sydney department store]

grand *n.* the sum of $1000.

grape *phr.*
1. **a grape on the business,** an interloper; an unwelcome person.
2. **in the grip of the grape,** addicted to drink, esp. wine.

grass *n.* 1. marijuana. –*v.* 2. to inform (on). 3. to land (a fish).

grasser *n.* an informer.

gravel rash *phr.* **get gravel rash,** to act in a sycophantic fashion, as if by crawling.

graveyard chompers *pl. n.* false teeth.

grease-ball *n.* 1. *Racist.* a person of Mediterranean or Latin-American origin. 2. a person with greased or slicked-back hair.

greaser *n. Racist.* a member of a Latin-American race, especially a Mexican.

greasies *pl. n.* fish and chips.

greasy *n.* 1. one who, in a camp, attends to the chores of cooking, cleaning, etc. 2. a shearer. 3. *Racist.* a Greek, Italian or other Mediterranean person. 4. Also, **greasy eyeball.** a disdainful or disapproving look.

greasy spoon *n.* a cheap restaurant or cafe, very plain, often unclean.

great Australian adjective *n.* the word *bloody*, especially as used for emphasis.

Greek *phr.*
1. **be all Greek,** (of someone's speech) to be unintelligible.
2. **go Greek,** to have anal intercourse.

green and gold *n.* the Australian national sports uniform colours: *She was thrilled to be wearing the green and gold.*

greenback *n. Surfing.* an unbroken wave.

greenie *n.* 1. a conservationist. 2. a lump of mucus ejected or picked from the nose. 3. *Surfing.* a large green unbroken wave. –*adj.* 4. sympathetic with moves to conserve the environment, live more simply, etc.

green room *n. Surfing.* the tube of a breaking wave.

Gregory Peck *n.* 1. neck. 2. cheque. [rhyming slang from *Gregory Peck*, a US film actor]

gremmie *n. Surfing.* a young surfer, usually in his or her early teens. Also, **gremlin, gremmy**.

grey ghost *n. NSW.* parking meter inspector. Also, *Vic.* **grey meanie**. [from the grey uniform]

grey nurse *n.* a $100 note. [from *grey nurse* a shark, with reference to the note's colour]

grief *n.* a type of low-quality marijuana. [rhyming slang for *leaf*]

groan *interj.* used after someone has

made a bad joke or pathetic pun: *'You can say that again!' 'That.' Groan!*

grody *adj. Originally US.* (*with teenagers*) disgusting; unacceptable: *grody to the max.* [? an alteration of *grotty*]

grog *n.* alcohol, particularly cheap alcohol. [from British slang; 'Old Grog' the nickname (from *grogram* the material his cloak was made of) of Admiral Vernon who in 1740 ordered water to be issued with sailors' pure spirits]

grogan *n.* a piece of excrement; a turd.

grog shop *n.* **1.** a shop selling alcohol. **2.** *Obsolete.* a cheap tavern.

grommet *n.* **1.** an idiot. **2.** a young surfer or snowboarder, usually in his or her early teens. Also, **grom, grommie**. [Old French *gromet, groumet* servant, valet, shop-boy]

groove *n.* **1.** a rhythm or beat: *it's got a funky groove to it; dig the groove on this one.* **2.** musical feeling: *I went for a more minimalistic groove.* **3.** a piece of music: *playing a wicked set of grooves.* –*v.* **4.** to dance or listen to music: *groove to some original tunes.* –*phr.* **5. in the groove,** feeling well content with everything going right.

groover *n.* **1.** a person who is cool; a dude; a groovy person. **2.** a person who enjoys music, as a musician, a dancer, a member of an audience at a concert: *all you groovers out there.* –*phr.* **3. groovers and shakers,** *Jocular.* dancers.

groovy *adj.* **1.** excellent; cool. **2.** fashionable; stylish. **3.** (of music) having a good groove; danceable. –*interj.* **4.** excellent! cool!

grope *v.* **1.** to fondle, embrace clumsily and with sexual intent. –*phr.* **2. go the grope,** to fondle with a sexual purpose.

Groper *n.* a West Australian. Also, **Sandgroper**.

gross *adj.* **1.** repulsive; disagreeable; objectionable. –*interj.* **2.** an exclamation indicating disgust, revulsion, etc. –*phr.* **3. gross me out!** I am disgusted! **4. gross (someone) out,** to disgust (someone).

gross-out *n.* something disgusting.

grot *n.* **1.** filth. **2.** a filthy person. [backformation from *grotty*]

grotty *adj.* **1.** dirty; filthy. **2.** of poor quality; nasty. [alteration of *grotesque* + -*y*; apparently originally Liverpool slang, and first widely popularised by The Beatles]

group grope *n.* sexual intercourse mutually undertaken at the same time by three or more people.

groupie *n.* **1.** a young person who has sex with members of a pop or rock group. **2.** an admirer of a personality, a band, etc.; a committed fan. [originally referring to a young woman who travelled with, and made herself sexually available to, the male members of a rock group, but nowadays also used of males, and with reference to homo- or heterosexual sexual relations]

group stoop *n. Crass.* an occasion on which a number of males have sexual intercourse with one female; gang bang.

grouse *adj.* **1.** very good. **2.** *Prison.*

genuine; not jail-issue. –*n.* **3.** *Prison.* tobacco or a cigarette that is not jail-issue. [origin unknown]

grouter *phr.* **come in** (or **be on**) **the grouter, a.** to take an unfair advantage of a situation. **b.** *Two-up.* to bet on a change in the fall of the coins. [origin unknown]

growl *n. Offensive.* **1.** Also, **growler.** the vagina or vulva. –*phr.* **2. growl out**, to perform cunnilingus. [from rhyming slang *growl and grunt* cunt]

grrl *n.* **1.** a respelling of the word *girl*, connoting aggression, strength, self-confidence, etc., and rejecting any connotation of weakness, meekness, prissiness, etc. **2.** *Internet.* a female Internet user who is up-to-date with the latest, coolest things. Also, **grrrl.** [blend of *girl* with the representation of a growl *grrr*]

grub *n.* food or victuals.

grumblebum *n.* a cantankerous and complaining person.

grundies *pl. n.* underwear. [rhyming slang for 'undies'. See *Reg Grundies*]

grunge *n.* **1.** any filthy substance. **2.** a world view and urban lifestyle of the post-AIDS, post-Baby-Boomer 1990s, characterised by dressing in a manner that according to conventional standards showed a disregard for appearance. **3.** a musical genre intimately associated with the grunge view of the world. See **Seattle sound**. **4.** a style of clothing associated with the grunge lifestyle. –*adj.* **5.** of or pertaining to the grunge lifestyle. [backformation of *grungy*]

grunger *n.* a person of living the grunge lifestyle; a fan of grunge music.

grungy *adj.* **1.** filthy; unclean. **2.** (of people) living the grunge lifestyle; dressing in the grunge style. **3.** (of music) in the grunge style. [? blend of *grimy* and *scungy*]

grunt *n.* **1.** (of an engine) torque; power. **2.** power; strength. **3.** *Military.* an soldier in the infantry.

gubba *n. Derogatory.* (used by Aborigines) a white person. Also, **gub, gubbah, gubber.** [origin unknown; ? corruption of *governor*]

guck *n.* slimy, objectionable matter. [? blend of *goo* and *muck*]

guernsey *phr.* **get a guernsey,** to succeed, win approval (originally to be selected for a football team). [from *guernsey* a close-fitting knitted jumper, worn by seamen, footballers, etc., from the Isle of *Guernsey* in the English Channel]

guff *n.* spoken nonsense.

guilt *phr.*
1. guilt trip, a strong feeling of personal guilt about something.
2. the guilts, feelings of remorse: *I've got the guilts about not writing.*

gumby *n.* a foolish and unfashionable person. [from British dialect, Yorkshire *gomby*]

gum-digger *n.* a dentist. Also, **gum-puncher.**

gummys *pl. n.* gumboots.

gumption *n.* **1.** initiative; resourcefulness. **2.** shrewd, practical commonsense. [originally Scottish]

Gumsucker *n.* a native of or resident in Victoria. [? from the habit of some colonial youths of chewing or sucking the transparent lumps of gum from the silver wattle]

gum tree *phr.* **up a gum tree, a.** in difficulties; in a predicament. **b.** completely baffled.

gun *n.* **1.** a champion, especially in shearing. **2.** a large surfboat for riding big waves. –*v.* **3. a.** to rev (an engine). **b.** to accelerate (a car, motorbike, etc.). –*phr.*
4. go great guns, to have a period of success at something.
5. gun for, a. to seek (a person) with the intention to harm or kill. **b.** to support; go for; barrack for.
6. stick to one's guns, to maintain one's position, beliefs, etc.; keep believing in oneself.

gundy *phr.* **gone to gundy** or **no good to gundy,** unsatisfactory; broken; beyond repair; ruined; worthless. Also, **Gundy.** [origin unknown]

gunge *n.* marijuana. [from US *gungeon*, alteration of *ganja*]

gung-ho *adj. Originally US.* **1.** warlike; keenly militaristic. **2.** wholeheartedly fervid about doing something: *Don't be so gung-ho.*

gurgler *phr.* **down the gurgler,** ruined; irretrievably lost or destroyed.

guru *n.* a person who is recognised as an expert in a given field: *fashion guru; sports guru; a Solaris 2.4 guru.*

gussie *n. Derogatory.* an effeminate man. [diminutive of *Augustus*]

gussied-up *adj.* smartly dressed.

gut *adj.* initial and strongly felt: *gut reaction; gut feeling.*

gut-buster *n.* an activity requiring great effort, especially great physical effort.

gutless *adj.* **1.** cowardly. **2.** lacking in power, especially of a car, etc.

guts *pl. n.* **1.** the stomach or abdomen. **2.** one greedy for food; a glutton. **3.** courage; stamina; endurance: *to have guts.* **4.** essential information: *the guts of the matter.* **5.** *Two-up.* wagered money in the centre of the ring. **6.** the essential parts or contents: *Let me get to the guts of the motor.* –*v.* **7.** to cram (oneself) with food. –*phr.*
8. drop one's guts, to fart.
9. good guts, correct information; the news.

gutser *phr.* **come a gutser, a.** to fall over. **b.** to fail as a result of an error of judgment. Also, **gutzer.**

guvvie flat *n. ACT.* a government-funded residence, usually offering low-cost accommodation. Also, **govie.**

guy *n.* **1.** a fellow or man: *that big guy over there.* **2.** (*usually pl.*) a person of either sex: *Hey you guys, wait up!* **3.** a boyfriend.

guy-magnet *n.* a sexually attractive female.

guy-watch *v.* to sexually ogle males.

gym junkie *n.* a person who visits the gym an inordinate amount.

gyno *n.* a gynaecologist.

gyp *v.* **1.** to swindle; cheat; defraud or rob by some sharp practice. **2.** to obtain by swindling or cheating; steal. –*n.* **3.** a swindle. **4.** a swindler or cheat. Also, **gip.** [origin unknown; possibly, as racial slur, from *gypsy*]

H

HIMBO

There are many words for those people who make up the empty-headed portion of the population, such as *airhead, brainless cretin* and *space cadet*. To these can be added two gender-specific terms, the *bimbo* and the *himbo*. *Bimbo* is actually the Italian word for "baby". In Australia the word was formerly used to mean a homosexual male. It is only really since the 80s that we have abandoned the earlier sense and started using it to refer to females. The wider acceptance of the basic principles of feminism in society has led to quite a bit of social change which can be seen reflected in linguistic change. If there is a word for an empty-headed female, then surely there ought to be a corresponding one for an empty-headed male – thus the birth of the *himbo* – a blend of *him* and *bimbo*.

HATTER

The *hatter* was the name given to a lonely prospector in the bush, and is popularly believed to come from the phrase "as mad as a hatter". The hatter was mad because, in the manufacturing of hats, mercury was used in the felt, so the poor old hatters suffered from mercury poisoning. But the Australian hatter is not in this tradition of madness at all. He was a man whose hat covered his family – a British colloquial expression of the 1800s which meant that he was all alone with no-one to look after but himself. The lonely prospector in the bush was remarkable in that most men worked in the bush in pairs – they were mates. This partnership was one of necessity – it took two people to work a mine comfortably, and both the mines and the bush were full of danger that was best handled by two men, rather than one man alone. But usually one of the results of the hatter's choice to go it alone was that he became "ratty" – if not insane then at least eccentric – and so the expression "his hat covers his family" was forgotten, and the phrase "mad as a hatter" more or less filled the etymological vacuum.

HOE INTO

bog in, demolish, dig in, down, eat like a horse, get into, get oneself outside, get stuck into, gobble down, guzzle, knock back, knock off, make a big hole in, nosh, pig, pig out, put away, scoff, slurp, toss off, tuck in, wolf down, wrap one's laughing gear around

STUCK FOR WORDS

hack *n.* **1.** *Hacky Sack.* a successful round in which every player kicks the hacky sack. **2.** *Ultimate frisbee.* a point scored in which each of the seven players on a team touches the frisbee. **3.** See **party hack**. –*v.* **4.** to put up with; endure: *I can't hack it.* **5.** to go exploring in a computer system. –*phr.* **6. hack into,** to gain unauthorised access to a computer system.

hacker *n.* **1.** one who hacks into a computer system, especially with malicious intent. This meaning, though still in popular use, is now deprecated by hackers, who prefer to use the term **cracker** for a person who breaks computer security systems. **2.** a computer enthusiast who enjoys programming, exploring computer systems, and how to get beyond the supposed limitations of a system. **3.** *Older slang.* a hard worker.

hacky sack *n.* **1.** a small, soft, spherical bag of pellets used in the game hacky sack. **2.** a game in which players attempt to keep a hacky sack airborne as long as possible by kicking or striking with only the feet and knees, and sometimes the head.

hair *phr.*
 1. get in (someone's) hair, to irritate or annoy someone.
 2. hair of the dog (that bit you), an alcoholic drink taken to relieve a hangover.
 3. have by the short hairs (or **the short and curlies**), to have a person in one's power.
 4. keep your hair on, keep calm; do not get angry.
 5. let one's hair down, to behave in an informal, relaxed, or uninhibited manner; abandon oneself to pleasure.
 6. put hair on (someone's) chest, (usually of a man) something, as a strong drink, etc., which will make one feel fitter, more virile, etc.

hair pie *n. Crass.* cunnilingus.

hairy *adj.* frightening: *a hairy drive.*

hairy chequebook *n. Crass.* the vagina as used by a woman to pay for something with sexual intercourse: *had to pull out the hairy chequebook.*

hairy eyeball *n.* a disdainful or disapproving look. Also, **greasy eyeball**.

hairy-legs *phr.* **rack off, hairy-legs!** an exclamation of dismissal, contempt, etc.

hairy Mary *n.* a hairy male homosexual.

half *phr.* **not half, a.** not really; not at all: *His first poems were not half bad.* **b.** certainly! indeed!

half-baked *adj.* **1.** not completed: *a half-baked scheme.* **2.** lacking mature judgment or experience: *half-baked theorists.*

half-caser *n. Obsolete.* half a crown.

half-seas-over *adj.* intoxicated.

half spot *n.* fifty dollars.

half-tanked *adj.* half drunk.

hambone *n.* a male striptease. Also, **hammie**.

hammer *n.* **1.** heroin. **2.** *Ultimate frisbee.* a throw in which the disc is released upside-down from over the head. –*v.* **3.** *Sport.* to beat by a large margin. –*phr.* **4. be on (someone's) hammer, a.** to watch (someone)

hammer … **happening**

closely; badger. **b.** to tailgate (another's) vehicle: *I can't pull over, the bloke behind me is on me hammer.* [defs 1 and 4 rhyming slang *hammer and tack* smack, and, back]

hammer and tongs *adv.* with great noise, vigour, or violence.

hammered *adj.* drunk.

hammie *n.* **1.** the hamstring: *an injured hammie.* **2.** See **hambone**.

handbag *n.* an attractive male used by a woman as a showpiece when going out to social functions.

handball *n.* a schoolyard game played with a tennis ball which is hit with the hands in a court, consisting usually of either four or six squares, drawn on the asphalt. Also, **king ping**.

handbrakie *n.* a turn made in a car by slamming on the handbrake when driving at speed, and turning the steering wheel sharply; a handbrake turn.

hand job *n.* a manual bringing to orgasm of a male. Also, **handie, hand-job**.

handle *n.* **1.** a title in front of a name. **2.** a person's name. **3. a.** a beer glass with a handle. **b.** the contents of such a glass. *–v.* **4.** to accept without being shocked, annoyed, etc.; accept (something) well: *Handle it, will ya? –phr.*
5. get a handle on, a. to be able to utilise something. **b.** to understand.
6. fly off the handle, to lose one's temper, especially unexpectedly.

handraulic *adj.* operated by hand.

handsies *phr.* **play handsies,** (of a couple) to touch one another's hands in amorous play.

hands up *n. Car sales.* an easy deal; a deal which did not involve bargaining.

hang *v.* **1.** used to add emphasis to a statement: *I'll be hanged if I do.* **2.** to frequent; spend time in: *to hang in Indonesia for a while.* *–n.* **3.** the place one frequently socialises at; one's hang-out. *–phr.*
4. hang five, to ride a surfboard standing on the nose of the board with the toes of one foot over the edge.
5. hang loose, to relax; fill in time.
6. hang out, to live at or frequent a particular place.
7. hang out for, a. to remain adamant in expectation of (a goal, reward, etc.): *I'll hang out for a higher price before I'll sell; hangin' out for the Chilli Peppers concert.* **b.** to be in need of; crave: *He's hanging out for a coffee.*
8. hang ten, *Surfing.* to ride a surfboard while standing on the nose of the board with all one's toes over the edge.
9. hang with, to spend time with; socialise with.
10. let it all hang out, a. to allow oneself to speak one's mind or show emotion freely. **b.** to be uninhibited in manner, dress, etc.

hanging *adj.* completely eager: *I'm hanging to see them when they make it to Sydney.*

hanky-panky *n.* **1.** trickery; subterfuge or the like. **2.** sexual play.

happening *adj.* **1.** having reached a pinnacle of coolness; having all elements and aspects working together perfectly; better than the best; absolutely cool; really going off: *This*

112

place is really happening; What a happenin' jacket; happenin' party; How ya doin'? Happenin'. –*phr.*
2. happening thing, a venue, party, place, which is currently very cool. Also, **happenin'**.

happy *adj.* **1.** showing an excessive liking for, or quick to use an item indicated (used in combination): *trigger-happy; sex-happy.* –*phr.*
2. happy as a bastard on Father's Day, See **bastard**.
3. happy little vegemite, See **vegemite**.

happy hardcore *n.* a type of dance music.

happy house *n.* a type of dance music.

happy pill *n.* an anti-depressant drug.

hard *phr.*
1. do it hard, *Prison.* **a.** to take prison life badly. **b.** to suffer badly, as at the hands of cruel warders, while in prison.
2. hard cheese (or **cheddar**) (or **luck**), **a.** bad luck. **b.** an off-hand expression of sympathy. **c.** a rebuff to an appeal for sympathy.
3. hard up, urgently in need of something, especially money.
4. hard yakka, see **yakka**.
5. put the hard word on, a. to ask a favour of. **b.** to ask another for sexual intercourse.

hardcore *adj.* **1.** pertaining to an unadulterated form; classic: *hardcore skating; hardcore rock.* **2.** a type of dance music.

hard house *n.* a type of dance music.

hard-on *n.* an erect penis.

hard stuff *n.* **1.** strong alcoholic liquor; spirits. **2.** hard drugs, as heroin, etc.

hard yards *phr.* **to put in the hard yards,** to go through with difficult and demanding work in order to achieve an end.

harp *n.* a harmonica; mouth-organ.

hash *n.* a preparation of the resin of the Indian hemp plant used as a drug. [abbreviation of *hashish*, from Arabic]

hash cookies *n.* biscuits made with hashish in them.

hassle *n.* **1.** a quarrel; squabble. **2.** a struggle; period of unease: *Today was a real hassle.* –*v.* **3.** worry; harass: *Don't hassle me!* [origin unknown]

hasta la vista *phr.* goodbye; so long. Also, **hasta la vista, baby.** [from Spanish; used in imitation of the character played by Arnold Schwarzenegger in the movie *Terminator II* (1991)]

hatchet face *n.* a sharp, narrow face.

hatrack *n.* **1.** a thin or scrawny animal, as a horse, cow, etc. **2.** a very thin person.

hatter *n.* **1.** *Mining.* a miner who works alone. **2.** a lonely and eccentric bush dweller.

have *v.* **1.** to hold at a disadvantage: *He has you there.* **2.** to outwit, deceive, or cheat: *She is a person not easily had.* **3.** to have intercourse with; to copulate with. **4.** to fight (someone): *I'll have you, any day.* **5.** to charge with an infringement of the law: *I could have you for obscene behaviour.*
–*phr.*

6. have it coming to one, to deserve an unpleasant fate.

7. have it in for, to hold a grudge against.

8. have it off, to have sexual intercourse.

9. have (someone) going, to successfully fool or dupe someone.

10. have (someone) on, to fight with (someone).

hawk *phr.* **hawk the fork,** to be a prostitute.

hay *phr.*

1. a roll in the hay, an act of sexual intercourse.

2. hit the hay, to go to bed.

3. make hay, to scatter everything in disorder.

Hay *phr.* **Hay, Hell and Booligal,** hot and uncomfortable places; places to be avoided. [popularised by the poem *Hay, Hell and Booligal* by AB (Banjo) Paterson; Hay and Booligal are towns in inland NSW]

hayburner *n. Jocular.* a horse, especially a racehorse.

head *n.* **1.** a person who uses drugs regularly, especially hard drugs. **2.** the tops of the marijuana plant, having a higher concentration of drug-containing resin: *Got any good head?* **3.** fellatio: *to give good head.* –*phr.*

4. have (someone's) head, to punish (someone) severely.

5. head them (or **'em**), *Two-up.* to make the coins land with heads upwards.

6. make heads roll, to demote or dismiss people as a punishment.

7. need one's head read, *Jocular.* to be insane.

8. off one's head, mad; very excited; delirious.

9. out of one's head, a. out of one's mind; demented; delirious. **b.** under the influence of some drug; stoned; whacked.

10. pull one's head in, to mind one's own business.

headbanging *n.* a style of dancing to heavy metal music in which the dancer shakes the head violently.

head case *n.* a person who is suffering from some kind of mental illness.

headie *n.* **1.** *Two-up.* a person who bets on heads. Cf. **tailie. 2.** Also, **heady.** a head job.

head job *n.* an act of fellatio.

head rush *n.* a thrilling sensation in the head.

head serang *n.* the person in charge; boss. Also, **head sherang, head shebang**. [*head* + Persian *serang* boatswain]

headshrinker *n.* a psychiatrist. Also, **shrink.**

head-turner *n.* **1.** an attractive person. **2.** a shoplifter's accomplice who distracts staff.

healy *n. Obsolete.* **1.** a confidence trick. **2.** the essential trick or ruse of a confidence trick or bodgy device used in a confidence trick. Also, **heelie, eelie, illy**. [? an aspirated variant of *eelie*]

heap *n.* **1.** something very old and dilapidated, especially a motor car. –*phr.*

2. for heaps, for a long time.

3. give (someone) heaps, a. express strong displeasure with (someone); criticise severely. **b.** to

heap **helm**

tease; provoke to anger, annoyance, etc., by banter or mockery.

heaps *adv.* extremely: *I will be heaps grateful; heaps curious; heaps barro.*

heart-starter *n.* **1.** an alcoholic drink, especially one taken early in the day, often as a remedy for a hangover. **2.** any drink, as strong coffee, etc., taken before one begins the day's activities.

heavens *interj.* an exclamation of surprise. Also, **heavens to Betsy, heavens to Murgatroyd.**

heavy *adj.* **1.** serious; intense: *The relationship was getting a bit heavy for my liking; It was a really heavy scene.* **2.** violent: *No need to get heavy with him.* –*n.* **3.** a person who is eminent and influential in the sphere of their activities, as an important business person, etc. **4.** a person of some status who unpleasantly exercises their authority or seeks to intimidate. **5.** a man who attempts to intimidate a woman into sexual submission. **6.** a criminal employed by another to do the dirty work; a stand-over man; a goon. **7.** a detective. –*v.* **8.** to confront; put pressure on.

heck *n., interj.* a euphemism for the word 'hell': *What the heck! Get the heck out of here.*

hector protector *n. Cricket.* a hard protective covering for the genitals, worn inside the pants. Also, **hector.**

heebie-jeebies *pl. n.* **1.** a condition of nervousness or revulsion. **2.** a violent restlessness due to excessive indulgence in alcohol, characterised by trembling, terrifying visual hallucinations, etc.; delirium tremens. [coined by W De Beck, 1890-1942, US cartoonist]

heel *n.* **1.** a despicable person; cad. –*phr.* **2. show a clean pair of heels,** to run away.

heifer paddock *n.* a girl's school.

heist *n.* a robbery; a theft; housebreaking. [variant of *hoist* lift, steal]

hell *adj.* **1.** extremely good; excellent: *a hell collection.* –*interj.* **2.** an exclamation of annoyance, disgust, etc. –*phr.*
3. hell for leather, at top speed; recklessly fast.
4. hell's bells, a mild oath.
5. hell's teeth, an exclamation of astonishment, indignation, etc.
6. hell to pay, serious unwanted consequences.
7. the hell, an intensifier: *get the hell out of here.*
8. the hell with it, an expression of disgust or rejection.
9. what the hell, an exclamation of contempt, dismissal, or the like.

hellish *adj.* great; wonderful; excellent: *a hellish time; a hellish resort.*

hell-man *n.* an aggressive, radical dude, especially a surfer, snowboarder, etc.

hello *interj.* an interrogative expressing disbelief: *We were told that if we laminated our citizenship certificates they would become invalid. Hello?*

helluva *adj.* a spelling of the phrase *hell of a,* used as an intensifier to denote a very good or extreme example of something: *We had a helluva good time; a helluva guy; a helluva shock.*

helm *v.* **1.** to direct or produce (a

helm film). **2.** to be in charge of (something).

helo *n.* a helicopter.

he-man *n.* a tough or aggressively masculine man.

Henry the Third *n.* a turd. Also, **Richard the Third**. [rhyming slang]

hens' night *n.* **1.** a party, exclusively for women, thrown for the bride on the night before the wedding day. See **buck's night**. **2.** an evening on which a group of women have a night out together; girls' night out. Also, **hen's party**.

hep *abbrev.* hepatitis: *hep A; hep B*.

herbal *adj.* having a world view that favours esoteric philosophies, traditional healing, etc.

het *n.* a heterosexual person.

hetero *adj.* **1.** showing or relating to sexual feeling for a person (or persons) of the opposite sex. *–n.* **2.** a heterosexual person.

het-up *adj.* **1.** anxious; worried. **2.** sexually excited; turned on. Also, **het up**. [originally a dialect form of *heated-up*]

hey-diddle-diddle *n.* **1.** the middle. **2.** urination; a piddle. *–phr.* **3. through the hey-diddle-diddle,** *Football, etc.* through the middle of the goal posts. Also, **hi-diddle-diddle**. [rhyming slang]

hickey *n.* **1.** a haematoma caused by erotic sucking of the skin; love bite. **2.** a pimple. [origin unknown]

hiddy *adj.* extremely: *hiddy rare*. [from *hideously*]

hi-five *n., v.* See **high-five**.

high *adj.* **1. a.** intoxicated or under the influence of drugs. **b.** elated, as from the effects of drugs or alcohol. *–n.* **2.** euphoric state induced by drugs. *–phr.*

3. high as a kite, a. under the influence of drugs or alcohol. **b.** in exuberant spirits.

4. on a high, experiencing a euphoric state, especially as one induced by drugs.

high camp *adj.* extremely camp; over-the-top; outrageous.

highfalutin' *adj.* pompous; haughty; pretentious. Also, **hifalutin, highfaluting**.

high-five *n.* **1.** a gesture of pleasure and camaraderie between two people in which one person holds up their palm up high and the other slaps it with their open palm. *–v.* **2.** to perform a high-five. Also, **hi-five**.

high jump *n.* **1.** *Criminal/Prison.* a higher court than a magistrate's court. See **low jump**. **2.** execution by hanging. *–phr.* **3. for the high jump(s), a.** about to face an unpleasant experience, especially a punishment or reprimand. **b.** *Prison.* up for trial.

hill *phr.*

1. as old as the hills, very old.

2. over the hill, past prime efficiency; past the peak of physical or other condition, etc.

himbo *n.* a superficial, stupid man, who is overly concerned with his looks. See **bimbo**. [from *him* + *bimbo*]

hi-NRG *n.* a type of fast beat dance music; Euro-dance. Also, **hi NRG, hi nrg, high energy**.

hip *adj.* having inside knowledge, or being informed of current styles, especially in jazz: *to be hip to swing* *music.* [originally also *hep*; from US black English; cf. Wolof *hepi* to be aware]

hip-hop *n.* **1.** the urban subculture, originating in the US, which spawned rap, break-dancing and graffiti art. **2.** a type of dance music stemming from this subculture.

hip-pocket nerve *n.* an imaginary nerve which is sensitive to demands for one's money, especially through government action to increase taxation or weaken one's economic security.

hipster *n.* **1.** *Originally.* a hippy. **2.** someone who is hip; a cool person, up with the latest.

history *phr.*
1. be ancient history, to be finished or gone irrevocably.
2. be history, a. to be dead. **b.** to be ruined or incapacitated. **c.** to be broken beyond repair.

hit *v.* **1.** to inject any form of drugs. **2.** to get extremely angry; fume. [shortening of the phrase 'hit the roof'] –*n.* **3.** a shot of heroin or any drug; a fix. **4.** a visit to a website via the Internet: *received over 300 hits last week.* –*phr.*
5. hit for six, to confuse or disturb greatly: *The bad news hit him for six.* [from cricket parlance]
6. hit it off, to get on well together; agree.
7. hit off, to make a beginning; commence.
8. hit the ceiling (or **roof**), to display extreme anger or astonishment.
9. hit the lip, to ride a surfboard off the extremity of a wave.
10. hit the road (or **bitumen**), to set out; depart.
11. hit the sack (or **hay**), to go to bed.
12. hit the spot, to fulfil a need; satisfy.
13. hit up, to take a drug, as heroin, usually by injecting it into the bloodstream.

hit and giggle *n.* uncompetitive tennis.

hitched *adj.* married.

hit list *n.* **1.** a list of names of the intended victims of assassins or terrorists. **2.** a list of people, organisations, etc., targeted in some way, as for cost-cutting, reform, criticism, etc.

hit man *n.* a hired assassin.

hiya *interj.* an exclamation used in greeting. [from *hi* hello + *ya* you]

hock *n.* **1.** *Prison.* a male who takes the active part in homosexual practices in prison, but does not consider himself homosexual. **2.** an active male homosexual. [origin unknown]

hodad *n.* a swimmer who annoys or impedes surfboard riders. Also, **hodad**. [US slang; origin unknown]

hoe *phr.*
1. hoe in, a. to commence to eat heartily. **b.** to begin something energetically.
2. hoe into, a. to eat (food) heartily. **b.** to attack (a person) vigorously, usually verbally. **c.** to undertake (a job) with vigour.

hog *n.* **1.** a selfish, gluttonous person; a person who takes more than their fair share. **2.** a large motorcycle, especially a Harley-Davidson. –*v.* **3.** to appropriate selfishly; take more than one's share of. –*phr.*
4. go the whole hog, to do com-

pletely and thoroughly; to commit oneself unreservedly to a course of action.

hoick *v.* **1.** to clear the throat and spit. [imitative] **2.** to throw: *Hoick it over here.*

hoist *v.* **1.** to steal, especially to shoplift. **2.** to throw. *–n.* **3.** a theft; housebreaking.

hoister *n.* a shoplifter.

hole *n.* **1.** an embarrassing position or predicament: *to find oneself in a hole.* **2.** a filthy, disgusting, boring, or otherwise objectionable place. **3.** any of certain apertures of the body, as the mouth, anus, or female genitals. *–phr.*
4. hole up, to hide, as from the police.
5. like a hole in the head, not at all: *Would you like some pate? Yeah, like a hole in the head.* [from Yiddish]
6. put a big hole in, to eat or drink a large proportion of: *Well, I may not have finished it, but I put a big hole in it.*

hollow *phr.* **have hollow legs,** to have a prodigious appetite for either food or alcoholic drink.

hols *pl. n.* holidays. Also, **hollies**.

holy cow *interj.* an exclamation indicating surprise, indignation, etc. Also, **Holy Christ, holy mackerel, holy moley, Holy Moses, Holy Mother, Holy Mother of God, holy shit, holy smoke.**

home *phr.*
1. home and hosed, a. (of a racehorse) having won by a great length. **b.** finished successfully.
2. home on the pig's back, certain to succeed.
3. nothing to write home about, not remarkable; unexciting; all right.
4. who is he/she when he/she is at home? an exclamation, usually scornful, indicating that the person referred to has an undeservedly high opinion of themselves.

home boy *n.* **1.** (with a possessive) a fellow member of an American-style gang of youths: *Hanging out with my homies.* **2.** any member of such a gang. Also, **homie.**

homo *n. Derogatory.* **1.** a male homosexual. *–adj.* **2.** homosexual.

hon *n.* a term of endearment; darling. [short for *honey*]

honcho *n.* a person in power; the boss. [from Japanese]

honey *n.* **1.** an extremely good-looking person. **2.** a term of endearment; sweet one; darling.

honey buns *n.* a term of endearment; sweet one; darling. Also, **honey bunch, honey-pie.**

honey pot *n.* **1.** sweet one; darling; honey. **2.** a toilet, especially a sanitary can. **3.** the female genitals.

honker *n.* a nose, especially a large one.

honky *n. Chiefly US. Racist.* a white person. [originally US Black English; see Wolof *honq* pink, the colour used to describe white people in many African languages]

hoo *interj.* See **whoo**.

hoodoo *n. Sport.* a jinx, especially when certain conditions are met, as playing at a particular ground, racing at a particular course, playing a particular team, etc.

hooer *n.* **1.** a prostitute. **2.** a term of general abuse applied to either sex.

[from a representation of the non-standard pronunciation of *whore*]

hooey *Originally US.* –*interj.* **1.** an exclamation of disapproval. –*n.* **2.** silly or worthless stuff; nonsense. [origin unknown]

hoof *n.* **1.** *Jocular.* the human foot. –*v.* **2.** to dance. –*phr.* **3. hoof it,** to walk.

hoofo *n. Derogatory.* a homosexual male.

hoo-ha *n.* a fuss; turmoil; argument. [probably from Yiddish *hu-ha* to-do, uproar]

hook *n.* **1.** a catchy musical strain or lyric phrase that keeps a person listening to a song. **2.** a plot device given near the beginning of a story, television drama, etc., intended to get the audience interested. –*v.* **3.** to seize by stealth, pilfer, or steal. **4.** to marry: *She's managed to hook a rich man.* –*phr.*
5. hook into, to become an integral part of.
6. hook it, to depart; clear off.
7. hook, line, and sinker, completely.
8. hook up, to meet again and spend time with (someone): *Let's get some numbers so we can hook up later on.*
9. off the hook, a. (of a garment) ready-made; off the peg. **b.** out of trouble.
10. on the hook, a. waiting; being delayed. **b.** in a difficult predicament.
11. put the hooks into, to borrow from; cadge.
12. sling one's hook, to depart.
13. the hooks, the fingers; the hands.

hooker *n.* a prostitute.

hookline *n.* a line of the lyrics of a song containing a hook.

hooky *phr.* **play hooky,** to be unjustifiably absent from school, work, etc. Also, **hookey.** [originally US; see *hook it*]

hooley-dooley *interj.* an exclamation of amazement, surprise, etc.

hooligan *n.* a hoodlum; young street rough. [origin unknown]

hoon *n.* **1.** *Originally.* a man who lives off the earnings of prostitution; a pimp; a bludger. **2.** a despicable person. **3.** a hooligan; a lout. **4.** a fast, reckless driver of a car, boat, etc. **5.** a speedy drive: *going out for a hoon tonight.* –*v.* **6.** to drive fast and recklessly. [origin unknown]

hoop *n.* a jockey.

hooroo *interj.* goodbye. Also, **hooray, ooray, ooroo.**

hoot[1] *n.* **1.** a thing of no value: *I don't give a hoot.* **2.** an amusing or funny thing; a good time.

hoot[2] *n.* money. [from New Zealand slang, from Maori *utu* payment]

hooter *n.* **1.** the nose. **2.** (*pl.*) *Crass.* a woman's breasts.

horizontal dancing *n.* sexual intercourse. Also, **horizontal hula.**

horn *n.* **1.** an erect penis. **2.** the telephone.

hornswoggle *v. Chiefly US.* **1.** to cheat or trick; confuse. –*phr.* **2. well, I'll be hornswoggled,** an exclamation of surprise, incredulity, etc.

horny *adj.* randy; sexually excited.

horse *n.* **1.** heroin.
–*phr*

2. back the wrong horse, to support the wrong or losing contender.
3. could eat a horse (and chase the rider) or **eat a horse if you took its shoes off,** very hungry.
4. horse about (or **around**), to act or play roughly or boisterously.

horse bite *n.* (*amongst schoolchildren*) a stinging slap on the thigh with a slightly cupped palm.

horse's doover *n. Jocular.* an hors d'oeuvre.

horseshit *n.* nonsense; rubbish; bullshit.

horse's hoof *n.* a homosexual. Also, **horse's**. [rhyming slang *horse's hoof* poof]

hospital pass *n.* **1.** *Football.* a pass given to a player who will inevitably be tackled on receiving the ball. **2.** *Ultimate frisbee.* Also, **hospital throw.** a throw that hangs in the air a long time before descending and for which many players crowd together and attempt to catch.

hot *adj.* **1.** sexually attractive; sexually stimulating. **2.** fashionable and exciting; cool. **3.** performing well; peaking: *The bassist is really hot tonight.* **4.** recently stolen or otherwise illegally obtained. **5.** (of a person) wanted by the police. **6.** the most favoured currently: *the hot favourite.* **7.** the latest and freshest: *the hot news is; a hot tip.* –*phr.*
8. hot to trot, extremely eager; raring to go.
9. hot under the collar, angry; annoyed.
10. hot up, a. to escalate: *He hotted up his attack.* **b.** to stir up: *to hot things up a bit.* **c.** to tune or modify (a motor vehicle) for high speeds.
11. in hot water, in trouble.
12. like a cat on a hot tin-roof (or **on hot bricks**), in a state of extreme agitation.
13. sell (or **go**) **like hot cakes,** to sell or be removed quickly, especially in large quantities.
14. the hots, a strong sexual attraction: *to have the hots for Jack.*

hot air *n.* empty, pretentious talk or writing.

hotpants *n.* **1.** strong sexual desires. **2.** one who has strong sexual desires: *She's a real little hotpants.*

hot property *n.* **1.** a person or thing highly valued for its commercial potential. **2.** a person or thing that is currently all the rage; the in thing or person. **3.** a sexually attractive person.

hot seat *n.* a position involving difficulties or danger.

hot-shot *adj.* **1.** exceptionally proficient. –*n.* **2.** one who is exceptionally proficient, often ostentatiously so.

hot stuff *n.* **1.** a woman or man who is sexually exciting. **2.** something or someone of great excellence or interest.

hottie *n.* a hot water bottle.

hot-wire *v.* to start (a car) using a wire to bypass the starting key.

house[1] *phr.*
1. like a house on fire, very well; with great rapidity.
2. safe as houses, completely safe.
3. the little house, an outside toilet.

house[2] *n.* a type of dance music.

how *n.* **1.** way or manner of doing: *to*

consider the hows of a problem. –*phr.*
2. and how, very much indeed; certainly.
3. how's it hanging? Also, **how're they hanging?** a form of greeting among men. [in reference to the state of the male genitals]
4. how's that? See **howzat**.

howdy *interj.* an exclamation of greeting; hello. Also, **howdy-do, howdy-doody.** [shortenings of *how do ye?* and *how do ye do?*]

howzat *interj. Cricket.* an appeal by the fielding side to the umpire to declare the person batting out.

hoy *v.* **1.** to throw. –*n.* **2.** bingo. [Middle English *hoy*, variant of *hey*]

Hoyts *phr.*
1. dressed up like the man outside Hoyts, to be elaborately overdressed.
2. the man outside Hoyts, the commissionaire outside Hoyts Theatre, Melbourne, in the early part of this century, used as **a.** an (obviously innocent) scapegoat for any crime, misdemeanour, rumour, or **b.** a stereotype of a disinterested observer.

hubba hubba *interj. Originally US. Crass.* (used leeringly by males) an exclamation expressing admiration of a sexually attractive person. [origin unknown]

hubby *n.* husband. Also, **hub.**

huck *n. Ultimate frisbee.* **1.** a long throw. –*v.* **2.** to make such a throw: *She hucked it for a goal.* [origin unknown]

huckfest *n. Ultimate frisbee.* (a disparaging term for) a game in which there are many hucks thrown.

Huey *n.* a jocular name for the powers above used when encouraging a heavy rainfall, good snow or good surf: *Send her down, Huey! Whip 'em up, Huey!* Also, **Hughie.** [origin of appellation unknown]

huge *adj.* exceedingly excellent; awesome; unreal.

Humbolt domestic *n.* a type of marijuana.

humdinger *n.* a person or thing remarkable of its kind.

hump *n. Crass.* **1.** an act of sexual intercourse. **2.** a person with whom one has sexual intercourse. –*v.* **3.** to have sexual intercourse.

humpy *n.* any rough or temporary dwelling; bush hut. [from the Aboriginal language Jagara]

humungous *adj.* of huge size or extent. [originally US; ? a blending of *huge* and *monstrous*]

hung *adj.* (of a male) with a large penis; well-hung.

hunk *n.* a solid, well-built, sexually attractive male. Also, **hunkster.**

hunky *adj.* (of a male) solid and attractively well-built; gorgeous.

hunky-dory *adj.* perfectly all right, satisfactory. Also, **hunky.**

hurl *v.* **1.** to vomit. –*n.* **2.** the act of vomiting.

husband-beater *n.* a very long, narrow, loaf of bread. Also, **wife-beater.**

hush money *n.* a bribe to keep silent about something.

hustle *v. Originally US.* **1. a.** to obtain (money) by questionable methods. **b.** to pursue sales with aggressive energy. –*n.* **2.** a confi-

hustle dence trick; a swindle. [from Dutch *husselen* to shake]

hustler *n. Chiefly US.* a person who swindles people out of money.

hydro *n.* **1.** a type of marijuana. *–phr.* **2. the hydro,** *Tasmania.* **a.** the Hydro-Electric Commission. **b.** power supplied by the Hydro-Electric Commission; electricity.

hype *n.* **1.** exaggeration; hyperbolic description, especially as produced by the media or in advertising: *all the hype about the Olympics.* **2.** excitement; thrill: *the hype of just being there.* **3.** excited activity; hustle and bustle: *getting away from the hype of Surfers' Paradise. –v.* **4.** to acclaim, announce or promote hyperbolically: *the book has been hyped into the bestseller lists. –phr.* **5. hype up,** to stimulate; make excited. [origin uncertain; earlier meanings are, 'a hypodermic needle', 'a drug addict', (thus *hype up* to become stimulated by a drug); but also meaning 'a swindle', 'to short change or swindle'; nowadays often thought of as being a shortening of *hyperbole, hyperbolic* or *hyperactive*]

hyped *adj.* totally excited; thrilled; all geed up; stoked. Also, **hyped-up**.

hyper *adj.* over-stimulated; hyperactive; on edge. Also, **hypo.**

INNIE

There are basically only two types of people in the world, the more common *innie*, those people whose bellybuttons are sunken below the surface of the stomach, and the rarer *outie*, those people whose bellybuttons protrude. Why these two tribes aren't equal in number is one of the world's great unsolved mysteries. Interestingly, there are two figures which cannot be aligned to either the *innie* or *outie* group – namely, Adam and Eve. The one thing Adam and Eve did not have that every other human being does possess is a navel. Since Adam and Eve did not spend time in utero they did not have to be sustained via the umbilical cord, and hence did not have navels. Indeed, in medieval iconography, Adam and Eve were often depicted navelless.

INDIE

If you think this word has something to do with India or the Indians then you are way behind the times. It is a shortening of the word *independent*, referring to music released by independent record companies rather than the larger labels devoted to the mainstream pop/rock music industry. It first was applied in this sense to certain record companies in the 1940s, but today it describes a particular style or genre of music. It generally refers to a type of pop/rock music from a band that uses conventional rock ensemble instruments, two electric guitars, electric bass, unsynthesised drum-kit, and, of course, the unpolished vocals. Often the guitars are given a characteristic fuzz sound. Lovers of *indie* music, or as it is commonly known, *indie pop* or *indie rock*, enjoy the fact that this music is less commercial as it shows that the musicians clearly have their music as their number one priority. This is opposed to the highly produced, highly commercial groups who are much more concerned with stardom and making megabucks.

INSANE

ace, awesome, bad, bitchin', booshit, bullshit, choice, classic, cool, deadly, def, dope, dudical, excellent, exo, fat, feral, filth, filthy, gnarly, groovy, hellish, huge, insane, kewl, kick-arse, kick-butt, kool, mad, mega, out there, phat, putrid, rad, radical, rancid, sick, sik, wicked

STUCK FOR WORDS

ice *n.* **1.** a diamond or diamonds. *–phr.* **2. cut no ice with,** to make no impression on; be unconvincing: *His excuses cut no ice with me.*

iceberg *n.* **1.** a regular winter swimmer. *–phr.* **2. tip of the iceberg,** a small part of a larger whole, usually a problem: *The leaking roof was only the tip of the iceberg.*

ID *n.* **1.** a document, etc., providing personal details, such as address or proof-of-age: *No entry without ID.* **2.** an identification of a person: *We got a positive ID.* *–v.* **3.** to identify (a person).

idiot box *n.* a television set.

idiot lights *pl. n.* warning lights on a dashboard.

idjut *n.* an idiot; fool. Also, **idjit.**

iffy *adj.* **1.** dubious; odd. **2.** unsure; undecided.

illy *phr. Obsolete.* **whack the illy,** to perform a confidence tricks; to be a con artist. [probably a variant of *eelie*]

illywhacker *n.* a con artist; a trickster. [agent noun from the phrase *whack the illy*]

imbo *n.* a simpleton; fool. [shortening of *imbecile* + *-o*]

impro *n.* improvisation.

imshi *v. WWI & II Military.* to go away. Also, **imshee.** [from Egyptian Arabic]

in *adj.* **1.** in favour; on friendly terms: *He's in with the managing director.* **2.** in fashion: *the in thing; Velour was never in.* *–n.* **3.** influence, pull; connection: *She has an in with the management - she married a director.* **4.** an opening; a way in: *provided a much sought-after in to the music industry.* *–phr.* **5. in for it,** about to be reprimanded or punished. **6. in it up to one's neck,** in big trouble. **7. in on,** having a share in or a part of, especially something secret, or known to just a few people. **8. in the poo** (or **shit**), in big trouble. **9. nothing in it,** (in a competitive situation) no difference in performance, abilities, etc., between the contestants.

incoming *interj.* a cry used to warn that something thrown is approaching. [from military use, as *incoming missile*]

indeedie *adv. Originally US.* indeed: *Yes, indeedie, here we are.* Also, **indeedie-do.**

Indian giver *n.* a person who gives something as a gift to another and later takes or demands it back. [originally US]

indie *adj.* **1.** of or pertaining to non-mainstream music produced on independent record labels. **2.** a specific genre of guitar-based pop or rock, characterised by relatively low-tech production, and seen as being more sincere because it is less like a business to the musicians and more like art. [from *independent*]

Indo *n.* **1.** *Derogatory.* a person from Indonesia. **2.** Indonesia.

industrial *n.* a musical movement speaking out against the propaganda of authority and the establishment, characterised by use of synthesisers, industrial machinery, found materials and other unconventional means of producing an antagonistic and confronting music. [named from *Industrial Records*, an independent label started in 1976 by members of the band Throbbing Gristle]

info *n.* information.

infobahn *n.* the information superhighway; the Internet. [from *info(rmation) + (auto)bahn*]

inked *adj.* drunk; intoxicated.

inky smudge *n.* a judge. [rhyming slang]

inner man *n.* the stomach or appetite.

innie *n.* **1.** a recessed belly-button; a navel that goes in, as opposed to an *outie*. **2.** a person with such a navel.

innings *phr.* **have had a good innings,** to have had a long life or long and successful career.

innos *interj.* (in schoolyard games) a call claiming that an interference occurred and upset play, thus requiring a restart of play.

ins and outs *pl. n.* the intricacies of something.

insane *adj.* fantastic; wonderful. See **mad**.

inside *adv.* to or in prison.

inside-out *n. Ultimate frisbee.* a throw that curves across the front of the body.

intestinal fortitude *n. Jocular.* strength of will; guts.

into *adj.* having an enthusiasm for; exceedingly interested in: *I am into health foods; He's fully into Nirvana.*

intro *n.* an introduction.

invite *n.* an invitation. Also, **invo**.

in-your-face *adj.* confronting. Also, **in your face**.

Irish *adj.* **1.** containing an inherent contradiction. *–phr.* **2. get one's Irish up,** to become angry. **3. Irish as Paddy's pigs,** extremely Irish in character.

Irish curtains *pl. n.* cobwebs.

iron *phr.* **1. iron out, a.** to smooth and remove (problems and difficulties, etc.). **b.** to flatten (someone); knock down. **2. iron (oneself) out,** to get drunk. **3. pump iron,** to work out with weights.

irrits *pl. n.* **1.** a feeling of annoyance or irritation: *have the irrits. –phr.* **2. give (someone) the irrits,** to make (someone) annoyed.

it *n.* **1.** (in chasings games) being the person currently tagged or tipped and having to chase the other players. **2.** sexual intercourse. **3.** sex appeal. **4.** the one chosen: *Okay, you're it. –phr.* **5. with it, a.** in accordance with current trends and fashions; fashionable. **b.** well-informed and quick-witted.

Italo house *n.* a type of dance music. Also, **italo house**.

item *phr.* **be an item,** (of two people) to be involved in a romantic relationship.

Itie *n. Derogatory.* an Italian. Also, **eyetie, eytie**.

ivory *phr.* **1. the ivories, a.** the keys of a piano, accordion, etc. **b.** dice. **2. tickle the ivories,** to play the piano.

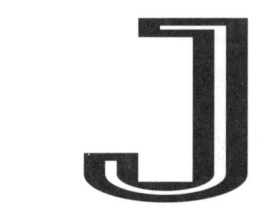

JOINT

Have you ever wondered why marijuana cigarettes are called *joints?* What on earth do they *join?* Well, nothing really. The origin of this term is related to the slang term *joint* meaning "place", "room", etc. Originally, in the US in the late 19th century, a *joint* was an opium den. Later, this sense was extended to mean any place where illegal drugs were taken, including marijuana. Finally, in the 1930s, the sense was transferred to the cigarette itself, and, showing similar semantic development, it was also applied to the apparatus for injecting drugs, more commonly known as a *fit* nowadays. Another term which has perplexed lexicographers is *roach* for the stub of the marijuana cigarette. Presumably this is so called from its resemblance to the *cockroach*. When a joint is passed around the end piece invariably becomes moist and shiny, and also very darkly coloured due to an accumulation of tar and oil from the smoke of the burning hemp.

JUMBUCK

Despite the comparatively short history of the English language in this country, there are some words that we know surprisingly little about – and *jumbuck* is one of them. A helpful Mr Meston, in the *Bulletin* of 18 April 1896, reported that *jumbuck* was a word borrowed from an Aboriginal language, and meant "white mist preceding a shower", to which, he maintained, a flock of sheep bore a strong resemblance. "It seemed the only thing the Aboriginal mind could compare it to." However, to equate a flock of sheep with a "white mist preceding a shower" is really just too great a stretch of the imagination to be believed. A later theory is that the word comes from Aboriginal pidgin and is a version of "jump up", which is what sheep do when you come across them. However, as far as I know, sheep don't "jump up" any more often or quickly than cows, wallabies, kangaroos, or any other animal, so why the special label? It's a mystery.

JOSH

chaff, chiack, dish it out, gee up, get a rise out of, heckle, mock, pay out on, poke borak at, poke mullock at, pull someone's leg, put a rocket under, razz, rev up, rib, roast, rubbish, scoff at, shit-stir, stir, take the micky out of, take the piss out of, twit

STUCK FOR WORDS

J *n.* a marijuana cigarette. [see *jay*]

jab *n.* an injection with a hypodermic needle.

jack[1] *n.* **1.** venereal disease. [from rhyming slang *jack in the box* pox] **2.** a police officer, especially a detective. –*v.* **3.** *Surfing.* Also, **jack up**, to become good; to pick up: *the swell jacked again mid-afternoon.* –*adj.* **4.** *Military.* highly undesirable; deserving contempt, especially for lack of effort or fairness; slack. –*phr.*
5. jack of, fed up with; sick and tired of.
6. jack off, to masturbate.
7. jack up, a. to refuse; be obstinate; resist. **b.** to raise or increase (something): *jacking up their prices; jacked up my level of horniness.*

jack[2] *n.* nothing: *I don't know jack about it.* [euphemistic shortening of *jack shit*]

Jack *phr.*
1. I'm all right Jack, an expression of selfish complacency on the part of the speaker.
2. Jack the dancer, cancer.
3. the house that Jack built, *Jocular.* a venereal disease clinic.

jacked-up *adj.* infected with venereal disease.

jackeroo *n.* **1.** an apprentice station hand on a sheep or cattle station. –*v.* **2.** to work as a trainee on such a station: *He's jackerooing in Queensland this year.* Also, **jackaroo.** [origin unknown]

Jack-'n'-Jill *n.* **1.** the bill. **2.** a dill; fool. **3.** a cash register; till. [rhyming slang]

Jacko *n.* the kookaburra. Also **jack,**
jacky. [shortening of (*laughing*) *jack(ass)* + *-o*]

jackpot *phr.* **hit the jackpot, a.** to win chief prize on a gambling machine. **b.** achieve great success; be very lucky.

jack shit *n. Offensive.* nothing: *We owe you jack shit.* Also, **jackshit.**

Jack the Painter *n. Hist.* a strong, green, tea, used in the bush, which discolours utensils.

Jacky Howe *n.* **1.** a navy or black woollen singlet worn by labourers, bushmen, etc. **2.** any similar singlet. Also, **Jimmy Howe.** [? from name of Australian world champion shearer of 1892]

jaffa *n. Cricket.* a very good delivery.

jag *n.* **1.** a drinking bout. **2.** any sustained single activity, often carried to excess: *an eating jag, a fishing jag, a crying jag.* [? from US *jag,* a load carried on the back; thus as much drink as one can carry]

Jag *n.* any Jaguar make car.

jail-bait *n.* a girl or boy below the legal age of consent. Also, **gaol-bait.**

jake[1] *adj.* all right: *She'll be jake, mate; everything's jake now.* [origin unknown]

jake[2] *n.* a toilet. [origin unknown]

Jane Doe *n.* (especially with police, lawyers, etc.) a name used to refer to any unknown or unspecified woman who is dead or unconscious. See **John Doe.**

Jap *n. Racist.* **1.** a Japanese person. –*adj.* **2.** of Japanese construction or origin. –*phr.*
3. Jap crap, Japanese made cars.

4. wouldn't feed it to a Jap on Anzac Day, See **wouldn't.**

Japper n. Derogatory. a Japanese motorcycle.

jar n. a glass of beer.

J Arthur n. an act of masturbation. [from rhyming slang *J Arthur Rank* wank]

Jatz crackers pl. n. the testicles. [from rhyming slang *Jatz crackers* (a brand of cracker biscuits) knackers]

jawbone v. to talk, especially at length, as in expounding an idea, presenting an argument, etc.

jaw-breaker n. **1.** a word hard to pronounce. **2.** a large, hard or sticky sweet.

jay n. a marijuana cigarette. [? from *j(oint)* or from (*Mary*) *J(ane)*]

jerk n. **1.** an annoying, stupid person. –phr.
2. jerk off, to masturbate.
3. jerk the gherkin, (of a male) to masturbate.

jerk-off n. **1.** an act of male masturbation. **2.** a very foolish person; an idiot.

jerry[1] n. **1.** a chamber-pot. **2.** lavatory. –phr. **3. full as a family jerry, a.** full (of food). **b.** drunk. [apparently from *jeroboam*, a very large wine bottle]

jerry[2] phr. **jerry to,** to understand, realise: *He jerries to what's going on.* [origin unknown]

jerry[3] n. See **geri.**

Jesus interj. an exclamation indicating surprise, indignation, etc.: *Jesus! What was that?* Also, **holy Jesus, Jesus Christ, Jesus Fucking Christ, Jesus H. Christ, sweet Jesus.**

Jesus-freak n. an overtly enthusiastic and obtrusive Christian.

jewels n. the testicles. Also, **crown jewels, family jewels.**

jiffy n. a very short time: *Hang on, I'll do it in a jiffy.* Also, **jif, jiff.**

jig[1] phr. **the jig is up,** the game is up; there is no further chance.

jig[2] v. **1.** to play truant: *jig school; jig class.* –phr. **2. jig it,** to play truant. [from British slang *jig* to cheat or delude]

jigger n. **1.** a name for any mechanical device, the correct name of which one does not know. **2.** *Prison.* an illegally made crystal radio set. **3.** *Horseracing.* an illegal apparatus which gives a shock to a horse during a race in order to increase its speed.

jig-jig n. sexual intercourse.

jilleroo n. a female station hand on a sheep or cattle station. [modelled on *jackeroo*, with *jill* representing the female, as in the nursery *Jack and Jill*]

jillion n. an inordinate amount. Also, **gillion, squillion, zillion.**

jim-dandy adj. remarkable; wonderful; superior.

Jimmy Brits pl. n. the shits. Also, **Jimmie Britt.** [rhyming slang, with reference to a former lightweight boxing champion of the world, *Jimmy Britt*, who was on vaudeville tour in Australia during WWI]

Jimmy dancer n. cancer.

Jimmy Riddle n. a piddle. [rhyming slang]

Jimmy Woodser n. **1.** one who drinks alone in a bar. **2.** an alcoholic drink consumed alone. [? from the name of a fictitious character, *Jimmy Woods,* who always drank alone]

jinx *interj.* a call made by someone when they say the exact same word simultaneously with a second person. The second person is thence forced to keep silent until relieved of the jinx by the saying of their name by the person who jinxed them. [originally US; from *jynx* a spell, from the ancient Greek name of the wryneck, a bird used in witchcraft]

jive *n. Originally US Black English.* 1. pretentious, empty talk. 2. Also, **jive talk**. a type of American Negro and jazz slang. –*v.* 3. tease; joke with: *Are you jiving me?* 4. to go or fit together; to make sense: *It just doesn't jive.* [cf. Wolof (an African language) *jev* to disparage someone in their absence]

Joan of Arc *n.* a shark. [rhyming slang]

job[1] *n.* 1. a theft or robbery, or any criminal deed. –*phr.*
2. **big jobs,** (*in children's speech*) defecation.
3. **do a job on (someone),** to bash (someone); assault.
4. **give up as a bad job,** to abandon as unprofitable an undertaking already begun.
5. **jobs for the boys,** See **boy**.
6. **just the job,** exactly what is required.

job[2] *v.* hit; punch: *Shut up or I'll job you.* [variant of *jab*]

jobbies *pl. n.* (*in children's speech*) defecation.

jock *n.* 1. a jockstrap. 2. (*pl.*) a type of men's underwear. 3. *Chiefly US.* a male athlete, especially one in college or university.

Joe *n.* (in Colonial times) a trooper; a military police officer. [from C *Joseph* La Trobe, whose mining regulations the troopers were enforcing on the gold diggings]

Joe Blake *n.* a snake. Also, **Joe**. [rhyming slang]

Joe Blakes *pl. n.* delirium tremens, characterised by trembling, terrifying visual hallucinations, etc., and caused by excessive indulgence in alcohol. Also, **Joes, joes**. [rhyming slang for 'shakes']

Joe Blow *n.* the man in the street; the average citizen. Also, **Joe Bloggs.**

joey *n.* 1. a baby kangaroo. 2. a young child. [origin unknown]

john[1] *n.* a police officer. Also, **John**. [from *John Dunn* or British *johndarm,* both renderings of the French *gendarme*]

john[2] *n.* 1. a toilet. 2. Also, **John.** a prostitute's client.

John Citizen *n.* the man in the street.

John Doe *n.* (especially with police, lawyers, etc.) a name used to refer to any unknown or unspecified man who is dead or unconscious. See **Jane Doe**.

John Henry *n. Originally US.* a signature. Also, **John Hancock.**

John Lennon glasses *pl. n.* small, round, steel-rimmed glasses. [from the fact that glasses of this type were favoured by John Lennon]

johnny *n.* fellow; man.

Johnny Bliss *n.* an act of urination. [rhyming slang *Johnny Bliss* piss]

Johnny Cash *n.* the drug hashish. [rhyming slang for *hash*]

joint *n.* **1.** a place of business, especially a stall, tent, etc. **2.** the house, unit, office, etc., regarded as in some sense one's own: *Come round to my joint.* **3.** a disreputable bar, restaurant, or nightclub; a dive. **4.** a marijuana cigarette.

joke *n.* **1.** something extremely bad, pathetic, awful, dreadful, etc.: *Their defensive play is a joke.* **2.** a hopeless, stupid, useless person: *You're nothing but a joke, an absolute joke; pack of hopeless jokes.* *–phr.*
3. the joke is on (someone), said of a person who has become the object of laughter or ridicule, usually after a reversal of fortune.

joker *n.* a fellow or bloke: *a funny sort of joker.*

jollies *phr.* **get one's jollies,** to get excited; to get one's cheap thrills.

José *phr.* **no way José,** an expression of denial or negation.

josh *v. Originally US.* **1.** to chaff; banter in a teasing way: *Don't worry, he was just joshing.* *–n.* **2.** a chaffing remark; a piece of banter. [origin unknown]

jostle *n.* an annoying person; a dickhead. Also, **jossel**.

jug *n.* **1.** a measure of beer served in a large glass jug. **2.** prison or jail. **3.** (*pl.*) *Crass.* the female breasts. *–v.* **4.** to commit to jail, or imprison.

juice *n.* **1.** electric power. **2.** petrol, oil, etc., used to run an engine. **3.** any alcoholic beverage. **4.** any sexual secretion.

juicy fruit *n.* an act of sexual intercourse. [rhyming slang for 'root']

jumbuck *n.* a sheep. [? Aboriginal corruption of *jump up*]

jump *v.* **1.** to board (a train, bus, ferry, etc.), without paying a fare. **2.** to have sexual intercourse with (someone). **3.** to attack suddenly without warning. **4.** *Horseracing.* (of a horse) to begin to race: *the bookie got caught with a large bet just before they jumped.* *–n.* **5.** an act of coitus. **6.** *Horseracing.* the beginning of the race. *–phr.*
7. go jump (in the lake or **creek),** an expression of dismissal.
8. go take a (running) jump (at yourself), an impolite dismissal indicating the speaker's wish to end the conversation.
9. jump on (or **upon**), to scold; rebuke; reprimand.
10. jump on (someone's) bones, to have sexual intercourse with (someone).
11. jump the box, *Criminal.* to give evidence in favour of a person being charged.

jumper *n. Police.* a person who has committed suicide by jumping off a building, bridge, cliff, etc.

jungle *n.* a type of rhythmically complex dance music employing breakbeat, arriving on the rave scene in the early 1990s; drum and bass.

junglist *n.* a jungle dance music enthusiast.

junk *n.* **1.** anything that is regarded as worthless or mere trash. **2.** any narcotic drug. *–v.* **3.** to cast aside as junk, discard as no longer of use.

junkie *n.* an addict, especially a person addicted to hard drugs. Also **junky.**

KEN DOLL

The constant companion of the plastic-curvaceous wonder-doll *Barbie* is the square-jawed, perfect-haired, flinty-eyed doll *Ken*. Not as popular or versatile as his female companion, *Ken* has happily remained in the background just hanging around and looking perfect. Of course such models of perfection are fine for little kiddies, but just as it is deemed silly for an adult to play with dolls, it is deemed equally silly for grown-ups to emulate these dolls in real life. Thus the term *Ken doll* gets applied to any male who satisfies the following criteria: has blow-dried hair, is clean-shaven, tanned, dressed conservatively, and is square-jawed with even features. In Australia this type of male is not often spotted, but when they are, you can rest assured they'll be branded a *Ken doll*.

KANGAROO

The first person to record *kangaroo* was Captain Cook who took time off from repairing his ship, which was holed on the Barrier Reef, to chat to the local Aborigines, the Guugu Yimidhirr, a tribe of northern Queensland. The next person to visit the Endeavour River was Captain King in 1820, and he also wrote down words from the Aboriginal language, but without mentioning *kangaroo*. Indeed he recorded a different word entirely. So who was right and who was wrong? There was endless speculation along the lines that the Aborigines and Cook had misunderstood each other, and that when Cook asked "What's that animal that looks like a greyhound?", the Aborigines really said, "I don't know what you're talking about", or even worse, gave him a rude word to take back as a joke on these strange white men. This speculation was finally ended in 1972 when a linguist, John Haviland, studied the language again and concluded that Cook and the Guugu Yimidhirr had had a meaningful exchange and that kangaroo was indeed the Aboriginal word for the strange animal that looked like a greyhound.

KAPUT

buggered, bung, cactus, clapped-out, done for, down the gurgler, down the plughole, gone a million, had it, had the dick, had the Richard, had the rod, jiggered, on the blink, ratshit, rooted, RS, snafued, stonkered, stuffed, up the spout, up to putty

STUCK FOR WORDS

K *n.* **1.** a thousand (dollars, etc.): *Her salary is well over 40K.* **2.** a kilometre. **3.** kilometres per hour: *We were only doing 100 k, officer.* **4.** a kilogram. Also, **k, kay.**

kack *n., v.* See **cack.**

kafuffle *n.* argument; commotion. Also, **kafoofle, kerfuffle, kerfoofle.**

kambrook *n. Car sales. Racist.* a group of four or more South-East Asian customers. [from the brand name of a make of powerboards; see *power point*]

kamikaze *n.* **1.** *Surfing.* a deliberate wipe-out. *–adj.* **2.** dangerous; suicidal: *his kamikaze driving.* [from the Japanese WWII *kamikaze* suicide squad pilots]

kanga *n.* a kangaroo.

kangaroo *v.* **1.** Also, **kangaroo-hop, bunny-hop**. to release the clutch of a car unevenly so that (a car) moves forward in a series of jerks. **2.** to squat over a toilet seat, while avoiding contact with it. *–phr.* **3. have kangaroos in the top paddock,** to be insane.

kaput *adj.* **1.** smashed; ruined. **2.** broken, not working; ruined. [from German]

kark *v.* See **cark.**

karma *n.* an intuition or feeling about the quality, mood or atmosphere of a person or place.

karma block *n. Ultimate frisbee.* a defensive play or block in which one causes the opposition to drop the frisbee by upsetting their equanimity rather than by actually touching the disc in flight.

kay *n.* See **K.**

keeper *n.* the ringkeeper of a two-up game.

keg *phr.* **spike the keg,** to urinate for the first time when participating in a drinking session.

keg-on-legs *n. Derogatory.* **1.** a person who drinks an inordinate amount of beer. **2.** an obese person.

keg party *n.* a party at which one or more kegs of beer are provided.

Ken doll *n. Derogatory.* a male who is superficially attractive in a conventional way but who lacks brains and personality. See **Barbie**. [Trademark: name of a children's doll]

kerb crawling *n.* the action of driving a car slowly along a street seeking out pedestrians in order to chat them up.

kerfuffle *n.* See **kafuffle**. Also, kerfoofle.

kewl *adj.* a cool spelling of the word *cool* (defs 1-3).

Khyber *n.* rump; buttocks: *a kick up the Khyber.* [rhyming slang *Khyber Pass* arse]

kick *n.* **1.** any thrill or excitement that gives pleasure; any act, sensation, etc., that gives satisfaction. **2.** a strong alcoholic taste and/or content in a drink. **3. a.** trouser pocket. **b.** financial resources: *nothing in the kick. –phr.*

4. a kick in the arse, a. a setback. **b.** retribution.

5. a kick in the pants, a sharp reprimand.

6. for kicks, for the sake of gaining some excitement or entertainment.

7. hit the kick, a. to pay up. **b.** to pay the bill.

8. kick about (or **around**), **a.** to be found (at a place). **b.** to hang about;

to loiter. **c.** to discuss or consider at length or in some detail (an idea, proposal, or the like).
9. kick arse, See **arse**.
10. kick back, to relax.
11. kick butt, See **butt**.
12. kick in, to contribute, as to a collection for a presentation.
13. kick off, to start, commence: *the band kicks off at 7.00.*
14. kick on, a. to carry on or continue, especially with just adequate resources: *We'll kick on until the fresh supplies get here.* **b.** to continue a party or other festivity: *We kicked on until the early hours.*
15. kick the bucket, to die.
16. kick the tin, to make a donation.

kick-arse *adj.* extremely excellent: *a real kick-arse track*. Also, **kick-ass, kick-butt**.

kick-flip *n. Skateboarding.* a manoeuvre in which the skateboard is flipped over whilst in motion, twisting lengthwise so that it lands back on the wheels enabling the skater to land and continue riding.

kick-off *n.* the beginning or initial stage of something.

kid *v.* **1.** to tease; banter; jest with. –*phr.* **2. I kid you not,** an assertion that one is speaking the truth.

kiddo *n.* a familiar form of address to a young person.

kidney wiper *n. Crass.* a large penis.

kids' beer *n.* **1.** low alcohol beer. **2.** the brand of beer KB, jokingly supposed by children to be the meaning of the initials.

kiff *n.* marijuana. Also, **kif**. [Moroccan and Algerian Arabic, from *kaif* pleasure]

killer *n.* **1.** something particularly effective: *That joke is a killer.* **2.** the final fact which makes a situation unbearable; the last straw. –*adj.* **3.** absolutely fantastic: *a killer mud cake; a killer mountain resort.*

kill file *n. Internet.* a file containing information about a particular person, or subject matter, that prevents any postings which match this information being shown by a newsreader.

kilos *pl. n.* bodily weight: *stacking on the kilos; those unwanted kilos.*

king hit *n.* **1.** a knock-out blow. **2.** a punch from behind. **3.** any sudden misfortune.

king-hit *v.* to punch forcibly and without warning.

king pair *n. Cricket.* falling first ball in both innings. See **pair**.

king ping *n.* a schoolyard game played with a tennis ball which is hit with the hands in a court, consisting usually of either four or six squares, drawn on the asphalt. Also, **KP, handball**.

king's ransom *n.* a large amount of money.

kink *n.* **1.** a deviation from normal behaviour; an eccentricity. **2.** a sexual predilection. **3.** a person with a sexual kink.

kinky *adj.* having unusual sexual tastes; perverted.

kip[1] *n.* **1.** a sleep. –*v.* **2.** to sleep. **3.** to stay (somewhere) on a temporary basis: *He's kipping at Tom's for a couple of days.* [earlier meaning 'bed', 'common lodging-house', 'brothel'; see Old English *cip* brothel]

kip² *n. Two-up.* a small, thin piece of wood used for spinning the coins. [? variant of *chip*]

kiss *phr.*
1. kiss my arse, an expression of contempt or incredulity.
2. kiss arse, to fawn; to behave sycophantically.

kisser *n.* the mouth.

KISS method *n.* a very simplistic method of explaining, teaching, etc. Also, **KISS principle**. [an acronym formed from the phrase *Keep It Simple, Stupid*]

kite *n.* **1.** a spinnaker. **2.** an aeroplane. **3.** a hang-glider. **4.** *Prison.* a newspaper. **5.** *Criminal.* a cheque, especially one forged or stolen. *–phr.*
6. fly a kite, to pass off a forged cheque.
7. go fly a kite, a phrase used as a peremptory dismissal.

Kiwi *n.* **1.** any New Zealander. **2.** a New Zealand soldier or representative sportsperson, especially a Rugby League representative. [from the bird unique to New Zealand]

Kiwiland *n.* New Zealand.

klutz *n.* a clumsy, awkward person; idiot. [originally US, from Yiddish *kluts* blockhead, literally, a wooden block]

knackered *adj.* exhausted; worn out.

knackers *pl. n.* testicles.

kneetrembler *n.* the act of sexual intercourse when both parties are standing.

knickers *phr.* **get one's knickers in a twist** (or **knot**), *Originally Brit.* to become agitated or flustered.

knob *n.* **1.** the penis or head of the penis. **2.** an annoying or stupid person; a dickhead.

knob-end *n.* **1.** the head of the penis. **2.** a prick; dickhead.

knock *v.* **1.** to criticise; find fault with: *People are always knocking the Government.* **2.** to have sexual intercourse with. **3.** *Prison Talk.* to kill. *–n.* **4.** an act of intercourse. *–phr.*
5. do a knock with, *Obsolete.* to go courting with.
6. knock about (or **around**), **a.** to wander in an aimless way; lead an irregular existence. **b.** to treat roughly; maltreat.
7. knock around with, to keep company with.
8. knock back, a. to consume, especially rapidly: *he knocked back two cans of beer.* **b.** to refuse. **c.** to set back; impede.
9. knock down, a. to reduce the price of. **b.** to spend freely, especially on liquor: *He knocked down his cheque at the local pub.*
10. knock it off, a. to desist; stop. **b.** (used imperatively) stop it!
11. knock off, a. to stop an activity, especially work. **b.** to deduct. **c.** to steal. **d.** to compose (an article, poem, or the like) hurriedly. **e.** to defeat, put out of a competition. **f.** to kill. **g.** to persuade (a person) to have sex; to seduce. **h.** to eat up; consume. **i.** (of police) to arrest (a person) or raid (a place).
12. knock oneself out, to exhaust oneself by excessive mental or physical work.
13. knock one's eye out or **knock one's socks off,** to cause one to feel excessive admiration.
14. knock out, a. to overwhelm with success or attractiveness. **b.** to

destroy; damage severely. **c.** to earn: *He knocked out a living as a station hand.* **d.** to make; produce: *Pete knocked out a few pots.*
15. knock rotten (or **silly**), to strike heavily.
16. knock spots off, to defeat; get the better of.
17. knock up, a. to arouse; awaken. **b.** to construct, cook, etc., (something) hastily or roughly. **c.** *Sport.* to score (runs, tries, etc.). **d.** to exhaust; wear out. **e.** to make pregnant. **f.** *Prison.* to attract the attention of the warder on duty by hammering on the cell door.
18. take a knock, to suffer a reverse, especially a financial one.
19. take the knock, *Horseracing, etc.* (of a punter) to admit that one is unable to settle one's debts with one's bookmaker.

knockabout *adj.* **1.** leading a rough life travelling about the country and living on one's wits: *a knockabout artist; a hard knockabout life.* **2.** rough and uncultivated: *a knockabout bloke.*

knock-back *n.* a refusal; rejection, especially of sexual advances.

knockdown *n.* **1.** a formal introduction. *–adj.* **2.** (of a punch, blow, etc.) strong enough to knock a person to the ground. *–phr.* **3. knock-down, drag-out,** (of a fight or brawl) particularly violent.

knocker *n.* **1.** a persistently hostile critic or carping detractor. *–phr.* **2. on the knocker, a.** at the right time, punctual: *He was there on the knocker.* **b.** immediately; on demand: *cash on the knocker.*

knockers *pl. n. Crass.* large breasts.

knockout *n.* a person or thing of over- whelming success of attractiveness.

knockover *n.* an easy success; pushover.

knotted *phr.* **get knotted,** go away; leave me alone.

knuckle *v.* **1.** to assault, with fists or knuckle-dusters. *–phr.*
2. fond of the knuckle, keen on fighting.
3. go the knuckle, to fight, especially with the fists.

knuckles *pl. n.* a game in which two contestants hold closed fists knuckle-to-knuckle and take turns at hitting the other player's knuckles. A change of turn takes place when one player misses a strike.

knuckle sandwich *n.* a punch in the mouth: *Are you looking for a knuckle sandwich, mate?*

KO *n.* **1.** a knockout. *–v.* **2.** to knock (someone) out.

k-one-w-one *n.* a New Zealander. [a fanciful spelling-out of *Kiwi* with *one* (1) substituted for *i*]

konk *n.* See **conk**.

kook *n.* **1.** a strange or eccentric person. **2.** *Surfing.* a beginner, especially one who imitates others badly. [from *cuckoo*]

kooky *adj.* eccentric; odd.

kool *adj.* a cool spelling of the word *cool* (defs 1-3).

KP *n.* See **king ping**.

LARRIKIN

Nowadays the term *larrikin* is used in a rather friendly way. A *larrikin* is someone who is mucking about or being playfully and good-humouredly annoying, someone who is *playing the lark* or *larking about*. Crocodile Dundee is a typical bush *larrikin*. However, the *larrikin* of the last century was not at all like that of today. They used to hang around in gangs called pushes or *larrikin pushes*. They didn't work, nor did they intend to, instead they just mooched about the streets causing trouble. Nat Gould, a prominent journalist and best-selling horse-racing novelist, described larrikins as "hideous-looking fellows, whose features bear traces of unmistakable indulgence in every loathsome vice". Thankfully the larrikin has cleaned up his act in recent times.

L A I R

Although many people think that Australian slang is merely a variant of good old English Cockney, there are very few words to back this theory up.

However, the great Australian *lair*, that flashy, dressed-up loudmouth, seems quite definitely to have Cockney origins. You see, a *lair* is someone who is *lairy*, and the word *lairy* comes directly from Cockney slang. Back in England a *lairy* character was someone who was "in the know", or "fly", and hence sometimes apt to be seen as conceited. When the word travelled to Australia in the last part of the 19th century, the negative connotations were brought to the fore, and word was used to describe showy, vulgar chaps. Another Australian innovation was the concoction of the verb *lairise* – to act or behave like a lair.

It is interesting to notice that *lairy* is actually a variant of the earlier *leery*, which probably comes from the Old English word *leor* or *hleor* meaning "cheek". This makes perfect sense, because, as we all know, *lairs* are "cheeky" buggers.

LOSER

bevan, bogan, dag, dork, drip, drongo, dweeb, Fred Nerk, goose, gumby, hick, loser, nerd, nerd-burger, neville, nigel, spac, square, turkey, twerp, wet sock

STUCK FOR WORDS

lad *n.* **1.** (in familiar use) any male. **2.** a devil-may-care, blokey man: *Watch out for him, they reckon he's a bit of a lad!*

lady *n.* **1.** (in cards) a queen. *–phr.* **2. lady of the night,** a female prostitute.

lady-killer *n.* a sexually attractive man popular with women.

lag *v.* **1.** to send to prison. **2.** to report (someone) to the authorities; inform on. *–n.* **3.** *Hist.* a transported convict. **4.** a prisoner, especially one who has had many convictions; a recidivist. **5.** a term of penal servitude. *–phr.* **6. old lag, a.** *Hist.* an ex-convict. **b.** Also, **old lagger.** a recidivist. [originally British slang, from 16th century *lag* to carry off, steal; origin unknown]

lair *n.* **1.** Also, **mug lair.** a flashily dressed young man of brash and vulgar behaviour. *–phr.* **2. lair about** (or **around**), to behave in a brash and vulgar manner. **3. lair it up,** to behave in a brash and vulgar manner. **4. lair up, a.** to dress up in flashy clothes. **b.** to renovate or dress up something in bad taste. [backformation from *lairy*]

lairise *v.* to behave like a lair; show off; indulge in brash, vulgar exhibitionism.

lairy *adj.* **1.** exhibitionistic; flashy. **2.** vulgar. [from Cockney slang *lairy* wise, knowing, awake up]

lammie *n.* a lamington. Also, **lammo.**

larrikin *n.* **1.** *Hist.* a lout, a hoodlum: *larrikins of the push.* **2.** a mischievous young person. **3.** a good-natured but independent or wild-spirited person, usually having little regard for authority, accepted values, etc. [British (Warwickshire and Worcestershire) dialect *larrikan* mischievous youth]

lash *n.* **1.** *Crass.* sexual intercourse. *–phr.* **2. have a lash at,** to attempt. **3. lash out, a.** to spend money freely. **b.** to burst into violent action or speech.

later *interj.* a common exclamation of farewell: *Later, dudes!*

Latin hip-hop *n.* a type of hip-hop dance music heavily influenced by Latin music; freestyle.

lats *pl. n. Weights.* the latissimus dorsi muscles.

laughing *phr.* **be laughing,** to be in a favourable or fortunate position: *One more result like that and you'll be laughing.*

laughing gear *phr.* **wrap one's laughing gear around** (**something**), to eat (something): *Here, wrap your laughing gear around this sanger.*

lavish *adj.* extremely good.

lay *v.* **1.** to have sexual intercourse with. **2.** to bet. *–n.* **3. a.** a person considered as a sex object: *a good lay, an easy lay.* **b.** the sexual act. *–phr.* **4. lay into, a.** to beat. **b.** to criticise severely. **5. lay off, a.** to desist doing or taking: *better lay off the booze.* **b.** to cease to annoy (someone). **c.** to protect a bet or speculation by taking some off-setting risk. **6. lay out,** *Ultimate frisbee.* to dive for the disc.

lay down misère *n.* something that is a certainty.

lead *phr.*
1. go down (or **over**) **like a lead balloon,** to fail dismally; fail to elicit the desired response.
2. have a lead foot, to be given to driving too fast.
3. put lead in one's pencil, (of a male) to increase sexual capacity.

lead-footed *adj.* given to reckless and speedy driving.

leaf *n.* the leaves of the marijuana plant dried and prepared for smoking.

leak *n.* **1.** an act of passing water; urination. *–v.* **2.** to pass water; urinate. *–phr.* **3. hang a leak,** to urinate.

leather dyke *n.* a homosexual woman who dresses in leather.

leatherman *n.* a homosexual man who dresses in leather.

lech *n.* **1.** a person preoccupied with sex. *–v.* **2.** to behave lecherously. [shortened from *lecher*]

ledge *n.* an absolutely cool person. [shortened from *legend*]

leech *v.* to download software via the Internet.

leery *adj.* **1.** doubtful; suspicious. **2.** knowing; sly. *–phr.* **3. leery of the brush,** (of a man) nervous about getting married.

left right out *n. Jocular.* a spurious position on a sporting field.

leg *n* **1.** *Sport.* (*pl.*) running ability; stamina: *run out of legs; haven't got any legs left. –phr.*
2. get a leg in, to make a start.
3. get a leg over, to have sexual intercourse with.
4. got legs, (used leeringly by males) to have long, thin legs: *She's got legs.*
5. have legs right up to one's bum (or **arse**), (used leeringly by males) to have long, thin legs.
6. leg it, to walk or run.
7. sex on legs, an extremely sexually attractive person.

legend *n.* **1.** Also, **ledge.** an absolutely cool person. *–phr.* **2. legend in one's own mind,** a totally conceited person.

legless *adj.* very drunk, to the point where walking steadily is not possible.

leg man *n.* a male who is sexually aroused by legs.

leg opener *n.* an alcoholic drink calculated to facilitate the seduction of a woman.

leg-over *n.* an act of sexual intercourse.

lemon *n.* **1.** a lesbian. **2.** *Car sales.* a car which looks all right but actually is mechanically unsound. **3.** anything that is no good.

lemonhead *n.* a surfie with bleached hair.

length *phr.* **slip** (**someone**) **a length,** *Crass.* (of a man) to have sexual intercourse with (someone).

lerve *n.* a jocular spelling of *love*. Also, **lurve.**

lesbie *n.* **1.** Also, **lesbo.** a lesbian. *–adj.* **2.** lesbian. *–phr.* **3. lesbie friends,** a lesbian couple (punning on the phrase 'let's be friends').

leso *n.* **1.** a lesbian. *–adj.* **2.** lesbian. Also, **lesso, lezzo.** See **lezzie.**

lezzie *n.* a lesbian. Also, **lezzy.** See **leso.**

Lib *n.* a member or supporter of the Australian Liberal Party.

lick *v.* **1.** to overcome in a fight, etc.; defeat. **2.** to outdo; surpass. *–phr.* **3. lick (someone's) arse (or boots),** to act in a subservient manner; fawn upon.
4. lick out, to perform cunnilingus on.

lid *phr.* **dip one's lid,** *Obsolete.* **a.** to lift one's hat as a mark of respect. **b.** to show respect or admiration for someone or something.

life *phr.*
1. get a life, a catchphrase expressing derision at another person's life, view of life, point of view, etc.; an exhortation that someone become worthwhile.
2. life sux (and then you die). Also, **life's a bitch (and then you die).** a catchphrase expressing a dismal outlook on life, used when one feels that things are peculiarly bad.
3. not on your life, absolutely not.
4. such is life! an exclamation indicating resignation or tolerance. [reputed to be the last words of Ned Kelly]

lifer *n.* a person sentenced to life imprisonment.

lift *v.* **1.** to steal or plagiarise. *–n.* **2.** a facelift.

light[1] *phr.*
1. out like a light, unconscious, especially after being struck, or receiving an anaesthetic.
2. see the light, a. to be converted, especially to Christianity. **b.** to suddenly understand something.
3. the lights are on but nobody's home, a phrase implying that someone is stupid.

light[2] *adj.* relating to a state of temporary financial embarrassment: *I'll pay you later, I'm a bit light today.*

like *adv.* **1.** (used after a clause to weaken the force of a direct statement) so to speak; as it were; sort of; kind of: *It was a bit tough, like; they've gone bad like.* **2.** more recently used frequently interspersed throughout speech with the same meaning, but sometimes also with little semantic force, and sometimes as a mere filler: *There was like this big guy, like really big...and he like said to me like 'G'day'; He would go like 'Shut up!' really loud; So you'd, like, lie on your tax form.*

lily *n.* **1.** *Derogatory.* a man who does not conform to some conventional notion of masculinity, as an artist, a homosexual, etc. *–phr.* **2. lily on a dustbin, a.** a person or thing rejected or neglected. **b.** something incongruous, as to be inappropriately or overdressed at an informal gathering.

limp-wristed *adj. Derogatory.* (of a man) **a.** homosexual. **b.** effeminate; wimpish.

line *n.* **1.** a pick-up line. **2.** a measure of cocaine laid out for inhalation.

line-up *n. Surfing.* a line of surfers waiting in the ocean for waves.

lip *n. Surfing.* the top edge of a wave.

lipstick lesbian *n.* a lesbian who wears conventional woman's clothing and make-up. Also, **lipstick dyke**.

liquid laugh *n.* vomit.

liquid lunch *n.* alcoholic drink, usually beer, consumed instead of food at the normal lunchtime.

little Aussie battler *n.* See **battler**.

little blister *n.* one's little sister. [rhyming slang]

little boy's/girl's room *n.* a toilet.

little Vegemite *n.* See **Vegemite**.

little white mouse *n.* a tampon.

Liverpool kiss *n.* a headbutt. Also, **Balmain kiss**.

livestock *n.* maggots infesting a dead body.

lizard *phr.*
1. **flat out like a lizard drinking,** working at full capacity; going at top speed.
2. **starve** (or **stiffen**) **the lizards,** an exclamation of mild surprise, astonishment, exasperation, etc.

load *n.* 1. an infection of venereal disease, usually gonorrhoea. 2. an ejaculation of semen. –*phr.* 3. **get a load of, a.** to look at; observe. **b.** to listen; to hear.

loaded *adj.* 1. Also, **loaded up.** unjustly incriminated; framed. 2. very wealthy. 3. under the effects of alcohol; drunk. 4. under the effects of marijuana or some other drug; stoned.

loadie *n. Derogatory.* a person under the influence of marijuana; a stoned person.

lob *v.* 1. to arrive, especially unexpectedly: *He lobbed here this afternoon.* 2. to land: *it lobbed on the rockery below.* 3. to win a race: *He was hoping the horse would lob.* –*phr.* 4. **lob in,** to arrive unannounced or unexpectedly.

lobster *n.* a $20 note. [from its colour]

local *phr.* **the local,** the closest or preferred hotel in the neighbourhood.

local yokels *pl. n.* the inhabitants of a town, suburb, etc.

London *phr.* **London to a brick on,** (of an outcome) extremely likely: *It's London to a brick on that he'll chicken out.* [popularised by race-caller Ken Howard who used it to unofficially announce winners in a tight finish while awaiting the official decision. In racing parlance it is a statement of betting odds in which a punter is so certain of the outcome that they are willing to bet London to win a measly brick. Many people unaware of betting lingo leave out the vital word *on*, thus making the phrase the opposite of what is intended, i.e. the odds of laying a brick to win all of London, not much of a risk]

long *adj.* 1. (of odds) returning a large dividend for the outlay. –*phr.* 2. **long in the tooth,** elderly.

long drop *n.* death; death by hanging. Also, **long jump**.

long neck *n.* a 750ml bottle of beer.

loo *n.* a toilet. [origin unknown]

look *phr.* **looking at,** liable for: *You'd be looking at $400 000 for a house in that area.*

looker *n.* a good-looking person. Also, **good-looker**.

look-see *n.* a visual search or examination.

looky *phr.* **looky here,** *Jocular.* look here!

loon *n.* a crazy person.

loony *adj.* **1.** lunatic; crazy. *–n.* **2.** an insane person. Also, **looney, luny**.

loony bin *n.* a lunatic asylum.

loop *n.* **1.** a musical sample repeated throughout a song. [originally referring to a tape loop] **2.** Also, **fruit loop.** a crazy person; weirdo. *–phr.* **3. out of the loop,** to be out of touch with one's surroundings; out of touch.

loopy *adj.* mad or eccentric.

loot *n.* **1.** money stolen in a robbery. **2.** money: *spend your hard-earned loot.* [from Hindi]

loppy *n.* a handyman on a station; rouseabout.

lose *v.* **1.** to stop wearing: *Lose the earring; He could definitely lose those yellow socks.* **2.** to cause (someone) to lose track of a story, explanation, or the like: *You lost me after the first sentence. –phr.*
3. lose it, a. to no longer have that quality which made one specially able or talented. **b.** to lose control of one's temper: *Mum really lost it when I pranged the car.* **c.** to lose control of a vehicle: *lost it big time coming round that last bend.* **d.** to lose the plot.
4. lose one's marbles, to go insane.
5. lose the plot, (of a person) to fail to act effectively any longer; to no longer understand fully what is going on in a certain situation, job, etc.
6. move it or lose it, a warning indicating that one should move whatever it is they have in the way.

loser *n.* **1.** a person who is socially unacceptable; a complete dag. **2.** a person who is hopeless at everything; an out-and-out no-hoper.

lost *phr.* **get lost,** (used in the imperative) go away; rack off!

lost weekend *n.* **1.** a weekend spent in drunken oblivion. **2.** a weekend spent in prison as part of a sentence.

lot *phr.*
1. a bad lot, a bad, reprehensible, or evil person.
2. the lot, a. all the available ingredients or toppings, as on a hamburger, pizza, etc. **b.** *Prison.* a life sentence.

louse *n.* **1.** a despicable person. *–phr.* **2. louse up,** to spoil.

lousy *adj.* **1.** mean, contemptible or unpleasant. **2.** well supplied: *He's lousy with money.* **3.** trifling; mere: *fighting over a lousy $20.* **4.** unwell.

love-'em-and-leave-'em *adj.* pertaining to a person who only has brief affairs with other people.

love glove *n.* a condom.

love handles *pl. n.* the sides of the roll of fat running around the abdomen which can be grasped during sex.

love-juice *n.* a sexual secretion.

lovely *n.* a sexually attractive woman.

love muscle *n. Crass.* the penis.

lover's balls *n.* See **blue balls**.

lovey-dovey *adj.* openly affectionate. Also, **lovey, dovey**.

lowie *n. Derogatory.* a despicable, deplorable person; a scumbag. [from *lowlife*]

low jump *n. Prison.* a magistrate's court. See **high jump**.

low-life *n.* **1.** the seamy elements of society, as those involved with drug trafficking, prostitution, etc. **2.** a despicable person; a scumbag. –*adj.* **3.** of or pertaining to such people: *a low-life scum*. Also, **lowlife**.

lowlight *n.* a low point; a point at which things are at their worst: *Being stranded at the airport was a lowlight of the holiday.*

lube *n.* **1.** a lubrication, especially of a motor vehicle. **2.** a lubricant, especially one used for sexual purposes.

lubricate *phr.* **lubricate the larynx**, to drink some alcoholic drink.

luck-out *v.* to run out of luck; to have bad luck.

Lucky Country *n.* (*often ironic*) Australia. [from the title of the book by Donald Horne, Australian writer]

lucky shop *n. Vic.* a government-run betting shop; TAB.

lug *n.* **1.** an ear. **2.** a big, clumsy person: *Out of my way, you great lug.* –*phr.*
3. blow down (someone's) lug, Also, **chew (someone's) lug**. to harangue someone.
4. lug it, (amongst musicians) to work out (a piece of music) by ear.

lulu *n.* **1.** an amazing person, event, or thing. **2.** a tall story. [origin uncertain]

lumber *v.* **1.** to foist off on or leave with, as with something or someone unwelcome or unpleasant: *to lumber with the bill*. **2.** to place under arrest. **3.** (of a prostitute) to take a client to a place for sexual services. **4.** to take a person to one's house for sex.

lummox *n.* a clumsy, stupid person, usually overweight. [origin unknown]

lump *n.* a fat, lazy person.

lunch *n.* **1.** the penis. –*phr.*
2. cut (someone's) lunch, to cuckold (someone).
3. do lunch, to have lunch with someone as a social or business occasion.
4. drop one's lunch, to fart.

lunkhead *n. Originally US.* a great, big stupid bloke.

lurgy *n.* **1.** a fictitious, very infectious disease. **2.** any illness. Also, **lurgi, dreaded lurgy**. [coined by the Goons on BBC radio]

lurk *n.* **1.** a dodge; a slightly underhand scheme. **2.** a convenient, often unethical, method of performing a task, earning a living, etc. –*v.* **3.** *Internet.* to only occasionally visit and respond to postings on a newsgroup. [from Middle English *lurken*]

lurker *n. Internet.* a person who is not a steady, regular user of a newsgroup, and only occasionally sends in postings.

lurve *n.* a jocular spelling of *love*. Also, **lerve**.

lush *adj.* **1.** extremely good; fantastic. **2.** sexually attractive. **3.** characterised by luxury and comfort.

lushy *adj.* drunk; tipsy.

lust *phr.*
1. lust after (someone), to want (someone) sexually.
2. in lust with (someone), strongly sexually attracted to (someone), but not in love.

MOSHING

For those who haven't been to see a live band for a while *moshing* is a type of dancing. The hyper-aggressive slam-dancing of the 80s has given way to *moshing*. In *moshing* the participants still bang into one another, but with less force. It occurs in a *mosh-pit,* an area, usually directly in front of the stage, where the keenest *punters* (audience members) congregate. Here the crowd is so tightly packed that each individual is touched on every side, body against body. Thus the *moshers* all *mosh* at once. Naturally this does usually make for some bruising and soreness the next day, but it also engenders a great sense of camaraderie amongst those in the pit. Associated with *moshing* is *stage-diving,* diving from the stage onto the top of the mosh, and *crowd surfing,* being carried over the top of the mosh supported on the hands of the other punters in the pit.

MOLLYDOOKER

A left–hander is a *mollydooker* or sometimes simply a *mollydook*. The first part of this word, *molly*, is probably the same word as that appearing in *mollycoddle*. In British dialect a *molly* was a fussy man who did women's work. The *dook* part is no doubt the slang word *dook* meaning a "hand" or "fist". This is now still used in the jocular invitation to fight, *put up your dooks*. When you put these two elements together you get *mollydooker*, a weak-handed person. Not that left-handed people are really weak-handed at all, as anyone who has lost a fight to a southpaw will know. Yet there has been this prejudice with us from time immemorial. In the Indo-European culture, from which Western culture developed, the "right" was considered lucky and the "left" unlucky. In fact the word for "left" is very different in all Indo-European languages which signifies that the original word was taboo and had to be substituted with another word from time to time. For instance, in Latin the word for left is *sinister*, which also meant evil and unlucky.

MATE

amigo, boozing buddy, boozing mate, bosom buddy, bro, brother, buddy, buddy-buddy, china plate, china, chum, cob, cobber, cohort, comrade, crony, dig, digger, homie, main man, mate, pal, pard (US), pardner (US), sidekick

STUCK FOR WORDS

ma *n.* **1.** one's mother. *–phr.* **2. the ma state,** New South Wales.

Mac-attack *n.* a strong desire to eat food from a McDonald's Family Restaurant.

Macca's *n.* **1.** a McDonald's Family Restaurant. **2.** food from a McDonald's Family Restaurant. Also, **Maccas, Mackers.**

machine *n.* a motorbike, car, truck, etc.

mad *adj.* **1.** extremely good; excellent; cool: *She's got a mad outfit.* *–adv.* **2.** madly: *mad keen to go.*

Madchester *adj.* See **Manchester**.

made *phr.* **have (got) it made (in the shade),** to be assured of success.

madwoman *phr.* **be all over the place like** (or **look like**) **a madwoman's breakfast** (or **custard**) (or **knitting**) (or **lunch box**) (or **piss**) (or **washing**), to be in complete confusion and disarray.

mag *v.* **1.** to chatter or natter; talk socially; to chat. *–n.* **2.** such a chat.

maggot *n.* a reprehensible or despicable person.

maggoty *adj.* angry.

magic mushroom *n.* any of various mushrooms, as the liberty cap or fly agaric, which contain psilocybin, a hallucinogenic substance. Also, **magic mushie**.

magic sponge *n. Football. Jocular.* the sponge or towel applied by trainers to slightly injured players.

-magnet *suffix.* **1.** a person who attracts much sexual interest from others due to their beauty and personality: *chick-magnet; stud-magnet.* **2.** a person who attracts people or things as specified by the first element: *an ugly-magnet.*

magpie day *n.* a day-time event in which there is a fifty-fifty assemblage of Aboriginal and white people.

magsman *n.* **1.** a person who tells stories; raconteur. **2.** a confidence man.

mainland *phr.* **the mainland,** *Tas.* continental Australia.

mainlanders *n. Tas.* residents of mainland states of Australia.

main man *n. Chiefly US.* **1.** the most important person; the person in control. **2.** (with a possessive) one's best friend, closest associate, etc. **3.** the front man of a band or rock group.

major *n.* **1.** *Australian Rules.* a goal. **2.** a major record label company: *majors vs independents.*

majorly *adv.* to a great extent; in a major way: *He was majorly upset.*

make *v.* **1.** to seduce or have sexual intercourse with. *–phr.*
2. make it, a. to achieve one's object. **b.** to arrive successfully.
3. make it (with), to have intercourse (with).
4. make off with, to steal; take.
5. make out, a. to have sexual intercourse: *I made out last night.* **b.** to kiss, pet and fondle sexually: *making out at the movies.*
6. on the make, a. intent on gain or one's own advantage. **b.** looking for a sexual partner.

makings *phr.* **the makings,** the tobacco and paper used to hand roll a cigarette.

male chauvinist pig *n.* a male who

discriminates against women by applying to them stereotyped ideas of female incompetence, inferiority, traditional female roles, etc.

mamma mia *interj.* an expression of surprise, admiration, etc. [from Italian, literally *My Mummy!*]

man *n.* **1.** a term of address to a man or woman. *–interj.* **2.** Also, **man oh man.** an exclamation of surprise, bewilderment, amazement, etc. *–phr.*
3. man (or **boy**) **in the boat,** the clitoris.
4. man outside Hoyts, See **Hoyts.**
5. the man on the land, farmers in general.
6. the men in white coats, the putative employees of a mental institution who collect people for incarceration.

Manchester *adj.* pertaining to a type of indie dance music coming about in the late 1980s and originating in Manchester, England. Also, **Madchester**.

mangare *n.* eating: *a place for serious mangare.* [from Italian *mangiare* to eat]

mangle *v.* to destroy or ruin: *It's mangled your surfing.*

mangulate *v.* to mangle; to bend or twist out of shape; to wreck.

man-hungry *adj.* in pursuit of sexual intercourse with a man.

mankad *v. Cricket.* (of a bowler) to run out the non-facing batter who is backing up, especially after pretending to bowl. Also, **Mankad**. [named after Indian cricketer Vinoo *Mankad* who was dismissed in this manner in Test series of 1947-8]

manual *n. Snowboarding.* a trick in which the tip of the board is lifted up whilst in motion, this stance being held for as long as possible.

manymak *n.* marijuana. [Aboriginal English, meaning literally 'good grass']

Maoriland *n.* New Zealand. [from *Maoris* the original inhabitants]

map of Tasmania *n.* the female pubic area. Also, **map of Tassie**.

marble *phr.*
1. lose one's marbles, to act irrationally; go mad.
2. make one's marble good (with), ingratiate oneself (with).
3. pass (or **throw**) **in one's marbles,** to die.

mark *n.* **1.** a person who is the target of a swindle. *–phr.* **2. easy mark,** *Criminal.* an easily duped victim of a confidence trick.

market *n.* **1.** *Horseracing, etc.* the totality of betting odds being offered on a particular race. *–phr.*
2. in the market, of a racehorse, etc., considered to have a chance of winning, consequently causing the betting odds to be short.
3. go to market, to become angry, excited, unmanageable.

Marrickville Mercedes *n. Sydney slang.* (a derisive term for) a Valiant car.

martini *n. Film.* the last shot taken before making it a wrap.

marvie *adj.* marvellous.

mary *n.* a homosexual male.

Mary Jane *n.* marijuana. Also, **Mary Jay.**

Mary Pickford *phr.* **a Mary Pickford in three acts,** a quick wash; perfunctory wash of the face, hands and crotch. [*Mary Pickford* was an early US film actress]

masher *n.* a man who makes aggressive sexual advances to women.

massive *adj.* tremendous; extraordinary; unusual.

mate *n.* **1. a.** an habitual associate; comrade; friend; equal; intimate: *They've been good mates from way back.* **b.** a form of address (originally amongst men, but now also with women): *How are you going, mate?* **c.** a form of address used to a man in a confrontational situation: *You got a problem, mate?* –*phr.* **2. mate rates,** specially cheap rates for friends.

matey *adj.* **1.** comradely; friendly. –*n.* **2.** a form of address; comrade; chum.

maths in space *n.* the simplest level of mathematics offered at high school.

matilda *n. Hist.* **1.** a swag. –*phr.* **2. waltz Matilda,** to carry one's swag. [from German *Mathilde* female travelling companion, bedroll, from the girl's name; possibly taken to the goldfields by German speakers from South Australia]

mattress muncher *n. Derogatory.* a male homosexual.

max *n.* **1.** the maximum. –*phr.* **2. max out,** to cease surfing when the waves are too big to ride. **3. to the max,** extremely; to the greatest extent possible: *to be hip to the max.*

mazuma *n.* money. [from Yiddish]

MC *n., v.* See **emcee.**

MCP *n.* male chauvinist pig. [from the initials]

meal ticket *n.* any means or source of financial support, as a pimp's prostitute, a spouse, a university degree, etc.

mean *adj.* **1.** (of a person involved in a competitive activity, as sport, business, etc.) sufficiently accomplished and determined to make success very difficult for an opponent: *a mean bowler.* **2.** powerful; effective; having a vicious energy: *a big mean motor.* **3.** extremely good; very cool; hot: *a mean dude; playing some mean bass.*

meat *n.* **1.** a person considered as a sexual object. **2.** male or female genitalia.

meat injection *n. Crass.* the penis, as used in sexual intercourse.

meat market *n.* a place where people frequent to seek sexual partners: *that bar is a real meat market.*

meat-pie *adj. Racing.* small-time: *a meat-pie bookie.*

meat tag *n.* an identity disc, especially those worn by members of the armed forces. Also, **meat ticket.**

Mediterranean back *n. Racist.* a supposed fake back injury in order to get out of work.

mega *adj.* excellent; great; unreal.

mega- a prefix denoting a very great degree: *a megahit; megatrendy.*

megababe *n.* **1.** a very attractive female. **2.** a very attractive male.

megabucks *n.* a large amount of money.

megahunk *n.* a very attractive male.

-meister *suffix.* used with a colloquialising force to create nicknames (sometimes prefaced by 'the'): *readermeisters* (the readers);

Brucie-meister (Bruce). See **-ster**. [from German *Meister* master, leader, chief]

Melba *phr.* **to do a Melba,** to make a habit of returning from retirement, in a number of 'farewell' performances. [from Dame Nellie *Melba* 1861-1931 who had several 'farewells']

mellow *v.* to relax; to chill out.

melon *n.* **1.** a head. **2.** a stupid person; fool.

melonhead *n.* a fool; idiot.

melt *v.* to swoon in response to someone else's sheer attractiveness.

member *n.* the penis.

mental *adj.* **1.** driven to distraction; acting crazy: *He'll go mental when he finds out.* **2.** extremely drunk. *–n.* **3.** (especially amongst children) a stupid person. *–phr.*
4. chuck (or **crack**) **a mental,** to lose one's temper in a violent manner.
5. mental attack, an occasion in which one gets extremely angry or starts acting very oddly.

me'n'u *n.* a restaurant menu. [punning on the phrase *me and you*]

Merc *n.* a Mercedes-Benz motor car.

merchant *n.* (*usually preceded by a defining term*) a person noted or notorious for the specified aspect of their behaviour: *panic merchant, standover merchant.*

merry monk *n. Obsolete.* the sum of 500 pounds.

metal *n.* heavy metal music: *70s metal still rules.*

metalhead *n.* a fan of heavy metal music.

meth *n.* methedrine.

metho *n.* **1.** methylated spirits. **2.** one addicted to drinking methylated spirits. Also, **meths.**

Mexican *n.* **1.** *NSW.* a person from Victoria. **2.** *Qld.* a person from New South Wales [i.e. one south of the border]

Mexican stand-off *n.* a situation in which two opponents threaten each other equally and thus are at an impasse.

mick *n.* See **micky**[2].

Mick *n.* **1.** a Roman Catholic (especially of Irish extraction). **2.** an Irishman or woman.

mickey finn *n.* **1.** a drink, usually alcoholic, which has been surreptitiously laced so as to cause to fall asleep, to discomfort or in some way to incapacitate the person who drinks it. **2.** *Obsolete.* the sum of five pounds. Also, **Mickey Finn.** [def 2 rhyming slang for 'spin', five pounds. See *spin*[2]]

mickey mouse[1] *adj.* cheap and not always reliable, as a piece of machinery, watch, etc. [? from the cheap toy goods sold with merchandising of the Walt Disney cartoon character *Mickey Mouse*]

mickey mouse[2] *adj.* splendid, excellent. [rhyming slang for 'grouse']

micky[1] *n.* **1.** Also, **mickey.** a young, wild bull. *–phr.*
2. chuck a micky, to throw a fit, panic.
3. take the micky out of, to make seem foolish; tease.

micky[2] *n.* the female genitalia. Also, **mick.** [apparently from the male name *Mick, Mickey*]

micky juice *n.* vaginal secretions produced during sexual arousal.

micky muncher *n. Crass.* one who practises cunnilingus.

microdot *n.* a type of LSD trip.

middy *n.* **1.** *NSW.* **a.** a 10 ounce size glass, primarily used for serving beer. **b.** a serving of this amount of beer. **2.** *WA.* **a.** a 7 ounce size glass, primarily used for serving beer. **b.** a serving of this amount of beer. [so called because it is *mid*way between a glass and a schooner]

mile-high club *n.* a supposed club of which the members have all had sexual intercourse in an aeroplane in flight.

miler *n. Horseracing.* a racehorse good at running races of a mile's length or thereabouts.

milk *v.* **1.** to steal petrol by siphoning it off. **2.** to obtain something bit by bit; to siphon off. **3.** to attempt to draw something out; to try and get a bit more out of something: *to milk a joke for more laughs.* –*phr.* **4. milk someone dry,** to cause a person to spend all their money.

milkie *n.* a white marble, usually with swirls of another colour.

milk moustache *n.* a residue of milk left on hairs above the lips after drinking milk.

milko *n.* a person who sells or delivers milk.

miller *phr.* **kill the miller,** to ruin pastry or bread by putting too much water in.

mimsey *adj.* twee; coy.

mind *phr.*

1. blow (someone's) mind, See **blow**.

2. fuck with (someone's) mind, *Offensive.* (commonly in sport) to upset (an opponent's) equanimity; to psych (an opponent) out.

3. legend in one's own mind, See **legend**.

mind-fuck *n. Offensive.* a brainwashing.

mingy *adj.* mean and stingy.

minute man *n. Derogatory.* a man who, in intercourse, ejaculates after a very short time.

miseryguts *n.* a person who is always whingeing or complaining.

missus *n.* **1.** one's wife. **2.** *Rural.* the female owner, or spouse of the owner, of a country property or station. Usually the wife of the **boss**, and traditionally having jurisdiction over the affairs pertaining to the homestead. [pronunciation spelling of *Mrs*]

missy *n.* a young girl, especially a pert or rude one.

mistake *n.* a person born from an unplanned pregnancy.

mitt *n.* a hand. [variant of *mitten*]

mix *v.* **1.** (of a deejay) to create a medley of different dance tunes; to work the decks; to beatmix. –*n.* **2.** a medley of dance tunes. –*phr.* **3. mix it.** to fight vigorously, as with the fists.

mix-up *n.* a fight.

mizzle *v.* **1.** (of rain) to drizzle. **2.** *Older slang.* Also, **mizzle off.** to depart; to leave. –*n.* **3.** drizzling rain.

mo[1] *n.* **1.** a moment. –*phr.* **2. half a mo,** just a moment.

mo[2] *n.* **1.** a moustache. –*phr.* **2. curl**

the mo! *Older slang.* an exclamation of admiration, delight, etc.

mob *n.* **1.** any assemblage or aggregation of persons, animals, or things; a crowd. **2.** a group of people, as friends, not necessarily large: *We'll invite the mob over for Saturday night.* –*phr.* **3. big mobs of,** a large number or amount: *I'll have big mobs of mashed potato, please.*

mobile *adj.* ready to leave immediately.

mocker *phr.* **put the mocker(s) on,** to bring bad luck to; jinx. Also, **put the mock(s) on.** [from *mock* ridicule]

mod *n.* **1.** *Originally.* a member of the mod sub-culture, an early 1960s, primarily British, sub-culture, which was influenced by the modernist movement in dress and music. Stylistically characterised by neat, clean design, and black and white colour use. Seen as a diametrical opposite to the contemporary **rocker**. **2.** a young person of later decades espousing similar dress, music taste, etc. Also, **Mod.**

mod cons *pl. n.* modern conveniences, especially household appliances.

modette *n.* a female of a mod revival subculture.

mods *pl. n. Motoring.* modifications, as made to a standard engine, etc.

moff *n. Rural.* any animal, as a kangaroo, born a hermaphrodite. [shortening from *morphodite*, from *hermaphrodite*; cf. South African slang *moffie* a male homosexual]

moggy *n.* a cat. Also, **mog, moggie.** [possibly variant of *Maggie*, pet form of *Margaret*]

moi *pron.* (*used jocularly as an affectation*) me. [from French]

moisty *n. Crass.* a nubile young female.

mole *n.* **1.** a spy. **2.** *Derogatory.* a variant spelling of *moll.*

moll *n.* **1.** the girlfriend or mistress, as of a gangster, crook, bikie, etc. **2.** *Derogatory.* a girl or woman, with the imputation that they are either nasty or ugly, or are overly liberal with their sexuality. **3.** *Derogatory.* a prostitute. [from the name *Moll*, short for *Molly*, a variant of *Mary*]

moll patrol *n. Derogatory.* a scathing term for a group of schoolgirls, especially as used by other schoolgirls.

mollydooker *n.* a left-handed person. Also, **mollydook.** [probably from British dialect *molly* an effeminate man + *dook* the hand]

Molly the Monk *adj.* drunk. [rhyming slang]

Mondayitis *n.* lassitude and general reluctance to work as is often experienced on Mondays.

mong[1] *n.* a mongrel dog.

mong[2] *n.* a stupid or annoying person; a dork. Also, **mongo.** [shortening of *mongoloid*]

mongrel *n.* **1.** a despicable person. **2.** something difficult: *It's a mongrel of a job.*

moniker *n.* **1.** a person's name; a nickname. **2.** a person's signature. Also, **monicker, monniker.** [blend of *monogram* and *marker*]

monkey *n.* **1. a.** *Obsolete.* the sum of fifty pounds or five-hundred

pounds. **b.** the sum of $50 or $500. *–phr.*
2. a monkey on one's back, any obsession, compulsion, or addiction, seen as a burden, as a compulsion to work or an addiction to drugs.
3. I'll be a monkey's uncle, an exclamation of disbelief, surprise, etc. [originally a slur at Darwinism]
4. monkey business, trickery; underhand dealing.

monkey suit *n.* a dinner suit.

monobrow *n.* a person with eyebrow hair between the eyebrows.

monster *v.* **1.** to harass or hassle. *–adj.* **2.** huge; enormous: *a monster headache; monster truck.*

month *phr.*
1. month of Sundays, a very long time.
2. that time of the month, a. the menstrual period. **b.** the time when pre-menstrual syndrome affects a woman.

monthlies *pl. n.* a woman's menstrual period.

moo *n.* a stupid person; a dork: *Give it here, ya stupid moo.*

mooch *v.* **1.** to hang or loiter about. **2.** to slouch or saunter along. [from Middle English]

moofo and foofti *n. Surfing.* a drink containing Black Sambuca, Bailey's Irish Cream, and Cherry Vok.

moo-juice *n.* milk.

moolah *n.* money. Also, **moola.** [originally US; origin unknown]

moon *v.* **1.** to wander (about) or gaze idly, dreamily, or listlessly. **2.** to display the buttocks publicly, as from out of a car window.

moonlighting *v.* working at a job in addition to one's regular, full-time employment.

moonshine *n.* **1.** smuggled or illicitly distilled liquor. **2.** any alcohol.

moon tan *n.* extremely pale skin.

moo poo *n.* cow manure.

moosh *n.* **1.** the mouth; the face. **2.** prison food, especially porridge. Also, **mush.** [origin unknown]

moot *n. Often offensive.* the female genitals. Also, **moote.** [origin unknown; cf. Spanish *mata* bush, vagina, and obsolete British slang *motte* vagina]

moppet *n.* a little girl. [from *moppet* a doll]

morning glory *n.* **1.** sexual intercourse had upon awakening in the morning. **2.** an erection of the penis upon awakening. **3.** *Horseracing.* a horse which performs well in morning track work, but not in races. [from *morning glory* a climbing plant with delicate flowers, which are at their peak in the morning]

morph[1] *v.* to alter shape. [extracted from *metamorphosis*]

morph[2] *n.* morphine.

Moscow *n.* **1.** a pawnshop. *–v.* **2.** to pawn. *–phr.* **3. gone to** (or **in**) **Moscow,** in pawn.

mosey *v. Originally US.* to amble; stroll; saunter: *Mosey on down; just moseying along.* [origin unknown]

mosh *v.* **1.** to dance in a mosh pit. *–n.* **2.** the crush of moshers in a mosh pit. [probably a variant of *mash* to squash]

mosher *n.* one who takes part in moshing.

moshing *n.* a form of dance, similar

to, but less violent than, slam dancing, in which the crowd is tightly packed together.

mosh pit *n.* the area in front of a stage at a concert where moshing takes place.

mossie *n.* a mosquito. Also, **mozzie**.

mother *n.* 1. the most extreme example of its kind: *the mother of all wars*. 2. *Offensive and derogatory.* a mother-fucker.

mother-fucker *n. Offensive and derogatory.* a person or thing which arouses exasperation, irritation, contempt, etc. Also, **mother; muthafucka**.

mother-fucking *adj, adv. Offensive.* an obscene intensifier: *You mother-fucking arsehole; a mother-fucking enormous sponge cake.*

motor-head *n.* a car enthusiast.

motor-mouth *n. Derogatory.* a person who talks too much, or talks very rapidly.

motza *n.* 1. a large amount of money, especially a gambling win. –*v.* 2. to bet a large amount of money: *to motser a horse*. Also, **motser**. [? from Yiddish *matse* bread; in English *bread* = money]

move *n.* 1. a choice or decision about a course of action: *So you've decided to forgive him? Bad move!* –*phr.*
2. **get a move on,** hurry up.
3. **if it moves, shoot it; if it doesn't, chop it down,** a jocular summing up of the Australian attitude to clearing and settling the land.
4. **move it or lose it,** a warning indicating that one should move whatever it is one has in the way.

mozz *phr.* **put the mozz on (someone)**, to jinx (someone); to cause (someone) to have bad luck. [short for *mozzle*]

mozzie *n.* a mosquito.

mozzle *n.* luck, especially bad luck. [Hebrew *mazzal* luck; which word also appears in *shemozzle*]

Mr Nice Guy *phr.* **no more Mr Nice Guy,** See **nice**.

Mrs Palmer *phr.* See **Palmer**.

muchly *adv.* very much: *ta muchly*.

muck-up day *n.* the last day of attendance at high school, traditionally a day of student pranks.

mudlark *n. Horseracing.* a horse that performs well on wet tracks. Also, **mudrunner**.

muff *n.* 1. the vagina or vulva. 2. a failure. –*v.* 3. to perform clumsily, or bungle: *He muffed it.*

muff-diver *n. Crass.* a person who practises cunnilingus. Also, **muff-muncher**.

mug *n.* 1. the face. 2. a fool; one who is easily duped. 3. one who is not of the underground fraternity. 4. a victim of a criminal. 5. a prostitute's client. 6. (amongst showies, carnies, etc.) a customer. –*v.* 7. to assault and rob. 8. *Older slang.* to smooch (someone). –*adj.* 9. stupid: *a mug copper*. –*phr.* 10. **mug up,** to study hard. [def 1 possibly in reference to drinking mugs with faces on them, as toby mugs]

mug lair *n.* (a term of general contempt) a flashily dressed young man of especially brash and vulgar behaviour.

mug shot *n.* a photograph of a person, usually of the head only, taken in compliance with an official or legal requirement.

mulga *phr.* **the mulga,** the outback.

mulga wire *n.* an unofficial communication, as by word of mouth; bush wire; bush telegram.

mull *n.* **1.** a preparation of dried leaves, as mint, comfrey, or tobacco, used to mix with marijuana or hash: *What are we gonna use for mull?* **2.** marijuana or hash mulled up or prepared for smoking. *–v.* **3.** Also, **mull up.** to prepare marijuana or hash for smoking, often by mixing it with some other substance as tobacco.

mull bowl *n.* a small bowl used to mull up marijuana.

mullet *n.* **1.** a stupid person. *–phr.* **2. stunned mullet.** See **stunned. 3. get a mullet up you,** an abusive expression; piss off; go to hell; fuck off!

mullet haircut *n.* a type of haircut, commonly worn by males, with the hair short all-over on top, but long at the back.

mull head *n.* a heavy marijuana user.

mull mix *n.* dried herbs for mulling with marijuana, used to soften to harsh effect of marijuana smoke on the throat.

mullock *n.* **1.** anything valueless; nonsense; rubbish. *–phr.* **2. poke mullock at,** to ridicule; make fun of. [from British dialect]

mullygrubber *n. Cricket.* a poorly executed bowl which bounces twice or more.

munchies *pl. n.* **1.** anything to eat, especially snacks between meals. *–phr.* **2. the munchies, a.** a craving for food resulting from smoking marijuana. **b.** any craving for food.

munchkin *n.* a person who is of small stature. [from the *Munchkins*, the dwarfish race in *The Wonderful Wizard of Oz* (1900), a novel by L Frank Baum, 1856-1919, American writer]

murder *n.* **1.** an uncommonly laborious or difficult task: *Gardening in the heat is murder. –v.* **2.** to ruin or wreck: *He absolutely murdered that song. –phr.* **3. get away with murder,** to avoid blame or punishment for (something).

Murphy's law *n.* a mock-scientific law which states 'If something can go wrong, it will go wrong'. [apparently with reference to a Captain E *Murphy* of the Wright Field-Aircraft Laboratory in 1949]

Murrumbidgee whaler *n. Hist.* a swagman frequenting the Australian inland rivers, who sustained himself by begging and fishing. [from *Murrumbidgee* a river in NSW and *whaler* a person who fishes for Murray cod]

muscle *n.* **1.** power: *institutional muscle; people muscle –phr.* **2. muscle in (on),** to force one's way in(to), especially by violent means, trickery, or in the face of hostility, in order to obtain a share of something. **3. flex one's muscles,** to display one's power.

muscle car *n.* a powerful car with aggressive detailing.

muscle man *n.* **1.** a very strong man; a man of unusually impressive and powerful physique. **2.** a man who regularly uses violence, or the

muscle man threat of violence, to further the interests of his employer or himself.

muscle Mary *n.* a strong, masculine male homosexual.

mush *n.* See **moosh**.

mushie *n.* a mushroom.

mushroom *n. Jocular.* a person who is deliberately kept ignorant and misinformed. [from the practice of growing mushrooms in the dark and feeding them with manure]

muso *n.* a musician.

muss up *v.* to make a mess of: *hair all mussed up.*

muthafucka *n. Offensive and derogatory.* See **mother-fucker**. [representing US Black English pronunciation]

mutt *n.* **1.** a dog, especially a mongrel. **2.** a simpleton; a stupid person. [from *mutton-head*]

mutton *n.* **1.** the penis. *–phr.*
2. dead as mutton, a. undeniably dead. **b.** dull; boring.
3. mutton dressed (or **done**) **up as lamb,** something made out to be better than it really is.
4. underground mutton, *Jocular.* rabbit meat used as food.

mystery bag *n.* **1.** a sausage. **2.** a meat pie.

myxo *n.* a highly infectious viral disease of rabbits, artificially introduced into Britain and Australia to reduce the rabbit population; myxomatosis. Also, **myxie.**

N

THE NET

The term *internet* is a blend of *international* and *network*, and has recently been shortened to simply *the Net*. The capitalisation is not really necessary, but it is very common, as is the form *the 'Net*, where the apostrophe is meant to stand for the missing *inter–*.

As more people are connected to the Net, more of its jargon will become familiar. Soon everyone will be talking about *netspot*, a site on the internet, *netsurfing*, looking for information on the internet, and even *netsex* which is similar to phone sex only conducted via the keyboard and terminal screen. Of course, when *surfing* the Net one should always keep within the limits prescribed by *netiquette*, the unwritten code of behaviour and protocol observed by seasoned users, or *netizens*.

N A R K

A *nark* was also known as a *copper's nark* and, amongst the criminal class, they were the worst of the worst, the dreaded police informer. This piece of slang comes originally from Britain and is one of a whole host of disparaging terms for this particular character. Apparently the word derives from the Romany *nak* meaning the "nose". This is presumably because they sniff out criminals for the police. They were also once called in Britain a *nose* or *noser*. Another disparaging Australian term for a *nark* was *police pimp*.

As a verb, to *nark* meant to exasperate or annoy. Thus anyone who was upset would say they were *narked*. And anyone who was liable to be easily annoyed or was just plain bad-tempered was known to be *narky*. In this way a *nark* is a wowser or party-pooper, anyone who puts a dampener on things, any stickler for rules that ruins the fun of a situation.

NOOKY

a bit of how's your father, a bit on the side, afternoon delight, banging, boffing, bonking, bouncy-bouncy, fucking, funny business, hanky-panky, jig-jig, knee-trembler, making babies, making whoopee, morning glory, naughty, poke, quickie, roll, roll in the hay, root, rumpy-pumpy, slap and tickle, the beast with two backs, tumble in the hay

STUCK FOR WORDS

nada *n.* nothing: *Best of all it's free, zip, zero, nada.* [from Spanish]

nads *pl. n.* the testicles. [shortened from *gonads*]

naff *adj. Chiefly Brit.* **1.** inferior; tasteless. *–phr.* **2. naff off,** to go away. [cf. northern British dialect *naffhead, naffin* a fool]

nail *v.* **1.** to secure by prompt action; catch or seize. **2.** to catch (a person) in some difficulty, a lie, etc. **3.** to kill. **4.** *Crass.* (of a male) to have sexual intercourse with. **5.** to perform an action or do something perfectly and confidently.

nail-biter *n.* an exciting game or match with a close finish: *The grand final was a real nail-biter.*

nana *n.* **1.** a banana. *–phr.*
2. do one's nana, to lose one's temper.
3. off one's nana, mad; deranged.

nancy boy *n. Derogatory.* **1.** an effeminate man. **2.** a male homosexual. Also, **nancy.**

nanny goat *n.* the tote. [rhyming slang]

nanosecond *n.* a very brief period of time: *With you in a nanosecond.*

narc *n.* a police officer from the narcotics squad. [from *narc(otics squad)*]

nark *n.* **1.** an informer; a spy, especially for the police. **2.** a whingeing, whining person; one who is always interfering and spoiling the pleasure of others; a spoilsport. *–v.* **3.** to irritate; annoy. **4.** to thwart; to upset someone's plans. **5.** to act as an informer. [from British underworld slang, originally meaning 'to watch', from Gipsy *nak* nose]

narky *adj.* irritable; bad-tempered.

narly *adj.* See **gnarly.**

Nasho *n. Obsolete.* **1.** national service. **2.** one who has been called up for national service.

natch *adv.* naturally.

national game, the *phr.* **1.** two-up. **2.** Australian Rules football.

Nats *pl. n.* members of the National Party or the National Party collectively.

natural foot *n.* a surfer who rides with the left foot in front of the right.

nature *phr.* **call of nature,** the need to urinate or defecate.

naughty *n.* an act of sexual intercourse: *a nightly naughty.*

NBG *adj.* no bloody good.

neato *adj.* excellent.

nebbie *n.* a nembutal, a form of sleeping pill.

neck *v.* **1.** to kiss, cuddle and pet, especially while seated. **2.** *Criminal.* to rob a person by seizing them about the neck. *–phr.*
3. get it in the neck, to be reprimanded or punished severely.
4. neck oneself, a. to hang oneself. **b.** to be the cause of one's own misfortune or downfall.

necking *n.* the act of kissing, cuddling and petting, especially while seated.

Ned Kelly *phr.* **as game as Ned Kelly,** very game; courageous.

neg *n.* a film negative.

neg driving *n.* the offence of negligent driving.

Nellie Bly *n.* **1.** a (meat) pie. **2.** a fly, either insect or trousers fly. **3.** a lie.

4. a tie. Also, **Nelly Bligh**. [rhyming slang]

nelly *phr.* **not on your nelly!** absolutely not!

Nelson's number *n.* a cricket score of 111; thought by the English to be unlucky. [because after his injuries Lord *Nelson* retained 1 arm, 1 leg, and 1 eye]

ner *interj.* an exclamation of ridicule, suggesting that what has just been said or done was stupid.

nerd *n. Originally US.* an idiot; fool. Also, **nerd-burger, nurd**. [origin uncertain; perhaps from the name of a character in Dr. Seuss's *If I Ran the Zoo* (1950)]

Net, the *n.* the Internet. Also, **the 'Net, the net**.

net chick *n.* a woman who uses the net.

netiquette *n.* the etiquette of good and bad behaviour on the Internet.

netizen *n.* a person who uses the Internet, especially one well-versed in the culture and etiquette of the Internet.

netsex *n.* the role-playing of engaging in sexual activities via the Internet.

netsurfing *n.* exploring the Internet.

neville *n.* an unpopular person; a nerd. Also, **Neville**.

never-never *n.* **1.** the hire-purchase system: *on the never-never.* –*phr.*
2. the Never-Never, sparsely inhabited desert country; a remote and isolated region.

newbie *n.* a new-comer to the Internet; one who is using the Internet but is not versed in its workings.

new chum *n.* **1.** a novice; one inexperienced in some field: *a new chum on the job.* **2.** *Hist.* **a.** a newly transported convict. **b.** a newly arrived British immigrant. Cf. **old chum**.

newshound *n.* a newspaper reporter.

newt *phr.* **pissed** (or **tight**) **as a newt,** extremely drunk.

NFI *abbrev.* no fucking idea.

Niagara Falls *pl. n.* the testicles. Also, **Niagaras**. [rhyming slang for 'balls']

nibs *phr.* **his nibs,** an arrogant or self-important man. [earlier also *nabs*; origin unknown]

nice *phr.*
1. no more Mr Nice Guy, no more acting nicely, being kind, generous, etc.
2. you'd be a nice (mate, friend, father, etc.), an ironic compliment.

nick[1] *n.* **1.** prison. –*v.* **2.** to capture or arrest. **3.** to steal. –*phr.*
4. in good nick, in good physical condition.
5. nick off, a. to leave, disappear. **b.** (used imperatively) piss off!
6. nick out, to go out for a short period.

nick[2] *phr.* **in the nick,** in the nude; naked.

nicked *phr.* **get nicked,** (used imperatively) piss off!

nifty *adj.* smart; stylish; fine: *a nifty little car.* [originally theatrical slang]

nig *n. Racist.* a Negro. [short for *nigger*]

nigel *n.* an unpopular person. Also, **Nigel**.

nigger *n. Racist.* **1.** a Negro. **2.** an Australian Aborigine. **3.** a member of any dark-skinned race. By extreme white racists extended to include Indians, Arabs, Mediterraneans, etc. –*adj.* **4.** denoting or pertaining to a Negro or dark-skinned person. –*phr.* **5. nigger in the woodpile,** a hidden snag.

nigger-lover *n. Racist.* a person who accepts Aborigines, Negroes, and dark-skinned people generally; a non-racist.

nightwatchman *n. Cricket.* a low order batsman, who is sent in to bat late in the afternoon when the batting-side captain wishes to preserve the better batsmen for the next day's play.

nig-nog *n. Racist.* a Negro or other black person.

nimby *n.* **1.** a person who protests against having necessary developments such as new prisons, hospitals, airports, military installations, homes for the disabled, etc., in the vicinity of their own home, although they would support such developments if they were located elsewhere. **2.** such a development. [acronym from the phrase *not in my back yard*]

niner *n.* a nine gallon keg of beer. Also, **nine.**

nineteenth hole *n.* the bar in a golf clubhouse.

ning-nong *n.* a simpleton.

Nip *n. Racist.* a Japanese person, especially a Japanese soldier. [short for *Nipponese*]

nipper *n.* **1.** a small child; a kid. **2.** a junior lifesaver. **3.** *Building Trades.* one employed on a construction site to do small odd jobs, as make tea, buy lunch, etc.

nippy *adj.* **1.** (of the weather) cold. **2.** nimble; active.

nit[1] *n.* a foolish or stupid person.

nit[2] *interj. Older slang.* **1.** a word used to warn people engaged in some illegal activity that the police are coming. –*phr.* **2. keep nit,** to keep watch while some illegal activity takes place; to act as lookout. [in British 19th century slang also *nix*]

nit-keeper *n. Older slang.* a person who keeps watch for authorities while illegal activities are taking place; a lookout.

nitty-gritty *n.* **1.** the hard core of a matter: *Let's get down to the nitty-gritty.* **2.** sexual intercourse, especially hot, horny love-making.

nitwit *n.* a slow-witted or foolish person.

nix *n.* **1.** nothing. –*adv.* **2.** no. [German, variant of *nichts* nothing]

Noahs *n.* a shark. Also, **Noah's ark.** [rhyming slang]

nob[1] *n.* **1.** the head. **2.** Also, **nob-end**, **a.** the head of the penis. **b.** an annoying, socially rejected person; a dickhead: *He sat there by himself, looking like a real nob.* [variant of *knob*]

nob[2] *n.* a member of a social elite. [in Scottish *nab, knabb*; origin unknown]

nobble *v.* to disable (a racehorse), as by drugging it.

nobby *n.* a rough nodule of opal covered with dirt.

nob-end *n.* **1.** the head of the penis. **2.** an annoying, socially rejected person; a dickhead.

nob-sucker *n. Offensive and derogatory.* a despicable person.

nod *phr.*
   1. nod one's head, *Prison.* **a.** to plead guilty. **b.** to accept blame or responsibility for something.
   2. on the nod, on credit: *to bet on the nod.*
   3. the nod, a. approval or permission. **b.** unofficial assurance of a job, position, etc.

nod bet *n.* a bet taken on credit.

noddle *n.* the head.

nog *n. Racist.* a coloured person, especially a Vietnamese.

noggin *n.* the head.

nogoodnik *n.* a bad person. [from the phrase *no good* + *-nik*, Russian name element]

no-hoper *n.* **1.** one who displays marked incompetence: *He is a real no-hoper at tennis.* **2.** a social misfit. **3.** an unpromising animal, as a second-rate racehorse, greyhound, etc.

nointer *n. Tas.* a mischievous child; a brat. [from British dialect: a mischievous fellow, from *anointer*, presumably meaning 'one who needs anointing', from obsolete *anoint* to chastise, thrash, i.e. to consecrate by beating]

nollie *n. Skateboarding.* a manoeuvre similar to an ollie but off the nose of the board, rather than the tail. See **ollie**. [blend of *nose* and *ollie*]

no-neck *n.* a muscular, stupid man.

nong *n.* a fool; an idiot. Also, **ning-nong.**

nonny *n. Obsolete.* an act of sexual intercourse.

no-no *n.* something not to be done on any account: *In this house smoking is a no-no.*

non-scene *adj.* (of a homosexual) not partaking or involved in the public homosexual world, such as frequenting gay bars, etc. See **scene**.

non-starter *n.* something which has no chance of success, as an idea that is discounted as inherently impracticable.

no-nuts *n.* an effeminate male; a wimp; a wuss.

noodle *n.* **1.** a silly, stupid person. *–phr.* **2. use one's noodle,** to think for oneself. [? variant of *noddle*]

nooky *n.* sexual intercourse. Also, **nookie.**

nope *adv.* an emphatic form of *no*.

nork *n.* a woman's breast. Also, **norg.** [origin unknown; the suggestion that it is from *Norco* butter, the wrapping of which at one time featured a cow's udder, is pretty farfetched]

Norm *n.* an average citizen viewed as a non-participant in any kind of physical exercise while addicted to watching spectator sports on television. [from the name *Norm* 'the normal man' of the cartoon character devised for the *Life. Be in it* promotion campaign]

north and south *n.* the mouth. [rhyming slang]

North Shore Holden *n. Sydney slang.* a Volvo car.

nose *phr.*
   1. get up (someone's) nose, to irritate or annoy (someone).
   2. have a (good) nose for, a. able to search out or locate: *a good nose for bargains.* **b.** a propensity for; good sense of: *a good nose for business; a nose for pretension.*

3. keep one's nose clean, to follow rules and regulations meticulously so as to avoid any blame.
4. on the nose, a. smelly; objectionable; decayed; stinking (especially of rotten organic matter, as food). **b.** unpleasant; distasteful.

nose job *n.* cosmetic surgery done to the nose.

nose rag *n.* a handkerchief.

nosh *v.* **1.** to eat; have a snack or a meal. *–n.* **2.** anything eaten, especially a snack. [from Yiddish]

noshery *n.* an eating house, restaurant or cafe.

nosh-up *n.* a meal.

nosy parker *n.* a person who continually pries; a meddler; a stickybeak. Also, **nosey parker.**

not *adv.* used after a sentence to negate the previous statement: *That's a nice shirt. Not!*

now *adj.* very fashionable, trendy: *a very now dress.*

nozzle *n.* the nose.

NRG *n.* See **hi-NRG**. Also, **nrg**.

nubile *n.* a young, attractive female.

nuddy *phr.* **in the nuddy,** in the nude.

nudge-nudge, wink-wink *interj.* an expression suggesting an innuendo, especially in relation to sexual activities. [from a Monty Python sketch]

nugget *n.* **1.** a short muscular man or animal. **2.** a hard knob of faeces.

nuggety *adj.* (of a person) solidly built; stocky.

nuh *adv.* no.

nuke *n.* **1.** a nuclear device. **2.** to destroy utterly by, or as if by, a nuclear bomb. **3.** to cook in a microwave oven.

nullabat *n.* See **alibi.**

number *n.* **1.** an article of clothing: *Her new dress is a cute little number.* **2.** an attractive woman: *that blonde number who lives out of town.* **3.** a theatrical piece; a routine. **4.** a song. **5.** a meal: *a nice pesto number. –phr.*
6. one's number is up, a. one is in serious trouble. **b.** one is due to die.

number one *n.* **1.** Also, **number ones.** urination. **2.** *Navy.* the first officer.

number two *n.* defecation. Also, **number twos**.

numbnuts *n.* an ineffectual man.

numbskull *n.* a dull-witted person; a dunce; a dolt. Also, **numskull.**

numero uno *n.* **1.** oneself. **2.** the leader or most important person in any situation. [Italian: number one]

nup *adv.* no.

nurd *n.* See **nerd.**

nut *n.* **1.** a foolish or eccentric person. **2.** an insane person. **3.** a testicle. **4.** an enthusiast. **5.** the head. *–v.* **6.** to headbutt. *–phr.*
7. do one's nut, to be very angry, anxious, or upset.
8. hard nut to crack, a. a difficult question, undertaking, or problem. **b.** a person who is difficult to convince, understand, or know.
9. nut out, to think out; solve (a problem, a plan of action, etc.).
10. off one's nut, a. mad; insane. **b.** crazy; foolish.

nuthouse *n.* a mental hospital. Also, **nut factory.**

nuts *pl. n.* **1.** the testicles. *–interj.* **2.** an expression of defiance, dis-

gust, etc.: *Nuts to you!* –*adj.* **3.** crazy; insane. –*phr.*
4. do one's nuts over, to become infatuated with.
5. nuts on (or **over**), overwhelmingly attracted to: *I'm nuts over her.*
nutso *adj.* crazy; mad.
nutter *n.* a crazy or foolish person.
nutty *adj.* **1.** silly or stupid; crazy. –*phr.* **2. nutty as a fruitcake,** completely mad.

nyet *adv.* no. [from Russian]

nympho *n. Derogatory.* a promiscuous woman; often used disparagingly of a woman who is not really promiscuous but whose sexual aggression frightens a man. [from *nymphomaniac*]

OLLIE

The first really big skateboarding craze was in the 1970s. The skateboarding tricks back then were quite simplistic compared with those of today. The coolest thing one could do was known as a *coffin*, this was performed by lying down flat on one's back on your deck and pretending to be a corpse in a coffin. Dag-o-rama! This sad state of affairs was changed however with the advent of the *ollie*. The term *ollie* derives from an American skater Alan Gelfand in 1979 – his nickname was Ollie. As the manoeuvres became more complex so did the jargon to describe them. Thus a typical description might run thus: *the dude nollie heel-flipped to nose slide down the handrail and blind side kick-flipped to fake over the bell curve on the bowl wall.* Clearly one has to be an adept to comprehend.

OPPOSITES

Teenagers have always enjoyed turning the language about-face and many have suggested that they do this in order to make their conversations inexplicable to adults, but, actually, this is not true – they have a far more sinister agenda…to annoy the hell out of adults. To use the word *bad* to mean *good* is the linguistic equivalent of wearing your baseball cap backwards, a thing that the older generation find inexplicably stupid since the sun-visor no longer forms any function. But then again most adults just don't know what *cool* is! Interestingly enough, the genesis of this quirk of the English language is not very well known. The use of *bad* to mean *good* originally is a feature of Black American English where it first meant "tough, mean, formidable", and hence it came to mean "wonderful". Here is a short list of words that were once relegated to describing the worst the world had to offer and are currently used to describe the ultimate in cool: **beastly, deadly, feral, hell, hellish, insane, killer, mad, outrageous, putrid, rancid, sick, vicious** and **wicked**.

OCKER

Alf (obsol.), ape, blockhead, bogan (Tas, WA), cougan, galoot, gorilla, hoon, larrikin (obs.), lunkhead, male chauvinist, male chauvinist pig, masher, MCP, meathead, no-neck, palooka, pig, real man, rugger-bugger, scozza, wide boy, yahoo, yob, yobbo

STUCK FOR WORDS

O *n.* **1.** *Sport.* offence. *–phr.* **2. the big O,** orgasm, especially female orgasm.

oater *n.* a western movie.

oath *phr.* **blood(y) oath,** a statement of emphatic agreement. Also, **my oath, my bloody oath, my colonial oath.**

obsess *v.* to become obsessive; to hold a fixation on (something).

ocker[1] *n.* **1.** the archetypal uncultivated Australian working man. **2.** a boorish, uncouth, chauvinistic Australian. **3.** an Australian male displaying qualities considered to be typically Australian, as good humour, helpfulness, and resourcefulness. *–adj.* **4.** relating to an ocker. **5.** distinctively Australian: *an ocker sense of humour.* [a nickname of *Oscar*, used by a character played by Ron Frazer in the television program *The Mavis Bramston Show* (1965-68)]

ocker[2] *n.* See **ockie strap.**

ockerdom *n.* the society of boorish, uncouth, chauvinistic Australians.

ockerina *n. Jocular.* an ocker's female counterpart.

ockie *n.* an octopus.

ockie strap *n.* a stretchable rope with hooks on either end used for securing luggage to roof-racks, etc.; an octopus strap. Also, **ocker.**

OD *n.* **1.** an overdose, especially of an injected addictive drug, as heroin. **2.** *Police, etc.* a person who has overdosed. **3.** a surfeit; oversupply: *a major chocolate OD. –phr.* **4. OD on, a.** to give oneself a drug overdose. **b.** *Jocular.* to have or consume to excess; have a surfeit of: *I OD'd on ice-cream; OD'ing on sex.*

odd bod *n.* an eccentric person, especially one with a particular fixation.

off *prep.* **1.** refraining from (some food, activity, etc.): *to be off gambling. –adj.* **2.** not functioning or working well: *having an off day.* **3.** offensive: *an off joke.* **4.** unwell; off-colour: *feeling a bit off. –phr.* **5. off like a bride's nightie,** off or away with the utmost speed. **6. off like a bucket of prawns (in the midday sun),** extremely rotten; stinking.

office bike *n. Offensive and derogatory.* a woman who has sex with many different men in her place of employment. [see *bike*]

offie *n. Cricket.* **1.** a ball bowled so as to change direction from leg to off when it pitches; off break. **2.** a bowler who specialises in off-break deliveries.

off-load *v. Rugby.* to pass the ball.

off-the-wall *adj.* bizarre; unusual.

oi *interj.* See **oy.**

oil *phr.* **the good** (or **dinkum**) **oil,** correct (and usually profitable) information, often to be used in confidence; the drum.

oiled *adj.* drunk.

oil rag *phr.* **live on the smell of an oil(y) rag,** to survive on the barest amount of food, money, etc.

oinker *n.* **1.** a pig. **2.** an ugly person; a person with piggish habits.

okey-doke *adv.* yes; all right; okay. Also, **okey-dokey.** [rhyming reduplication of *okay*]

old chum *n. Hist.* an experienced

colonist; one who had spent some years in the colony, especially in the outback. Cf. **new chum**.

old fart *n.* any old person: *even old farts, like myself.*

old lady *n.* **1.** one's mother. **2.** one's wife.

old maid *n. Derogatory.* a person with the alleged characteristics of an elderly spinster, such as primness, prudery, fastidiousness, etc.

old man *n.* **1.** one's father. **2.** one in a position of authority, as an employer. **3.** the penis. **4.** a very large kangaroo.

oldster *n.* an old or older person.

old-timer *n.* **1.** one whose residence, membership, or experience dates from a long time ago. **2.** an old man.

old-timer's disease *n. Jocular.* Alzheimer's disease.

old woman *n.* **1.** one's wife. **2.** one's mother. **3.** a fussy, silly person of any age or sex.

ollie *n. Skateboarding and snowboarding.* a manoeuvre in which one drives the board up into the air off a flat surface without holding the board, often in order to perform a jump over an obstacle. See **nollie**. [invented by Florida skater Alan 'Ollie' Gelfand in 1979]

on *phr.*
1. be on, a. to be willing or in agreement. **b.** to have placed a bet. **c.** habitually taking a drug: *on heroin.* **d.** currently under the effects of a drug: *could tell he was on eccy that night.*
2. have oneself on, to think oneself better, more skilled, or more important than one really is.
3. not on, not a possibility; not allowable: *To buy a car now is just not on.*
4. on for young and old, in a state of general disorder and lack of restraint.
5. on to, in a state of awareness; knowing or realising the true meaning, nature, etc.: *The police are already on to your little game.*

once-over *n.* **1.** a quick or superficial examination, inspection, treatment, etc., especially of a person viewed as a sexual object. **2.** a beating-up; act of physical violence.

oncer *n.* **1.** something done or made only once; something for the nonce. **2.** *Obsolete.* a one pound note.

one *phr.*
1. to one them, *Two-up.* to throw a head and a tail.
2. one for the road, a last alcoholic drink before beginning a journey.
3. only interested in one thing, (usually said as a warning about males) only interested in sex.

one-handed *adj.* (of literature, a magazine, etc.) pornographic: *one-handed reading.* [i.e. the other hand is engaged in masturbation]

one-hit wonder *n.* a band or musician who has only one big hit and then fades into obscurity.

one-two *phr.* **give (someone) the old one-two,** to punch (someone) with a left and a right.

onkaparinga *n. Older slang.* a finger. Also, **onka**. [rhyming slang from *Onkaparinga* the propriety name of a blanket]

onya *interj.* good on you! See **good**. Also (in the plural), **onyas**.

oodles *pl. n.* a large quantity: *oodles of money.*

oo-er *interj.* an exclamation of ironic remonstrance.

oont *n. Obsolescent.* **1.** a camel. **2.** an ugly boy. [originally Anglo-Indian, from Hindi]

oozle *v. Older slang.* **1.** to steal. **2.** to insinuate: *to oozle one's way into a party.*

op *n.* **1.** a surgical operation. **2.** an operator.

opener *phr.* **for openers,** to begin with; for starters: *Well, for openers, the guy is a known Melrose Place watcher.*

open slather *n.* a situation in which there are no restraints, often becoming chaotic or rowdy; free-for-all.

operator *n.* one who successfully manipulates people or situations: *He's a pretty smooth operator.*

optic *n.* a look; an ogling look. Also, **optic nerve.** [rhyming slang *optic nerve* perve]

optics *pl. n.* the eyes.

-o-rama *suffix.* **1.** a word element meaning surrounded by or inundated by a specified thing: *tack-o-rama.* **2.** a word element denoting a superb or extreme example of a specified thing: *spunk-o-rama.* Also, **-a-rama.** [as used in the names of products, denoting 'all around', extracted from *panorama, diorama*]

orchestras *n.* the testicles. [rhyming slang *orchestra stalls* balls]

order of the boot *n.* the sack; dismissal.

oscar *n.* cash, money. [rhyming slang *Oscar Asche*, Australian actor, 1871-1936]

osteo *n.* an osteopath.

ouch *n.* something that hurts, especially financially: *But the $500 fine was the big ouch.*

out *v.* **1.** to publicly expose someone's homosexuality. **2.** to admit publicly to some misdemeanour, etc.: *a number of public figures have outed themselves as having smoked pot.* **3.** *Sport.* to suspend from playing or partaking: *outed for the rest of the season.* **4.** to dismiss; exclude; sack. *–adv.* **5.** *Criminal.* (used with a specifying number) in a group of that number; thus *one out* - alone, *two out* - in company with another, *five out* - in a group of five, etc. *–phr.*
6. get (the fuck) out of here, an expression of disbelief.
7. out of here, Also, **outta here.** to be leaving: *I'm outta here, see ya tomorrow.*
8. out of it, a. incapacitated as a result of taking drugs or alcohol. **b.** in a dreamy or vague state of mind, as if under the influence of drugs or alcohol.
9. out to it, a. unconscious. **b.** asleep. **c.** dead drunk. **d.** completely exhausted.
10. run of outs, a succession of bad luck or unfortunate happenings.

out-dipper *n. Cricket.* a ball bowled so that it swings from leg to off.

outer *n.* **1.** an open betting place near a racecourse. *–phr.* **2. on the outer, a.** excluded from the group; mildly ostracised. **b.** penniless.

outfit *n.* a band or group of musicians.

out-gun *v.* to beat convincingly in a contest.

171

outie *n.* **1.** a protruding belly-button; a navel that sticks out, as opposed to an *innie*. **2.** a person with such a navel.

outing *n.* **1.** *Horseracing.* a race taken part in (by a horse): *It was his first outing since a spell of 3 months; continues to improve with each outing.* **2.** an instance of public exposure of someone's homosexuality.

outrageous *adj.* cool; excellent; unreal.

outside *n.* **1.** *Prison.* the world outside prison. *–phr.* **2. get (oneself) outside,** to eat or, especially, drink: *Get yourself outside this beer.*

out there *adj.* **1.** extremely cool; excellent; unreal. **2.** actively participating in life, an event, etc.; taking part.

over *phr.*
 1. be all over, to show great affection towards; be excessively attentive to: *She was all over him as soon as he entered the room.*
 2. over the top, excessive.

over-the-shoulder boulder-holder *n.* (*amongst children*) a joking term for a bra.

Oxford scholar *n.* a dollar. Also, **Oxford.** [rhyming slang]

oy *interj.* **1.** an exclamation calling for attention. **2.** an exclamation used after a statement. Also, **oi**.

Oz *n.* **1.** Australia. *–adj.* **2.** Australian.

PRAT

The term *prat* for an annoying person, a jerk, or someone you just can't stand has been heard in Australia since the 80s. In Britain it is a very common term, and in America it turns up occasionally. The ultimate origin is not known, but its current sense comes from its earlier meaning of "buttock". This was a slang word of the 16th century amongst the criminal and vagabond class. It is first recorded in a book from 1567 which detailed the language, the scams and devious tricks used by tramps and other itinerants of the day. This early meaning of *prat* of course is still current in the theatrical slang term *prat-fall* a staged, heavy fall on the buttocks.

PONCE

Ponce was originally a word for a pimp, a man who lived off the earnings of a prostitute. The word comes from Yiddish, and ultimately from the north German coarse slang word *Punze* meaning "vagina". The typical *ponce* was also a bit of a dandy who enjoyed dressing up in a flash manner. In Australia it was often changed to *poonce* (pronounced with the vowel sound of *foot*). Also, here it was used to mean an effeminate man or a male homosexual. Thus it was a term of general abuse amongst ocker males for many years. Another possible variant of this is the word *poon*. In the Australian vernacular this means a fool or idiot, a stupid or useless person. An early appearance of this word is in Eric Curry's *Hysterical History of Australia* (1940) where the jocular schoolteacher who is given to insulting his pupils calls them "peripatetic poons". This may not seem to be closely related to the flashy *ponce*, but to be *all pooned up* meant to be dressed in a flashy manner, just as the *ponce* was wont to do.

PEDAL TO THE METAL

all stops out, at a rate of knots, at warpspeed, barrelling along, belting along, breaking the sound barrier, burning rubber, fanging, going flat out, going flat-chat, going full pelt, going like a cut cat, going like a rocket, going like billy-o, hell for leather, hooning, like a bat out of hell, ripping along, scorching

STUCK FOR WORDS

P *phr.* **silent like the P in swimming** (or **the ocean**) (or **the sea**) (or **the surf**) **etc.,** a pun on the word *pee*, used humorously to explain the pronunciation of words beginning with a silent *p*, such as *psalm, pseudo,* etc. See **pee**.

pack *v.* **1.** to place drugs into a cone, bong, etc., preparatory to smoking them. *–phr.*
2. go to the pack, a. to degenerate; collapse. **b.** to give up; admit defeat.
3. pack death (or **'em**) (or **it**) (or **shit**), to be afraid.
4. pack it in, Also, **shit it in.** to win easily.
5. pack up (or **in**), to cease to function; to become useless.

packet *n.* a large sum of money: *to lose a packet at the races; earn a packet.*

pad *n.* a dwelling, especially a single room.

paddle face *n. Racist.* a person of South-East Asian extraction.

paddock *n.* a sporting field.

paddock-basher *n.* an off-road vehicle.

Paddy *n.* **1.** an Irishman. *–phr.* **2. as Irish as Paddy's pigs,** very Irish. [familiar variant of Irish *Padraig* Patrick]

Paddy's lantern *n. Rural.* the moon.

Paddy's poke *n.* a cut made to a deck of cards by pushing out the middle section with a finger and placing those cards on top.

pair *n. Cricket.* getting out for zero in both innings. See **king pair**.

Paki *n.* **1.** *Often racist.* a Pakistani. *–phr.* **2. the Pakis,** the Pakistani Test Cricket team.

pal *n.* a good friend; a chum. [from Romany *plal* brother]

pally *adj.* friendly.

Palmer *phr.* **Mrs Palmer and her five (lovely) daughters,** a metaphor for the hand used in male masturbation.

palooka *n.* **1.** a stupid or clumsy boxer or wrestler. **2.** a dull, stupid male. [originally US; origin unknown]

palsy-walsy *adj.* overly and often sycophantically friendly.

panic button *phr.* **hit** (**press, etc.**) **the panic button,** to begin panicking or over-reacting.

pansy *n. Derogatory.* **1.** a male homosexual. **2.** Also, **pansy boy,** an effeminate man. *–v.* **3.** (of a male) to move in an effeminate way: *pansying along the street.*

pants *v.* **1.** to pull the pants off (someone), as a prank. *–phr.*
2. beat the pants off, to beat convincingly.
3. get into (**someone's**) **pants,** to have sexual intercourse with (someone).
4. have ants in one's pants, to be restless.
5. wear the pants, to be in charge; dominate.

pants man *n.* a woman-chaser; a womaniser.

panty-waist *n. Chiefly US. Derogatory.* an effeminate male; a wimp or wuss.

paperbag *phr.*
1. paperbag job, someone physically unattractive, especially facially, so that if one were to have

sex with them, one would need a paperbag to hide the head.
2. unable to fight one's way out of a (wet) paperbag, ineffectual; lacking strength; lacking spirit.

paralytic *adj.* completely intoxicated with alcoholic drink; very drunk. Also, **para**.

parking *n.* kissing, petting, and other amorous activities done in a parked car.

parra *n. Derogatory.* a tourist or visiting non-resident of a beach area. [? from *parasite*, or *Parramatta*, Sydney, considered as indicative of the classic type of westie visitor]

party *v.* **1.** to take part in a party; to really get into a party. *–phr.*
2. party hard, or **party hearty,** to party enthusiastically and for the duration of the party.
3. party on, to continue to party.

party animal *n.* **1.** a person who parties hard. **2.** a person who is always going to parties.

party hack *n.* a long-time, loyal member of a political party, especially one who does menial work for the party.

party pooper *n.* a person who has a discouraging or depressing effect, especially at a party.

pash *n.* **1.** a session of passionate kissing, especially French kissing. **2.** a long, passionate, deep kiss. *–v.* **3.** Also, **pash off.** to kiss passionately; to French kiss; to suck face.

pass *n.* a request, often couched slyly, for sexual intercourse: *Do you think that was a pass he just made? That was definitely a pass!*

pasting *n.* **1.** a beating or thrashing. **2.** a tirade of abuse.

pat *phr.* **on one's pat,** all by oneself; alone. Also, **Pat**. [rhyming slang *Pat Malone* alone]

Pat *n.* an Irishman. Also, **Paddy**. [shortened form of common Irish name *Patrick*]

patch *n.* the club colours or insignia of a motorcycle club or bikie gang.

patsy *n.* **1.** a scapegoat. **2.** a person who is easily deceived, swindled, ridiculed, etc. [? Italian *pazzo* fool, lunatic]

pav *n.* a pavlova.

paw *n.* **1.** the human hand. *–v.* **2.** to handle clumsily. **3.** to fondle sexually, especially in an ungentle way.

pay *v.* **1.** to admit the truth of; acknowledge that one has been outwitted, especially in repartee or argument: *I'll pay that. –phr.*
2. pay one's dues, See **due**.
3. pay (someone) out, Also, **pay out on (someone). a.** to stir (someone), especially when they have made a blunder. **b.** to berate or scold (someone).

PB *n.* a sporting record that is one's personal best.

PC *adj.* **1.** politically correct. *–n.* **2.** political correctness.

peabrain *n.* an idiot; fool.

peach *n.* a person or thing especially admired or liked.

peachy *adj.* excellent; wonderful.

peak *v.* **1.** to climax sexually. **2.** to reach the height of drug-induced euphoria. **3.** to reach a climax of enjoyment.

peanut *n.* **1.** (*pl.*) any small amount, especially of money. **2.** an insignificant person. **3.** *Derogatory.* a small penis.

pearler *adj.* **1.** excellent; pleasing. *–n.* **2.** something impressive: *That new dress is a real pearler.* **3.** *Cricket.* a very good delivery. Also, **purler.**

pearl necklace *n. Crass.* blobs or beads of sperm ejaculated on the chest of a sexual partner. Also, **string of pearls.**

pecker *n.* **1.** the penis. *–phr.* **2. keep one's pecker up,** to remain cheerful; maintain good spirits, courage, or resolution.

pecs *pl. n. Weights.* the pectoral muscles.

ped *n.* a paedophile.

pedal *phr.* **be pedal to the metal,** to be driving a vehicle at top speed: *We were pedal to the metal when we passed a cop.*

pee *v.* **1.** to urinate. *–n.* **2.** an act of urination. [originally a euphemistic pronunciation of the first letter of the word *piss*]

peepers *pl. n.* the eyes.

peg *n.* **1.** *Obsolete.* a shilling. *–v.* **2.** to throw or toss (something). **3.** to observe; identify the true nature of: *to have someone pegged. –phr.*
4. peg out, to die.
5. take down a peg, to humble.
6. square peg in a round hole, a misfit.

pelf *n.* money or riches. [from Middle English, from Old French]

pelican shit *phr.* **a long streak of pelican shit,** a very tall and thin person.

pen *n.* prison.

pen and ink *n.* an alcoholic drink. [rhyming slang]

pencil *v. Horseracing.* to work as a bookmaker's clerk.

penciller *n. Horseracing.* a bookmaker's clerk, who writes out the betting tickets.

penguin *n. Derogatory.* a nun. [from the similarity of the markings of the bird to the black and white nun's habit]

penguin suit *n.* a dinner suit.

pen-pusher *n.* one who works with a pen, especially a clerk engaged in work considered to be drudgery. [also formerly *quill-pusher*]

pep *n.* **1.** spirit or animation; vigour; energy. *–phr.* **2. pep up,** to give spirit or vigour to. [short for *pepper*]

pep pill *n.* a stimulant drug in pill form.

Percy *n.* **1.** the penis. *–phr.* **2. point Percy at the porcelain,** (of a male) to urinate.

perfection *n. Surfing.* perfectly formed waves.

perk[1] *v.* (of percolator coffee) to percolate.

perk[2] *n.* a fringe benefit or bonus; something given in addition to one's normal salary. [from *perquisite*]

perk[3] *v.* to vomit; to puke. Also, **perk up.** [imitative]

perve *n.* **1.** *Originally.* a sexual pervert, either **a.** a person, especially a man, whose interest or indulgence in sex is outside of that socially sanctioned, or, **b.** a person with a sexual interest that is considered perverted or unnatural; a person with a particular sexual kink. **2.** a person who is being sexually obtrusive; a person who is leering: *Rack off, you old perve.* **3.** an act of voyeurism; a look taken for the sake of sexual observation: *having a bit of a perve*. **4.** a person who is in the habit of watching others voyeuristically; a person addicted to perving. **5.** an attractive person; one who is worth perving at. –*adj.* **6.** suitable for perving; pornographic: *real perve material*. –*v.* **7.** *Obsolete.* to act in a sexually perverted way; to be a sexual pervert. **8.** to watch a person lustfully; to look at someone in order to assess their sexual attributes. Also, **perv**. [a shortening of *pervert*]

pestiferous *adj.* mischievous, troublesome, or annoying.

peter *n.* **1.** a till; cash register. **2.** *Prison.* a prison cell. –*phr.*
3. black peter, *Prison.* a punishment cell devoid of light or furniture.
4. tickle (or **rat**) **the peter,** to ring up false amounts on a cash register, so as to pocket the extra money.

peth *n.* pethidine, an analgesic.

petrolhead *n.* a person who is an enthusiast for driving or racing motor cars.

pew *n.* a chair; any place to sit down: *take a pew*.

phase *n.* See **faze**.

phat *adj.* excellent; cool; all okay: *Everything is phat*. [a respelling of *fat* (def 3)]

phizzgig *n.* See **fizgig**.

phone phreak *n.* a person who hacks into a telephone system.

phoney *adj.* **1.** not genuine; spurious, counterfeit, or bogus; fraudulent. –*n.* **2.** a counterfeit or fake. **3.** a person who pretends to be something other than what they are; a poseur; a fake. Also, **phony**. [originally US; ? originally black English, and thus possibly from Mandingo *foni, fani* to be false, to lie]

phooey *interj.* an exclamation denoting contempt, disbelief, rejection, etc. [variant of *phew*]

phreak *v.* **1.** to break into a telephone network. **2.** to break into a secure computer system; to crack.

phunk *n.* funk music.

phunky *n.* See **funky**.

phut *phr.* **go phut,** to collapse, become ruined.

physio *n.* **1.** physiotherapy. **2.** a physiotherapist.

piano *n.* one thousand dollars. [presumably a shortening of *grand piano*, from *grand* a thousand dollars]

piccie *n.* picture, as a photograph, illustration, etc. Also, **piccy, pickie**.

pick *v.* **1.** to begin a fight with (someone): *Do you know who you're picking?* –*phr.*
2. don't pick your nose or your head will cave in, an expression deriding another's intelligence.
3. pick a winner, to pick snot from one's nose.
4. pick (someone's) brains, to find out as much as one can, from someone else's knowledge of a subject.
5. pick up, to acquire (a partner) for a sexual encounter.

pickle *phr.* **in a pickle,** in a predicament.

pickled *adj.* drunk.

pick-up *n.* **1.** a casual acquaintance for sexual intercourse. **2.** a pick-up truck. **3.** a player who is not a regular part of the team. *–adj.* **4.** composed of whoever happens to be around: *a pick-up game; a pick-up jazz band.*

pick-up line *n.* a prepared opening line of conversation intended to get someone interested in having a casual sexual relationship.

picnic *n.* **1.** an enjoyable experience or time. **2.** an easy undertaking. *–phr.*
3. a few sandwiches short of a picnic, See **short**.
4. be no picnic, (of an event, chore, etc.) to be difficult or unpleasant, despite not being considered so by many: *Organising a fashion parade is no picnic.*

piddle *v.* **1.** to urinate. *–phr.*
2. piddle around, to do anything in a trifling or ineffective way; dawdle.

piddling *adj.* very small; insignificant.

piece *n.* **1.** *Derogatory.* a woman: *She's a nice little piece. –phr.*
2. a piece of cake, an easily achieved enterprise or undertaking.
3. a piece of piss (to a trained digger), an easily achieved enterprise or undertaking.
4. take a piece out of, to reprimand severely.

pie-eyed *adj.* drunk.

piffle *n.* **1.** nonsense; idle talk. *–v.* **2.** to talk nonsense.

piffling *adj.* trivial; petty; nonsensical.

pig *n.* **1.** a person or animal of piggish character or habit, especially one who eats too much, or eats messily. **2.** someone who does not share things out evenly; a hog. **3.** *Derogatory.* a police officer. **4.** *Rugby Union.* a forward. **5.** *Car sales.* a dirty car. *–v.* **6.** Also, **pig it,** to live, lie, etc., as if in a pigsty; live in squalor. *–phr.*
7. pig out, to eat a great deal.
8. pigs! Also, **pig's arse** (or **bum**) (or **ear**)! an exclamation of contempt, derision, denial, etc.

pig dog *n.* **1.** a bull terrier. **2.** *Rural.* a dog used for hunting wild pigs.

pig ignorant *adj.* extremely ignorant.

pig-out *n.* **1.** a session or period of overeating. **2.** a meal at which there is excessive eating. Also, **pigout**.

pig-swill *n.* inferior or unpleasant food.

pike *phr.*
1. pike on (**someone**), to let (someone) down; abandon: *Don't pike on me now.*
2. pike out, to go back on an arrangement; opt out: *He piked out on the deal.* [from old cant *pike off* depart, from Middle English *pike* to go away, cf. Danish *pigge af* to hasten off]

piker *n.* **1.** one who opts out of an arrangement or challenge or does not do their fair share. **2.** one who lacks courage. **3.** *Obsolete.* one who gambles, speculates, etc., in a small, cautious way.

pile *n.* **1.** a large number, quantity, or amount of anything: *A pile of things to do.* **2.** a large accumulation of money. *–phr.*
3. pile it on. to exaggerate.
4. pile up, to accumulate; to form a backlog.

pile-driver *n.* a powerful punch, kick, stroke, etc.

pile-up *n.* **1.** a crash or collision, usually involving more than one vehicle. **2.** an accumulation; backlog.

pill *n.* **1.** a disagreeable, insipid person. **2.** *Sports.* a ball, especially in football, tennis, etc.

pillow *n.* **1.** a person who is a wimp, especially when playing sport. **2.** a type of biscuit, a 'Spicy Fruit Roll', made by the Arnott's company, and resembling a pillow in shape.

pillow biter *n. Crass.* the passive partner in anal intercourse.

pimp *n. Derogatory.* **1. a.** one who lives off the earnings of a prostitute, often being also a lover or boyfriend and providing protection. **b.** a man who has a number of prostitutes working for him. **2.** *Older slang.* **a.** a police informer; a police pimp. **b.** one who informs on others; a dobber. *–v.* **3.** to act as a pimp for a prostitute. **4.** *Older slang.* to inform; tell tales. [from 17th century English]

pimples *pl. n.* (a derogatory term for) breasts that are either small, or (of an adolescent) not fully developed.

pin *n.* **1.** (*pl.*) the legs. *–phr.* **2. pull the pin,** to stop; to cut short.

pinch *v.* **1.** to steal. **2.** to arrest. *–n.* **3.** an arrest. **4.** a tight situation: *if it came to a pinch; at a pinch. –phr.* **5. with a pinch of salt,** with some reserve; without wholly believing.

pineapple *n.* **1.** a $50 note. [from its colour] *–phr.* **2. rough end of the pineapple,** a raw deal; the worst part of a bargain.

ping *v.* **1.** to penalise: *got pinged for being off-side. –phr.* **2. ping off,** a euphemism for *piss off.*

pinhead *n.* **1.** a stupid person; a jerk. **2.** a person with a small head.

pink *adj.* **1.** of or pertaining to homosexuals or the homosexual community: *the pink dollar; the pink vote.* **2.** having Leftist tendencies.

pink elephants *n.* a hallucination reputedly experienced by alcoholics.

pink-eye *n. Obsolete.* **1.** cheap alcoholic liquor. **2.** a drinking bout.

pink fit *n.* a burst of anger; a tantrum.

pinko *n.* **1.** a Communist or Leftist sympathiser. *–n.* **2.** politically Left, or Communist. Also, **pinkie.**

pinnie *n.* a pinball machine.

pipe-opener *n.* See **heart-starter.**

pipes *pl. n.* the respiratory passages.

pipsqueak *n.* a small or insignificant person or thing.

piss *v. Sometimes offensive.* **1.** to urinate. **2.** to rain heavily: *It was pissing down. –n.* **3.** urine. **4.** an act of passing water; urination. **5.** alcoholic drink, especially beer. *–phr.* **6. all piss 'n' wind,** loquacious, but insincere.
7. a piss in the ocean, an insignificantly small amount or part.
8. on the piss, on a drinking spree.
9. piece of piss, See **piece.**
10. piss about (or **around**), to mess about.
11. piss (something) away, to waste; squander.
12. piss down, to rain heavily.
13. piss in (someone's) pocket, to behave obsequiously towards (someone).
14. piss in(to) the wind, to embark on a futile course of action.
15. piss it in, to do something with ease.

16. piss off, *Offensive.* **a.** to leave; go away. **b.** (used imperatively) go away!

17. piss (someone) off, a. to send (someone) away. **b.** to annoy (someone) intensely.

18. piss on, to beat convincingly.

19. piss (all) over, to beat or confound utterly.

20. take the piss out of (someone), to stir or make fun of (someone).

21. wouldn't piss on (someone or **something),** an expression proclaiming that (someone or something) is totally worthless, hopeless, etc.

22. wouldn't piss on (someone) if they were on fire, an expression of utter contempt.

23. wouldn't piss in (someone's) ear if their brain was on fire, an expression of utter contempt.

[from Middle English, from Old French *pisser* to urinate; onomatopoeic]

piss- *prefix.* very: *piss-awful; piss-easy.*

pissant *n.* **1.** a small, aggressive person. –*phr.*

2. drunk as a pissant, very drunk.

3. game as a pissant, very brave.

4. pissant around, to waste time; to fart about. [from *pissant* an ant, from *piss* urine, due to the smell given off by the ant; in Middle English *pissemyre,* from *mire* ant]

pissed *adj.* **1.** drunk. **2.** *Originally US.* extremely annoyed; pissed-off. –*phr.* **3. pissed as a fart, pissed as a newt, pissed as a parrot, pissed to the eyeballs,** very drunk.

pissed-off *adj.* disgruntled; fed up; thoroughly discontent.

piss-elegant *adj.* with pretensions to elegance.

pisser *n.* **1.** something bad; a bad outcome; a bummer. **2.** a pub. **3.** a urinal.

piss-fart *v.* to waste time.

piss fat *n. Crass.* a morning erection caused by a full bladder.

piss flaps *pl. n. Crass.* the labia of the vulva.

pisspot *n.* a drunkard; alcoholic. Also, **piss-head.**

pissproud *adj.* (of a penis) erect as a result of an overfull bladder.

piss-take *n.* **1.** a satirical version; a send-up. –*v.* **2.** to send up; to make fun of. [noun formed from the phrase *take the piss out of*]

piss-up *n.* an occasion on which a large quantity of alcohol is consumed by a group of people, as at a party, etc.

piss-weak *adj.* **1.** mean; despicable; shabby: *a piss-weak thing to do.* **2.** inadequate; disappointing; not up to standard. **3.** of weak character; cowardly; irresolute. Also, **piss-poor.**

pissy *adj.* **1.** unpleasant. **2.** mildly drunk. **3.** irritable. **4.** insignificant: *a pissy little thing.*

pit *n.* **1.** *Surfing.* the hollow tube of a breaking wave. –*phr.*

2. the pit, a. a mosh pit. **b.** a bowl for skateboarding.

3. the pits, a. the most unpleasant or most obnoxious (place, circumstance, condition, etc.). **b.** the armpits.

pitch *n.* **1.** a contrived piece of banter

pitch | **plonk**

used by salespeople to get a customer to buy. –*v.* **2.** to offer or suggest (an idea or concept). **3.** to vie or compete for or against. –*phr.*
4. pitch into, to attack verbally or physically.
5. queer (someone's) pitch, to upset (someone's) plans.

Pitt Street farmer *n. NSW.* one who owns a country property, often for purposes of tax avoidance, but who lives and works in Sydney. See also, **Collins Street cocky, Queen Street bushie**. [from *Pitt Street* a major street in Sydney]

pixie *phr.* **away (or off) with the pixies** (or **fairies**), **a.** daydreaming. **b.** mentally unsound. **c.** incapacitated by alcohol.

PJs *pl. n.* pyjamas. Also, **pjs**.

planet *phr.* **off the planet, a.** fantastic; wonderful. **b.** daydreaming. **c.** mentally unsound or eccentric. **d.** not in touch with reality. **d.** under the influence of a mind-altering drug.

plank *n.* a type of long and old-fashioned surfboard.

plant *n.* **1. a.** something or someone intended to trap, decoy, or lure. **b.** a spy. **2.** something hidden, often illegally. **3.** a place where stolen goods are hidden. **4.** a scheme to trap, trick, swindle, or defraud. –*v.* **5.** to deliver (a blow, etc.). **6.** to hide or conceal, as stolen goods. **7.** to place (evidence) so that, when discovered, it will incriminate an innocent person. –*phr.* **8. plant one's foot,** to quickly accelerate a car, etc.

plastered *adj.* drunk.

plastic *adj.* **1.** (of people, society, etc.) artificial; fake. **2.** Also, **plastic money**. a credit or ATM card, or such cards collectively: *Have you brought your plastic?*

plate face *n. Racist.* a South-East Asian.

plates of meat *pl. n.* feet. [rhyming slang]

platform game *n.* a video or computer game in which characters move through a two-dimensional world made up of various horizontal playing areas. Also, **platformer**.

platter *n.* a record.

play *phr.*
1. play around, a. to philander. **b.** to be sexually promiscuous. **c.** to engage in sexual play or sexual intercourse.
2. play ball, to cooperate.
3. play for keeps, to expect a decision, result, etc., to be permanent.
4. play (it) cool, to act cautiously.
5. play silly buggers, to act the fool.
6. play the field, a. to have as many flirtations as possible. **b.** to keep oneself open to advantage from a number of sources.
7. play up, a. to behave naughtily or annoyingly. **b.** to philander.
8. play up to, to attempt to get into the favour of.

played-out *adj.* exhausted; used up.

pleb *n.* **1.** a commonplace or ordinary person. [shortened form of *plebeian* from Latin *plebs* the commons of ancient Rome as contrasted with the patricians]

plonk *n.* **1.** any alcoholic liquor, especially cheap wine. –*phr.* **2. plonk artist** (or **fiend**) (or **freak**) (or **merchant**), an addict of cheap wine.

182

plonko *n.* a wine addict. Also, **plonkie**.

plop *n.* (*with children*) faeces. Also, **plop plop**.

plot *phr.* **lose the plot,** See **lose**.

plug *n.* **1.** the favourable mention of a product or the like on radio, television, etc.; an advertisement, especially unsolicited. **2.** a punch. **3.** a tampon. **4.** *Crass.* an instance of sexual intercourse. *–v.* **5.** to mention (a publication, product or the like) favourably and, often, repetitively as in a lecture, radio show, etc. **6.** to punch. **7.** to shoot. **8.** *Crass.* (of a male) to have sexual intercourse with. *–phr.* **9. plug away,** to work steadily or doggedly.

plugged-in *adj.* **1.** up with the latest technology; wired. **2.** having close ties; closely connected with and aware about: *very plugged-in with respect to the art world.*

plughole *phr.* **down the plughole,** wasted (as effort, money, etc.); ruined.

plug-ugly *adj.* extremely ugly.

plumb *adv.* **1.** completely or absolutely. *–n.* **2.** *Car sales.* a good car.

plum pud *adj.* good. Also, **plum pudd**. [rhyming slang]

plunder *v. Crass.* (of a male) to have sexual intercourse with.

plunge *v.* **1.** to bet a large sum of money. *–n.* **2.** a bet, especially a large bet.

plurry *adj., adv.* a euphemism for *bloody*.

po *n.* **1.** a chamber-pot. *–phr.* **2. full as a family po,** extremely full. [from French *pot (de chambre)*]

PO *abbrev.* a euphemism for *piss off*.

pocket *v.* **1.** to secrete in one's pocket. **2.** to steal (money or some small item). *–phr.* **3. in each other's pockets,** (of two people) constantly together.

pocket billiards *phr.* **play pocket billiards,** *Jocular.* (of a male) to fondle the testicles through the pants pockets. Also, **pocket pool**.

pocket boxer *n. Jocular.* a male who continually has his hands in his pockets in order to fondle the testicles.

poet's day *n.* Friday, the day on which people often leave work a little early. [acronym from the phrase *piss off early tomorrow's Saturday*]

pogo *n.* **1.** an annoying or despicable person. **2.** *Military.* any member of the clerical staff. [rhyming slang from *pogo-stick* prick]

point *phr.*
1. point Percy at the porcelain, See **Percy**.
2. point the bone, See **bone**.

poisoner *n.* a cook, especially a shearers' cook, etc.

poke *v.* **1.** *Crass.* (of a male) to have sexual intercourse with. **2.** to punch: *poked him one in the eye. –n.* **3.** a blow with the fist. **4.** *Crass.* the act of sexual intercourse.

pokey *n.* jail.

pokie *n.* (usually used in the plural) a poker machine.

Polack *n. Chiefly US. Derogatory.* a person of Polish descent. [from Polish *Polak* a Pole]

poley cup *n.* a cup which has lost its handle. [from *poley* (of an animal) dehorned or hornless]

police pimp *n. Older slang.* a police informer. See **pimp** (defs 2 and 4).

pollie *n.* a politician. Also, **polly**.

pommy *n. Derogatory.* **1.** an English person. *–adj.* **2.** English. Also, **Pommy, pom**. [probably from *pomegranate*, rhyming slang for 'immigrant'. Definitely not from the purported acronym POME, supposedly standing for Prisoner Of Mother England]

pommyland *n.* England.

ponce *n. Derogatory.* **1.** a male homosexual. **2.** an effeminate man; a wimp. **3.** *Older slang.* a pimp. **4.** *Obsolete.* the vagina or vulva. *–v.* **5.** to act as a pimp. *–phr.*
6. all ponced up, dressed up smartly; spruced up.
7. ponce about, to flounce; behave in a foolishly effeminate fashion. See **poonce**. [from British slang, from Yiddish *punse*, from German slang *punze* the female genitals]

poncy *adj. Derogatory.* effeminate; like a ponce.

pongo *adj.* **1.** smelly. *–n.* **2.** a smelly person.

pony *n.* **1. a.** *Obsolete.* the sum of 25 pounds. **b.** the sum of $25. **c.** the sum of $50. **2.** a small glass for beer or spirits.

poo *n.* **1.** (a euphemistic term for) faeces. **2.** manure. *–phr.*
3. in the poo, in trouble or bad favour.
4. poo oneself, to be vary scared.
5. the poos, (euphemistically) the shits. Also, **pooh, poo-poo**.

poo-brown *adj.* of a yucky brown colour reminiscent of faeces.

poo bum *n.* **1.** an annoying person; one who causes mild annoyance. *–interj.* **2.** an expression of mild annoyance or exasperation.

pooch *n.* a dog. [originally US; origin unknown]

pooey *adj.* disagreeable; unpleasant.

poofteen *n.* any number of; umpteen.

poofteenth *n.* a very small quantity or measure: *move it just a poofteenth.*

poofter *n. Derogatory.* **1.** a male homosexual. **2.** an effeminate male. Also, **poof**. [an early meaning of *poof* was 'a male prostitute' and is possibly derived from the French *pouffiasse* a prostitute; the form *poofter* appears later and is an extension of *poof*]

poofter-bashing *n.* **1.** assault on a male homosexual. **2.** verbal attacks on men in public life reputed to be homosexuals.

poofter-rorter *n.* **1.** *Prison.* a prisoner who gets other men to have sex with him. **2.** one who assaults and robs homosexual men.

poofy *adj. Derogatory.* effeminate; wimpy.

pooh *n.* See **poo**.

poo-jabber *n.* **1.** *Derogatory and offensive.* a male homosexual. **2.** a mild term of abuse.

poon *n.* **1.** *Derogatory.* a stupid, useless person; an idiot; fool. *–phr.*
2. pooned up, all dressed up to go out; togged out in one's finest. [? from *poonce*]

poonce *n. Derogatory.* **1.** a male homosexual. **2.** an effeminate male. *–phr.*

3. poonced up, dressed up smartly; spruced up.

4. poonce about, to flounce; behave in a foolishly effeminate fashion. See also **ponce**. [variant of *ponce*]

pooncey *adj. Derogatory.* effeminate.

poop[1] *v.* to tire or exhaust. [origin unknown]

poop[2] *n.* **1.** excrement. –*v.* **2.** to void excrement: *pooped his pants.* [from British dialect, earlier, to fart]

poopcatchers *pl. n.* **1.** loosely fitting short breeches, gathered at the knee. **2.** any loose-fitting pants with a low-hanging crotch. Also, **poocatchers**.

pooped *adj.* exhausted.

poove *n. Derogatory.* a male homosexual. [affecting a camp pronunciation]

pop *v.* **1.** (of a pimple) to break through the outer layer of skin and thus form a small open wound. **2.** to burst a pimple with applied digital pressure. **3.** (of the ears) to suddenly adjust to a new level of air pressure. **4.** to hold the nose and close the mouth and force air into the Eustachian tubes so as to adjust the pressure on the ear drums. **5.** to take a recreational drug orally: *popping eccy.* **6.** *Sport.* to kick (a ball) smartly, and usually only a short distance. –*n.* **7.** each: *They cost five dollars a pop.* –*phr.*

8. pop off, a. to depart, especially abruptly. **b.** to die, especially suddenly.

9. pop up, to appear suddenly: *He disappeared for a while and then 3 years later popped up in Hong Kong.*

10. pop the question, to propose marriage.

pop-out *n.* a mass-produced surfboard.

poppycock *n.* nonsense; bosh. [possibly from Dutch *pappekak* soft dung]

popster *n.* a pop musician.

p.o.q. *v.* to depart in a hurry. Also, **POQ.** [initialism from the phrase *piss off quick*]

pork *v. Crass.* (of a male) to have sexual intercourse with.

pork barrel *n.* **1.** a government appropriation, bill, or policy which supplies funds for local improvements designed to ingratiate legislators with their constituents. –*v.* **2.** to supply an inappropriate share of government funding to a project, etc., in order to gain support from constituents.

porker *n.* a pig.

porkie *n.* a lie. [rhyming slang *pork pie* lie]

porky *adj.* fat.

porn *n.* pornography. Also, **porno**.

porn queen *n.* a female pornography star. Also, **porno queen**.

port *n.* **1.** a suitcase. **2.** *Qld.* a shopping bag. [shortened form of *portmanteau*]

posh *adj.* **1.** elegant; luxurious; smart; first-class. [origin uncertain, probably from obsolete *posh* a dandy, also, money; almost certainly not from a supposed acronym of the phrase *Port Out; Starboard Home,* with reference to the better (i.e. cooler) accommodation on vessels sailing from Britain to India, Australia, etc.]

posse *n.* **1.** a gang of graffiti artists. **2.** any group of people.

possie *n.* a place; position: *Save me a possie next to you.* Also, **pozzy.**

possum *n.* **1.** a term of affectionate address: *Hello, possums; How are you possum?* **2.** *Criminal.* a victim of a swindle, con trick, etc. *–phr.* **3. play possum,** to feign illness or death.
4. stir the possum, See **stir.**

poster *n. Australian Rules.* a kick which hits one of the goalposts, scoring a point.

postie *n.* a mail deliverer.

pot *n.* **1.** marijuana. **2.** a medium sized beer glass; middy. **3.** the contents of such a glass. **4.** (*pl.*) a large quantity. **5.** a large sum of money. **6.** *Horseracing.* a heavily backed horse; favourite. **7.** a trophy or prize in a contest, especially a silver cup. *–v.* **8.** to take a pot shot; shoot. **9.** to capture, secure, or win. *–phr.* **10. go to pot,** to deteriorate.

pot and pan *n.* a man; one's man or boyfriend. [rhyming slang]

potato *n.* **1.** a woman or girl. [rhyming slang *potato peeler* sheila] **2.** a small hole in a sock through which skin is showing. **3.** See **couch potato**.

potatoes *phr.*
1. strain the potatoes, to urinate.
2. what's that got to do with the price of potatoes, a phrase used to question the relevance of a piece of information.

pot-head *n. Derogatory.* a person who smokes marijuana frequently; a marijuana addict.

potluck *n.* a random or haphazard choice. [from *pot luck* whatever food happens to be at hand without special preparation or buying]

potty *adj.* foolish; crazy.

pound *n. Prison.* the punishment cells in a prison.

pow *n.* powdery snow, good for skiing on.

powder *phr.*
1. powder one's nose, a. (of a female) to visit the ladies' room or toilet. **b.** *Jocular.* to snort cocaine.
2. take a powder, to depart; disappear.

powder puff *n.* a weak or effeminate male.

powerhouse *adj.* strong; powerful: *a powerhouse tackle.*

power-point *n. Racist.* a South-East Asian or Chinese person.

powwow *n.* any conference or meeting. [from Narangansett, an American Indian language]

pox *n.* **1.** any venereal disease: *a dose of the pox.* *–phr.*
2. a pox on (someone or **something)!** an expression of annoyance directed towards (someone or something): *a pox on panty-hose; a pox on the Council.*
3. pox off, (used imperatively) go away; piss off!
[an early spelling of *pocks* small pustules on the skin or the indents left by them, from Middle English *pokke*, from Old English *poc*]

pox doctor *phr.* **dressed up like a pox doctor's clerk,** dressed flashily, but in poor taste.

pox-head *n.* an unpleasant person.

poxy *adj.* unpleasant; distasteful; rubbishy.

pozzie *n.* See **possie**.

prang *v.* **1.** to crash (a car or the like). –*n.* **2.** a crash, especially a minor one, in a motor vehicle or the like. [onomatopoeic]

prat *n.* **1.** *Originally.* the buttocks; the arse. **2.** a fool; a jerk; an annoying person. –*phr.* **3. prat (oneself) in,** to intrude; to butt in. [British cant of the 16th century; origin unknown]

pratfall *n.* **1.** a heavy fall onto the buttocks. **2.** a specially practised fall onto the buttocks, as by a clown.

prawn *n.* **1.** a weak, spiritless, insignificant person: *He's a bit of a prawn.* –*phr.*
2. come the raw prawn (or **uncooked crustacean**), to try to deceive; delude: *Don't come the raw prawn with me.*
3. off like a bucket of prawns (left in the midday sun), extremely rotten; stinking.
4. prawn and porn night, a social event for men in which pornography is shown and prawns are served.

preggers *adj.* pregnant. Also, **preggie, preggies, preggo**.

pregnant rollerskate *n.* a Volkswagon car of the first type produced.

premmie *n.* **1.** an infant born prematurely. –*adj.* **2.** of or pertaining to such an infant. Also, **prem, premie**.

pressie *n.* a present. Also, **prezzie**.

pretty boy *n.* a young man with good looks but no strength of personality.

prick *n. Offensive.* **1.** a penis. **2.** an unpleasant or despicable person.

prick-features *n. Offensive.* a contemptible person.

prickle farmer *n.* a suburban or urban resident who takes up working a small block of land in a rural area.

prick-nose *n. Offensive.* an obnoxious person.

prickteaser *n. Offensive.* one who withholds sexual favours from a man after having encouraged expectation of them. Also, **cockteaser**.

prig *n.* a fastidious, self-important, smug person. [dating from the 18th century; origin unknown]

primo *adj.* first class; top quality.

pro *n.* **1.** a professional. **2.** a prostitute. **3.** problem: *No pro bro.* –*adj.* **4.** professional.

prob *n.* a problem.

problem *phr.* **no problems,** a conventional way of maintaining that there is nothing at all to worry about, everything is in hand and under control. Also, **no problemo, no probs**.

prole *n.* a member of the proletariat. Also, **prol**.

prong *n. Offensive.* the penis.

pronto *adv.* promptly; quickly. [from Spanish: quick]

prop *v.* to stop suddenly.

prossie *n.* a prostitute. Also, **prozzie**.

proverbial *phr.* **the proverbial,** used as a polite substitute for the word *shit*: *like a pig in the proverbial.*

provo *n.* a military police officer. [short for *provost-marshal*]

psst *interj.* a sibilant utterance used

to secretively gain someone else's attention.

psych v. **1.** to prepare psychologically, especially for a competition, stressful situation, etc.: *psyched themselves into it; psyching up the players for the final.* –*phr.* **2. psych out,** to cause an opponent to become flustered; to upset an opponent's mental composure.

psyched *adj.* fully enthused and excited; really going off.

psycho *n.* **1.** an insane person. **2.** a psychopath. –*adj.* **3.** insane or obsessional. **4.** psychopathic. **5.** wildly angry: *They went absolutely psycho.*

pub *n.* a hotel. [short for *public house*]

pub band *n.* a band that regularly plays at pubs.

pubbo *n.* a kid from a public school.

pub crawl *n.* an outing in which a series of pubs are drunk at in succession.

pube *n.* a pubic hair.

pudding *n.* **1.** Also, **pud, pudden.** a small, fat person. **2.** Also, **pudding head.** a stupid person. –*phr.* **3. in the pudding club,** pregnant. **4. pull one's pudding** (or **pud**), (of a male) to masturbate.

puffer *n.* **1.** a device used by asthmatics to assist inhalation of medication; inhaler. **2.** (*with children*) a steam locomotive. **3.** someone smoking a cigarette.

puke *n.* to vomit. [probably imitative]

pull *v.* **1.** *Horseracing.* Also, **pull up.** to prevent (a horse) from running on its merits. **2.** to successfully attract (someone) in order have sexual intercourse with: *pulling chicks.* **3.** to draw back on a bong and smoke a cone of marijuana. –*n.* **4.** influence, as with persons able to grant favours. **5.** the ability to attract or draw audiences, followers, etc.: *An actor with box office pull.* **6.** a drag on a cigarette, bong, etc. –*phr.*
7. pull in, a. to arrest. **b.** to earn (as a wage or salary).
8. pull off, to succeed in achieving or performing (something).
9. pull oneself (**off**), to masturbate.
10. pull one's finger out, to stop being lazy, idle, or a waster.
11. pull one's head in, to withdraw; to mind one's own business.
12. pull one's pud (or **pudding**), See **pudding**.
13. pull the other one, or (**the other leg**), an expression of disbelief, etc.
14. pull the plug on, to prevent (someone) from continuing their present activities as by making some damning revelation, issuing an order, etc.
15. pull up, a. to finish an activity, etc.: *How did he pull up after the weekend?* **b.** *Horseracing* (of a jockey) to prevent (a horse) from running a race to the best of its ability.

pullie *n.* a pullover.

pulverise *v.* to defeat overwhelmingly, as a fighter.

pump *v.* **1.** *Crass.* to have sexual intercourse. **2.** Also, **pump out. a.** (of dance music) to be played loudly with the bass beat being so loud as to be felt physically: *the*

funk pumps loud and hard. **b.** (of a DJ, or a venue) to play music in this manner: *pumping out the latest toons; the place was really pumping.* **c.** to dance en masse: *the crowd was pumping.* **3.** *Surfing.* (of waves) to be frequent and large enough for good riding: *the sets are pumping.* –*phr.*
4. pump iron, to exercise with weights in order to build muscles.
5. pump up, a. to increase (the volume of recorded music). **b.** to inflate; to hype up.

pumped up *adj.* **1.** having the musculature engorged with blood from weight training. **2.** physically invigorated, as after strenuous exercise. **3.** brought to a peak of exhilaration and confidence; psyched up. Also, **pumped**.

Punch *phr.*
1. pleased as Punch, delighted; highly pleased.
2. no show without Punch, a. a phrase used to lament that a party, or other social event, was not very good because the most important guest was not present. **b.** a phrase used to suggest wryly that a particular person is always the centre of attention at social events. [from *Punch* the chief character in the puppet show 'Punch and Judy']

punchy *adj.* **1.** punch-drunk. **2.** forceful; vigorously effective.

punk *n.* **1.** *Obsolete.* a small-time criminal; a hoodlum. **2.** a punk rocker.

punt *v.* **1.** to wager. –*n.* **2.** a bet or wager. –*phr.*
3. take a punt, to take a chance.
4. on the punt, engaged in gambling: *spent a good weekend on the punt.*
5. the punt, gambling: *a love affair with the punt; went back to the punt full time.*

punter *n.* **1.** a customer; the person who is paying out money for something. **2.** a person attending a concert, entertainment, etc. **3.** a bettor on horse or dog races. **4.** *Derogatory.* (amongst snowboarders) a skier.

pup *phr.*
1. be sold a pup, to be the victim of some deception.
2. the night is (still) a pup, it is (still) early in the night.

puppy *phr.* **to be one sick puppy**, to be a very depraved person: *When he told me what he'd done, I said 'Hey man, you are one sick puppy.'* [from the image of a psychologically disturbed puppy who enjoys being spanked with a newspaper]

purler *n.* See **pearler**.

purple heads *n.* a type of marijuana.

purse-carrier *n. Derogatory.* a male homosexual.

pus-ball *n.* a pimple.

pus-face *n. Derogatory.* a person badly affected with acne.

push *v.* **1.** to place excessive or dangerous strain on: *You're pushing your luck.* **2.** to sell illegal drugs. –*n.* **3.** *Obsolete.* a gang of vicious city hooligans: *the Rocks push.* –*phr.*
4. push it, to be exorbitant in one's demands.
5. push off, to leave; go away.
6. push shit uphill (with a pointy stick), to attempt the impossible.
7. push the envelope, See **envelope**.

8. push up daisies, to be dead and buried.

9. push up zeds, See **zed**.

10. the push, dismissal; rejection; the sack: *She gave him the push.*

pushing *phr.* **be pushing (an age),** to be getting close to a specified age: *pushing 30; he's pushing 40.*

puss[1] *n.* **1.** a girl or woman. **2.** an ineffectual or weak person; a wimp or wuss.

puss[2] *n.* **1.** the face. **2.** the mouth. [from Irish *pus* lip, mouth]

pussy *n.* **1.** *Offensive.* the vagina or vulva; the female genitals. **2.** an ineffectual or weak person; a wimp or wuss.

put *phr.*

1. put away, a. institutionalised for reasons of mental illness: *He should be put away.* **b.** sent to jail. **c.** to eat voraciously.

2. put the boot in, a. to attack savagely by kicking. **b.** to attack without restraint. **c.** to take unfair advantage.

3. put in the fangs (or **hooks**) (or **nips**) (or **screws**), to borrow.

4. put out, (of a woman) to have sexual intercourse.

5. put the acid on, to put pressure on (someone) for a favour, especially a loan.

6. put the hard word on, See **hard**.

7. put up or shut up, to be prepared to support what one says or else remain silent.

putrid *adj.* excellent; cool; unreal.

pyjama game *n.* one-day cricket. [so called because of the colourful uniforms worn]

pyro *n.* a pyromaniac.

python *phr.* **siphon the python,** See **siphon**.

QUADS

This is shortening of the anatomical term *quadriceps*, the large muscle at the front of the thigh. Amongst body-builders this term has been used for decades, but it is only with the recent development of the gym culture that the word has become known by the wider population. The erudite anatomists who first dissected the human body and devised the now completely-ensconced medical nomenclature had no thought for the future body-builders and weight-trainers. Having to use such a silly word as *quadriceps* (which looks like a plural but isn't) is beyond the pale. Shortening is the natural thing to do. Thus we also get *abs* for the abdominal muscles, *delts* for the deltoid muscles, *lats* for the latissimus dorsi muscles. And don't forget the *pecs* for the pectoral muscles of the chest.

QUICHE-EATER

The original *quiche* was the *quiche Lorraine,* from the north-eastern French region of Alsace and Lorraine. This dish of savoury custard in a open pastry shell was originally a delicacy found only in fine French restaurants. During the 80s this item of cuisine was identified with the newly-emerging model of the modern male, that is, the sensitive, gentle, kind male who was in tune with the politically correct social issues and definitely not aggressive – the antithesis of the macho, Rambo type, the so-called *real man.* In 1982 the book *Real Men Don't Eat Quiche,* written by Bruce Feirstein, was released in the States, and an Aussie-oriented version, adapted by Alex Buzo, was released in Australia. It was a huge success, and the word *quiche-eater* was added to the long list of disparaging words for "effeminate" males – *wimp, pansy, poonce,* etc. The real *real men* of course loved having this new weapon in their arsenal. Joh Bjelke-Petersen, for instance, is reported to have said "The National Party is a real man's party – there are no *quiche-eating,* sandal-wearing trendies and no small 'l' Nationals." You can't argue with that.

QUOIT

berk, bonehead, boofhead, buffer, clod, clot, dill, dingbat, dolt, dope, drongo, dumbcluck, galah, goober, jerk, mug, sap, schmuck, twerp, twit, wally, waste-of-space

STUCK FOR WORDS

q.t. *adj.* 1. quiet. *–phr.* 2. **on the q.t.,** secretly.

quack *n.* any medical practitioner, not necessarily an inferior one.

quacker *n.* a Kawasaki bike.

quandong *n.* a person who cadges or imposes upon another.

queen *n.* 1. Also, **quean**. an effeminate male homosexual. *–phr.* 2. **queen it,** (of a woman) to act as a queen; to lord it over. See also, **beat queen, drag queen, drama queen, porn queen, size queen**.

Queen Street bushie *n. Qld.* one who owns a country property, often for purposes of tax avoidance, but who lives and works in Brisbane. See also, **Pitt Street farmer, Collins Street cocky**. [from *Queen Street* a major street in Brisbane]

queeny *adj.* effeminate; camp.

queer *adj.* 1. not simply straight-up-and-down heterosexual. 2. (of a male) homosexual. 3. mentally unbalanced or deranged: *queer in the head.* *–v.* 4. to spoil; jeopardise; ruin: *queer one's pitch.* *–n.* 5. a person who is not strictly heterosexual. 6. a male homosexual. *–phr.* 7. **queer for,** keen on; in love with. [def 2 of this word was probably originally US, and while used in the gay community, was never an exclusively gay term. Amongst homophobes it was used disparagingly, and still is. It has recently been reclaimed as a positive term by the gay/lesbian/transgender community and is now applied as in senses 1 and 5]

queer street *n.* a state of financial embarrassment. Also, **Queer Street.**

quiche-eater *n. Derogatory.* a man who is kind, gentle, and sensitive in his personal relationships and has a politically correct social consciousness; a male who holds a world view that is the antithesis of that held by a rugger-bugger or traditional ocker. [from the book *Real Men Don't Eat Quiche* (1982) by Bruce Feirstein]

quiche-eating *adj. Derogatory.* having the qualities of a quiche-eater.

quick-and-dirty *adj.* (of a computer program) hastily written, but still doing the job required, just not in an elegant way.

quickie *n.* 1. an act of sexual intercourse performed in a short space of time, often without getting fully naked. 2. anything taken or done quickly, as a quick drink. 3. something produced in a short space of time on a low budget and therefore of inferior quality. 4. *Cricket.* a fast bowler.

quid *n.* 1. (formerly) one pound in money; a pound note. 2. Also, **quids.** money, especially a large amount: *I'll bet that cost a quid or two.* *–phr.*

3. **a quick quid,** money earned with little effort, often by dishonest means.

4. **not for quids,** never; for no inducement at all: *wouldn't have missed it for quids.*

5. **not the full quid,** mentally retarded; dull-witted.

6. **wouldn't be dead for quids,** an phrase expressing great enjoyment of life. [from British slang; origin unknown]

quim *n.* the female genitalia. [origin unknown; possibly from Scottish *quim*, variant of Old English *queme* pleasure]

quince *n.* **1.** *Derogatory.* a male homosexual. *–phr.*

2. do one's quince, to lose one's temper.

3. get on someone's quince, to annoy, irritate.

quiver *n.* **1.** *Surfing.* a set of surfboards for different conditions. *–phr.* **2. a full quiver,** a large family.

quod *n. Older slang.* a prison. [originally British thieve's cant; origin unknown]

quoit *n.* **1.** the anus. **2.** the buttocks or arse. **3.** an annoying or obnoxious person. Also, **coit**. [from resemblance of the sphincter to the shape of a rope *quoit*]

RAINCOAT

The humble prophylactic sheath has numerous slang names, one of the earliest being *condom*. Dating back to the beginning of the 18th century the word was recorded, in the form *cundum*, in the *Lexicon Balatronicum, or, A Dictionary of Buckish Slang, University Wit and Pickpocket Eloquence* – a scandalous tome originally compiled by a Captain Grose, and later enlarged by a number of gentlemen including one fellow calling himself Hell-Fire Dick. This dictionary asserts that the device was invented by one Colonel Cundum, however, no-one has yet been able to verify this claim. A more recent term, dating to the mid-19th century, is *French letter*. As with *condom,* the origin of this term is also a bit of a mystery. One not very plausible story is that contraceptive sheaths became scarce in Britain and were only able to be obtained from France via the post – hence *French letter*. Interestingly, one French term for the *condom* is *capote anglaise*, which translates as "English hood". Despite the mystery with these terms, some other words are quite obvious. *Rubber* clearly refers to the material of construction, and *raincoat* is as plain a metaphor as you can get.

RAZOO

The *razoo*, brass or otherwise, made its appearance in Australian English in World War I, where it was part of the soldiers' slang. No-one knows what the origin of this word is – some suggest Egyptian, others nominate the British Army in India as the source. Another suggestion is that it is a playful variation on "sou", as in the expression "not a sou", which dates back to the late 1700s. Mind you, various helpful people have attempted to fill in this gap in our history by creating a coin, usually with inscriptions along the lines of "the original one-and-only authentic brass razoo". I suppose that it is intriguing to manufacture a material coin, the purpose of which is to state that it has absolutely no value whatsoever, except its wealth of historical allusion.

RUDDY

bally, blamed, blankety, blanky, blasted, bleeding, bloody, blooming, blowed, confounded, damned, darned, doggone (US), dratted, effing, flaming, flipping, flogging, freaking, frigging, fucken, fucking, fugging, mother-fucking, plurry, son-of-a-bitching

STUCK FOR WORDS

rabbit[1] *n.* **1.** a fool. **2.** *Cricket.* a player who is not very good at batting. –*phr.* **3. root like a rabbit,** to have a great deal of sex.

rabbit[2] *phr.* **rabbit on,** talk nonsense, usually at length. [rhyming slang *rabbit and pork* talk]

rabbit ears *pl. n.* an indoor television antenna with two adjustable arms. Also, **rabbit's ears.**

rabbit-killer *n.* a short, sharp blow on the nape of the neck or lower part of the skull. Also, **rabbit-punch, rabbit-chop.**

race *phr.*
1. race (someone) off, to take (someone) to a secluded spot for sexual intercourse.
2. race off with, a. to leave a place, party, etc., with (a person) for sexual intercourse. **b.** to elope with.

racehorse *n.* a thinly rolled cigarette or joint.

rack *n.* **1.** a passionate kiss or French kiss. **2.** large breasts. –*v.* **3.** to rob; to steal or shoplift. **4.** to French kiss; kiss passionately. –*phr.*
5. rack off, to leave; go: *He racked off ages ago; Rack off, hairy legs!*
6. rack up, to amass.

racket *n.* **1.** an organised illegal activity such as the extortion of money by threat or violence from legitimate businessmen: *the protection racket.* **2.** a dishonest scheme, trick, etc. **3.** one's legitimate business or occupation: *He's in the advertising racket.*

radical *adj.* **1.** wonderful; fantastic. –*interj.* **2.** an exclamation expressing great approval. Also, **rad.**

Rafferty's rules *pl. n.* no rules at all. [British dialect *rafferty* irregular, linked by association with the Irish surname *Rafferty*]

rag *n.* **1.** a newspaper or magazine, especially a local one. **2.** a handkerchief. **3.** *Derogatory.* a woman, usually implying that they are promiscuous. –*phr.*
4. chew the rag, a. to argue or grumble. **b.** to brood or grieve.
5. on one's rags, (of a woman) menstruating.

rage *n.* **1.** an event at which people have unadulterated fun; an event that really goes off; a really good time: *That party was a rage; had a rage of a weekend.* –*v.* **2.** to partake in a rage; to have a really excellent time: *going out raging; Rage with us man!*

rager *n.* a person who parties hard and long.

ragga *n.* a type of dance music, similar to jungle and featuring reggae samples.

rag-top *n.* a convertible car.

rail *phr.*
1. off the rails, insane; out of control.
2. on the rails, a. *Horseracing.* running on the inside of the field, against the inner railings. **b.** functioning in a normal manner.

railroad *v.* to send or push forward with great or undue speed: *to railroad a bill through parliament.*

railway tracks *pl. n.* dental braces.

raincoat *n.* a condom.

rainmaker *n.* *Australian Rules.* a very high kick.

rake *n.* *Rugby.* a hooker.

rake-off *n.* **1.** a share or portion, as of a sum involved or of profits. **2.** a

rake-off   **ratbag**

share or amount taken or received illicitly.

ralph *v.* to vomit. Also, **ralf**. [imitative]

ram *n. Older slang.* **1.** a trickster or confidence man, especially one who sets up victims for another. –*v.* **2.** to work as a con artist's accomplice. [origin uncertain]

Rambo *n.* an aggressive, macho male. [from *Rambo*, the hero of the film *First Blood* (1982) based on the novel *First Blood* (1972) by David Morrell]

rammies *n.* pants; trousers. [representing a broad Australian pronunciation of *round mes*, from rhyming slang *round me houses* trousers]

ramp *v. Prison.* **1.** to search a prisoner or prison cell. –*n.* **2.** such a search. [origin uncertain; ? from *rampage*]

rancid *adj.* cool; excellent; unreal.

randy *adj.* **1.** interested in sex and sexuality beyond the level generally seen as normal; extremely lustful; lecherous. **2.** sexually aroused.

rank *adj.* very bad; pathetic; daggy; disgusting.

rap *n.* **1.** Also, **rap-up**. an appraisal, especially a favourable one: *gave it a real rap*. **2.** punishment or blame, especially for a crime one did not commit: *to take the rap*. **3.** a criminal charge: *a housebreaking rap*.

rapster *n.* a rap musician; a person into rap music or rap dance.

rap-up *n.* a criticism, especially a favourable one: *gave it a great rap-up*.

rash *phr.* **to be all over (someone) like a rash, a.** to excessively and sycophantically attentive to (someone). **b.** to smother (someone) in kisses and cuddles; feel or fondle (someone).

rashie *n. Surfing.* a lycra garment worn under a wetsuit for prevention of wettie rash. Also, **rashy, rash vest**.

raspberry *n.* **1.** a sound expressing derision or contempt made with the tongue and lips. –*v.* **2.** to make such a sound. [rhyming slang *raspberry tart* fart]

rat *n.* **1.** one who abandons their friends or associates, especially in time of trouble. **2.** *Derogatory.* a chihuahua. **3.** a person considered as wretched or despicable. –*v.* **4.** to desert one's party or associates, especially in time of trouble: *three of the delegates ratted this morning*. **5.** to continue at work during a strike; to work as a scab. **6.** *Mining.* **a.** to pilfer opal from a miner's hiding place. **b.** to enter someone's mine and take out opal rock. –*interj.* **7.** (*pl.*) an exclamation of annoyance, incredulity, denial, or disappointment. –*phr.*
8. like a rat up a rope (or **a drainpipe**), very quickly.
9. not to give a rat's (**arse**), not to care at all.
10. rat on, a. to inform (on); betray. **b.** to go back on a statement, agreement, etc.
11. rat on stilts, a greyhound.
12. rat through, to sort through in a careless or hasty manner.
13. smell a rat, to be suspicious.

ratbag *n.* **1.** a worthless, despicable, unreliable person. **2.** a person of eccentric or nonconforming ideas or behaviour; a queer person; a weirdo.

rat cunning *n.* shrewdness; slyness.

rat-fink *n. Originally US.* a despicable person.

rathouse *n.* a psychiatric hospital.

ratshit *adj. Sometimes offensive.* **1.** useless; broken. **2.** depressed or unwell. **3.** no good: *That exam was ratshit.* Also, **R.S.**

rat tamer *n.* a psychologist or psychiatrist.

rattle *v.* **1.** to disconcert or confuse (a person). *–phr.* **2. rattle your dags,** (a command to) hurry up!

rattler *n.* **1.** a train. *–phr.* **2. jump** (or **scale**) **the rattler,** to board a train illegally.

rattletrap *n.* **1.** a shaky, rattling object. **2.** a run-down vehicle that makes rattling noises when in locomotion.

ratty *adj.* **1.** worn-out; shabby. **2.** slightly eccentric.

rave *n.* **1.** an entertainment event in which the patrons are primarily provided with a large dance space (typically a warehouse or an outdoor clearing), typical raver dance music, and the presence of amphetamines. Normally as a once-off event as opposed to a regular event at a fixed venue. **2.** a type of dance music as played at raves. **3.** a wild or hectic party or the like. **4.** a long and animated conversation. **5.** an event or time that was particularly exciting: *Last weekend was a real rave. –v.* **6.** to attend a rave. [Middle English, probably from Old French *raver* wander, be delirious]

raver *n.* a person who attends a rave; a person into the rave scene.

raw *adj.* **1.** harsh or unfair: *a raw deal. –phr.*
2. come the raw prawn, See **prawn.**
3. the raw, a. a crude, uncultured state: *The play portrayed life in the raw.* **b.** naked; nude: *She sleeps in the raw.*

razoo *phr.* **1.** (used in negative contexts) a (fictional) coin of little value. *–phr.*
2. not have a (brass) razoo, to have no money at all.
3. not worth a (brass) razoo, to be of no value. [origin unknown; not actually the name of any particular coin]

razor gang *n.* a government committee which reviews all expenditure with the aim of cutting back wherever possible.

razz *v.* **1.** to deride; make fun of; chiack. *–n.* **2.** severe criticism; derision. [short for *raspberry*]

razza *n.* a Returned Services League (RSL) club.

RDO *n.* a rostered day off.

real *adv.* **1.** really; very: *It was real good. –phr.*
2. for real, a. actual; definite: *That overseas trip is for real.* **b.** genuine; sincere: *He's for real; Are you for real?*
3. real man, *Often derogatory.* an overtly masculine male.
4. the real McCoy (or **thing**), the genuine article.

ream *v.* See **rim.**

recovery party *n.* a party held after a big event at which people who have been out all night can continue partying.

red *adj.* **1.** politically Left or Communistic. *–n.* **2.** Also, **Red.** a person with strong political leanings to the Left; a Communist.

redback *n.* a $20 note.

Redfern *phr.* **get off at Redfern,** to practise coitus interruptus. [from *Redfern* a railway station immediately before Central Railway Station, Sydney]

red-hot *n.* **1.** enthusiastic; keen; avid. **2.** extreme; outrageous. **3.** highly sexually aroused or arousing. **4.** currently the most favoured: *a red-hot favourite.* Also, **red hot**.

red hots *pl. n. Horseracing.* harness racing. [rhyming slang *red hots* the trots]

red-line *v.* to rev an engine beyond the prescribed limits. [referring to the red line on a tachometer]

red-ragger *n.* a person who holds a Communist or socialist political point of view.

reefer *n.* a marijuana cigarette. [from *reef* a part of a sail which is rolled up]

ref *n.* referee.

reffo *n. Racist.* a refugee.

Reg Grundies *pl. n.* underwear. Also, **reggies, reginalds, grundies**. [rhyming slang for 'undies', from *Reg Grundy* a well-known television producer]

rego *n.* registration.

rehab *n.* **1.** rehabilitation. **2.** the rehabilitation ward of a hospital.

reject *n.* a socially unacceptable person; a nerd.

rellie *n.* a relative. Also, **rello, relly**.

rels *pl. n.* one's relatives: *The rels are coming over on Sunday.*

rent-a-crowd *n.* an audience which is induced to attend a function for reasons other than their own entertainment; an audience procured directly by the organisers of an event.

rent boy *n.* a young male homosexual prostitute.

reo *n. Surfing.* a surfing manoeuvre performed on the top of a wave.

rep *n.* **1.** a representative: *union rep.* **2.** reputation: *worried about your rep.* *–adj.* **3.** representative: *a rep match.*

repro *n.* a reproduction, as of an antique.

Reps, the *n.* House of Representatives.

reptile *n.* an unscrupulous news reporter.

resto *n.* a restored antique, vintage car, etc.

retard *n.* **1.** an awkward or clumsy person. **2.** a socially unacceptable person; a nerd.

retent *n.* See **anal retent**.

retread *n.* a person who has come out of retirement to take up work again.

retro *n.* **1.** a fashion and music taste harking back to the previous decades. *–adj.* **2.** (of music) dating anywhere from the 1950s to the 1980s.

rev *n.* **1.** a revolution of an engine. **2.** (*pl.*) engine power: *running out of revs.* *–v.* **3.** to engage an engine while in neutral or with the clutch disengaged. *–phr.* **4. rev up,** to turn a disengaged engine over. **b.** to excite; to stir up: *revving up the supporters.*

revhead *n.* a motor car enthusiast.

rhubarb *n.* **1.** confused gabbling noise, as of people talking in the background. **2.** nonsense; rubbish. [from the word *rhubarb* supposedly spoken by actors to simulate noisy conversation in the background]

ribuck *adj. Obsolete.* **1.** very good, genuine: *a ribuck shearer. –interj.* **2.** an exclamation of agreement; all right. Also, **ryebuck**. [earlier in British slang *rybeck* profit, from Yiddish or German *reibach* profit]

rice grinder *n. Derogatory.* a Japanese motorcycle.

Richard *phr.*
1. have had the Richard, a. to be ruined. **b.** to be worn out.
2. Richard the third, a. a piece of excrement. **b.** an act of defecation. [def 1 a euphemistic version of the phrase *had the dick*; def 2 rhyming slang for 'turd']

ride *v. Crass.* **1.** to have sexual intercourse with. *–n.* **2.** an act of sexual intercourse. *–phr.* **3. ride the tan track,** to be the active partner in anal intercourse.

rider *n.* a snowboarder.

ridgy-didge[1] *adj.* all right; true; correct; genuine; dinkum. [reduplicative of earlier *ridge*, from thieve's slang *ridge* gold or gold coinage]

ridgy-didge[2] *n.* refrigerator. [rhyming slang for 'fridge']

R-ie *n.* an RSL Club: *They have an under-18s disco every Friday night at the R-ie.*

rig *n.* **1.** Also, **rig-out**. costume or dress, especially when odd or conspicuous. *–phr.*
2. rig out (or **up**), to fit or deck with clothes, etc.
3. See **Territory rig**.

righto *interj.* an expression indicating approval or agreement. Also, **rightio, right-oh, righty-ho.**

rim *v.* **1.** Also, **ream**. to suck or lick another's anus for sexual gratification. *–phr.* **2. rim out,** *Basketball.* (of a shot) to roll around the rim of the hoop but not go in for a basket.

ring *n.* **1.** the anus. *–phr.* **2. ring in, a.** to substitute a racehorse or greyhound for another in a race. **b.** *Two-up.* to substitute a double-sided coin for a genuine one: *If you got caught trying to ring a two-header in, you'd probably be kicked to death.*

ringdinger *n. Derogatory.* a two-stroke motorcycle. [imitative of the noise (*ring-ding-ding-ding-ding*) of a two-stroke motorcycle engine starting up]

ringie *n. Two-up.* the person in charge of a two-up school.

ring-in *n.* **1.** a racehorse or greyhound substituted for another in a race. **2.** the act of making such a substitution. **3.** a person or thing substituted for another at the last moment: *Joe couldn't come, so I'm the ring-in.* **4.** a fraudulent person; a person pretending to be someone else; a phoney. **5.** someone from another place; an outsider.

rip *v.* **1.** to move along with violence or great speed. **2.** to be excellent. **3.** to surf, ski, skate, snowboard, etc. outstandingly. *–phr.*
4. let it (or **her**) **rip,** to begin, start, set in motion, an engine, etc.

rip / **rock**

5. let rip, a. to give free rein to anger, passion, etc. **b.** to utter oaths; swear.

6. rip into, begin rapidly, eagerly: *Let's rip into the housework.*

7. rip off, a. to overcharge. **b.** to swindle money out of.

8. wouldn't it rip you? an expression of annoyance, exasperation, etc.

ripe *adj.* **1.** ready; keen; eager. **2.** drunk. **3.** obscene or pertaining to obscenity.

rip-off *n.* **1.** something not worth the amount placed on it; an overpriced item. **2.** a system or situation in which people are unfairly done out of money.

ripped *adj.* heavily under the influence of drugs or alcohol; stoned.

ripper *n.* **1.** a surfboard rider, skater, snowboarder, etc. **2.** something or someone exciting extreme admiration: *You little ripper!* –*adj.* **3.** absolutely excellent: *a ripper movie.*

rip-snorter *n.* a person or thing made remarkable by some outstanding characteristic, as great strength, excellence, liveliness, beauty, etc.

rip-snorting *adj.* incredibly good; excellent.

risk *phr.* **no risk!** an exclamation of reassurance or approval.

rissole *n.* **1.** a Returned Services League (RSL) Club. –*phr.* **2.** *Theatre.* **do the rissoles,** (of entertainers) to perform shows in Returned Services League (RSL) Clubs.

roach *n.* **1.** a cockroach. **2.** the butt of a marijuana cigarette.

road *phr.*
 1. one for the road, a final alcoholic drink consumed before setting out on a journey.
 2. hit the road, to set out on a journey.

road-hog *n.* a motorist who drives without consideration for other road users.

roadie *n.* **1.** a person associated with a pop group who arranges road transportation, sets up equipment, etc. **2.** a bottle or can of beer consumed while driving. **3.** a bottle or can of beer consumed while driving used as a measure of distance: *It's a three-roadie trip.* **4.** the last alcoholic drink consumed before leaving: *Have you got time for a roadie?* [def 4 from the phrase *one for the road*]

road-test *v.* to test something by using it for a short while: *road-testing several types of letterhead.*

robber's dog *phr.* a dog such as would be owned by a petty thief, used as a metaphor for **a.** speed: *off like a robber's dog; run like a robber's dog.* **b.** ugliness: *head on 'im like a robber's dog.*

rock[1] *n.* **1.** a jewel, especially a diamond. **2.** (*pl.*) the testicles. –*phr.*
 3. get one's rocks off, a. (of a male or female) to orgasm. **b.** to gain pleasurable experience from: *He gets his rocks off on heavy metal.*
 4. on the rocks, a. close to a state of disaster or ruin. **b.** (of a marriage or relationship) liable to end soon. **c.** (of drinks) with ice-cubes: *Scotch on the rocks.*

rock[2] *v.* **1.** to upset someone's equanimity with a cutting remark, witty come-back, etc. **2.** to play rock'n'roll music: *Let's rock.* –*phr.*

3. rock on, to continue to play, listen or dance to rock'n'roll.
4. rock out, to play rock'n'roll music.
5. rock up, to arrive: *Look who's just rocked up.*
6. rock along, to go; visit; travel to: *Just rock along to the movies on Saturday.*

rock and roll *n.* **1.** the dole. *–interj.* **2.** to set out or go: *Okay everyone, let's rock'n'roll.* [def 1 rhyming slang]

rocker *n.* **1.** a young person of the early 1960s rocker sub-culture, characterised by delinquent behaviour and American-influenced dress, such as leather jackets, greased-back hair, etc. Seen as diametrically opposite to the **mod. 2. a.** a rock'n'roll performer. **b.** a fan of rock'n'roll.

rocket *v.* **1.** to move or travel quickly. *–phr.*
2. go like a rocket, a. to move fast. **b.** (of a machine) to function well.
3. put a rocket under, to stir (someone) to action.

rock hopper *n.* a person who fishes from coastal rocks.

Rockie *n.* a member of the Royal Australian Naval Reserve.

rock spider *n. Prison.* a child molester.

rod *n.* **1.** revolver; pistol. **2.** the erect penis. *–phr.* **3. have had the rod,** to be completely ruined.

rod-walloper *n.* a male who masturbates.

roger *interj.* **1.** an expression of agreement, comprehension, etc. *–v.* **2.** (of a man) to have sexual intercourse with (someone). [def 1 *Roger* (personal name) used in telecommunications as a name for *r*, used as an abbreviation for *received*; def 2 18th century British slang, from the personal name]

rogue *n. Horseracing.* a racehorse that is difficult to handle.

rogues' gallery *n.* a collection of portraits of criminals, as at a police station.

roid rage *n.* an attack of aggressive or violent behaviour characteristic of steroid abuse.

roids *n. pl.* steroids, especially when used as a drug of abuse.

roll *v.* **1.** to arrive at a place: *rolling up at six o'clock; just roll along whenever you like.* **2.** to upset someone's equanimity with a cutting remark, witty come-back, etc. **3.** to assault and rob a person. *–n.* **4.** a wad of paper currency. **5.** any amount of money. **6.** an act of sexual intercourse. *–phr.*
7. on a roll, enjoying a series of successes.
8. roll in the hay, an act of sexual intercourse.
9. roll over, a. (of a politician) to resign gracefully. **b.** to decide to confess to corrupt activities and at the same time inform against others.

Roller *n.* a Rolls Royce car.

rollie *n.* a hand-rolled cigarette. Also, **roll-your-own.**

rolling *phr.*
1. rolling drunk, very drunk.
2. rolling in money (or **it**), very rich.

romp *phr.*
1. romp in, to finish a race easily.
2. romp it in, to win a game easily.

Ron *phr.* **one for Ron,** a cigarette borrowed for later on. [punningly from *Ron* a man's name, standing for *'ron*, extracted from the phrase *(late)r on*]

roof *phr.*
1. **hit the roof,** become very angry; lose one's temper.
2. **raise the roof,** to create a loud noise.

rookie *n.* a raw recruit, originally in the army, and hence in any service, sporting team, etc. Also, **rooky.**

Rookwood *phr.* **crook as Rookwood,** extremely ill. [from *Rookwood* Cemetery in Sydney]

roost *v.* to kick (a football, etc.) very high.

rooster *phr.* **a rooster one day and a feather duster the next,** an expression describing the uncertainty of continued popularity or success.

root *n. Sometimes offensive.* 1. an act of sexual intercourse. 2. a person measured in terms of their sexual ability: *a good root.* –*v.* 3. to have sexual intercourse with. 4. a. to exhaust. b. to break; ruin. 5. to kick. –*phr.*
6. **root for,** *Originally US.* to give encouragement to, or applaud, a contestant, etc.
7. **root like a rabbit,** to have a great deal of sex.
8. **wouldn't it root you,** an expression of annoyance, exasperation, etc.

rooted *adj.* 1. exhausted. 2. frustrated; thwarted. 3. broken; ruined. –*phr.* 4. **get rooted,** *Offensive.* go away.

rootin'-tootin' *adj. Chiefly US.* noisy and high-spirited.

root rat *n.* a person who is notable for their sexual endeavours.

roots *adj.* of grassroots origin: *basic roots rock'n'roll.*

rort *n.* 1. a trick; lurk; scheme. 2. a wild party. –*v.* 3. to perform a rort. 4. to gain control over (an organisation, as a branch of a political party) especially by falsifying records. [backformation of *rorty*]

rorter *n.* a con artist operating on a small scale, as with worthless goods.

rort horse *n.* a horse whose form has been kept secret; a smokie.

rorty *adj. Obsolete.* wild; rowdy [from 19th century London slang; origin unknown]

roseleaf *v. Chiefly gay slang.* 1. to perform anilingus. –*n.* 2. an act of anilingus. [probably from French *faire feuille de rose* to lick the anus]

rotate *phr.*
1. **wouldn't it rotate you,** an exclamation of annoyance, disgust, etc. [euphemism for *wouldn't it root you*]
2. **go rotate,** (used in the imperative) an offensive request that someone leave you alone.
3. **go sit on that** (i.e. a held up finger) **and rotate,** (used in the imperative) an offensive request that someone leave you alone.

rotgut *n.* alcoholic liquor of interior quality.

rotten *adj.* extremely drunk.

rotten egg gas *n.* the gas hydrogen sulphide.

rottie *n.* a rottweiler.

rough *adj.* **1.** severe, hard, or unpleasant: *to have a rough time of it.* **2.** unpleasant or ugly: *a rough head.* *–n.* **3.** a rough person; a rowdy. *–phr.*
4. a bit rough, unfair, unreasonable.
5. cut up rough, to behave angrily or violently; be upset.
6. rough end of the pineapple, See **pineapple**.
7. rough it, to live without even the ordinary comforts or conveniences: *We roughed it all month long.*
8. rough up, to beat up or smack around, especially in order to intimidate.
9. rough trot, a spell of bad luck or misfortune.
10. sleep rough, to sleep in the street when homeless.

rough diamond *n.* a person without refinement of manner but having an essentially good or likeable personality. [a *rough diamond* is one that is uncut]

rough-house *n.* **1.** noisy, disorderly behaviour or play; rowdy conduct; a brawl. *–v.* **2.** to disturb or harass by a rough-house. *–adj.* **3.** tough and rugged; rowdy.

roughie *n.* **1.** one who is rough or crude. **2.** a shrewd trick; a cunning act. **3.** *Greyhound and horseracing.* a starter with little chance of winning the race; a long shot.

rough trade *n. Homosexual slang.* **1.** *Originally.* a non-identifying male homosexual who takes the active part in casual homosexual encounters, but never the receptive role. **2.** (now used in a less strict sense) casual sexual partners or pick-ups. See **trade**.

rouse *phr.* **rouse on,** to castigate; criticise severely. [from Scottish *roust* to shout, roar]

rozzer *n.* a police officer. [cf. French *rousse, roussin* a detective, police]

RS *adj.* ratshit.

rub *phr.*
1. rub it in, to remind someone repeatedly of their mistakes, failures or short comings.
2. rub out, to kill.
3. rub shoulders (or **elbows**), to come into social contact.
4. rub uglies, See **ugly**.
5. rub (up) the right way, to please.
6. rub (up) the wrong way, to annoy.

rubber *n.* **1.** a condom. **2.** car tyres: *putting new rubber on.* *–phr.* **3. burn rubber,** to drive a motor vehicle extremely fast.

rubber bands *phr.* **betting with rubber bands,** *Horseracing.* desperation betting or betting with the very last of one's money after a day of losses. [i.e. betting the rubber bands which at the beginning of the day held wads of money]

rubberneck *n.* **1.** an extremely or excessively curious person. **2.** a tourist.

rubber van *n.* a van which, in popular fancy, takes people to a lunatic asylum. Also, **rubber cart, rubber truck.**

rubbery *adj.* unreliable: *The budget estimates are a bit rubbery.*

rubbish *n.* **1.** *Sport.* any poor pass,

throw, kick, etc. **2.** *Cricket.* bowling that is easy to hit.

ruby-dazzler *n.* an excellent thing or person. Also, **bobby-dazzler**.

ruddy *adv., adj.* a euphemism for 'bloody': *I've a ruddy good mind to hit him.*

rude *adj.* **1.** inconsiderate; unfair; dismissive: *That's a bit rude.* **2.** unpleasant or ugly: *a rude head.*

rude finger *n.* the index finger. [so called because it is used when making *the finger*; see *finger*]

rugger-bugger *n. Derogatory.* a player (or former player) of Rugby Union or Rugby League who is keenly interested in Rugby and actively partakes in the ethos of the sport, which is noted for boisterous social behaviour, excessive beer-drinking, and a macho image.

rug-rat *n.* a small child, especially one at the crawling stage.

rule *v.* to be the best or greatest: *wogs rule okay; Rob ruled with the cleanest ollie kick-flip of the day.*

Rules *n.* Australian Rules Football. Also, **rules.**

rum *adj.* **1.** Also, **rummy.** odd, strange, or queer. *–phr.* **2. rum go,** harsh or unfair treatment.

rumble *v.* **1.** to take part in a fight, as between gangs. *–n.* **2.** a group fight, as between gangs. **3.** a milder version of this practised in the schoolyard. *–interj.* **4.** a call signalling the start of a schoolyard rumble.

rumpy-pumpy *n.* sexual intercourse.

run *phr.*
  1. have runs on the board, to be ahead or in a favourable position.
  2. run a book, to work as a bookmaker.
  3. run around, to behave promiscuously.
  4. run (around) with, to keep company with.
  5. run away with, a. to elope with. **b.** to win easily: *They ran away with the election.*
  6. run in, arrest.
  7. run off with, a. to steal. **b.** to elope. **c.** to leave one's spouse in order to co-habit with another person.
  8. run out on, to desert; abandon.
  9. run rings (a)round (someone), to perform with far greater success.
  10. the runs, diarrhoea.

run-around *phr.* **1. give (someone) the run-around,** to fob (someone) off with evasions and subterfuges. Also, **runround.**

run-in *n.* disagreement; argument; quarrel.

runner *phr.* **do a runner, a.** to escape by running, especially from a difficult situation. **b.** to leave a restaurant quickly to avoid paying the bill.

run-through *n. Crass.* an act of sexual intercourse.

runway *n.* the catwalk of a fashion parade.

rush *n.* a strong feeling of exhilaration and pleasure felt after taking a narcotic or stimulant drug.

Ruski *n. Derogatory.* a Russian. [from Russian]

rust bucket *n.* a badly rusted motor vehicle.

ryebuck *adj. Obsolete.* See **ribuck.**

S

SPAM

This word, a blend of *spiced* and *ham,* was coined by a New York actor by the name of Kenneth Daigneau, who reckoned that he had invented the terrific name for a product first, and then searched around for an appropriate product to attach it to. This story sounds apocryphal, but who are we to disbelieve? Certainly the name caught on. As apparently did the product itself. In Monty Python's second series of their *Flying Circus* there was a sketch set in a railway cafe where every single item on the menu contained *spam* as an ingredient. The sketch ended with the singing of a thoroughly silly song which repeated the word *spam* over and over again. This sketch, and its song, was well-beloved by the computer hackers and enthusiasts who were corresponding via the Internet way before the rest of the world had even heard of it. Hence, on the Internet *spam* is the equivalent of junk mail, though it is not usually advertising anything.

SCUMBAG

This word is one of a suite of words with interchangeable parts. The beginning parts are either *scum-*, *scuzz-* or *slime-*. To any of these may be added *-bag*, *-ball* or *-bucket*. Thus a *scumbag* may equally be called a *scuzzball* or a *slimebucket*, or a *slimebag* or a *scumbucket* – the choice is yours. This neat invention of three productive prefixes matched together with three productive suffixes allows the swearer to call a person by the same name without seeming repetitive. Of the suffixes it seems that the most useful is *-bag* since it also is used to form the words *sleazebag* and *wussbag*.

SLAUGHTER

annihilate, beat the stuffing out of, beat the tripe out of, cane, clobber, do, do like a dinner, donkey-lick, down, drub, get the best of, piss all over, polish off, pulverise, punish, shit all over, slay, thrash, trounce, wallop, whitewash, whop, wipe the floor with

STUCK FOR WORDS

sack *n.* **1.** dismissal or discharge, as from employment. **2.** a bed. *–v.* **3.** to dismiss or discharge, as from employment.

sacred site *n. Jocular.* a place of great significance: *that sacred site of Australian sport - the SCG.*

sad *adj.* so pathetic as to cause sadness; pitiful; hopeless; worthless: *That's a sad haircut, man.*

saddling paddock *n.* a place where sexual activities take place.

salami *phr.* **(play) hide the salami,** *Crass.* to have sexual intercourse.

Sallie *n.* **1.** a member of the Salvation Army. *–phr.* **2. the Sallies,** the Salvation Army.

salmon *n.* **1.** Also, **red salmon.** a twenty dollar note. **2.** *Obsolete.* a fifty pound note.

saltcellar *n.* either one of the hollows above the collarbones of thin people.

saltie *n.* a saltwater crocodile.

salt mine *n. Jocular.* (*usually plural*) a workplace in which work is fast-paced and gruelling.

Salvo *n.* **1.** a member of the Salvation Army. *–phr.* **2. the Salvos,** the Salvation Army.

sambo *n.* a sandwich. Also, **sammie, sammo.**

sammidge *n.* a sandwich. Also, **sangwich, sangwidge.**

Sandgroper *n.* a West Australian. Also, **sandgroper.**

sandshoe crusher *n. Cricket.* a ball aimed at the feet of the person batting. Also, **sandshoe ball.**

sanger *n.* a sandwich. Also, **sango.** [from *sang(wich)* + *-er*]

sangwich *n.* a sandwich. Also, **sangwidge.**

sarky *adj.* sarcastic.

sarvo *phr.* **the sarvo,** this afternoon.

sassy *adj.* impudent; saucy.

sauce *n.* **1.** impertinence; impudence. *–phr.* **2. fair suck of the sauce bottle,** See **suck.**

sausage *n.* **1.** Also **silly sausage.** (*used affectionately, especially to children*) silly person. **2.** the penis. *–phr.*
3. (play) hide the sausage, (of a male) to have sexual intercourse.
4. not a sausage, absolutely nothing.
[def 4 perhaps from rhyming slang *sausage and mash* cash]

savvy *v.* **1.** to know; understand. *–n.* **2.** understanding; intelligence; commonsense. [18th century, from pidgin English, from Spanish *sabe usted* you know]

scab *n.* **1.** a strike-breaker; a blackleg. **2.** a person who is mean or stingy. **3.** a person who asks for something for free, especially when they are able to afford it. *–v.* **4.** to work as scab labour. **5.** to ask for something for free; to bludge (something) from someone.

scabby *adj.* **1.** poor quality; bad; pathetic. **2.** mean or contemptible: *That was a scabby trick.*

scab-face *n.* an ugly, horrible person.

scads *pl. n.* a large quantity: *He has scads of money.* [origin unknown]

scag *n.* **1.** heroin. *–phr.* **2. scagged out,** wasted from taking drugs. [origin unknown]

scale *v.* **1.** to ride on public transport without paying a fare: *scale a rattler; scaling trains.* **2.** *Obsolete.* to defraud or cheat out of money.

scalp *v.* to buy tickets and sell them at other than official rates.

scalper *n.* one who buys tickets and sells them at other than official rates.

scam *n.* **1.** an illegal or unscrupulous business operation; a racket. **2.** a swindle; a confidence trick. **3.** current, relevant information: *What's the scam?* *–v.* **4.** to orchestrate an illegal or unscrupulous business or deal. **5.** to cheat or swindle (someone). [origin unknown]

scaredy-cat *n.* (*especially in children's speech*) a coward.

scarer *phr.* **put the scarers on (someone),** to frighten (someone).

scene *n.* **1.** the public places or establishments and life associated with a particular subculture: *the clubbing scene; the drug scene.* **2.** public homosexual life as that of gay bars, etc. **3.** a sexual relationship: *they had a scene going a while back.* *–adj.* **4.** (of a homosexual) partaking or involved in the public homosexual world: *a scene dyke; scene queen.* See **non-scene**. *–phr.* **5. a good (bad) scene,** a place or situation which has a good (bad) ambience.

scheisse *interj.* a euphemism for the exclamation *shit!* [from German *Scheisse* shit]

Schindler's *adj.* drunk. [rhyming slang *Schindler's List* pissed]

schizo *n.* **1.** a schizophrenic. **2.** (loosely) a person having an unpredictable character. *–adj.* **3.** suffering from schizophrenia; schizophrenic. **4.** (loosely) unpredictable in behaviour; liable to suddenly change disposition. Also, **schizoid**.

schlep *v.* **1.** to carry; cart or lug. *–phr.* **2. schlep around,** to traipse. [originally US, from Yiddish *shlep(pen)* drag, carry, also, to go somewhere unwillingly]

schlock *n.* low-grade material; rubbish, especially referring to entertainment. Also, **shlock**. [originally US, from Yiddish *shlak* a curse]

schlong *n. Crass.* a penis. [originally US, from Yiddish *shlang* penis, literally, snake]

schm- *prefix.* substituted for the beginning of consonants of a specific word when forming a reduplicative pair, and used to reject or deny the importance of that word: *I can't come I'm too old. Old, schmold! You can't get out of it that easily.* [originally US, from the beginning of many Yiddish words]

schmear *phr.* **the whole schmear,** the totality of a scheme, activity, etc. Also, **schmeer**. [originally US, from Yiddish *shmeer,* from *schmeeren* to spread]

schmick *adj.* **1.** very classy; done up amazingly well: *a really schmick car.* *–v.* **2.** to do up beautifully. Also, **smick**. [cf. German *schmuck* neat, spruce, smart]

schmo *n.* a foolish person; a goose. Also, **shmo**. [originally US; origin unknown; perhaps euphemistic alteration of *schmuck*]

schmooze *v.* **1.** to chat idly. **2.** to be servile and fawning in order to gain some personal benefit from those in influential positions. [originally US, from Yiddish *shmuesn* to chat, from Hebrew]

schmuck *n.* a stupid person; idiot;

schmuck fool. Also, **shmuck**. [originally US, from Yiddish *shmok* penis]

schnookums *n.* See **snookums**.

schnozzle *n.* the nose. Also, **schnoz, snoz**. [originally US, from Yiddish *shnoz*, from German *Schnauze*]

schoolie *n.* a holidaying school student who has just completed their final year exams; a teenager on a holiday during schoolies' week.

schoolies' week *n.* a week or so of holiday, especially at Surfers Paradise, Qld, taken by year 12 students after their final exams.

schtick *n.* a theatrical entertainment, especially one exhibiting gimmickry. Also, **shtick**. [originally US, from Yiddish, literally, 'piece', 'bit']

schtup *v.* to have sexual intercourse. Also, **shtup**. [originally US, from Yiddish *shtup* screw, literally, 'push', 'press', 'shove']

scooby *n.* a marijuana joint.

scope *v.* **1.** to look about; to look for. **2.** to watch.

score *n.* **1.** latest news or state of progress: *What's the score on Malcolm?* **2.** a prostitute's customer. **3.** the sum of twenty dollars. **4.** *Obsolete.* the sum of twenty pounds. –*v.* **5.** to get or obtain: *scored the job.* **6.** to be successful in obtaining a partner for casual sex. **7.** to obtain illegal drugs for personal use. **8.** *Horseracing, etc.* to win a race.

scour *v.* to search for sexual partners.

scozza *n.* a person who drinks a lot of alcohol and is very rowdy; a party animal; a yobbo. Also, **scozzer**.

scrag *n.* **1.** *Derogatory.* a woman, especially conceived of as unattractive. **2.** *Crass.* an act of sexual intercourse. –*v.* **3.** *Crass.* to have sexual intercourse. [variant of obsolete *crag, cragge* neck]

scrape *n.* **1.** an embarrassing situation. **2.** a fight; struggle; scrap. **3.** an act of sexual intercourse. [apparently originally in Aboriginal usage] **4. a.** a dilation and curettage of the uterus. **b.** an abortion.

scratch *adj.* **1. a.** a rhythmic scratching sound created by manually moving a vinyl record back and forth on a turntable causing the stylus to run in the record groove at speeds different to that intended. **b.** a genre of music utilising this technique. –*v.* **2.** to play music using scratch technique.

scratchie *n.* **1.** an instant lottery ticket. **2.** *Vic.* a type of public transport ticket.

screamer *n.* **1.** someone who is very vocal during sexual intercourse. **2.** *Surfing.* a very large wave. **3.** *Australian Rules.* a very high mark: *to pull down a screamer.*

screw *n.* (*often offensive when used for words equivalent in sense to* 'fuck'). **1.** an act of sexual intercourse. **2.** a person gauged according to their sexual prowess: *a great screw.* **3.** a prison warder. **4.** wages; money. –*v.* **5.** to have sexual intercourse (with). **6.** to ruin or wreck: *You've screwed it this time.* **7.** to swindle or cheat: *screwed me for ten bucks.* **8.** to upset, mistreat, or otherwise act unfairly to someone. –*interj.* **9.** an exclamation of mild surprise, anger, rejection, etc. –*phr.*

screw | **sell-out**

10. put the screws on, to apply pressure; intimidate; coerce: *to put the screws on a debtor.*

11. screw about (or **around**), **a.** to treat (someone) unfairly; deceive, or cause inconvenience, distress, etc., to. **b.** to behave stupidly or insanely.

12. screw around (on), to have sexual intercourse outside of a relationship; to be unfaithful.

13. screw the legs off (someone), to have sex with someone energetically; to have sex with someone to the point of exhaustion.

14. screw (someone) up, to cause (someone) to become mentally and emotionally disturbed.

15. screw up, to make a mess of; impair; frustrate.

16. screw with, to meddle with; tamper with.

17. screw you, an exclamation of rejection, dismissal, etc.

screwy *adj.* eccentric; crazy.

scrote *n.* the scrotum.

scrounge *v.* **1.** to borrow, sponge, or pilfer. *–phr.* **2. scrounge around,** to gather, as by foraging; search out.

scrub bashing *n.* See **bush bashing**.

scrubber *n. Derogatory.* an ugly girl or woman.

scrummy *adj.* scrumptious; attractive. Also, **scrum**.

scum *n.* **1.** *Cricket.* a score of 36 runs. **2.** Also, **scum of the earth. a.** a despicable person; a sleaze. **b.** despicable, lowlife people in general. *–phr.* **3. scum on,** to scold or rebuke severely.

scumbag *n.* a contemptible or despicable person. Also, **scumball, scumbucket**. [originally a word for a condom, from *scum* semen]

scummy *adj.* pathetic; rotten; no good.

scum-sucker *n.* a contemptible or despicable person.

scunge *n.* **1.** an unkempt, slovenly person. **2.** dirt, mess, slime, etc. **3.** messy, untidy objects: *I'll clear the scunge off this desk.*

scunge-face *n.* a contemptible or despicable person.

scungies *pl. n.* a type of woman's full brief underpants worn whilst playing sport.

scungy *adj.* mean, dirty, miserable, unpleasant. Also, **skungy.**

scuzz *adj.* **1.** vulgar; seamy; disgusting. *–n.* **2.** Also, **scuzz-bag, scuzzball.** an unpleasant person. Also, **skuzz**. [possibly extracted from *disgusting*]

seat *v. Prison.* **1.** to perform anal intercourse on. *–n.* **2.** anal intercourse.

seatman *n. Prison.* a male homosexual who takes the active part; a hock.

Seattle sound *n.* a guitar-based form of rock using simple minor-chord progressions; the style of music typified by the grunge bands of Seattle, Washington, which became internationally popular in the early 1990s.

secko *n.* a sex pervert or a person charged with a sexual offence. Also, **secco**.

seedy *adj.* **1.** dirty; shabby; worn-out. **2.** out of sorts physically, as when hung-over. **3.** sleazy; leering.

sell-out *n.* a betrayal.

sensible shoes *n.* practical, comfortable women's shoes, with low heels and completely covered uppers.

septic tank *n.* an American. Also, **septic, seppo**. [rhyming slang for 'Yank']

serious *adj.* complete and unadulterated: *serious chocolate cake; having serious fun.*

seriously *adv.* exceedingly: *seriously rich.*

serve *n.* a strong rebuke; a tongue lashing: *She gave her a real serve when she came home at 4 o'clock in the morning.*

servo *n.* a service station.

session *n.* 1. an occasion of smoking marijuana, hash, etc. 2. an occasion of beer drinking. 3. an occasion of love making. 4. a period of surfing, normally a couple of hours.

set *n.* 1. *Surfing.* a series of larger than normal waves. 2. *Weights.* a series of weight exercises. –*adj.* 3. having a bet placed: *Make sure I'm set for a tenner.*

set-up *n.* 1. a racket; swindle. 2. a trap; ambush.

sex *phr.*
1. **sex, drugs and rock'n'roll,** a catch-phrase expressing adherence to an ethos of partying, drinking, indulging in sex and basically having a good time above all else.
2. **sex on legs,** Also, **sex on a stick,** a person who is extremely sexually attractive.

sex-fiend *n.* a person who has a lot of sex.

sex-god *n.* a sexually attractive man.

sex-goddess *n.* a sexually attractive woman.

sexpot *n.* a blatantly sexually attractive person

sexy *adj.* 1. sexually attractive. 2. sexually exciting. 3. appealing; cool looking; classy: *it has sexy front-end spoilers; let's try and make the document a bit more sexy; the sexiest topic last year.*

s.f.a. *n.* very little; next to nothing. [initialism of *Sweet Fanny Adams* or *Sweet Fuck All*]

shack *phr.* **shack up, a.** to live at a place; reside: *You can come and shack up with us till your house is ready.* **b.** to live together in a sexual relationship.

shades *pl. n.* sunglasses.

shaft *n.* 1. *Crass.* the erect penis. –*v.* 2. *Crass.* (of a male) to have intercourse with (someone). 3. *Crass.* (of a male) to sodomise (someone). 4. to betray (someone) for one's own gain; to opportunistically take (someone else's) place, position, kudos, benefits, etc.: *got shafted by his workmate.*

shag *v.* 1. to have sexual intercourse with. –*n.* 2. an act of sexual intercourse. [old British slang; origin unknown]

shagged-out *adj.* exhausted.

shagger's back *n.* any pain in a person's back, jocularly attributed to the strains of indulging in sexual intercourse.

shaggin' wagon *n.* a panel van, often luxuriously appointed with carpet, curtains, etc., as a suitable place for sexual intercourse; a fuck truck. Also, **shag-wagon**.

shakedown *n.* extortion, especially by blackmail or threatened violence.

shanghai *v.* **1.** to involve someone in an activity, usually without their knowledge or against their wishes. **2.** to steal. **3.** *Prison.* to transfer without warning to another jail. *–n.* **4.** *Prison.* an unexpected transfer to another jail. **5.** a child's catapult; a sling-shot.

shanks's pony *n.* one's legs used for walking: *How'd you get here? Shank's pony.*

shark bait *n.* one who swims where there is danger of a shark attack.

shark shit *phr.* **lower than shark shit,** (of behaviour, etc.) low; mean; despicable.

sharp *adj.* **1.** cunning and clever; shrewd and crafty; knowledgeable of devious ruses and underhand activities; fly: *a sharp lad.* **2.** stylishly smart: *a sharp dresser. –n.* **3.** Also, **sharper.** a swindler, con artist or the like.

sharpie *n.* a teenage or young adult hoodlum of the 1970s. Generally used of males, but also of females.

shat *v.* **1.** past tense of *shit. –phr.* **2. be shat off,** to have had enough of; to be upset.

shebang *phr.* **the whole shebang,** the totality of something; the works; the lot; everything. [origin unknown]

sheep-fucker *n. Derogatory and offensive.* a New Zealander.

sheesh *interj.* a euphemism for the exclamation *shit!*

sheet anchor *n. Cricket.* a player whose batting is very reliable.

sheila *n.* a woman: *a couple of sheilas told me; a great-looking sheila.* [probably from *Sheila* an Irish girl's name]

shekels *pl. n.* money. [a measure of weight and money used by the ancient Hebrews]

shelf *n.* **1.** an informer. *–v.* **2.** to inform on (someone). *–phr.* **3. (left) on the shelf,** unattached or unmarried, and without prospects of marriage.

shemozzle *n.* **1.** a confused state of affairs; muddle. **2.** an uproar; row. [originally US, from Yiddish *shlim mazel* a person who always has bad luck]

shenanigan *n.* nonsense; deceit; trickery. Also, **shenanigans.** [perhaps from Irish *sionnachuighim* play tricks]

shickered *adj.* drunk; intoxicated. Also, **shicker.** [from earlier *shicker* drunk, from Yiddish *shiker* drunk]

shiner *n.* a black eye.

shingle *phr.* **be a shingle short,** to be eccentric; mentally disturbed.

shiralee *n. Hist.* a swag. [origin unknown]

shirt-front *n.* **1.** *Australian Rules.* Also, **shirt-fronter.** a head-on charge aimed at bumping an opponent to the ground. *–v.* **2.** to bump (an opponent) in such a manner.

shirt-lifter *n. Derogatory.* a male homosexual.

shish-kebab *interj.* a euphemism for the exclamation *shit!*

shit *v. Often offensive.* **1.** to defecate. **2.** to anger or disgust. *–n.* **3.** faeces; dung; excrement. **4.** the act of defecating. **5.** a contemptible or despicable person. **6.** nonsense; rubbish;

lies. **7.** marijuana or hashish. **8.** *Prison.* tobacco. *–adj.* **9.** very bad quality: *This is shit beer, man.* *–interj.* **10.** an exclamation expressing anger, disgust, disappointment, disbelief, etc. *–phr.*

8. dump shit on, to denigrate; criticise.

9. get the shits, to become angry or annoyed.

10. give (someone) shit, to stir (someone).

11. give (someone) the shits, to arouse dislike, resentment, annoyance in (someone).

12. have one's shit together, to be in complete control of one's life, emotions, etc.

13. have shit for brains, to be extremely stupid.

14. have the shits, a. to have diarrhoea. **b.** to feel annoyed; to be in a bad mood.

15. have the shits (with), to feel angry or annoyed (with).

16. holy shit, an exclamation of surprise.

17. in the shit, a. in trouble. **b.** in an angry or resentful mood.

18. not worth a pinch of shit, completely worthless.

19. pack shit, See **pack.**

20. piece of shit, a despicable person.

21. put shit on, to denigrate; criticise.

22. sack of shit, *Derogatory.* a lazy, fat person.

23. shit eh! (or **shit hey!**), an expression of surprise.

24. shit happens, a catch-phrase expressing acceptance of some injustice or other problem.

25. shit happens (and then you die), a catch-phrase expressing a dismal outlook on life, used when one feels that things are peculiarly bad.

26. shit it in, win or succeed easily.

27. shit (itself), (of mechanical devices) to break down: *The radiator shit itself while I was driving to work today.*

28. shit off, to annoy; to give the shits to.

29. sure as shit, absolutely sure; positive.

30. sure beats shovelling shit, an exclamation noting that things could be worse.

31. the (living) shit, an intensifier: *beat the living shit out of it; annoying the shit out of.*

32. the shit hits the fan, the trouble begins.

33. up shit creek (without a paddle), in trouble; in difficulties.

34. up to shit, worthless; useless. [Middle English *shiten*, Old English *scitan* to defecate]

shitcan *v.* to denigrate unmercifully.

shit-easy *adj.* extremely easy.

shit-faced *adj.* drunk.

shit-for-brains *n.* a stupid, annoying person.

shithead *n.* **1.** a mean contemptible person. **2.** a no-hoper; dullard. **3.** a person who smokes marijuana regularly.

shitheap *n.* a motor vehicle in poor condition.

shitheel *n.* a despicable, annoying person.

shit-hot *adj.* extremely good.

shithouse *n.* **1.** a toilet. *–adj.* **2.** foul; wretchedly bad. Also, **shouse.** [from 18th century British slang]

shitkicker *n.* **1.** an assistant, especially one doing menial or repetitive jobs. **2.** a person of little consequence.

shitless *adv.* completely; utterly (used to add emphasis to a statement): *scared shitless; bored shitless.*

shitload *n.* a great deal. Also, **shitloads**.

shits *pl. n.* **1.** diarrhoea. **2.** a mood characterised by anger, quick temper, etc.

shit-scared *adj.* very frightened.

shit-stirrer *n.* **1.** a trouble-maker, especially one who is only stirring in jest. **2.** an activist, especially in a political context.

shitter *phr.* **the shitter,** used as an intensifier: *They beat the shitter out of them.*

shitty *adj.* **1.** annoyed; bad tempered. **2.** unpleasant; disagreeable; of low quality.

shitwork *n.* hack work.

shmo *n.* See **schmo**.

shocker *n.* **1.** an unpleasant or disagreeable person or thing. **2.** *Sport.* a bad game: *Had a shocker last Saturday.* **3.** (*pl.*) shock absorbers.

shocks *n.* shock absorbers. Also, **shockers**.

shod *adj.* (of a vehicle) fitted with (a particular brand or type of) tyres: *Dunlop shod; shod with top quality Michelins.*

shoe *phr.* **(a specified man) can put his shoes under my bed any day,** a phrase used by women to indicate that they are sexually attracted to a particular man. [from a once customary placement of shoes when going to bed]

shonk *n.* a dishonest person; a swindler or con artist. [? from *shonk*, offensive name for a Jew]

shonky *adj.* **1.** of dubious integrity or honesty. **2.** mechanically unreliable. *–n.* **3.** a dishonest person. Also, **shonkie**.

shooftee *n.* a look; an inspection. Also, **shoofty, shooftey, shufti**. [from Egyptian Arabic]

shoo-in *n.* a certainty to win a competition, election, etc.

shoot *v.* **1.** to begin, especially to begin to talk. *–interj.* **2.** a euphemism for the exclamation *shit! –phr.* **3. shoot one's bolt, a.** to do one's utmost. **b.** to ejaculate. **4. shoot the moon, a.** to abscond. **b.** to go all out. **5. shoot up,** to take drugs intravenously.

shoot-'em-up *n.* **1.** a book, movie, television show, etc. with much gun-fire and violence. **2.** a video or computer game simulating moving targets which the players have to shoot.

shooter *n.* **1.** a mixed alcoholic drink in a shot glass. **2.** *Cricket.* a bowl that hits the pitch and then rolls.

shooting gallery *n.* a place where people go to shoot up heroin.

shooting iron *n.* a firearm, especially a pistol or revolver.

shop *phr.* **shop till you drop,** to go on a shopping spree.

short *adj* **1.** (of odds) returning a small dividend for the outlay. *–phr.* **2. a few alps short of a range; a few bites short of a biscuit; a few bricks short of a load; a few bangers** (or **snags**) **short of a**

short / **sickie**

barbie; a few sandwiches short of a picnic: stock phrases used to describe a stupid person.

short and curlies *pl. n.* See **hair**.

shot *n.* **1.** an injection of a drug, vaccine, etc. –*v.* **2.** to toss or throw; to chuck unceremoniously: *Just shot it out the window.* –*phr.*
3. be shot of, to be fed up with; to no longer countenance.
4. call the shots, to be in command.
5. that's the shot! an exclamation of approval.

shotgun *n.* **1.** Also, **shotty**. a small hole at the back of a bong which is uncovered in order to get the smoke that has accumulated in the bowl. –*v.* **2.** to drink a can of beer by first shaking it up a little, puncturing a small hole near the base with some pointed object, and then placing the mouth over the hole and releasing the tab or ring-pull.

shove *phr.*
1. shove it! an expression of dismissal, contempt, etc.
2. shove off, to leave; depart.

shovel-ware *n.* hastily packaged and compiled CD-ROM software.

showie *n.* **1.** one who works in a travelling carnival doing agricultural shows around the country; a showman; a carnie. **2.** a person who attends or takes place in an event at an agricultural show.

show pony *n.* a person, car, etc. for which appearance is more important than ability.

shrapnel *n.* small change, especially silver.

shred *v. Surfing, snowboarding.* to surf or snowboard outstandingly.

shredder *n. Surfing, snowboarding.* a very good surfer or snowboarder.

shrimp *n.* **1.** a diminutive or insignificant person. –*phr.* **2. throw another shrimp on the barbie,** *US.* a phrase supposed, quite wrongly, to be indicative of the Australian idiom.

shrink *n.* See **headshrinker**.

shtick *n.* See **schtick**.

shtoom *phr.* **keep shtoom,** to keep quiet about; remain silent. [from Yiddish, from German *stumm* silent]

shuffle *phr.* **shuffle off this mortal coil,** to die. [quoting Shakespeare's *Hamlet*. Often erroneously thought to be some metaphorical use of *coil* meaning 'the earth' or 'the body', but actually coming from a quite different, and now obsolete, word *coil* a tumult, commotion, trouble, bustle]

shufti *n.* See **shooftee**.

shut-eye *n.* sleep.

shyster *n.* **1.** a dishonest person or con artist. **2.** a lawyer who uses unprofessional or questionable methods. [apparently alteration of *Scheuster,* an unscrupulous 19th century New York lawyer]

sick *adj.* **1.** Also, **sik**. totally excellent; totally cool; unreal. **2.** disgusting; revolting: *that was a sick movie.* –*n.* **3.** vomit. –*phr.*
4. sick as a dog, very sick.
5. sick in the head, mentally deranged.
6. sick up, to vomit.
7. to be one sick puppy, See **puppy**.

sickie *n.* a day taken off work with

217

pay, because of either genuine or feigned illness.

sicko *n.* **1.** a disgusting or disturbingly revolting person. *–adj.* **2.** depraved.

side-splitter *n.* (*often ironic*) a joke.

sig file *n.* a file containing one's name, e-mail address, and often a small ascii art picture and/or quotation, added to the end of e-mail messages. [short for *signature file*]

sik *adj.* See **sick**.

silent *phr.*
1. silent but deadly, a phrase used to describe a fart that while inaudible is extremely unpleasant to the nose.
2. silent like the P in swimming, See **P**.

sim *n.* a video or computer game which simulates a real world activity, such as flying a plane, playing golf, a soccer match, etc. [short for *simulator*]

simmer *interj.* an exclamation requesting someone to curb their temper or calm down.

simp *n.* **1.** a stupid or dull person. **2.** a weakling; a wimp.

sin-bin *n.* **1.** a panel van, often luxuriously appointed, as a suitable place for sexual intercourse; shaggin' wagon. **2.** (in team sports) an area adjoining the playing field set aside for penalised players; penalty box. *–v.* **3.** to consign a player to the sin-bin.

sing *v. Prison.* to turn informer.

siphon *phr.*
1. siphon off, to take little by little.
2. siphon the python, (of a male) to urinate.

siree *phr. Jocular.* **yes/no siree,** yes/no indeed. [a variant of the word *sir*]

sitter *n.* something easily accomplished, as a catch in cricket, a mark to be shot at, etc.

sitting duck *n.* **1.** one who is easily duped or defeated. **2.** something easily accomplished.

sixer *n. Prison.* a jail sentence of six months.

six-finger country *n.* a remote area in which the inhabitants are imagined to be inbred.

six o'clock swill *n. NSW.* (formerly) a hectic session of buying and drinking beers by men in a public bar near to closing time, which from 1916 to 1955 was, for many hotels, 6 p.m.

sixpack *n.* a male's stomach, with rippling muscles.

six-stitcher *n.* a cricket ball.

sixty-nine *n.* **1.** Also, **sixty-niner, 69er.** simultaneous oral sex by two people. *–v.* **2.** to perform a sixty-nine. Also, **69**. [translation of French *soixante-neuf*, referring to the body positioning]

size queen *n.* a male homosexual obsessed with penis size.

sizzle *v.* **1.** (of the weather) to be very hot. **2.** (of a person) to be extremely sexually attractive. **3.** to be extremely good; to be excellent.

skater *n.* a skateboard rider. Also, **sk8r**.

skatey *n.* a skateboard.

skeeter *n.* **1.** a mosquito. **2.** a nickname for a man of small build.

skeg *n.* a surfer. Also, **skeghead**. [from *skeg* the fin of a surfboard, the afterpart of a ship's keel, from Dutch, from Old Norse]

skid *phr.*
1. hit the skids, to brake fast; to stop in one's tracks.
2. on the skids, deteriorating fast.
3. put the skids under, to place in a precarious position; to ensure the downfall of.

skid-lid *n.* a helmet worn by a cyclist.

skidmark *n.* a mark or smudge of faeces on underwear.

skin *n.* **1.** a skinhead. *–phr.*
2. by the skin of one's teeth, scarcely; just; barely.
3. get under one's skin, a. to irritate one. **b.** to fascinate or attract one.
4. slapping skins, having sexual intercourse.

skin and blister *n.* sister. Also, **blister**. [rhyming slang]

skin and bones *n.* (a nickname for) a very thin person.

skin-dog *n.* an uncircumcised male.

skin flick *n.* a pornographic movie.

skinful *n.* a large amount, especially of alcoholic drink.

skinhead *n.* **1.** a person with head hair shaved very short or off all together; a mild derogatory term for anyone who has had their hair cut short. **2.** a young man or woman of any of the various skinhead sub-cultures, identified by shaven heads. The aggressive, anti-social, right-wing, boot-wearing type is the one most commonly referred to in the press, and in popular conservative belief nearly all shaven-headed people are categorised as such.

skinner *n. Horseracing.* **1.** a horse which wins a race at very long odds.
2. a betting coup.

skins *pl. n.* drums; bongos.

skint *adj.* completely without money; broke. [variant of *skinned* stripped of money or belongings]

skip *n. Derogatory.* an Anglo-Celtic Australian. Also, **skippy**. [from *Skippy* the name of a kangaroo in a television series]

skipper *n. Chiefly Sport.* **1.** a captain or leader, as of a team. *–v.* **2.** to captain a team.

skirt *phr.* **bit** (or **piece**) **of skirt.** *Derogatory.* a woman who a male is only interested in for sexual purposes.

skol *v.* to consume (a drink) at one draught. Also, **skoal**. [Scandinavian]

skun *v.* (as a jocular past tense of *skin*) skinned.

skungy *adj.* See **scungy**.

skunk *n.* **1.** a thoroughly contemptible person. **2.** a type of marijuana that has a strong odour.

skuzz *adj., n.* See **scuzz**.

sky *v.* **1.** to raise aloft; strike (a ball) high into the air. *–phr.*
2. sky the towel, to give up, admit defeat.
3. the sky's the limit, there is no limit.

skyhook *n.* an imaginary hook hanging from the sky, used as an example of something unobtainable or impossible.

slab *n.* **1.** a carton of two dozen cans or bottles of beer. **2.** a thousand dollars. **3.** an examination or preparation table at a mortuary or morgue.

slack *adj.* **1.** unkind, cruel, unfair:

Don't be slack, he can't help being tall. **2.** lazy: *Why don't you ever visit, you slack bastard?*

slacker *n.* one who avoids work, effort, etc.

slag *n.* **1.** a gob of phlegm. **2.** *Derogatory.* a girl or woman who is unattractive, dirty, or promiscuous. *–v.* **3.** to spit. *–phr.* **4. slag off,** to bad-mouth; criticise severely.

slam *v.* **1.** to criticise severely. **2.** to slam dance. *–n.* **3.** a severe criticism. **4.** *Skateboarding, blading, etc.* a heavy fall, especially one resulting in bodily harm.

slam dance *v.* to take part in slam dancing.

slam dancing *n.* a type of rough dancing in which participants slam into each other.

slam dunk *n. Basketball.* **1.** a shot in which a player jumps and puts the ball through the hoop by releasing it above the height of the ring. *–v.* **2.** to perform such a shot.

slammer *n.* **1.** jail. **2.** a slam dancer.

slant-eye *n. Racist.* a South-East Asian person. Also, **slant-eyes, slanty-eyes**.

slant-eyed *adj. Racist.* of South-East Asian extraction. Also, **slanty-eyed**.

slap *n. Racist.* a South-East Asian.

slap and tickle *n.* sexual intercourse; sexual play.

slaphead *n. Racist.* a South-East Asian.

slaps *pl. n.* a game in which two contestants hold out their hands in prayer-position, fingertip to fingertip, and take turns at slapping the other player's hands. A change of turn takes place when one player misses a strike.

slash *n.* the act of urinating.

slaughter *v.* **1.** to defeat thoroughly. **2.** to ruin totally: *completely slaughtered the original film in a re-make.*

slaughtered *adj.* extremely drunk.

slave-labour *n.* work considered as very badly paid.

slay *v.* **1.** to amuse (someone) greatly. **2.** *Sport.* to defeat convincingly.

sleaze *n.* **1.** low life; squalor; etc. **2.** overt sexual activity of a sordid nature; sleaziness. **3.** a person who only relates to others on a sexual level; one who constantly attempts to crack on to others, especially in an obnoxious and leering manner. *–v.* **4.** to attempt to entice someone into having sex. *–phr.* **5. sleaze on to (someone),** to entice someone into having sex.

sleazebag *n.* **1.** a despicable person. **2.** a person, especially a male, who constantly attempts to crack on to others, especially in an obnoxious and leering manner. Also, **sleazeball, sleazebucket**.

sleazepit *n.* a place inhabited by sleazy people.

sleazoid *adj.* **1.** Also, **sleazoidal**. of the nature of a sleaze. *–n.* **2.** a sleazy person; a sleaze.

sleazy *adj.* **1.** (of behaviour) sexually sordid and disgusting; leering. **2.** overtly sexual. **3.** shabby, shoddy, untidy or dirty.

sledging *n.* **1.** *Sport.* the practice of heaping abuse and ridicule on members of the opposing team in an effort to upset their game. **2.** any sustained ridiculing; paying out on someone.

slew *n.* **1.** a large number: *a slew of leadership hopefuls.* *–v.* **2.** *Criminal.* **a.** to turn one's head in order to look. **b.** to watch furtively; to spy. *–phr.*
3. slew and blue, *Criminal.* to incriminate oneself by suspiciously looking at the wrong time.
4. that slews you, *Obsolete.* a phrase used to indicate that you have been confounded.

slewed *adj.* lost, especially in the bush.

slice *n.* **1.** *Obsolete.* a one-pound note. **2.** two dollars.

sliced bread *phr.* **the best** (or **greatest**) **thing since sliced bread,** excellent; first-rate: *He thinks he is the greatest thing since sliced bread.*

slick *adj.* **1.** shrewdly adroit; glib: *a slick operator.* *–n.* **2.** *(pl.) Car sales.* bald tyres.

slime *n.* **1.** an unpleasant person: *Some slime stole my bike.* **2.** a person who only relates to others on a sexual level. *–v.* **3.** to act in a despicable, sleazy manner, especially to attempt to flatter someone in order to entice them into having sex. **4.** to attempt to ingratiate oneself. *–phr.* **5. slime on to** (**someone**), to entice someone into having sex.

slimebag *n.* a despicable person. Also, **slimeball, slimebucket.**

slimy *adj.* unpleasantly ingratiating.

sling *n.* **1.** money given as a bribe; protection money. **2.** money given as a gratuity. *–v.* **3.** to give money as bribe. **4.** to give money as a tip, or as a friendly gesture when they have worked hard, helped out, etc.: *to sling someone $20.* *–phr.*
5. sling a tip, to offer a racing tip to someone.
6. sling off at, to speak disparagingly of (someone): *He slings off at his teachers.*

slinging *n. Australian Rules.* the act of catching a player by the neck and throwing them on the ground.

slip *n. Two-up.* the price of a cab or bus fare home given by the ringkeeper to a person who has lost all their money.

slit *n. Crass.* the vagina or vulva.

slog *v.* **1.** to hit hard, as in boxing, cricket, etc. **2.** to toil. *–n.* **3.** a strong blow with little finesse or technique. **4.** a spell of hard work or walking.

slogger *n. Cricket.* a batter who just slogs the ball.

slo-mo *n.* slow-motion.

sloop *n.* the penis.

slop *n.* choppy sea.

slope *v.* **1.** to move or go: *just sloping along.* *–phr.* **2. slope off,** to go away, especially furtively. *–n.* **3.** *n. Racist.* a South-East Asian.

slopehead *n. Racist.* a South-East Asian.

slops *pl. n.* **1.** beer. **2.** *Crass.* the second or subsequent partner in a gang sex situation.

sloshed *adj.* drunk.

slot *n.* prison.

slug *n.* **1.** a lazy, indolent person. **2.** a bullet. **3.** a drink or swallow of something, especially spirits. **4.** *Crass.* the penis. *–phr.* **5. slug it out, a.** to fight. **b.** to contend vigorously.

slugger *n.* **1.** one who strikes hard, as

slugger

with the fists or a baseball bat. **2.** a prize-fighter.

slug-slewer *n. Prison.* one who voyeuristically views penises, such as at a lavatory, communal shower, etc.

slum *phr.* **slum it,** to be living in circumstances below one's usual or expected standard of living.

slush box *n. Motor.* a derogatory name for a car with automatic transmission.

slushy *n.* a cook's assistant; kitchen worker.

slut *n.* **1.** *Derogatory.* a woman deemed to be promiscuous. **2.** (often used by heterosexual males in self-reference as a brag) a promiscuous man.

smack *n.* heroin.

smacked-out *adj.* heavily under the influence of heroin.

smacker *n.* **1.** a dollar. **2.** *Obsolete.* one pound.

smackeroo *n.* a dollar. Also, **smackeroonie.**

smackie *n.* a person who takes or is addicted to taking heroin. Also, **smackhead.**

s-mail *n.* See **snail mail.**

smart alec *n.* one who is ostentatious in the display of knowledge or skill, often despite basic ignorance or lack of ability. Also, **smart aleck.**

smart arse *n.* a smart alec; know-all.

smarty pants *n.* a smug know-all; a show-off. Also, **Mister Smarty Pants, Miss Smarty Pants.**

smashed *adj.* incapacitated as a result of taking drugs, alcohol, etc.

smick *adj.* See **schmick.**

snag

smiley *n.* **1.** a simple graphic representation of a smiling face. **2.** the emoticon :-) or :) - representing a smile. **3.** any emoticon. Also, **smilie.**

smoke *n.* **1.** Also, **smokey.** marijuana dried and prepared for smoking: *Anybody got any smoke? –phr.* **2. smoke it,** *Crass.* to perform fellatio.

smokie *n.* a horse whose form has been kept secret; a rort horse.

smoking *adj.* really excellent; hot.

smoko *n.* **1.** a rest from work; tea-break. **2.** any informal gathering. Also, **smoke-o, smoke-oh.**

smooey *n. Offensive.* **1.** the vulva or vagina. *–phr.* **2. bit of smooey,** sexual intercourse with a woman. Also, **smooy.** [origin unknown]

smother *v.* **1.** to stand so as to conceal a crime taking place. *–n.* **2.** a criminal's accomplice who does this. **3.** such a concealment.

smurf *n.* a short person. [from the name of a small elf-like cartoon character and toy]

snack-attack *n.* a craving for something to eat between normal meals.

snaffle *v.* **1.** to steal. **2.** to take away quickly before anyone else: *Early shoppers snaffled up the sales bargains.* Also, **snavel.**

snafu *n. Originally US Military.* **1.** chaos; a muddled situation. *–v.* **2.** to throw into disorder; muddle. [acronym from the initial letters of *Situation Normal: All Fucked* (or, euphemistically, *Fouled*) *Up*]

snag[1] *n.* a sausage. [? British dialect *snag*, variant of *snack* a light repast, morsel of food, from *snack* a bite]

snag² *n.* a man who embodies all the attributes of the New-Age philosophy, such as sensitivity to others, an ability to articulate feelings, an attitude to life which is not macho. Also, **SNAG**. [acronym from *Sensitive New-Age Guy*]

snail mail *n.* the normal postal service (as opposed to e-mail messages). Also, **s-mail**.

snail trail *n.* dried mucus or semen on clothing.

snake *v. Surfing.* to paddle inside someone who has priority.

snakebite *n.* a drink of Guinness stout and apple cider.

snake oil merchant *n.* a quack or a person selling phoney medical treatments. Also, **snake oil doctor, snake oil salesman.**

snake's belly *phr.* **lower than a snake's belly,** unpleasant; mean; despicable.

snarky *adj.* irritable or annoyed. [? British dialect *snark* nag, complain]

snatch *n.* **1.** a robbery by a quick seizing of goods. **2.** *Crass.* **a.** a woman's vagina or vulva. **b.** a woman as a sexual object.

sneaker net *n. Jocular.* an office data transferral system in which computer files are copied onto a floppy disc and then taken to other computers on foot. [punning on computer networking terms such as *telnet*, *ethernet*, etc.]

snit *n.* a fit of rage or bad temper. [origin unknown]

snitch¹ *v.* to snatch or steal. [? variant of *snatch*]

snitch² *v.* **1.** to turn informer. *–n.* **2.** an informer. [from 18th century slang for 'nose'; origin unknown]

snog *v.* **1.** to kiss and cuddle; canoodle. *–n.* **2.** an act of kissing and cuddling: *a quiet snog in the corner.* Also, **snoog**. [origin uncertain; see obsolete *snug* to copulate, or cant *snoodge*, variant of *snooze* to sleep with a woman]

snooker *n.* **1.** a hiding place. *–v.* **2.** to obstruct or hinder (someone), especially from reaching some object, aim, etc. **3.** to hide.

snookums *n.* a term of endearment. Also, **schnookums, snookieookums, snooks**. [cf. 19th century *snooks* the name of an imaginary practical joker]

snooze *v.* **1.** to sleep; slumber; doze; nap. *–n.* **2.** a rest; nap. **3.** *Prison.* a period of imprisonment of three months.

snort *v.* **1.** to laugh outright or boisterously. **2.** to sniff (a powdered drug, as cocaine). *–n.* **3.** an alcoholic drink.

snorter *n.* **1.** anything unusually strong, large, difficult, dangerous, as a fast ball in cricket, a gale, etc.: *a snorter of a day*. **2.** an alcoholic drink.

snot *n.* **1.** mucus from the nose. *–v.* **2.** to eject mucus from the nose. [Middle English *snotte*; Old English *gesnot*]

snotrag *n.* a handkerchief.

snotty *adj.* **1.** snobbish; arrogant. **2.** ill-tempered; cranky.

snotty-nosed *n.* **1.** (of adults) snobbish or affected. **2.** (of children) too young to wipe their noses, and hence, annoying.

snowdrop *v.* to steal laundry from clothes lines. [from cant *snow* linen hung out to dry]

snow job *n.* 1. an attempt to distract attention away from certain aspects of a situation by supplying an overwhelming amount of often extraneous information; a cover-up. 2. a quick and superficial attempt to improve the state or appearance of (something).

snoz *n.* the nose. Also, **schnozz, snozz.** [see *schnozzle*]

snuff *phr.* **snuff it,** to die. [i.e. to put one's light out, snuff out one's flame]

so *interj.* 1. an expression indicating rejection, lack of interest, refusal to understand: *So? –phr.* **2. so what,** what does that matter?

soak *n.* a heavy drinker of alcohol.

soapbox *n.* any place, means, or the like, used by a person to make a speech, voice opinions, etc.

soapie *n.* a radio or television drama series. Also, **soapy, soap opera.** [so called because originally sponsored on US radio by soap manufacturers]

soapy *adj.* 1. flattering; given to using smooth words. 2. (*ironic*) not predisposed to washing oneself; smelly and dirty.

sod *n.* 1. a disagreeable person. *–phr.* **2. sod all,** nothing.
3. sod it, an exclamation of annoyance, disgust, etc.
4. sod off, an exclamation of rejection, dismissal, etc.; piss off! [shortened form of *sodomite*, used as a insult]

soft-cock *adj. Offensive.* (of a male) weak; wimpy; unmasculine.

soft touch *n.* a person who is easy to borrow money from due to their generous nature; a person who is not mean with their money.

soggy Sao *n.* a game in which a group of men simultaneously begin masturbating onto a Sao biscuit, the last to ejaculate having to eat the biscuit.

soldier *n.* a strip or finger of bread or toast, especially for dipping into a soft-boiled egg.

solid *adj. Criminal.* loyal to the underworld, especially when under pressure from the police.

-something *suffix.* 1. used to make adjectives denoting an age falling within a certain decade: *twentysomething; thirty-something.* 2. used to make nouns: *a bunch of thirty-somethings.*

sonny Jim *n.* an affectionate appellation to a male, often used in remonstrance: *Listen here, sonny Jim.*

son of a bitch *n. Derogatory and offensive.* 1. a mean and contemptible man. 2. any person, object or thing which has incurred one's wrath.

sool *v.* to incite or urge (someone).

sop *n.* a weak or cowardly person.

sort *n.* 1. **a.** a good-looking woman: *a real sort.* **b.** a person described in terms of attractiveness: *a good sort, a drack sort. –phr.*
2. a good sort, a. a sexually attractive woman or man. **b.** one who is likeable, trustworthy, reliable.
3. (one) would be a nice sort of mate (or **father**) (or **bludger**) etc., an ironic compliment.

soup *phr.* **soup up,** to modify (an

engine, especially of a motor car) in order to increase its power.

souse *v.* **1.** to intoxicate. **2.** to drink to intoxication. *–n.* **3.** a drunkard. [from *souse,* to steep in pickling liquid]

souvenir *v.* to steal some minor item as a souvenir.

sozzled *adj.* drunk. [obsolete *sozzle* drunken stupor (akin to *souse*)]

spac *n.* **1.** an idiot; a person who dresses or behaves in an unfashionable or unstylish manner. *–adj.* **2.** daggy and uncool; stupid. Also, **spack, spacko, spak**. [derived from *spastic*]

space cadet *n.* a person who is vague or dull.

spaced-out *adj.* **1.** in a euphoric or dreamy state, as if under the influence of a hallucinogen, extremely tired, etc. **2.** under the influence of a mind-altering drug. Also, **spaced, spaced out.**

spacey *adj.* dreamy; hallucinatory.

spacies *n.* computer arcade games in general. [from *Space Invaders* one of the first very popular models in the 70s; modelled on *pinnies, pokies*]

spade *n.* **1.** *Racist.* someone of very dark skin, as a Negro, Aborigine, etc. [from *spade* a black figure used on playing cards] *–v.* **2.** to try to set up the necessary conditions for beginning an amorous or sexual relationship with someone; to attempt to impress a potential sexual partner: *He was over by the bar spading for his life.*

spade-face *n.* *Racist.* a South-East Asian. Also, **spade-head**.

spadework *n.* social interaction preliminary to sexual advance. Also, **spading**.

spag[1] *n.* **1.** spaghetti. **2.** *Racist.* an Italian. **3.** *Racist.* the Italian language.

spag[2] *n.* **1.** saliva or spittle with mucus that is spat out. *–v.* **2.** to spit out a gob of saliva and mucus; slag. [a blend of *spit* + *slag*]

spag bol *n.* spaghetti bolognaise. Also, **spag bog**.

spam *n. Internet.* **1.** large amounts of useless, meaningless information sent via the Internet to annoy someone. **2.** any unwanted e-mail, newsgroup postings, or the like, especially cross-postings sent to many varied and different newsgroups. *–v.* **3.** to send spam. **4.** to repeat one particular term in the text of a homepage in order to give that homepage a high rating in an Internet search engine. [from a Monty Python sketch in which the word *spam* is repeated over and over again]

spam can *n. Aeron.* a mass-produced light aircraft with a thin metal skin.

spammer *n. Internet.* a person sending spam.

Spanish dancer *n.* cancer. [rhyming slang]

spanner *phr.* **spanner in the works,** any cause of confusion or impediment.

spanner water *n.* extremely cold water. [so called since it tightens the nuts]

spare tyre *n.* a roll of fat around a person's midriff.

sparrow fart *n.* dawn; very early

sparrow fart / **spin**

morning: *Up at sparrow fart.* Also, **sparrow's fart**.

sparrowgrass *n.* asparagus.

spas *n.* See **spastic**.

spas-attack *n.* an instance of losing one's temper, going crazy, or the like.

spastic *n.* 1. someone who behaves foolishly or crazily. 2. someone who has lost self-control. 3. a clumsy person. Also, **spas, spaz, spazzo**.

spear *n.* 1. a surfboard. *–v.* 2. to move rapidly, especially in a restricted passage: *a racehorse spearing down the rails. –phr.* 3. **get the spear,** to be dismissed, as from employment, etc.

spec *n.* 1. speculation. *–adj.* 2. speculative: *spec builder. –phr.* 3. **on spec,** as a guess, risk, or gamble: *to buy shares on spec.*

speccy *adj.* remarkably good; impressive; spectacular.

special K *n.* the drug ketamine. [humorous reference to the breakfast cereal *Special K*]

specs *pl. n.* 1. spectacles; glasses. 2. technical specifications: *I've checked all the specs.*

speed *n.* a stimulant drug, as an amphetamine; goey.

speedball *n.* 1. a mixture containing cocaine and heroin. 2. a rissole.

speed-cop *n.* a police officer, often a motorcyclist, who enforces the observation of speed-limits.

speed demon *n.* a person who likes to drive fast. Also, **speed-merchant**.

speed hump *n. Jocular.* (amongst boaties) a skindiver.

speedo *n.* speedometer.

speed pump *v. Surfing.* to rock the board back and forth in order to gain speed.

spesh *adj.* special.

spew *v.* 1. to vomit. 2. to become extremely angry and vent that anger verbally. *–n.* 3. an instance of vomiting. 4. vomit. [from Middle English *spewe*, from Old English *spiwan, speowan*]

spewiferous *adj.* so unpleasant as to cause nausea; yucky; off.

spewy *adj.* 1. unpleasant; yucky; off: *a spewy meat pie.* 2. angry.

spic *n. Originally US. Racist.* a person of Spanish or Latin American descent. Also, **spick, spik**. [meant to represent the Spanish pronunciation of *speak*, as used in phrases such as *No spic a de English*]

spiel *n.* 1. a persuasive speech designed to explain and hopefully sell a product; a sales talk. 2. a speech on a particular subject: *I was given this huge spiel about honesty and stuff. –v.* 3. to deliver a patter or sales talk. [Yiddish *shpiel*, from German *spiel* play]

spike *v.* 1. to add alcoholic liquor to a usually non-alcoholic drink. 2. to add a hard drug to a soft drug. 3. to add anything to any drink or food. *–n.* 4. a hairdo in which the hair is cut short and stands up all over. 5. a person with such a haircut.

spill *v.* to divulge, disclose, or tell: *spill the beans; spill one's guts.*

spin[1] *n.* 1. a playing of a record or CD: *give this one a spin and see if you like it. –v.* 2. to play a record. 3. to play dance music as a deejay. *–phr.*

4. spin a yarn (or **dit**), **a.** to tell a tale. **b.** to tell a false or improbable story or version of any event.

5. spin out, a. to become greatly amazed. **b.** to cause to become greatly amazed; to stun (someone).

spin² *n.* **1.** *Obsolete.* the sum of five pounds. **2.** the sum of $5. **3.** *Prison.* a prison sentence of five years' duration. [abbreviation of *spinnaker*]

spinebash *v.* **1.** to rest; loaf. –*n.* **2.** a rest.

spinnaker *n. Obsolete.* the sum of five pounds; a five pound note.

spinner *n.* **1.** the person tossing the coins in two-up. –*phr.* **2. come in, spinner! a.** *Two-up.* a call made to signify that all the bets are laid and it is time to spin the coins. **b.** a phrase used to inform someone that they have just been successfully duped.

spin-out *n.* **1.** a skid in which a vehicle spins off the road. **2.** something that causes amazement, shock, etc.

spit *n.* **1.** Also, **dead spit**, the image, likeness or counterpart of a person, etc. –*phr.*
2. spit chips, to be very annoyed.
3. spit it out, speak up.
4. spit the dummy, See **dummy**.
5. the big spit, vomit.
6. swap spit, to French kiss.

spiv *n. Originally Brit.* one who lives by their wits, without working or by dubious business activity, and usually affecting ostentatious dress and tastes. [back-formation from British dialect *spiving* smart]

split *v.* **1.** to divide something with another or others. **2.** to leave hurriedly. –*n.* **3.** an act or arrangement of splitting, as of a sum of money. **4.** one's share or divvy of such a split.

splosh *n.* money.

spondulicks *n.* money. Also, **spondulix, spons, spon.** [19th century slang; originally meaning 'paper money'; obviously somehow a use of the Ancient Greek word *spondulikos*, adjective of *spondulos* a vertebra, a round stone, a round weight, a voting pebble, though the sense connection cannot be established; possibly it was based on an error]

spoof *n.* **1.** semen; come. –*v.* **2.** to ejaculate; to come.

spook *n.* **1.** an agent of an intelligence organisation; a spy. **2.** a police informer.

spot *n.* **a.** *Obsolete.* the sum of 100 pounds. **b.** the sum of $100.

spot-on *adj.* **1.** absolutely right or accurate; excellent. –*interj.* **2.** an exclamation of approbation, etc.

spout *n.* **1.** the chamber of a rifle. –*v.* **2.** to utter or declaim in an oratorical manner. –*phr.* **3. up the spout, a.** ruined; lost. **b.** pawned. **c.** pregnant.

spread *phr.*
1. chuck a spread, (of a woman) to spread her legs in a sexual way.
2. spread 'em, to hold the arms and legs out straight and place them as wide apart as possible in order to facilitate a search for concealed weapons, drugs, etc.
3. spread it on thick, to exaggerate.

spring *v.* **1.** to catch out; to come upon unexpectedly: *We were sprung* *last Tuesday.* **2.** to cause or enable (someone) to escape from prison.

spring chicken *n.* (*usually with a negative*) a very young person: *I'm no spring chicken.*

springy *n. Surfing.* a wetsuit covering the body to the knees, elbows and neck. [originally designed for use in spring weather]

sprog *n.* **1.** a child or youngster. **2.** a new recruit, as in an air force. **3.** semen. *–v.* **4.** to ejaculate; to come.

spruiker *n.* a person who harangues prospective customers. [probably from Yiddish *shpruch* a saying or charm]

spud *n.* **1.** a potato. **2.** a hole in a sock through which the skin shows. [earlier a type of digging fork or weeding implement, from Middle English *spudde* a kind of knife]

spunk *n.* **1.** a good-looking person, male or female. **2.** *Chiefly Brit.* semen. **3.** pluck; spirit; mettle. [blend of *spark*, a fiery particle and obsolete *funk*, spark, touchwood]

spunkette *n.* a sexually attractive female.

spunk-rat *n.* a sexually attractive person.

spunky *adj.* **1.** good-looking; attractive. *–n.* **2.** a good-looking person, male or female.

spun-out *adj.* **1.** totally amazed; stunned. **2.** out of one's mind on a drug; tripping.

square *n.* **1.** one who is ignorant of or uninterested in up-to-date popular culture; an uncool person; a dag. **2.** *Derogatory.* Also, **squarie.** (*amongst homosexuals*) a heterosexual person. *–adj.* **3.** *Derogatory.* (*amongst homosexuals*) heterosexual. **4.** law-abiding; honest.

squat *v.* **1.** to occupy a building without title or right. *–n.* **2.** a building which is occupied without title or right: *He shares a squat in Glebe.*

squatter *n.* **1.** *Hist.* one who settled on Crown land to run stock, especially sheep, initially without government permission, but later with a lease or licence. **2.** one of a group of rich and influential rural landowners. **3.** one who occupies a building without right or title.

squeaky-clean *adj.* **1.** very clean. **2.** morally irreproachable.

squeal *n.* **1.** a protest or complaint. *–v.* **2.** to turn informer. **3.** to protest or complain. **4.** to disclose or reveal, as something secret.

squeeze *n.* **1.** a situation from which extrication is difficult: *in a tight squeeze.* **2.** a boyfriend or girlfriend; lover. *–v.* **3.** to put pressure upon (a person or persons) to act in a given way, especially by blackmail.

squillion *n.* an extremely large amount. Also, **gillion, jillion, squintillion, zillion**.

squirrel *v.* to subject someone to a squirrel grip.

squirrel grip *n. Football.* an illegal tackle in which pressure is applied to the testicles of the tackled player; Christmas hold. [so called because a *squirrel* collects 'nuts' (i.e. testicles)]

squirt *n.* **1.** an insignificant, self-assertive fellow. **2.** a short person. **3.** a little child or kid. **4.** an act of male urination.

squitters *n.* diarrhoea. [from obsolete *squitter* to squirt]

squiz *v.* **1.** to look at quickly but closely. –*n.* **2.** a quick but close look. [? a blend of *squint* and *quiz*]

stack *n.* **1.** a combination of amplifiers and speaker boxes. **2.** a crash or accident involving a motor vehicle, bicycle, etc. **3.** (*pl.*) a great amount. –*v.* **4.** to crash a motor vehicle, bicycle, etc. **5.** *Snowboarding.* a fall.

stacked *adj. Crass.* (of a woman) having large breasts. Also, **well-stacked.**

stackhat *n.* a safety helmet to be used with bike riding, skateboard riding, etc. [Trademark]

stage-dive *v.* to dive from the stage into the audience.

stage diving *n.* diving from the stage into the audience.

stag film *n.* a pornographic film. Also, **stag movie.**

stag party *n.* a party, exclusively for men, with entertainment such as strippers, prostitutes, pornographic films or other things involving the exploitation of women. Also, **stag night.**

stakes *pl. n.* an assumed condition of competitiveness: *beauty stakes*. [from *stakes* a prize in a race or contest]

stalk *n. Crass.* an erect penis.

stallion *n.* a very sexually active man, especially a well-endowed one.

stand *v.* **1.** to bear the expense of; pay for. –*phr.*
  2. stand on one's dig, to claim respect for (one's rights, dignity, etc.).
  3. stand out like dogs' balls (or **a sore thumb**) (or **a sore toe**), to be prominent or conspicuous.

standover merchant *n.* one who bullies or intimidates; one who threatens violence to gain a desired result; a hoodlum. Also, **standover man.**

starkers *adj.* **1.** totally naked. **2.** absolutely mad; insane. [from *stark* absolutely, utterly, as used in the phrases *stark naked* and *stark raving mad*]

stash *n.* a cache of drugs for personal use.

stat dec *n.* a statutory declaration.

stax *n.* a great deal; lots. Also, **stacks**.

steamer *n.* a lightweight one-piece wetsuit with long sleeves and legs.

steer *phr.*
  1. bum steer, a misleading idea or suggested course of action.
  2. steer clear of, to avoid.

step-ins *pl. n.* a woman's elasticised foundation garment, without fastenings.

-ster *suffix.* used with a colloquialising force to create nicknames (often prefaced by 'the'): *the Magster* (Margaret); *the Gregster* (Greg); *Goughster* (Gough Whitlam); *the Igster* (Iggy Pop). See **-meister**.

stewed *adj.* intoxicated or drunk.

stick *n* **1.** a very thin person. **2.** a surfboard. **3.** *Crass.* the penis. –*phr.*
  4. the sticks, a. an area or district regarded as lacking in the amenities of urban life. **b.** the outback. **c.** *Football.* the goal posts.
  5. up the stick, *Crass.* pregnant.

stick-book *n.* a pornographic magazine. Also, **stick mag**.

sticky *n.* a look: *Have a sticky at this.* [from *stickybeak*]

stickybeak *n.* **1.** an inquisitive, prying person. **2.** a look merely to satisfy one's own inquisitiveness: *We went to the inspection just to have a stickybeak.* –*v.* **3.** to pry or meddle.

stiff *adj.* **1.** drunk. –*n.* **2.** a dead body; corpse. **3.** a drunk. **4.** a racehorse that is certain to lose. **5.** Also, **stiffy, stiffie.** an erect penis. **6.** *Prison.* an illegal letter sent out of jail without being censored. –*interj.* **7.** an exclamation of derision, used to point out that someone has got what they deserved; serves yourself right! –*phr.*
8. stiff cheese (or **cheddar**) (or **luck**), **a.** bad luck. **b.** serves yourself right! **c.** an off-hand expression of sympathy.
9. stiff with, full of; bristling with: *The area was stiff with cops.*

stiffener *n.* an alcoholic drink.

stiffo *interj.* tough luck!

stiffy *n.* an erect penis. Also, **stiffie.**

stink *v.* **1.** to be very inferior in quality. –*n.* **2.** a commotion; fuss; scandal: *kick up a stink.* –*phr.* **3. play stink finger,** *Crass.* to engage in erotic play of the female genitals with the fingers.

stinker *n* **1.** a dishonourable, disgusting, or objectionable person. **2.** something difficult, as a task, problem, etc. **3.** a very hot and humid day.

stinko *adj.* **1.** stinking. **2.** drunk.

stinkpot *n.* **1.** one who stinks. **2.** an objectionable person.

stipe *n.* a stipendiary steward at a racecourse.

stir[1] *v.* **1.** to make trouble; provoke; tease; upset the equanimity of others, especially just for the sake of stirring; shit-stir. –*n.* **2.** a commotion. –*phr.* **3. stir the possum,** to instigate a debate on a controversial topic, especially in the public arena; create a disturbance.

stir[2] *n.* prison.

stir-crazy *adj.* crazy as a result of being institutionalised in jail.

stoked *adj.* amazed; thrilled; delighted; blown away.

stomach *phr.* **one's stomach** (or **belly**) **thinks one's throat is cut,** to be very hungry.

stone *n.* **1.** *Mining.* opal-bearing material. **2.** (*pl.*) the testicles. –*phr.* **3. stone the crows,** an exclamation of surprise, amazement, etc. [def 2 dating from the 12th century; def 3 referring to the former occupation of watching over cornfields and stoning crows that attempt to plunder the crop]

stoned *adj.* completely drunk or under the influence of drugs, especially marijuana.

stonkered *adj.* **1.** defeated; destroyed; overthrown. **2.** exhausted. **3.** drunk. **4.** extremely lethargic or incapacitated, as after a large meal.

stooge *n.* **1.** an entertainer who feeds lines to a comedian and is often the object of ridicule. **2.** one who acts on behalf of another, especially in an obsequious, corrupt, or secretive fashion. –*v.* **3.** to act as a stooge.

store jack *n.* a store security officer.

stoush *n* **1.** a fight; a brawl. –*v.* **2.** to

fight (someone or something). [? Scottish *stashie, stushie* uproar, commotion]

stow *phr.* **stow it,** an impolite request to someone to be quiet. [from 16th century cant]

straight *adj.* **1.** conforming to orthodox, conservative forms of behaviour, as heterosexuality, avoidance of illegal drugs, etc. **2.** reliable, as reports, information, etc. –*n.* **3.** one who conforms to orthodox forms of behaviour. **4.** a heterosexual. –*phr.* **5. go straight,** to lead an honest life, especially after a prison sentence.

straight-acting *adj.* (of a homosexual) not openly gay or lesbian.

straight-up *adj.* **1.** honest; fair. **2.** (of sexual intercourse) conventional; employing the missionary position with little variation; avoiding oral sex, etc.: *She likes only straight-up sex.* Also, **straight-up-and-down**.

strap-on *n.* a dildo which can be worn strapped around the waist and hence moved by pelvic thrusts.

strapped *phr.* **strapped for cash,** low on funds; broke.

strawb *n.* a strawberry.

street cred *n.* credibility or status amongst people of the urban counter-culture or the trendy, fashionable set.

streetie *n.* a street kid.

streetwalker *n.* one who walks the streets, especially a soliciting prostitute.

street-wise *adj.* **1.** skilled in living in an urban environment; knowing how to survive on the streets. **2.** up with the latest trends or fashions; having street cred.

stress-head *n.* an extremely stressed person; a person easily stressed.

stretch *n.* **1.** a term of imprisonment. **2.** a jocular form of address to a tall person.

strewth *interj.* See **struth**.

strides *pl. n.* trousers.

Strine *n.* the form of Australian English which appeared in the books of Alastair Morrison, penname 'Afferbeck Lauder' (that is, 'alphabetical order'), where it was written in a form meant to represent broad pronunciation, but with spelt with shifted word boundaries so as to give the impression that other words were being used, as in *Gloria Soame* for *glorious home; sly drool* for *slide rule; Emma Chisit* for *how much is it?* [the Strine rendering of *Australian*, used in the title of Morrison's first book 'Let Stalk Strine' (i.e. *Let's talk Australian*) 1965]

strip *n.* a sporting uniform.

stroppy *adj.* rebellious and difficult to control; awkward; complaining.

strung-out *adj.* emotionally and nervously exhausted.

strut *phr.* **strut one's stuff,** to display one's skills, favourable attributes, etc., especially in an ostentatious manner.

struth *interj.* an exclamation expressing surprise or verification: *Did he say that? Struth!; Struth he did!* Also, **strewth, 'struth**. [short for *God's truth*]

stud *n.* **1.** an attractive male. **2.** a male who sleeps around or fancies himself as extremely sexually attractive.

stud-magnet *n.* a woman who many men find sexually attractive.

stuff *n.* **1.** property, as personal belongings, equipment, etc. **2.** one's own trade, profession, occupation, etc.: *to know one's stuff.* –*v.* **3.** to cause to fail; render useless; to ruin. **4.** (of males) to have sexual intercourse with. –*phr.*
5. do one's stuff, to do what is expected of one; show what one can do.
6. not to give a stuff, to be unconcerned.
7. stuff it! an exclamation indicating anger, frustration, etc.
8. stuff this for a lark (or **joke**), an exclamation denoting dissatisfaction with something.
9. stuff up, to blunder; fail.

stuffed *v.* **1.** exhausted; ruined. –*phr.*
2. get stuffed, (used imperatively) go away; piss off!

stuff-up *n.* a failure which has arisen from a foolish or thoughtless error.

stung *adj.* **1.** drunk. **2.** tricked; cheated.

stunned *phr.* **like a stunned mullet, a.** in complete bewilderment or astonishment. **b.** in a state of inertia.

stunner *n.* a person or thing of striking excellence, beauty, attractiveness, etc.

stupido *n.* a stupid person. [from Italian]

stu vac *n.* vacation from school, college, university, etc. [short for *stu*(*dent*) *vac*(*ation*)]

subbie *n.* **1.** a subcontractor, especially a sub-contracting truck operator or building tradesperson. **2.** *Derogatory.* a dull or stupid person. Also **subby**. [def 2 from '*sub*normal intellect']

suck *v.* **1.** to be contemptible, bad, despicable, disgusting, dreadful, etc.; to be utterly dreadful: *westies suck badly; homework sucks!* See **sux**. **2.** *Crass.* to perform fellatio or cunnilingus. –*interj.* **3.** an exclamation of derision, used to point out that someone has got what they deserved; serves yourself right! –*phr.*
4. fair suck of the sav (or **saveloy**) (or **sausage**) (or **sauce bottle**) (or **Siberian sandshoe**), an appeal for fairness or reason; fair go!
5. life sucks, and then you die, See **life**.
6. suck cock, *Crass.* to perform fellatio.
7. sucked in! Also, **suck a rat! suck eggs! suck fuck! suck it harder! suck my arse! suck on that! suck shit!** an exclamation of derision, used to point out that someone has got what they deserved; serves yourself right!
8. suck face, *Crass.* to French kiss; to swap spit.
9. suck off, *Crass.* to cause orgasm by fellatio.
10. suck the big one, to be utterly dreadful.
11. suck up to, to flatter; toady; fawn upon.

sucker *n.* a person easily deceived or imposed upon; dupe.

suckhole *n. Crass.* **1.** an obsequious or ingratiating person; toady –*v.*
2. to treat in a servile or obsequious manner: *to suckhole to the boss.*

sucko *interj.* an exclamation of derision.

suds *n.* **1.** the head of glass of beer, etc. **2.** beer.

sugar *n.* **1.** Also, **sugar-pie**. a term of endearment. *–interj.* **2.** a euphemism for the exclamation *shit!*

suicidal *adj.* **1.** quite dangerous and outrageously gutsy: *That was absolutely suicidal driving; taking that wave was suicidal.* **2.** absolutely excellent: *That skater dood's got suicidal gear.*

suicide blonde *n.* a woman who has dyed her own hair blonde rather than have it done by a hairdresser, with predictable results. [a pun on the phrase *died (dyed) by her own hand*]

suit *n. Derogatory.* a person wearing a business suit.

sun *phr.* **think the sun shines out of one's arse,** to have a very high opinion of oneself.

sunbeam *n.* a plate, utensil, etc. which is not used at a meal, and does not need to be washed.

sunnies *pl. n.* sunglasses.

sup *interj.* a greeting. [abbreviation of *whassup*]

supercool *adj.* **1.** extremely sophisticated, fashionable, smart, etc. **2.** very calm; controlled.

super mum *n.* a woman who displays exceptional competence in managing her career, her home and her children.

supremo *n.* a ruler; leader.

sure *adv.* **1.** surely, undoubtedly, or certainly: *He was sure fat. –interj.* **2.** a sarcastic agreement denoting disbelief. *–phr.* **3. a sure thing, a.** a certainty; something assured beyond any doubt. **b.** a racehorse or greyhound tipped to win. **c.** a woman who is a definite prospect for sexual intercourse. **4. sure thing,** assuredly; certainly.

surf *v.* to look for information on the Internet: *spend a few hours surfing the Net.*

surface *v.* **1.** to wake up. **2.** to appear after a period of being out of contact with people.

surfboard *n.* a large sanitary napkin.

surfie *n.* a devotee of surfing, especially of surfboard riding.

surfie chick *n.* a female who is part of the surfie subculture.

suss *adj.* **1.** unreliable; needing confirmation: *Her story sounded very suss to me. –phr.* **2. suss out,** to attempt to determine the possibilities of a situation, especially one involving a particular challenge or presenting probable difficulties: *Before the minister proposed his bill, he sussed out the likely reaction of the opposition.* Also, **sus.** [shortened from *suspect* or *suspicious*]

sux *v.* **1.** (often used in graffiti) to be contemptible, bad, despicable, dreadful, etc.; to suck: *school sux; you sux! –phr.* **2. life sux, and then you die,** See **life.** [originally a respelling of *sucks*, the third person present singular of *suck*, but also used for first and second person and the plural, where, despite its spelling, it is pronounced *suck*; such a spelling is purposefully designed to flout spelling rules as spelling is part of the authoritarian regime that teenagers rebel against]

swag *n.* **1.** *Hist.* a bundle or roll carried across the shoulders or otherwise, and containing the personal belongings of a traveller through the bush, a miner, etc.; shiralee; bluey. **2.** any similar bundle of belongings. **3.** plundered property; booty. **4.** an unspecified but large number or quantity: *a swag of people*. [British dialect]

swagman *n. Hist.* **1.** a man who travels about the country on foot, living on his earnings from occasional jobs, or gifts of money or food. **2.** one who carries a swag. Also, **swagger, swaggie, swagwoman**.

swanky *adj.* **1.** conceited; boastful. **2.** expensive; smart; luxurious.

swap *n.* **1.** Also, **swappie**. a card in a collection which one is willing to swap, usually because it is a duplicate. *–phr.* **2. swap spit,** to French kiss; to suck face.

sweat *v.* **1.** to exert oneself strenuously; work hard. **2.** to feel distress, as from anxiety, impatience, vexation, etc. *–n.* **3.** a state of perturbation, anxiety, or impatience. **4.** a sweatshirt. *–phr.*
5. no sweat! it's no problem!
6. sweat blood, to be under a strain; be anxious; worry.
7. sweat it out, to hold out; endure until the end.
8. sweat on, to await anxiously.

sweet *adj.* **1.** satisfactory as arranged: *She's sweet*. **2.** beautifully executed, as a skateboard trick, a pass in football, a frisbee throw, etc.

sweetener *n.* **1.** a bribe. **2.** a financial or other benefit added to something on offer.

Sweet Fanny Adams *n.* very little; next to nothing. Also, **sweet FA**. [euphemism for *sweet fuck-all*]

sweet fuck-all *n. Offensive.* nothing: *He's done sweet fuck-all about it.*

swiftie *n.* **1.** an unfair act; a deceitful practice; a confidence trick. **2.** a con artist; a devious operator. Also, **swifty**.

swill *n. Ultimate frisbee.* a really bad pass.

swinger *n.* **1.** an active, lively, or modern person. **2. a.** a person who exchanges sexual partners frequently. **b.** a member of a group of people who agree to exchange sexual partners on a casual basis. **3.** (in motorcycle side-car racing) the rider in the side-car.

swipe *v.* to steal.

switched-on *adj.* with heightened awareness.

switcheroo *n.* a change; a turnabout.

switch hitter *n.* a bisexual person.

swiz *n.* **1.** a disappointment. **2.** a fraud; swindle. Also, **swizz**. [earlier *swizzle*; origin uncertain]

swy *n.* **1.** the game two-up. **2.** *Prison.* a two ounces of tobacco. **3.** *Prison.* a two-year jail sentence. **4.** *Obsolete.* a two-shilling coin; florin; two shillings. [probably from a Yiddish use of German *zwei* two]

synchro *n. Motor.* synchromesh.

TIN LID

Rhyming slang has been a feature of Australian slang forever. Everyone knows the classic oldies: *Khyber (pass)* – arse; *Noah's (ark)* – shark; *china (plate)* – mate; *frog (and toad)* – road; *(Reg) Grundies* – undies; *optic (nerve)* – perve; and *horse's (hoof)* – poof. Some of these are borrowings of English rhyming slang, others our own invention. New to the scene are the recent inventions *billy lid* and *tin lid*, both meaning "kid". Also, as heard on the telecast of the 1996 Olympic Games, there is the term *Jatz crackers*, for knackers, a pair of which needed polite reference to when they copped a beating in a badly executed high-dive. Ouch! Another invention of a few years back was *Schindler's (list)*, for "pissed". This was recorded in 1994 when Steven Spielberg's movie of Thomas Keneally's novel first hit Australian screens.

TWO – BOB

In former times *two bob* was two shillings, since a *bob* was a shilling. The coin worth two bob was called a florin. This coin was almost identical in size to the modern twenty cent piece, brought in with the changeover to decimal currency in 1966, and which is also still known as *two bob*. Unhappily this slang is dying out. Something worth *two bob* was pretty cheap and thus we get the phrase *to go like a two-bob watch* which means to work or perform badly. Clearly watches in this price range were not very reliable. Amongst lairs there was the *two-bob lair* – a particular breed of lair who tried to be flashy and ostentatious, who put on the dog, but with only the cheapest and tackiest of accoutrements. A *two-bob boss* is a petty official, a bureaucratic microbe, who swaggers around throwing his weight about in a highly officious manner. Finally, inexpert or slap-dash hammerers often strike wide of the mark and leave ugly circular indentations in the wood surface, from their shape and size these are called two-bobs.

TIN – POT

bodger (obs.), bodgie, bodgy, bogus, brummy, chatty, crap, crappy, crook, crud, cruddy, crummy, el cheapo, grotty, junky, lousy, naff (Chiefly Brit.), no-good, rough, rubbishy, scummy, shit, shitty, shoddy, tacky, trashy

STUCK FOR WORDS

tab *n.* **1.** a tablet of some drug. *–phr.*
2. keep tabs on, to keep account of or a check on: *keep tabs on your expenses.*
3. pick up the tab, to pay the bill.

table *phr.*
1. drink (someone) under the table, to out-drink (someone).
2. under the table, a. drunk to the extent of being incapable. **b.** given as a bribe or other secret dealing.

tacho *n.* a tachometer. Also, **tach**.

tack *n.* food; fare: *hard tack.* [origin unknown]

tacker *n.* a young kid. [originally from Devon and Cornwall dialect]

tack-o-rama *adj.* completely tacky.

tacky *adj.* in extremely poor taste; *a tacky remark; tacky decor.* [originally US; originally meaning 'small, useless horse']

tad *n., adj.* a little bit: *It won't make a tad of difference; I'm a tad late.* [originally US meaning 'small boy', possibly from *tadpole*]

ta-da *interj.* an expression used to present some feat or surprise. [reduplicating the musical notes conventionally used for a short introductory fanfare]

taddie *n.* a tadpole.

tadpoling *n.* catching tadpoles and keeping them in a jar, etc., a common children's pastime.

Taffy *n.* a Welshman. [Welsh form of *Davy,* shortened form of *David,* proper name and name of patron saint of Wales]

tag *n.* **1.** a graffiti artist's signature. **2.** a person following someone: *couldn't shake the tag. –v.* **3.** to follow closely. **4.** *Australian Rules.* to follow or mark (an opponent) closely in order to limit their play. [from *tag* an attached label]

tagger *n.* **1.** *Australian Rules.* one who follows an opponent closely with the hope of spoiling the opponent's play. **2.** a graffiti writer.

tail *n.* **1.** the buttocks; rump; arse.
2. a person who follows another, especially one who is employed to do so in order to hinder their escape or observe their movements.
3. *Offensive.* a woman considered as a sex object: *a nice bit of tail. –v.*
4. to follow close behind. **5.** to follow a person surreptitiously: *tailing a suspect.*

tailie *n.* *Two-up.* a person who consistently bets on tails.

tailor-made *n.* a cigarette made by machine, i.e., not hand rolled.

tail spin *n.* a state of utter confusion; flat spin.

take *n.* **1.** a cheat; a swindle. **2.** a profit, as from a short term business venture, a day's gambling, etc.: *The take was $100. –phr.*
3. on the take, receiving bribes, as a dishonest police officer, politician, etc.
4. take (someone) apart, a. to berate or abuse (someone). **b.** to physically assault (someone).
5. take down, to take advantage of; cheat; swindle.
6. take in, to deceive, trick or cheat.
7. take it out of, to exhaust; sap (one's) strength or energy.
8. take it out on, to vent wrath, anger or the like.
9. take off, a. to become popular: *The show really took off in Mel-*

bourne. **b.** to begin to move or increase quickly: *Prices took off; the play takes off in the second act.* **c.** to imitate or mimic.

10. take on, a. to start a quarrel or fight with. **b.** to stand up to in a position of conflict, especially political.

11. take on board, to accept and use: *They took that idea on board.*

12. take out, a. to destroy, eliminate, render harmless: *to take out a military post.* **c.** to win: *The Windies took out the series.*

13. take to, to attack: *He took to the bloke with a cricket bat.*

take-down *n.* a fraudulent transaction.

take-off *n.* **1.** an imitating or mimicking; caricature. **2.** *Surfing.* **a.** standing on the board to begin a ride. **b.** the point on a wave where one does this, or should do this.

take-out *n.* take-away food: *We had take-out last night.*

talent *n.* **1.** women or men viewed as possible sexual partners: *Check out the guy talent on page 48.* **2.** *Obsolete.* the members of the underworld.

talk *v.* **1.** to reveal information: *We have ways to make you talk.* *–phr.*
2. be talking, an idiom used to denote an outstanding example, either positive or negative, of a particular thing under discussion: *I'm talking mega-bucks; we're talking major dag.*
3. talk about! used to add emphasis to a statement: *Talk about laugh.*
4. talk big, to speak boastfully.
5. talk down to, to speak condescendingly to.
6. talk the leg off an iron pot (or **a chair**), or **talk the ears off** (**someone**), to talk at great length.

Tallarook *phr.* **things are crook in Tallarook** (or **Muswellbrook**), the situation is not good.

tall poppy *n.* a person who is preeminent in a particular field; a person with great wealth or status.

tangle *n.* **1.** a conflict, quarrel, or disagreement. *–phr.* **2. tangle with,** to conflict, quarrel, or argue with.

tank *n.* **1.** *Prison.* a safe. *–v.* **2.** to deliberately lose (a match or a contest). *–phr.*
3. built like a tank, See **built**.
4. tank up, a. to fill the tank of a motor vehicle with fuel. **b.** to drink heavily.

tanked *adj.* intoxicated, especially with beer. Also, **tanked up**. See **half-tanked**.

tank man *n.* *Prison.* a person who specialises in stealing from safes.

tanner *n. Obsolete.* a sixpence. [19th century British slang; origin unknown]

tan track *phr.* **ride the tan track,** *Crass.* to practise anal sex. [punning on the *tan track* at a racecourse]

tap dancer *n.* cancer. [rhyming slang]

tart *n.* **1.** *Originally.* (used positively) a girlfriend. **2.** *Derogatory.* **a.** a woman deemed to be promiscuous. **b.** any woman. **3.** *Derogatory.* a prostitute. *–phr.* **4. tart up,** to adorn; make attractive, especially with cheap ornaments and cosmetics. [originally also *jamtart*, i.e. a sweet woman; see *honey-pie, sugar*]

Tasmania *phr.* **map of Tasmania,**

the female pubic area. Also, **map of Tassie**.

tassel *n.* the penis.

tat *n.* a tattoo.

team cream *n. Crass.* an occasion on which a number of males have sexual intercourse with one female; gang bang.

tear *v.* **1.** to move or go with violence or great haste: *to tear along the expressway.* *–phr.* **2. tear into,** to attack violently, either physically or verbally. **3. tear strips off,** to reprove severely.

tear-arse *v.* to run or drive exceedingly fast.

tearaway *n.* **1.** an impetuous or unruly person. *–adj.* **2.** uncontrolled; impetuous. **3.** (of a sporting win, etc.) won by a long distance or a high score: *They had a tearaway victory.*

tease *n.* someone who sexually teases or leads others on.

tech *n.* **1.** a technical college or school. **2.** Also, **tech-head**. someone with a professional or passionate interest in technology, especially computing.

teched-up *adj.* having or being familiar with the latest technical equipment.

techie *n.* a technical services employee.

technical *phr.* **get technical,** to propound or apply a strict interpretation of the rules.

technicolour yawn *n.* the act of vomiting.

techno *n.* a type of electronic dance music.

technobabble *n.* seemingly meaningless technological jargon.

techno-head *n.* an enthusiast of techno dance music.

telegraph *v.* to give prior indication of (one's moves).

telephone *phr.* **call God on the big white telephone,** a metaphor for vomiting into a toilet bowl, especially from having drunk too much alcohol.

telly *n.* television. Also, **tellie**.

ten-four *interj.* an exclamation signifying agreement, acceptance, etc. Also, **10-4**. [originally a code used by CB radio operators]

tenner *n.* **1.** *Obsolete.* a ten-pound note. **2.** a ten-dollar note.

teno *n.* tenosynovitis; inflammation of the tendon sheath, especially inflammation of the sheath in the wrists, resulting from RSI.

terrif *adj.* wonderful; terrific.

Territory confetti *n.* ring pulls from beer cans.

Territory rig *n. NT.* the dress which men adopt in the Northern Territory on official occasions comprising long trousers, shirt and tie. Also, **Darwin rig**.

terrorists *pl. n. Jocular.* tourists (perceived as being nuisances).

tetchy *adj.* irritable; touchy. Also, **techy**.

thang *n. Jocular.* thing: *the latest thang; a happenin' thang; do one's thang.*

thatch *n.* **1.** the hair covering the head. **2.** the pubic hair, especially of a woman.

thick *adj.* slow of mental apprehension; stupid; dull; slow-witted.

thickhead *n.* a stupid or slow person.

thing *n.* **1.** an unaccountable attitude or feeling about something, as of fear or aversion: *I have a thing about spiders.* **2.** a sexual feeling for: *She's got a thing for Mr Darcy.* *–phr.*
3. do one's thing, to act in a characteristic manner; to do what is most satisfying to oneself.
4. make a (big) thing of, to turn into a major issue: *OK, so I made a mistake, there's no need to make a thing of it.*
5. one of those things, an event or situation which is unavoidable or which is no longer remediable.

thingie *adj.* overly sensitive; anxious; tense: *He gets all thingie with the children on a long car trip.* Also, **thingy**.

thingummyjig *n.* an indefinite name for a thing or person which a speaker cannot or does not designate more precisely. Also, **thingo, thingummybob, thingummy, thingumabob.**

third degree *n.* **1.** intense questioning, often with rough treatment, used by authorities to extract information from a person. **2.** any intense questioning: *I was given the third degree about the scratch on the side door of the van.*

third leg *n.* the penis.

thou *n.* **1.** a thousand (dollars, kilometres, etc.). **2.** one thousandth of (an inch, etc.).

thread *n.* **1.** (*pl.*) clothes. **2.** *Internet.* a series of newsgroup postings and replies.

three-dog night *n.* a very cold night. [from the practice of bushmen of sleeping with their dogs; the colder the night, the more dogs needed]

three-on-the-tree *n.* a column shift for a motor vehicle with three forward gears (opposed to *four-on-the-floor*).

throne *phr.* **the throne,** the toilet.

throw *v.* **1.** to permit an opponent to win (a race, contest, or the like) deliberately, as for a bribe. **2.** to astonish; disconcert; confuse. **3.** *TV.* to cross to another presenter. *–phr.*
4. throw away, to fail to use; miss (an opportunity, chance, etc.).
5. throw in, to add as an extra, especially in a bargain.
6. throw in one's hand, to concede defeat; surrender. [from poker]
7. throw in the towel (or **sponge**), to give in; accept defeat. [from boxing]

throwdown *n.* **1.** a small firework which explodes when thrown onto a surface. **2.** a stubby or small bottle of beer.

thruster *n.* a type of surfboard with three fins.

thumb *v.* to hitch-hike: *to thumb one's way around Queensland.*

thumb fight *n.* a contest in which two people hold interlocked fists and each attempt to pin down the other's thumb.

thumbs down *n.* a rejection or disapproval: *a big thumbs down for the presidency.* Also, **thumbs-down**.

thumbs up *interj.* **1.** an exclamation indicating encouragement. *–n.* **2.** a gesture made by clenching the fingers and holding the thumb vertical, symbolising success. **3.** a similar, but now out-of-date, gesture made with a vigorous upward thrust of the hand, symbolising contempt. **4.** Also, **thumbs-up**. an approval: *gave it the thumbs-up.*

thunderbox *n.* a toilet.

thunder thighs *n.* a person with large, fat legs.

thunk *v.* a jocular past tense or past participle of 'think': *I thunk and thunk.* [actually originally a mid-Yorkshire dialect form]

thusly *adv.* in this manner.

tick¹ *n.* **1.** a moment or instant: *Hang on a tick.* *–phr.* **2. what makes one tick,** what motivates one's behaviour.

tick² *n.* **1.** credit or trust: *to buy on tick.* *–phr.* **2. tick up,** to obtain on credit. [dating from the 16th century; from *ticket*]

ticker *n.* **1.** a watch. **2.** the heart.

tickle *v.* **1.** to amuse or please greatly. *–phr.*
2. tickle the peter, to rob the till.
3. tickle the ivories, to play the piano.

tick-tack *n.* **1.** Also, **tick-tacking**. a type of manual, and illegal, semaphore once popularly used at racetracks between bookmakers and their touts. **2.** a type of skateboard manoeuvre of the 1970s in which the front wheels are made to hit the ground to the right and left alternatively. *–v.* **3.** to communicate via tick-tack; to practise tick-tacking.

tiddly *adj.* slightly drunk; tipsy. [originally meaning 'a drink', from rhyming slang *tiddlywink* drink]

tiggy *n.* **1.** a children's game involving chasing and catching. *–phr.* **2. tiggy (tiggy) touch wood,** *Australian Rules.* a game characterised by many free kicks awarded because of minor infringements.

tight *adj.* **1.** close; nearly even: *a tight race.* **2.** *Music.* played exceedingly well; clean and polished in quality: *this band is tight.* **3.** stingy or parsimonious. **4.** Also, **tight as a newt.** drunk; tipsy. *–phr.* **5. tight as a bull's arse in fly-time, tight as a duck's arse, tight as a fish's arse, tight as a mouse's ear,** to be extremely mean with money; tight-arsed.

tight-arsed *adj.* **1.** mean; parsimonious. **2.** haughty.

tightwad *n.* a close-fisted or stingy person.

tike *n.* See **tyke**.

time *n.* **1.** a term of imprisonment. *–phr.*
2. do time, to serve a prison sentence.
3. kill time, to occupy oneself in some manner so as to make the time pass quickly.

time warp *n.* **1.** a reminiscence of past times. **2.** a feeling of being in a former time. **3.** a place which has changed little over the years. **4.** a person who has changed little over the years, or who holds out-moded values, notions, attitudes, etc. *–phr.* **5. the time warp,** a dance originating in *The Rocky Horror Picture Show*, done to the song *Time Warp*. [from the science fiction *time warp* a supposed warp in the space-time continuum allowing passage to other times]

timothy *n.* a brothel. [probably from rhyming slang *Timothy Titmouse* house]

tin arse *n.* a lucky person. Also, **tin bum, tin back**. [from *tin* money]

tingle *n.* a telephone call.

tin hares *pl. n.* the greyhounds; greyhound racing.

tinkle *v.* **1.** to urinate. *–n.* **2.** the act of urinating. Also, **twinkle**.

tin lid *n.* a child. [rhyming slang for *kid*]

tinned dog *n.* canned meat.

tinnie *n.* **1.** a can of beer. **2.** a light, aluminium-hulled boat. Also, **tinny**.

tinny *adj.* lucky. [from *tin* money; see *tin arse*]

tin-pot *adj.* inferior; petty; worthless.

tinsel town *n.* **1.** Hollywood. *–adj.* **2.** artificial; ephemeral.

tin teeth *pl. n.* dental braces.

tip *n.* **1.** the tips of the marijuana plant dried and prepared for smoking. **2.** Also, **tips**. the game of chasings; tippy. *–phr.* **3. tip off, a.** to give (someone) private or secret information; inform. **b.** to warn of impending trouble, danger, etc.

tip-off *n.* a hint or warning: *They got a tip-off about the raid.*

tippy *n.* the game of chasings; tag. Also, **tip, tips**.

tipster *n.* one who makes a business of furnishing tips, as for use in betting, speculation, etc. Also, **tipper, tip slinger**.

tiptop *adj.* of the highest quality or excellence: *in tiptop condition.*

tired *phr.* **tired and emotional**, a euphemistic description of a person who is drunk.

tit *n.* **1.** a female breast. *–phr.* **2. off one's tits, a.** very drunk. **b.** high on a drug or drugs, especially speed. [variant of *teat*, from Old English *titt*]

titfer *n.* a hat. [rhyming slang *tit for tat* hat]

tit fuck *n. Offensive.* a rubbing of the erect penis between and over the breasts of a sexual partner.

tit-off *v.* to grope or fondle the breasts of a female.

tits and bums *adj.* denoting a type of film in which females are exploited sexually by emphasis on their figures, breasts, etc.

tit torture *n.* sado-masochistic torture of the chest and nipples.

titty *n.* **1.** a female breast. *–phr.* **2. titty hard-ons**, erect nipples of a woman's breasts usually resulting from cold temperature, especially when showing through clothing.

tix *pl. n. Travel Industry.* tickets.

tizz *n.* a state of somewhat hysterical confusion and anxiety, often expressed in frantic but ineffectual activity: *Don't get in a tizz.* Also, **tizzy**.

tizzy *n.* **1.** a tizz. *–adj.* **2.** gaudy; vulgar; tinselly. [origin unknown]

TLC *n.* sympathetic attention. [initialism from *Tender Loving Care*]

toad *n. Internet.* (in a MUD) to close down (someone's) account or access; to kill off (a character).

to-and-from *n.* an English person. [rhyming slang *to and from* pom]

toasting *n.* lyrical speech spoken over dub tracks, the Jamaican precursor to rap.

tockley *n.* the penis. [apparently invented by the *Picture* magazine, Sydney]

todger *n.* the penis. [origin unknown]

to-die-for *adj.* extremely desirable: *the biggest to-die-for hunk at school; to-die-for tickets.*

toecutter *n.* **1.** a criminal thug who intimidates and brutalises people for a crime boss. **2.** a particularly ruthless person, especially in politics.

toey *adj.* **1.** anxious; apprehensive; edgy. **2.** keen, ready to go. **3.** (of a horse) having an excitable temperament; fast. *–phr.* **4. toey as a Roman sandal,** extremely anxious.

toff *n.* a rich, upper-class, usually well-dressed person.

toffee-nosed *adj. Originally Brit.* snobbish; pretentious; upper-class.

tog *v.* to clothe; dress: *all togged up.* [see *togs*]

together *adj.* **1.** capable and calm; in control of oneself: *She was a very together person. –phr.* **2. get/have one's shit together,** See **shit**.

togs *pl. n.* clothes: *football togs, swimming togs.* [from *tog* a coat, from cant *togeman* a coat, from either French *toge* or Latin *toga* toga]

toilet roll doll *n.* a doll with a dress constructed so that the skirt portion forms the cover of a spare toilet roll in a toilet.

toke *n.* a puff of a cigarette or joint. [origin unknown]

tomato *n.* a cricket ball.

tombowler *n.* a large marble.

tombstone *n.* a wheelie-bin.

tomtits *pl. n.* **1.** diarrhoea. **2.** anger; exasperation. [rhyming slang *tomtits* the shits]

ton[1] *n.* **1.** a heavy weight: *That book weighs a ton.* **2.** (*pl.*) very many; a good deal: *tons of things to see.*

ton[2] *n.* **1.** one hundred. **2.** *Cricket.* the score of one hundred runs. **3.** (formerly) a speed of one hundred miles an hour.

tonk[1] *n. Derogatory.* **1.** a homosexual male. **2.** the penis. [from rhyming slang *tonka bean* queen]

tonk[2] *n. Cricket.* **1.** a hit. *–v.* **2.** to give the ball a tonk. [imitative]

tonka tough *adj. Jocular.* extremely tough. [from an advertising slogan for *Tonka* toys, a brand of heavy duty toy trucks, back-hoes, etc.]

tonsil hockey *n.* French kissing; tongue kissing.

toodle-loo *interj.* an expression of farewell. Also, **tiddle-pip, toodle-pip.** [possibly from the French expression of farewell *tout à l' heure*]

too-hard basket *n.* an imaginary basket in which papers coming into an office are placed if the recipient finds them difficult and wishes to delay making a decision.

tool *n. Crass.* the penis. [dating back to the 16th century]

toon *n.* a tune; a song: *the latest toons.*

tooroo *interj.* goodbye.

tooshie *adj.* angry or upset: *Don't get tooshie with me.* [? see *tush*]

toot *n.* a toilet. [euphemistic pronunciation of *toilet*]

toot sweet *n. Jocular.* immediately. [humorous spelling of French *tout de suite*]

tootsy *n.* **1.** a foot. **2.** a lesbian. **3.** Also, **toots, tootsie-wootsie.** (a demeaning or belittling term of address to) a woman. *–phr.* **4. play tootsy, a.** (of two people) to touch feet secretly under a table as part of amorous play. **b.** (of a man) to have an affair. Also, **tootsie.**

top *adj.* **1.** the best; excellent: *a top bloke; top fun.* *–n.* **2.** Also, **top-man.** a male homosexual who takes the active role. *–phr.*
3. top off, a. to inform on; tell on. **b.** to finish; cap: *He topped off the sports day with a win in the marathon.*
4. top oneself, to kill oneself.

top dog *n.* person in the highest position; leader; boss.

top-ender *n.* a person living in the northern part of the Northern Territory of Australia. Also, **Top-Ender.**

top-heavy *adj. Crass.* (of a woman) having large breasts.

top-off *n. Older slang.* one who informs on another; an informer.

tops *adj.* wonderful; great: *We had a tops time; The party was tops.*

torch *v.* **1.** to set on fire. **2.** *Sport.* to completely outplay the opposition. *–phr.* **3. carry a torch for,** to be still madly in love with someone despite not being in a relationship with them.

tosh *n.* nonsense. [origin unknown]

toss *n.* **1.** an act of masturbation. *–phr.*
2. argue the toss, to go on arguing after a dispute has been settled.
3. to not give a toss, to be unconcerned; not care.
4. toss off, a. (of a male) to ejaculate sperm; have an orgasm. **b.** (of a male) to masturbate. **c.** to produce casually: *to toss off a poem.*
5. toss up, to weigh up in order to make a decision.

tosser *n.* a stupid or annoying person; a jerk; a wanker.

tossle *n.* the penis. Also, **tossil.** [variant of *tassel*]

toss-up *n.* an even chance: *The election is a toss-up.*

tot[1] *phr.* **tot up,** to add up. [short for *total*]

tot[2] *n.* **1.** a small glass of spirits. **2.** a small child.

total *v.* **1.** to wreck (a vehicle) through crashing it. **2.** to completely ruin.

t'othersider *n. WA.* a person living on the other side of the Nullarbor Plain.

touch *v.* **1.** to beg for money from. **2.** to borrow money and not give it back. *–n.* **3.** the act of applying to a person for money, as a gift or loan. **4.** an obtaining of money thus. **5.** the money obtained. **6.** a person from whom such money can be obtained easily.

touched *adj.* slightly crazy; weird. [from *touch* to affect mentally]

touchy-feely *adj.* much given to touching other people; generally physically affectionate.

tough *n.* **1.** a rough bully; a mean, abusive man. *–interj.* **2.** an exclamation of contempt; sucked in! tough luck! *–phr.* **3. tough it out,** to persevere to the end against difficulties, especially while under possibly justified criticism.

tough shit *interj.* **1.** bad luck; hard luck. **2.** a rebuff to an appeal for sympathy. Also, **tough titties.**

tout *n.* **1.** a racecourse tipster; specifically one who tips many different horses in a race to different people in the hope of receiving a gratuity from one of the winning punters. **2.** a person who watches and times practising racehorses in order to gain information for giving tips. **3.** a spy or informer. **4.** a person engaged to find customers for a business. –*v.* **5.** to work as a tout at a racecourse. **6.** to spy or inform on. **7.** to offer wares or services: *touting for customers; touted cheap jewellery.* **8.** to proclaim (as something): *chocolate was once touted as an aphrodisiac.* **9.** to put forward: *Only a third of the touted figure was made.* [old thieve's slang, to spy, from Middle English *tuten* to look out, peer, from Old English *tytan* to peep]

towie *n.* **1.** a tow truck. **2.** a tow truck driver.

town bike *n. Offensive and derogatory.* a woman who has sex with many different men in a certain locale, as a suburb, town, etc.; a woman with a reputation for sleeping around. [see *bike*]

townie *n.* one who comes from a town and is ignorant of country ways.

toy *phr.* **have taken away the toys but left the playground,** have had a hysterectomy.

toy boy *n.* the young male partner of an older woman or homosexual male, especially one who receives financial favours in return for services rendered.

trac *n. Prison.* a stubborn, unmanageable prisoner.

track *n.* **1.** *Prison.* a prison warder who will carry contraband messages or goods out of or into a prison for a prisoner. **2.** (*pl.*) Also, **track marks.** scars or marks on the arms or legs caused by habitual use of a hypodermic needle. –*phr.* **3. on the (wallaby) track,** *Hist.* itinerant; on the move, as a swagman, etc.

trackie *adj.* **1.** tracksuit: *trackie pants; trackie top.* –*n.* **2.** (*pl.*) a tracksuit.

trade *n.* (amongst gays and lesbians) a pick-up for casual sex. See **rough trade**.

train surfing *n.* the practice of standing on top of a moving railway carriage and imitating the pose of a surfboard rider.

trance *n.* a type of dance music.

trannie *n.* **1.** a transistor radio. **2.** a transformer. **3.** a transparency. **4.** Also, **trany.** a transvestite. **5.** Also, **trany.** a transsexual.

trap *n.* **1.** the mouth: *Shut your trap!* **2.** *Hist.* a trooper; a colonial police officer.

trash *n.* **1.** nonsense; rubbish: *Don't talk such trash!* **2.** *Derogatory.* an abusive term for people that one views as worthless or inferior types, especially if of another race, social stratum, etc.: *I've seen enough of that trash; black trash; white trash.* **3.** *Sport.* Also, **trash talk.** verbal abuse designed to hassle the opposition and put them off their game; sledging. –*v.* **4.** to speak unfavourably of; to rubbish. **5.** to get extremely drunk: *getting trashed at the Imperial.* **6.** to utterly wreck or mess up: *trashed his car; they totally trashed the joint.* **7.** *Sport.* to hassle or abuse someone verbally, especially in order to put them off their game.

trashed *adj.* 1. under the effects of much alcohol; drunk. 2. under the influence of marijuana or some other drug; out of it.

trawl *v.* to search for a sexual partner.

trax *n.* dance tracks.

Trekkie *n.* an avid fan of the television series *Star Trek*. Also, **Trekker**.

trendoid *n.* a trendy person.

trendy *n.* 1. one who embraces an ultrafashionable life-style. 2. one who adopts a set of avant-garde social or political viewpoints.

trey *n.* 1. *Obsolete.* a threepenny piece; threepence. 2. (*pl.*) the shits. 3. (*pl.*) a woman's breasts; tits. Also, **tray, tray-bit, trey-bit.** [def 1 from British slang, from *trey* three, from Old French; def 2 rhyming slang]

trick *n.* 1. a prostitute's customer. –*adj.* 2. classy; very fine; extremely well done up: *a really trick engine.*

trip *n.* 1. a certain quantity of LSD prepared for taking. 2. a period under the influence of a hallucinatory drug. 3. something that amazes; a spin-out. –*v.* 4. Also, **trip out. a.** to experience the effects of LSD or other drugs. **b.** to have an exhilarating or totally amazing experience similar to that of an LSD trip.

trip hop *n.* a type of dance music.

tripod *n. Crass.* a man with a large penis.

trippy *adj.* exhilarating, as of a hallucinogenic trip.

triss *n.* 1. an effeminate homosexual male. –*phr.* 2. **triss about,** to behave in the manner of an effeminate homosexual male. Also, **trish, trizz.**

trissy *adj.* in the manner of an effeminate homosexual male.

trojan horse *n. Computing.* a program that ostensibly does one thing, but actually performs some hidden or covert task.

troll *v.* 1. to go about looking for a casual sexual partner; cruise. 2. *Internet.* to post a provocative message to a newsgroup in order to stimulate a series of follow-up postings.

troppo *adj.* mentally disturbed. [shortened form of *tropical* from mental illness resulting from long military service in the tropics]

trot *phr.*
  1. **a good (bad) trot,** a run of good (bad) luck.
  2. **hot to trot,** extremely eager; raring to go.
  3. **on the trot, a.** in a state of continuous activity. **b.** one after another; in quick succession: *He won three races on the trot.*

trots *pl. n.* 1. diarrhoea. 2. harness racing.

trouble and strife *n.* a wife. [rhyming slang]

truckie *n.* a truck driver. Also, **trucker**.

true *phr.*
  1. **true blue,** loyal; faithful; genuine.
  2. **true dinks,** fair dinkum!

trumpy *n.* a Triumph motorcycle.

try *phr.* **try it on, a.** to attempt to deceive, hoodwink or test the patience of someone; to attempt to work a ruse or con. **b.** to try to induce someone to have sex.

try-hard *n.* **1.** one who attempts to be like someone: *a Madonna try-hard.* **2.** one who trys, failingly, to gain social acceptance, or to be cool, etc. *–adj.* **3.** of the nature of a try-hard; trying unsuccessfully: *a try-hard rock star; typical try-hard stuff.* Also, **tryhard**.

try-on *n.* **1.** an attempt to hoodwink, deceive; an attempted con job. **2.** an attempt to induce someone into having sex; a come on.

TS *abbrev.* transsexual.

TT *abbrev.* (in personal ads) tit torture.

tub *n. pl.* drums.

tube *n.* **1.** *Surfing.* the barrel of a breaking wave. **2.** a can of beer: *Let's sink a few tubes. –phr.*
3. go down the tubes, to go to ruin.
4. the tube, television.

tube time *n. Surfing.* the amount of time a rider has spent riding tubes of waves, used as a measure of experience.

tucker[1] *n.* food: *bush tucker; good tucker.* [i.e. that which is *tucked into* or *tucked away*]

tucker[2] *phr.* **tucker out,** to weary; tire; exhaust. [from *tucked up* (of an animal) having the flanks drawn in from fatigue]

tuckerbag *n. Hist.* a bag used for carrying food, as by a swagman.

tug *v.* **1.** (of a male) to masturbate. *–n.* **2.** an act of male masturbation.

tummy-banana *n.* the penis.

tune *v.* **1.** to successfully gain another's sexual favours; to crack on to. *–phr.*
2. call the tune, to be in a position to give orders, dictate policy, etc.; command; control.
3. change one's tune, to change one's mind; reverse previously held views, attitudes, etc.
4. to the tune of, to the amount of.

turd *n. Offensive.* **1.** a piece of excrement. **2.** *Derogatory.* a despicable person. [from Middle and Old English *tord*]

turd-burglar *n. Offensive and derogatory.* a male homosexual. Also, **turd-surfer**.

turd strangler *n. Offensive.* a plumber.

turf *n.* **1.** territory belonging to a gang. *–phr.*
2. the turf, the world of horseracing.

turkey *n.* **1.** a foolish person; an absolute goose. **2.** something which is unsuccessful; a flop.

turn *n.* **1.** a party. *–phr.*
2. turn it on, a. to start a fight. **b.** to engage in sexual intercourse enthusiastically: *She really turns it on.* **c.** to engage in some activity enthusiastically, as dancing, complaining, etc.
3. turn it up! (used imperatively) stop it! shut up!
4. turn off, a. to stop listening, thinking, etc. **b.** to cause revulsion, especially sexual: *He really turns me off.*
5. turn on, to arouse or please, especially sexually.

turn-off *n.* that which or one who excites disgust, revulsion, disinterest, etc., especially sexual.

turn-on *n.* that which or one who excites interest, enthusiasm, etc., especially sexual.

turn-up *n.* 1. a surprise; an unexpected reversal of fortune. Also, **turn-up for the books**.

turps *n.* 1. turpentine. –*phr.* 2. **on the turps,** drinking intoxicating liquor excessively.

tush *n.* the buttocks; the arse or rump. [probably an abbreviation of Yiddish *toches*]

TV *abbrev.* transvestite.

twat *n. Offensive.* 1. the vagina or vulva. 2. a stupid person. Also, **twot.** [dating from the 17th century; origin unknown; perhaps a reflex of an Old English borrowing of Old Norse *thveit* slit, forest clearing]

tweak *n.* 1. *Cricket.* extra spin imparted to a bowl: *He gives the ball a good tweak.* –*v.* 2. *Surfing.* to luckily find good surf; to fluke some good surf.

tweaker *n.* a finger-spinner in cricket.

twerp *n.* an insignificant or stupid person. Also, **twirp.**

twinkle *v.* 1. to urinate. –*n.* 2. the act of urinating. Also, **tinkle.**

twistie *n.* a twist-top bottle of beer.

twit *n.* a fool; twerp.

two bob *n.* 1. the sum of twenty cents. 2. a twenty-cent piece. 3. *Obsolete.* the sum of two shillings. 4. *Obsolete.* a silver coin of this value; a florin. –*phr.*
5. **have two bob each way,** to support contradictory causes at the same time, often in self-protection.
6. **not the full two bob,** weak of intellect.
7. **two bob's worth** or **two cent's worth,** opinion, say or advice: *He got in his two bob's worth before the end of the meeting.* Also, **two-bob.**

two-bob *adj.* 1. of poor quality; useless; unreliable: *goes like a two-bob watch.* –*phr.*
2. **mad** (or **silly**) **as a two-bob watch,** stupid; idiotic; erratic.
3. **two-bob boss,** a minor official who delights in exerting authority in an overbearing manner.
4. **two-bob millionaire,** a person temporarily flush with money.

two-header *n.* a double-headed coin.

two-pot screamer *n.* someone who gets uproariously drunk after consuming very little alcohol.

2SM *n.* a cup of coffee, or tea, made with two sugars and milk. [*2 s*ugars and *m*ilk; punning on the name of a Sydney radio station]

two-up *n.* a gambling game in which two coins are spun in the air and bets are laid on whether they fall heads or tails; swy.

tyke *n.* 1. a Roman Catholic. 2. a small kid. Also, **tike.** [def 1 from Northern Ireland Protestant name for a Catholic *Taig*, from the Irish name *Tadhg*; def 2 earlier meaning 'dog', from Old Norse *tik* bitch]

typical *interj.* an exclamation of disgust at some bad turn of events or when someone has acted according to some negative stereotype.

U - IE

The Australian penchant for shortening words and whacking the suffix *–ie* to the end is perhaps brought to perfection in this word. This is about as short as you get, just a single letter plus the suffix. That's minimalism for you. Of course, what makes this possible is the fact that the base word *U-turn* actually has the single letter *U* as its first syllable. This extremity in brevity can only be matched by one other term…the *R-ie*, a familiar term for your local *RSL Club*, also known as the *Razza* or the *Rissole*.

U N C O

Pity the poor *unco*. In the schoolyard anyone who displays even the slightest inability to move smoothly and gracefully is branded an *unco*, or an *unk*. If you drop a ball you're *unco*, if you trip on a step you're *unco*, etc., etc. Since nearly all teenagers have to go through that gangly, awkward, outsized phase, such a word gets a lot of use. Clumsiness is part and parcel of the age. But that's no reason not to sling off at someone is it? Of course, *unco* is just a shortening of *uncoordinated*. However, since this abbreviation ends in –o it matches up with the common Australian –o suffix used to form nouns, such as *garbo, journo, sambo,* etc. This –o ending comes from the interjection *oh!* which used to get tacked onto the end of words in order to make them heard better when yelled out loud. Thus *bottle-o* comes from the cry of the bottle-vendor, who used to yell out loudly *bottle-oh!* in the streets to announce that he was around. Similar to this was *milk-oh!* the cry of the milkman, and *rabbit-oh!* the cry of the rabbit-seller. Later on, this –o ending was added to other words, such as *arvo, sambo, derro,* and don't forget the unfortunate *unco*.

UNREAL

bang-up, beaut, bonzer, bosker (obs.), brill, brillo, castor, fab, fabbo, fantabulous, fazzo, great, grouse, marvey, mickey mouse, neato, not bad, rip-snorting, sensational, super, super-duper, terrif, top, tops, untold, you-beaut

STUCH FOR WORDS

uey *n.* See **u-ie**.

ugly *phr.* **bump** (or **rub**) **uglies,** to have sexual intercourse.

uh-huh *interj.* a representation in writing of various articulations expressing assent; yes.

uh-oh *interj.* an exclamation indicating that something has gone wrong.

uh-uh *interj.* a representation in writing of various articulations expressing negation; no.

U-ie *n.* **1.** a U-turn. *–phr.* **2. chuck a U-ie,** to do a U-turn. Also, **U-ey**.

um *phr.* **um and ah, a.** to be indecisive. **b.** to prevaricate.

umpteen *n.* an indefinite, especially a very large or immeasurable, number.

umpteenth *adj.* an indefinite but large number of: *for the umpteenth time; her umpteenth interview*.

unbelievable *adj.* absolutely excellent; unreal.

unco *adj.* **1.** awkward; clumsy. *–n.* **2.** a clumsy person. [short for *uncoordinated*]

uncool *adj.* **1.** not socially acceptable due to one's behaviour, interests, dress, etc.; totally lacking in cool; daggy: *He didn't want to appear uncool.* **2.** unfashionable and unsophisticated; not acceptable with regard to current fashions; not 'in'; daggy: *paisley is way uncool.*

uncut *adj.* uncircumcised.

underdaks *pl. n.* underpants.

undergunned *adj. Surfing.* riding with a surfboard that is too small for the conditions.

underwhelm *v.* to cause dissatisfaction by not performing to expectations.

unfazed *adj.* untroubled; unperturbed.

unhip *adj.* not cool; daggy.

unhung *adj. Jocular.* (of a person) having committed some outrageous misdemeanour for which they should be hanged. Also, **unhanged**.

unload *v. Football.* to successfully pass the ball.

unreal *adj.* excellent; unbelievably wonderful.

untold *adj.* excellent; unbelievably wonderful: *We had untold fun.*

up *prep.* **1.** (of a male) engaged in sexual intercourse with: *He's probably up her right now.* **2.** angry with: *She was up him for being late.* *–phr.*
3. be up oneself, to have an unjustifiably high opinion of oneself; be self-deluding.
4. get up (someone's) nose, See **nose**.
5. up each other or **up one another,** behaving in a sycophantic or toadying fashion to each other.
6. up for, liable to pay: *You'll be up for $100 if you break that.*
7. up the duff, pregnant.
8. up you (for the rent)! Also, **up yours; up your arse!** an exclamation indicating insolent or disgusted dismissal.
9. who's up who (and who's paying the rent), a. an inquiry as to the personal alliances in a political or business group, etc. **b.** an inquiry as to the alliances and sexual relationships within a particular group of people.

upper *n.* a stimulant as amphetamine, etc.

upter *adj.* no good; broken down; of

poor quality; worthless. Also, **upta**. [euphemistically short for *up to shit*]

upya *interj.* an offensive exclamation; up you. Also (*pl.*) **upyas**.

urger *n.* a racecourse tipster.

use *v.* to take narcotics: *He's been using for about three years now.*

use-by-date *n.* a time at which one is no longer needed, necessary, useful, cool, in fashion, etc. Also, **used-by date**.

useful *phr.* **useful as a bucket under a bull, useful as a dead dingo's donger, useful as a dry thunderstorm, useful as a glass door on a dunny, useful as an arsehole on a broom, useful as an ashtray on a motorbike** (or **pushbike**)**, useful as a piss in a shower, useful as a pocket on a singlet, useful as a roo-bar on a skateboard, useful as a sore arse to a boundary rider, useful as a spare dick at a wedding, useful as a submarine with screen doors, useful as a third armpit, useful as a wart on the hip, useful as a wether at a ram sale, useful as a witch's tit, useful as the bottom half of a mermaid, useful as tits on a bull, useful as two knobs of billy-goat poop**, (*ironic*) completely useless.

user *n.* **1.** a drug addict. **2.** a person who exploits other people in interpersonal relationships with complete disregard for the emotional damage caused. **3.** a person who only forms relationships with others for their own sexual gain.

ute *n.* a utility truck or utility van.

VEGEMITE

This thick, black, salty extract of yeast, a by-product of beer making, has been part of the Australian cuisine since its invention by Cyril Callister in the early days of this century. It is mostly used as a spread on sandwiches and toast, though there is such as thing as *vegemite broth,* made by spooning some *vegemite* straight from the jar into some boiled water. It is also spread with margarine or butter onto a type of crispbread biscuit known as Vita-Weats. These biscuits have neatly spaced holes and when two of these are spread with *vegemite* and squished together, long tubes of yellowy-black spread ooze out the holes. These are known throughout the land as *worms*. Americans cannot stand the stuff, and on the Net are sites in which they whinge and whine about it at length.

Not only is the spread indispensable, so too are the jars! Coming in various shapes and sizes, some with screw lids, some without, the humble *vegemite jar* is used as an all-purpose glass, for drinking softdrink, water, beer, etc., and found in most kitchens across the country. They are also found in the shed holding all sorts of caustic liquids, oils, and slimes, as well as screws, nails, rusty nuts and bolts, etc. And they make very useful collector jars for the budding, young, backyard entomologist. Many a red-back, funnel- web, or other spider has found its resting days at the bottom of a *vegemite jar* shoved into some dark recess of the laundry.

The advertising jingle which rang out across the nation's airwaves, and later, television channels, *We're happy little vegemites, As bright as bright can be,* has spawned the colloquial expression *happy little vegemite* to mean someone who is extremely pleased.

VINO

amber fluid, booze, bubbly, drinky-poos, firewater, fizz, grog, gutrot, hard stuff, home-brew, hooch, juice, jungle juice, lunatic soup, lush, moonshine, mountain dew, piss, plonk, rot-gut, sherbet, shicker, skinful, snake juice, slops, the bottle, the grape, turps

STUCK FOR WORDS

V *prep.* versus: *Pakistan V India.*

vag *n.* **1.** a vagrant. *–v.* **2.** to arrest on a vagrancy charge. *–phr.* **3. on the vag,** charged with vagrancy.

vamoose *v. Chiefly US.* to make off; decamp; depart quickly. [Spanish *vamos*, let us go]

vamp *n. Derogatory.* **1.** a woman who uses her charms to seduce and exploit men. *–v.* **2.** to act as a vamp. [short for *vampire*]

Vatican roulette *n.* the rhythm method of contraception.

Vee Dub *n.* a Volkswagen car. [from the initials *VW*]

veg *v.* to relax and become mentally inactive. Also, **veg out**.

vege-head *n.* a dull, stupid person.

vegemite *n.* **1.** a child, especially one who is good or well-behaved: *You're a clever little vegemite, aren't you. –phr.* **2. happy little vegemite,** a person in a good mood: *Look at the happy little vegemites working away in there.* [from the tradename and advertising jingle of *Vegemite,* a yeast extract used as a spread]

vegie *adj.* (of school subjects) considered to be easy or of a lower academic standard: *vegie maths; vegie subjects.*

vego *adj.* **1.** vegetarian: *great vego dishes; vego menu. –n.* **2.** a vegetarian.

velch *v.* See **felch**.

verandah *phr.* **verandah over the toy shop,** *Jocular.* a beer gut.

verbal *n. Prison.* **1.** a verbal confession, usually made to the police and recorded by them, and sometimes alleged to be fabricated. *–v.* **2.** (of the police) to insert into a prisoner's statement admissions which they did not make, and present it to a court as evidence.

verbal diarrhoea *n.* a tendency to talk too much; talkativeness.

veronica *n.* a search engine for the Internet. [acronym from *Very Easy, Rodent-Oriented, Net-wide, Index of Computerised Archives*]

verse *v.* (*amongst children*) to play against (a team): *Who are you versing this week?*

VI *adj. Police, etc.* (of a dead body) putrefied and infested with maggots; fly-blown. [standing for *Vermin Infested*]

vibe *n.* **1.** rhythm: *It's got a great vibe; latin vibes.* **2.** any musical aspect or quality indicative of a genre: *it has a commercial vibe.* **3.** mood or atmosphere; feeling: *The place had a nice vibe to it.* **4.** (*pl.*) signals or messages sent out to someone: *giving him bad vibes; He just doesn't know how to pick up vibes.*

vicious *adj.* cool; excellent: unreal.

vid *n.* a video.

Vinnies *n.* an opportunity shop run by the St Vincent de Paul Society: *I got this great bargain at Vinnies today.*

vino *n.* wine. [from Italian]

vinyl *n.* **1.** music recorded on vinyl, as opposed to CDs. *–adj.* **2.** (of music) recorded or released on vinyl: *played a mean set of vinyl house.*

virgin *n.* a person who has not experienced something: *I'm an opera virgin, and intend to remain that way; a skateboard virgin.*

virus *phr.* **the virus,** the HIV virus: *He's got the virus.*

vitamin E *n.* the drug ecstasy.

Volksie *n.* a Volkswagen car.

vomit-making *adj.* unattractive or unpleasant, as an idea, colour, etc.: *I think the whole concept is pretty vomit-making.*

vote *phr.* **vote with one's feet, a.** to express one's disapproval by leaving. **b.** a public exhibition of sympathy, opposition, etc., as a mass meeting, demonstration or march.

VPL *n.* the edge of underwear seen through the overgarment. [initialism of *Visible Panty Line*]

WUSS

The *wimp* of the 80s is the *wuss* of the 90s. Its origin is unknown but there is a theory that it could be a shortening from the term *wooza* meaning a "young woman" or a "girlfriend". This word was in use as early as 1920 and is still around today but has never had much currency. It possibly comes from the World War I slang term *Wazza* or *Wazzir*, the red-light district in Cairo, called in Egyptian Arabic *Haret el-Wassur*. However, there is one slight problem with this purported origin – it requires that the word *wuss* is strictly Australian. Unfortunately the term is also used extensively in America. If the word originated there, it is probably just a blend of the words *wimp* and *puss*, both with the same meaning. The suggestion that it is a shortening of *woman* is quite unlikely.

WIGWAM

The phrase *a wigwam for a goose's bridle* is used to rebuff someone who has asked you a question that you wish not to answer. Imagine a rude individual asking: "What is under that tarp in the backyard?". Outrageous! To this one should obviously retort: "A wigwam for a goose's bridle". That'll shut them up quick smart! Although this peculiar saying is actually from British dialect, its usage on this continent is steeped in Aussie history. The story goes that the bushranger Ben Hall used it when he held up a hotel in Tarago, near Goulburn, NSW. In his own inimitable style, after demanding food and drink, he kindly offered to hold the baby while the lady of the establishment was in the kitchen preparing his meal. Upon the arrival of the food he exclaimed: "Fair exchange! A wing-wong for a goose's bridle." In British dialect a *whim-wham* was a trinket or knick-knack, something that could be put on a horse's bridle, but not a goose's. It was only later that the term was changed to *wigwam* as a familiar if, in context, meaningless word, probably under the influence of too many Western movies and novels consumed by the Australian public.

WHATSIT

doodackie, doodad, doodah, doofer, doohickie, doover, dooverlackie, gismo, jigger, thingo, thingummy, thingummybob, thingummybobbit, thingummyjig, thingummyjiggit, whatchamacallit, what-d'ye-call-it, whoosie, whoosie-whatsit

STUCK FOR WORDS

wacked *adj.* See **whacked**.

wacker *n.* See **whacker**.

wacko *interj., adj.* See **whacko**.

wacky *adj.* erratic, irrational, or unconventional; crazy. Also, **whacky**.

wad *n.* **1.** *Chiefly Military.* a stupid or annoying person; jerk. *–phr.* **2. shoot one's wad,** *Crass.* (of a male) to ejaculate. [from *wad* the wadding used in loading cartridges]

wag *v.* to deliberately stay away from school, work, etc., without permission; to play truant.

wake *phr.*
1. wake up to oneself, to adopt a more sensible and responsible attitude.
2. wake up to (someone), to become aware of the motives, true nature, etc., of (someone).

wake-up *phr.*
1. a wake-up, fully aware of what is going on; alert.
2. a wake-up to, aware of someone's ruse, deceitfulness, hidden agenda, etc.: *I'm a wake-up to your game.* [possibly originally a jocular nominalisation in which the phrase *awake up* was re-analysed as *a wake-up*, much the same as the recent joke 'Be alert. We need more lerts!']

wakey-wakey *interj.* wake up!

walk *phr.*
1. walk all over, a. to be domineering towards someone. **b.** to defeat.
2. walk away with, to win easily.
3. walk off with, a. to remove without permission; steal. **b.** to win, as in a competition. **c.** to outdo one's competitors; win easily.

walking *adj.* (of a person) having the quality typical of some specified thing: *a walking calculator; a walking dictionary; a walking disaster area; a walking garbage disposal.*

walkover *n.* **1.** *Racing.* a going over the course at a walk or otherwise by a contestant who is the only starter. **2.** an easy victory.

wallie *n.* a wallet.

walloper *n.* a police officer.

wally *n.* a fool; a stupid person. [contraction of *Walter*, man's name]

waltz *phr.* **waltz Matilda,** *Hist.* to wander about as a tramp with a swag. [? German *walzen,* to move in a circular fashion, as of apprentices travelling from master to master + German *Mathilde,* female travelling companion, bed roll, from the girl's name]

wandering *phr.* **have wandering hands,** (of a male) to touch (women) in a sexual way.

wang *n.* See **whanger**.

wangle *v.* to bring about, accomplish, or obtain by contrivance, scheming, or often, indirect or insidious methods. [blend of *wag* and *dangle*]

wank *v.* **1.** to masturbate. *–n.* **2.** an act or instance of masturbation. **3.** something which belies self-indulgent or egotistical behaviour: *This movie is a complete wank; A three thousand dollar weekend too get in touch with yourself – what a wank!* **4.** a person exhibiting self-indulgent behaviour; a wanker. *–phr.*
5. wank off, (used imperatively) go away; piss off!
6. wank on, to talk at length.
7. wank oneself, to maintain an

wank ... illusion; deceive oneself. [a nasalised variant of *whack* to masturbate]

wankasaurus *n.* a very egotistical, self-important or obnoxious person; a wanker who is worse than most wankers.

wanker *n.* 1. an obnoxious or annoying person. 2. a self-indulgent or egotistical person.

wankery *n.* nonsense; rubbish. Also, **wankerism**.

wanky *adj.* 1. pretentious. 2. stupid; foolish.

wannabe *n. Derogatory.* 1. a person who aspires to be like a specified person, usually someone famous: *a Dolly Parton wannabe*. 2. a person who aspires to a particular role in life but has not achieved it: *an Olympic wannabe*. –*adj.* 3. trying very hard but not succeeding. Also, **wanna-be**.

warez *n. Internet.* versions of commercial software that have had the copy-protection erased or have been otherwise tampered with so as to make them available non-commercially. [respelling of *wares* in order to distinguish this sense from the ordinary sense of the word; the use of *z* for a voiced final *s* is common on the Internet]

war paint *n.* make-up; cosmetics.

warp speed *n. Jocular.* an exceedingly fast speed. [a term borrowed from the science fiction television show *Star Trek* where warp speed is beyond the speed of light]

warts *phr.* **warts and all,** including all defects.

warwicks *pl. n.* the arms. [rhyming slang, *Warwick Farm* (a racecourse in Sydney) arm]

washboard stomach *n.* a stomach with well-defined, well-toned, rippling muscles.

washer-upperer *n.* one who washes the dishes.

WASP *n. Derogatory.* 1. a member of the First World establishment conceived as being white, Anglo-Saxon and Protestant. –*adj.* 2. of or pertaining to this establishment. [acronym from *White Anglo-Saxon Protestant*]

waste *v.* to murder or kill, especially by shooting.

wasted *adj.* 1. completely exhausted. 2. under the effects of alcohol or drugs.

waste of space *n.* a stupid or useless person.

water sports *n.* sexual activities involving urination.

waterworks *n.* 1. the bladder or its functioning. –*phr.* 2. **turn on the waterworks,** to cry loudly and profusely, especially for the sake of gaining sympathy or getting one's own way.

waxhead *n.* a surfboard rider. Also, **waxie**. [in reference to the wax used on surfboards]

way *adv.* 1. extremely: *She's way cool; That was way good; Open 'til way late*. –*phr.*
2. **no way,** not at all; never.
3. **way back when,** a long time ago.

WC *n.* a toilet. Also, **wc**. [initialism from *water closet*]

weakie *n.* a weak or cowardly person. Also, **weaky.**

wear *v.* **1.** to accept, tolerate, or be convinced by: *He told me a lie but I wouldn't wear it.* **2.** to take as a blow: *You wore that hockey stick right across the face.*

wedding tackle *n.* the male genitalia.

wedgie *n.* a prank in which someone's pants are grabbed and pulled up sharply in order to wedge the clothing uncomfortably into the anal cleft.

wee *n.* **1.** urine. *–v.* **2.** to urinate. Also, **wee-wee, wee-wees.** [imitative of the sound of a stream of urine onto the side of a chamberpot]

weed *n.* **1.** a thin, weak person, esp. a male. **2.** *Older slang.* a cigar or cigarette. *–phr.* **3. the (evil) weed,** marijuana.

weedy *adj.* skinny and weak; tall, thin and puny.

weirdo *n.* one who behaves in a strange, abnormal, or eccentric way.

well *adv.* extremely; totally; completely: *a well dodgy piece of work; that's like a well stupid answer.*

well-endowed *adj.* **1.** (of a man) with large genitalia. **2.** (of a woman) with large breasts.

well-hung *adj.* (of a male) with large genitalia.

well-oiled *adj.* drunk.

werris *n.* **1.** an act of passing water; urination. **2.** a Greek person. [rhyming slang *Werris Creek* leak; Greek]

westie *n.* **1.** *Derogatory.* a person from the western suburbs of Sydney, usually characterised as being unsophisticated, uncouth, and typically wearing certain distinguishing items of clothing, as flannelette shirts and ugh boots. The word is applied negatively to any people living west of one's own suburb, thus a Bondi inhabitant may call a person from Ryde a westie, but Ryde inhabitants would not consider themselves such, and instead apply the term to people from Parramatta, who in turn apply it to people from Penrith, etc. *–adj.* **2.** pertaining to a westie; characteristic of a westie. Also, **westy.**

wet fart *n.* a fart in which some liquid waste is also ejected.

wet patch *n.* a wet area left on bedding after sexual intercourse.

wet sock *n.* a characterless person.

wettie *n. Surfing.* a wetsuit.

wettie rash *n. Surfing.* a rash caused from wearing a wetsuit.

whack *v.* **1.** to place in a rough or slap-dash manner: *Just whack it down in the corner; whacked a dirty big line through it. –n.* **2.** a go or attempt: *to take a whack at a job.* **3.** a portion or share: *pays his whack; Give me my whack now.* **4.** an act of male masturbation; a wank. *–phr.*
5. whack off, to masturbate.
6. whack off with, to steal: *Who whacked off with me pencil sharpener?*
7. whack up, to divide up; share.

whacked *adj.* **1.** exhausted; defeated: *I am whacked from all that work.* **2.** Also, **whacked out.** under the effects of alcohol or drugs; out of it. Also, **wacked.**

whacker *n.* a stupid person. Also, **wacker.**

whacking *adj.* large: *a whacking great smack on the lips.*

whacko *interj.* **1.** Also, **wacko, whacko-the-diddle-oh, whacko-the-did.** an expression denoting pleasure, delight, etc. –*adj.* **2.** eccentric; crazy; bizarre.

wham *phr.* **wham bam thank you ma'am, a.** the act of sexual intercourse, especially when quick and unromantic. **b.** anything done quickly and without fuss.

whammy *n.* **1.** a supposed supernatural blow or spell. –*phr.*
2. double whammy, an unfortunate occurrence which happens in two stages or is made up of two clearly defined negative elements or events.
3. triple/quadruple whammy, a whammy which is more forceful than a double whammy since it contains more than two negative elements.
4. put the whammy on (someone or **something),** to render useless, motionless or powerless. [originally US; from *wham* to hit, i.e. a powerful striking curse; popularised by the comic strip *Li'l Abner* (created by Al Capp in the 1950s) in which a character named Evil-Eye Fleegle can paralyse with a *single whammy* (a look with one evil eye) or a *double whammy* (a look with both evil eyes)]

whanger *n.* the penis. Also, **whang, wang**.

whassup *interj.* a form of greeting. [respelling of the phrase *what's up*]

what *phr.*
1. do I what! an exclamation used to express a positive answer to a question; certainly: *'Do you remember?' 'Do I what!'*
2. or what! an exclamation implying exaggerated agreement: *Stoked or what! Brilliant or what!*
3. so what? an exclamation of contempt, dismissal, or the like.
4. what about, an interrogative requesting someone's opinion: *What about that guy the other night? Wasn't he freaky?*
5. what can I do you for? *Jocular.* what can I do for you?
6. what for, severe treatment, punishment, or violence: *He hit me, so I gave him what for.*
7. what it takes, the necessary ability, personality, or the like: *He may look stupid, but he's got what it takes to hold the job down.*
8. what's up? what is happening; what is the latest news: *What's up down in Melbourne?*
9. what's what, the true position.

whatsit *n.* a name used in place of one temporarily forgotten; thingummyjig. Also, **whosie-whatsit**.

what's-their-face *n.* a term for someone who's name you cannot remember. Also, **what's-her-face, what's-his-face**.

wheelie *n.* **1.** a violent, usually noisy skidding of the driving wheels of a motor car while accelerating as around a corner or from a standing start: *to do a wheelie.* **2.** a manoeuvre performed on a bicycle, motorbike, etc., in which the front wheel is lifted and held off the ground whilst in motion.

wheelman *n.* the driver of a getaway car.

wheels *pl. n.* a motor vehicle.

whiffy *adj.* smelly.

whim-wham *n.* 1. any odd or fanciful object or thing; something showy or useless. *–phr.* 2. **whim-wham for a goose's bridle,** See **wigwam**.

whingeing Pom *n. Derogatory.* an English person thought to be always criticising and complaining about life in Australia.

whip *n.* 1. a jockey. *–v.* 2. to beat, outdo, or defeat, as in a contest. *–phr.*
3. **crack the whip,** to urge to greater effort.
4. **fair crack of the whip!** an appeal for fairness.
5. **whip around,** to make a collection of money.
6. **whip the cat, a.** to make a fuss or commotion. **b.** to reproach oneself.
7. **whips of,** an abundance: *whips of room; whips of money.*

whip-round *n.* an impromptu collection of money. Also, **whip-around**.

white head *n.* a pimple that has formed a head of pus.

whitey *n. Racist.* a person of a fair-skinned race.

whomp *v.* to beat convincingly. Also, **womp**.

whoo *interj.* an exclamation of pleasure and excitement: *Whoo yeah!* Also, **hoo, whoo-ee, wooh**.

whoop *phr.*
1. **big whoop,** a derisive exclamation used to note that one is not impressed.
2. **whoop it** (or **things**) **up, a.** to raise an outcry or disturbance. **b.** to have a party or celebration.

whoopee *phr.* **make whoopee, a. to engage in uproarious merry-making. b.** to have sexual intercourse. [extended variant of *whoop*]

whoopy-do *interj.* a derisive exclamation used to note that one is not impressed.

whopper *n.* 1. something uncommonly large for its kind. 2. a big lie.

whosie-whatsit *n.* a name used in place of one temporarily forgotten; thingummyjig. Also, **whosie**.

WHS *n.* (used by women of men) the Wandering Hands Society. See **wandering**.

whynaf *n.* an attractive female. [? backslang from *fanny* the vagina or vulva]

wick *phr.*
1. **dip one's wick,** (of a man) to have sexual intercourse.
2. **get one's wick wet,** (of a man) to loose their virginity.
3. **get on someone's wick,** to irritate someone.

wicked *adj.* 1. extremely good; cool: *a wicked coat. –adv.* 2. excellently: *I hope you do wicked in your exams.*

wicket *phr.*
1. **sticky wicket, a.** *Cricket.* a wet but drying wicket that promotes slow bounce in which the ball sticks and then pops. **b.** a delicate, difficult or disadvantageous situation: *He's on a sticky wicket now that his father has disinherited him.*
2. **a good wicket,** an advantageous situation or set of circumstances.

wide boy *n.* a larrikin, lout or tough.

widgie *n.* (in the 1950s and 60s) a

young woman belonging to an anti-social subculture (known as **bodgies and widgies**) that rejected the morality and general world-view of the time. Widgies were especially noted for wild behaviour, free sexuality, and dressing in tight, revealing skirts and sweaters, and having short, duck-tailed haircuts. See **bodgie**. [originally also spelled *weegie*; ? blend of *women* and *bodgie*]

widow-maker *n.* **1.** a dead branch on a tree which is likely to snap off. **2.** *Australian Rules.* a very high kick which, as it descends, puts the player taking it in danger from both the force of the ball and from the converging members of the opposing team.

wife *phr.* **the wife's best friend,** the penis.

wife-beater *n.* a long thin loaf of bread. Also, **husband-beater.**

wigged out *phr.* under the effects of marijuana; stoned.

wigger *n. Racist.* a white person who has adopted aspects of black culture. [blend of *w(hite)* + *(n)igger*]

wigwam *phr.* **a wigwam** (or **whim-wham**) **for a goose's bridle,** a fanciful, non-existent object, used as an answer to an unwanted question. [from British dialect (Antrim and Down), from *whim-wham, wim-wam, wim-wom* a trinket or trifle; altered in modern usage through association with the word *wigwam*]

willie *n.* the penis. Also, **willy.** [from *Willy*, variant of the name *William*]

willies *phr.* **give one the willies, a.** to give feelings of uneasiness or fear. **b.** to annoy, frustrate, or vex.

willing *adj.* zealous; violent; aggressive; willing to fight.

wimp *n.* **1.** a meek, non-aggressive, weak, spineless person, especially a male. *–phr.* **2. wimp out,** to fail or renege on a commitment as a result of lack of character or determination. [? from the meek character *Wimpy* in the 'Popeye' comic strip]

wimpish *adj.* of the nature of a wimp. Also, **wimpy.**

windbag *n.* an empty, voluble, pretentious talker.

wing-nut *n.* a person with large, protruding ears.

winkey *n.* the emoticon ;) - representing a winking face. Also, **winky.**

winner *n.* **1.** something successful or highly valued. *–phr.* **2. pick a winner,** to pick a large piece of snot from the nose with one's finger.

wino *n.* one addicted to drinking wine.

wipe *v.* **1.** to refuse to have anything to do with; dismiss; reject. *–phr.*
2. wipe out, to kill.
3. wipe the floor with, to defeat utterly; overcome completely.

wipe-out *n.* **1.** a failure; fiasco. **2.** *Surfing.* a fall from a surfboard. **3.** *Snowboarding.* a collision. **4.** any fall or crash.

wired *adj.* **1.** technologically aware and up-to-date, especially with computers and the Internet. **2.** fully versed in some topic, industry, area of expertise, etc.; tuned-in.

wise *adj.* **1.** Also, **wise to,** in the know (about something implied): *They tried to keep it secret, but he*

was wise; I'm wise to your tricks. –phr.
2. put wise, a. to explain something (to someone, especially a naive person). **b.** to warn.
3. wise up, to become aware or alerted; face the realities.

wish *phr.* **you wish!** an expression denoting that someone has unrealistic expectations or ideas: *Beat me in a race? Yeah right, you wish!*

wish list *n.* a list of things desired.

with *adj.* **1.** comprehending of: *Are you with me? –phr.*
2. be (or **get**) **with it, a.** to become aware of a situation. **b.** to concentrate. **c.** to be able to cope. **d.** to become fashionable or up-to-date.
3. get with (someone), a. to pet with (someone). **b.** to have sexual intercourse with (someone).

with-it *adj.* trendy; sophisticated; up-to-date: *with-it gear.*

wobbly *phr.* **chuck** (or **throw**) **a wobbly, a.** to become angry; have a tantrum. **b.** (of a machine, etc.) fail to function properly; break down.

wog[1] *n. Racist.* **1.** a person of Mediterranean or Middle Eastern extraction, or of similar complexion and appearance. **2.** (especially in WWII) a native of North Africa or the Middle East. **3.** (loosely) any foreigner. [origin unknown; probably not short for *golliwog*, and definitely not an acronym for Westernised (or Worthy or Wily) Oriental Gentleman]

wog[2] *n.* **1.** a germ, especially a germ leading to a minor ailment such as a cold or a stomach upset. **2.** such a cold, stomach upset, etc.

wogball *n. Racist.* soccer. [*wog* + (*foot*)*ball*; soccer being seen as especially popular with Australians of Mediterranean descent]

woman *phr.*
1. old woman, a. a woman or man who is pedantic or tends to fuss, gossip, etc. **b.** one's wife. **c.** one's mother.
2. woman's troubles, gynaecological problems.

wombat *n.* someone who is slow-moving or slow-witted. [from the stocky marsupial, seen to be slow and dull]

woodie *n.* an erect penis.

woofering *n. Military.* an initiation punishment for a male cadet in which the nozzle of a vacuum cleaner is applied to the genitals.

woo-hoo *interj.* an exclamation of pleasure, excitement, etc.

woolly woofter *n.* a male homosexual. [rhyming slang for *poofter*]

Woop Woop *n.* any remote or backward town or district. Also, **woop woop.**

wooza *n. Derogatory.* **1.** a young female who is silly and frivolous. **2.** a girlfriend. **3.** a woman's genitals. Also, **wooz, woozie.** [origin uncertain; however cf. earlier *wozzer* prostitute, from *wasser* brothel, from *The Wazzir* or *Haret el Wassir* the red-light district in Cairo during both WWI and WWII]

wop *n. Racist.* **1.** an Italian or any foreigner thought to be of Italianate appearance. *–adj.* **2.** of or pertaining to any Latin country, its culture, or inhabitants. [? from Italian *guappo* bold, showy, from Spanish *guapo* dandy, from Latin *vappa* worthless fellow]

word *phr.*
  1. the (letter) word, *Often jocular.* a euphemistic way of mentioning a rude, contentious, or taboo topic that begins with the specified letter: *Not the 'C' word!* (i.e. commitment); *the 'F' word* (i.e. fuck).
  2. the word, news or information: *The hot word is that she'll be here soon.*

worry *phr.* **no worries!** or **not a worry!** an expression of confidence that everything will go well. See **wucking furries**.

worrywart *n.* one who constantly worries unnecessarily.

wouldn't *phr.*
  1. wouldn't feed it to Jap on Anzac Day, *Racist.* (of food) absolutely disgusting.
  2. wouldn't it! an exclamation indicating dismay, disapproval, disgust, etc.

wow *interj.* **1.** Also, **wow-wee, wowee.** an exclamation of surprise, wonder, pleasure, dismay, etc. –*n.* **2.** something that proves an extraordinary success. –*v.* **3.** to amaze, astonish or greatly impress.

wowser *n.* **1.** a killjoy or spoilsport. **2.** a prude who publicly complains about the supposed deleterious effects of other people's behaviour on society. [? British dialect *wow,* to make a complaint; whine; popularly supposed to be an acronym of *We Only Want Social Evils Remedied,* a slogan invented by John Norton, Australian journalist and politician, 1862-1916]

w.p.b. file *n.* the wastepaper basket, viewed as a place for filing useless or unwanted material.

wrap *n.* enthusiastic approval; a wrap-up.

wrapped *adj.* **1.** totally amazed by; enthusiastic about: *He's not wrapped in the idea.* –*phr.* **2. wrapped up in,** involved with: *She's totally wrapped up in the new baby.*

wrap-up *n.* an enthusiastic approval or recommendation: *He gave the new product a good wrap-up.*

wrinklie *n.* an elderly person. Also, **wrinkly.**

write *phr.*
  1. have (something) written all over one (or **it**), to show as a clear characteristic: *Delight was written all over her face.*
  2. write off, to consider as dead, finished or useless.
  3. write oneself off, a. to get very drunk. **b.** to have a motor accident.

write-off *n.* **1.** something irreparably damaged, as an aircraft, car, etc. **2.** a person who is incapacitated through drunkenness, injury, etc. **3.** an incompetent person; a no-hoper. [from *write-off,* something written off in account books]

wucking furries *phr.* **no wucking furries,** an expression of confidence that all will go well. Also, **no wucks, no wuckers.** [spoonerism of *no fucking worries*]

wuss *n. Originally US.* an overly timid or ineffectual person; wimp. Also, **wus, wooz.** [probably a blend of *woman* + *puss*]

wuss-bag *n.* an exceedingly pathetic wuss.

·XYZ·

YOBBO

The British underground of bygone days developed a specialised crypti-language known as "backslang". This was basically a technique of pronouncing words as though spelt backwards. Thus the word *boy* in backslang becomes *yob*. The more familiar *yobbo* is an extended form. Of course what passes for a *yobbo* in England is not the same as the familiar Aussie *yobbo*. The British member of the species is more of a young lout or lair, usually with a strong antisocial streak, a loud mouth, and a monomania for the football club he supports. The Australian relative is more likely to be a bit older, even middle-aged, and to have a well-developed beer gut, thongs, a bad tan, and a perpetual stubbie holder glued to his palm. The only *snags* he knows are the ones he incinerates on the barbie.

STACKING UP ZEDS

It may come as a surprise to some people that the sound of the snoring human is one that has perplexed our language for many years. The problem seems to be in just how to represent the sound using the letters of our language. Nowadays the common term is *snore* but this is comparatively recent and prior to this it was more common to use *snort* to describe this sound. In Middle English times, however, the commonplace term was *fnort* – a word which doesn't exactly roll off the tongue. Similarly there was *fneeze* for *sneeze*. Other attempts have been *drone,* properly used to describe the buzzing of bees, and the inkhorn term *stertor* which is mainly a technical word. However, with the advent of the comic strip, a new way to represent this sound was born – a long and wavy line of the letter *zed* repeated was drawn issuing from the nose of the slumbering character. This quickly became a convention. One good thing about it was that the cartoonist could alter the size of the individual *zeds* in order to give the effect of increasing and decreasing volume. Thus the phrase *stacking up zeds* or *pushing up zeds,* meaning "to sleep", came into being.

YES-MAN

arse-licker, arse-sucker, bootlicker, brown noser, bum crawler, bum licker, bum sucker, bumboy, fawner, flunkey, greaser, groveller, lackey, lickspittle, sponger, suckhole, toady

STUCK FOR WORDS

X *n.* **1.** any unknown factor, agency or thing. **2.** someone whose identity is unknown, or who wishes to keep their identity a secret: *Mr X; Madame X.* *–phr.* **3. the X factor, a.** any unknown quality, aspect or thing. **b.** the aspect or factor that causes people to be attracted to one another, but which is seemingly inexplicable.

X-phile *n.* a fan of the television show *The X-Files*.

Y *phr. Chiefly US.*
1. the Y, the YMCA or YWCA.
2. dine at the Y, to perform cunnilingus.

ya *pron.* a representation in writing of *you*.

yack *v.* to vomit.

yahoo *n.* **1.** a rough, coarse or uncouth person. *–interj.* **2.** an exclamation expressing enthusiasm or delight. *–phr.* **3. yahoo around,** to act in a rough, loutish manner. [from *Yahoo,* one of a race of brutes having the form of human beings and embodying all the degrading passions of humanity, in *Gulliver's Travels* (1726) by Jonathan Swift]

yair *adv.* yes. Also, **yeah.**

yak *v.* to talk or chatter, especially pointlessly and continuously. Also, **yack, yacker, yakety-yak.** [imitative]

yakka *n.* manual labour; work. Also, **yacker, yakker.** [from the Aboriginal language Jagara]

Yank *n., adj.* American. Also, **Yankee.**

Yankee shout *n.* a social outing where each person pays their own way; Dutch treat.

Yank tank *n.* a large car of American manufacture.

yardie *n. Car sales.* a person employed to do the running around in a car yard; the yard gopher.

yard pet *n. Car sales.* a car which doesn't sell.

yarn *n.* **1.** a story or tale of adventure, especially a long one about extraordinary events. **2.** a lie. *–v.* **3.** to chat. **4.** to tell stories.

yartz *phr.* **the yartz,** *Jocular.* (the uncultivated Australian pronunciation of) the Arts.

yawn *n.* a boring event; a bore.

yay *interj.* an exclamation of glee.

yea *adv.* (accompanied by a hand gesture to indicate size) this; so: *She's a little girl, only about yea high.* Also, **yay.** [origin unknown]

yeah *adv.* **1.** Also, **yair, yeh.** yes. *–phr.* **2. yeah right,** an expression of agreement, used **a.** (with a tentative tone) to admit ostensible agreement, but with a lot of reservation, or, **b.** (with an sarcastic tone) to express disagreement.

yecch *interj.* an exclamation of disgust, aversion, horror, or the like.

yee-haa *interj. Originally US.* **1.** an exclamation of abandonment when commencing some exciting activity. **2.** used ironically to denote that one is not excited.

yellow *adj.* **1.** cowardly; mean or contemptible. *–adj.* **2.** *Racist.* Chinese. **3.** *Racist.* of mixed Aboriginal and white blood.

yeow *interj.* See **yowie.**

yep *interj.* yes.

yers *pron.* See **youse.**

yes siree *phr.* yes indeed.

yez *pron.* See **youse**.

yike *n.* a brawl, argument. [origin unknown]

yikes *interj.* a mild exclamation of surprise or concern. Also, **yipes**.

yippee *interj.* an exclamation used to express joy, pleasure, or the like.

yips *pl. n.* **a.** *Originally.* nervousness which can cause a golfer to miss an easy putt: *a case of the yips.* **b.** a similar complaint affecting any person playing a sport. [origin unknown]

yo *interj. Originally US.* **1.** an exclamation used to indicate a person's present at roll call. **2.** an exclamation used to call someone's attention. **3. a.** an exclamation used to show approval, excitement, etc. **b.** (used sarcastically) to indicate that someone has done something stupid or daggy. **4.** an expression of agreement; yes.

yob *n.* a loutish, aggressive, or surly youth or man. Also, **yobbo**. [19th century backslang of *boy*]

yokel *n.* **1.** a person from a rural area; a country bumpkin. *–phr.* **2.** See **local yokels**.

yonks *pl. n.* ages or a long time: *We haven't seen them for absolutely yonks.* [origin unknown; ? possibly from a spoonerism of *donkey's years*]

yonnie *n.* a stone or pebble. [origin unknown; possibly from an Aboriginal language]

yoo-hoo *interj.* a call used to attract someone's attention.

yorker *n. Cricket.* a well-up delivery pitched so that it will go under the bat.

you *n.* **1.** something resembling or closely identified with the person addressed: *That dress simply isn't you. –phr.* **2. up you,** See **up**. **3. you get that,** an expression of resignation to a bad situation: *The toilet's blocked again! Oh well, you get that.* **4. you wish,** See **wish**.

youse *pron.* **1.** plural form of *you*. **2.** a singular form of *you*. Also, **yers, yez, yous**. [def 1 originally in Irish English *yez*, translation of the Irish Gaelic second person plural pronoun; def 2 originally appearing in fiction where it was erroneously used by writers attempting to reproduce a social dialect (that is, working class speech) which was not their own, but now having some oral currency]

yow *interj.* **1.** Also, **yeow**. a cry of pain. **2.** *Obsolete.* a warning cry that the police are coming. *–phr.* **3. keep yow,** *Obsolete.* to keep watch for police when an illegal activity is taking place; to act as look-out. See **nit**[2].

yowie *interj.* a cry of pain. Also, **yeow, yow**.

yuck *interj.* **1.** an expression of disgust. **2.** an expression denoting that one is physically or sexually repulsed by someone. *–adj.* **3.** disgusting; unsavoury; unpleasant. **4.** physically unattractive. Also, **yuk**.

yucko *adj.* **1.** disgusting; unpleasant; repulsive. *–interj.* **2.** an exclamation of repulsion. Cf. **yummo**. [from *yuck(y)* + *-o*]

yucky *adj.* disgusting; unpleasant; repulsive. Also, **yukky**.

yum *adj.* **1.** having a very nice taste.

2. beautiful; gorgeous; sexually attractive. *–interj.* **3.** an exclamation of delighted approval. **4.** an expression denoting that someone is exceedingly physically or sexually attractive. Also, **yummy**.

yummo *adj.* **1.** having a very nice taste. **2.** beautiful; gorgeous. *–interj.* **3.** an exclamation of delighted approval. [from *yumm(y)* + *-o*]

yuppie *n.* a young urban professional person, typified as having a high disposable income to spend on luxury consumer goods. Also, **yup**. [acronym from *Young Urban Professional* + *-ie*; also considered to stand for *Young Upwardly-mobile Professional*]

zack *n.* **1.** *Obsolete.* a sixpence. **2.** *Older slang.* a five cent piece. Also, **zac**. [? from Scottish *saxpence* sixpence]

zap *v.* **1.** to destroy with a sudden burst of violence; annihilate. **2.** to give an electric shock: *zapped by the toaster*. **3.** to cook in a microwave oven. **4.** to discontinue watching (a television program or commercial) by changing stations with a remote control.

zapped *adj.* tired to the point of exhaustion.

zapper *n.* the remote control which operates a video cassette recorder, television, etc.

zappy *adj.* lively and interesting.

zed *phr.* **push** (or **stack**) **up zeds,** to sleep; snooze.

zilch *n. Originally US.* nothing.

zillion *n.* an unimaginably large amount. Also, **gillion, jillion, squillion**.

zine *n.* a magazine, especially one about an alternative subculture, or one in electronic form published on the Internet. Also, **'zine**.

zip *n.* nothing; zero: *a score of zip*.

zit *n.* **1.** a pimple. **2.** (*pl.*) acne. [perhaps onomatopoeic representation of the eruption of pus caused by squeezing a pimple]

zizz *n.* a nap; sleep. [cf. *zzz* an onomatopoeic representation of the sound of snoring]

zombie *n.* **1.** a dull, brainless person; a person having no independent judgment, intelligence, etc. **2.** *Older slang.* marijuana.

zone *phr.*
1. the zone, *Sport.* a period in which everything comes together and one plays perfectly.
2. zone out, to mentally remove oneself from a situation; to close one's mind.

zoned out *n.* under the influence of marijuana, or some other similar acting drug; spaced out.

zonked *adj.* **1.** exhausted; faint with fatigue. **2.** drunk. **3.** under the influence of drugs. Also, **zonked-out**.

zoo *phr.* **feeding time at the zoo,** a disorderly rabble.

zooter *n. Cricket.* a deceptive type of wrist-spin delivery, a variation of a leg-break bowl similar to a flipper. Also, **zoota**. [agent noun of *zoot*, blend of *zip* and *shoot*, both meaning 'travel fast']

zowie *interj.* an exclamation of surprise, excitement, etc.

K*I*D

[Kids Internet Dictionary]

http://www.dict.mq.edu.au

Collecting information about words, especially slang words, has always been one of the challenges of lexicography. Many slang words exist primarily in the spoken language and only make it into print very rarely. For a number of reasons reliable information about the slang language used by children is particularly scarce. Firstly, it is usually recorded by adults who are unfamiliar with the expressions being recorded. Secondly, children's slang is very volatile, changing much from suburb to suburb, school to school, year to year, and even grade to grade – thus a collection made at one time, and in one place, provides only the tiniest of windows from which to view the whole picture.

In order to collect children's language, the Macquarie Dictionary has set up a free Internet site entitled *K*I*D* (the Kids Internet Dictionary). Here children can record their own language in their own words.

Basically *K*I*D* provides a blank form in which children can enter words, definitions, pronunciations, and comments about whichever words they like. This information is left exactly as typed in, warts and all, in order to preserve the feeling that this dictionary is actually the work of children and not some adult's version of their language.

Of course, *K*I*D* has a search engine so that anyone visiting the site can look up a word they are interested in. Also, there is a clickable map of the world which lets you find all the words recorded by children of a particular area of the globe.

Here is a selection of kids' words and definitions which children from various parts of the world have entered into K*I*D.

AUSTRALIAN ENTRIES

a bit of alright visually satisfying; good looking.
abominable an explosive device in a male cow.
as if like "yeah right".
as stupid as a bucket god damn stupid!
awesome fantastic; great.
babe a word used as a compliment for a girl. It means that the girl is very good looking.
babs someone who tries to be cool but fails.
berko to be incredibly irate and angry.
burn to embarrass somebody through jokes, etc.
busted caught in the act, typically by a teacher.
chump someone who has a little bit more body fat than another person.
cobber a very cool person.
cool good looking; great; excellent.
crusty barnacle an ugly person.
crusty undies someone who is a filthbag.
dag someone who's not real cool.
deadly totally awesome; out of this world; really good; cool.
der stating the obvious.
dig to love someone.
dip an idiot.
dog someone to stand someone up, (to leave someone waiting).
dude a cool or nice person.
dudeness! used when saying something is cool.
dudical excellent; cool; fantastic; exciting.
dundaclumpen when someone is being particularly silly.
dunny it's an Australian expression for a toilet.
egghead a dag or a dork.
ego-tripper someone who gets high on their self-image and appearance.
feral disgusting or gross.
festy an ugly or unpleasant sight.
fezz disgusting; not nice looking.
fully very.
geebin someone who is geekish and is a clutz.
geek a crazy brain who is mad about technical stuff and can't get on with other people.
genie a compliment to someone - calling them cool.
gimp a really small person, a runt.
gnarly something that's really good.
greg a square; a person with no life.
groovy totally hip!!
grotty chops a messy eater.
grouse! a word meaning cool, or something that you might call excellent.
gumby a loser; a daggy person who can't do anything right.
guru legend; unreal person and someone to look up to.
hell it means very good.
inbreeder a country hick suspected of belonging to a rather loving family.
leg of lamb a legendary person.
legend you are the best. A really cool person.
mong an idiot (general derogatory term).
mullet to be stunned as a result of an object impacting the cranium at a

dangerous velocity. If the object is self-administered, the term 'auto-mullet' may be used.
na-der when something is already known or obvious.
nerd a stupid and daggy person.
neville a nobody, someone who has no friends, similar to nigel.
nigel a person who doesn't have no friends and always walks by themselves.
ninja! an exclamation for something really good.
plut your butt sit down.
psycho hose beast a hyperactive person.
rock someone to embarrass someone.
rock job to say something that is wrong, or to do something embarrassing.
roll someone to embarrass someone.
sheesh unbelievable.
shlep someone stupid.
sick to look good, nice, intelligent, hot and sexy.
silly as a two bob watch a very stupid, crazy, mad person.
skeg people who are into surfing and dress in surfing fashions.
slam it's sort of like rock job except even worse.
spark up light up a cigarette.
textile beach the opposite to a **nudist beach** a beach where people wear clothing and bathing costumes.
tiger a name for a friend.
tooshie upset and angry.
tripper a cool person; someone popular.
unco not with it.
vegee someone whose really dumb, stupid; someone who has no life and sits on their butt all day.
wallygon somebody who has done or said a silly thing.
wicked cool; grouse; real good.
yeah right! sure you did.
yokel it is somebody that lives in a local area, usually not your own area: they are under the 'yoke' of that area's ideas and beliefs.

SINGAPORE ENTRIES

alamak exclamation in Malay meaning 'oh my god!'
chin chai anything will do.
gasak - to fake.
Go and die, lah! Hey, go to hell!
kan chiong anxious, agitated.
kaypoh being a busybody.
lauyah lousy, bad quality.
pai sey embarrassing (from Hokkien, a Chinese dialect).
pak tor to go on a date.
relack relax, cool it.
ring, ring indication that your brassiere strap is showing.
sian boring; tiring.
tikam tikam to do something sloppily.

CANADIAN ENTRIES
gasha completely, totally, entirely.
gone attractive, sexy.
killed it! wrecked it or messed it up, usually by showing off.
malling hanging out in the mall for long periods of time, basically loitering.
skater someone who is into skateboarding, wears the clothes and is good at it, or pretends to be.
wicked totally awesome
xyz your zipper's undone, examine your zipper.

SOUTH AFRICAN ENTRIES
gimba (pronounced gimbu) to be greedy, eat a lot.
goop vomit
homeboy someone who is popular.
let's chuck sit or go somewhere.
schollie idiotic, stupid.
shade to embarrass somebody
yak (pronounced yuk) to dress.

AMERICAN ENTRIES
bites the big bootie something that is not good.
bogality the act or fact of being totally bogus.
butter cool, with it, hip.
dank a synonym for 'good'.
flack a nerd, or a geek, or a dork.
foofy happy, joyful, excited, silly.
ganshis it means very nice.
incrediburgable really cool.
kooshed when a guy gets racked.
pathetic stupid.
rocks the big bootie something that is good.
spiffy really awesome or cool.
wanned very crazy.